The Value of Privacy

For Rebecca, even though it's a book without pictures

The Value of Privacy

Beate Rössler

Translated by R. D. V. Glasgow

polity

The publication of this work was supported by a grant from the Goethe-Institut

Polity Press
65 Bridge Street
Cambridge CB2 1UR, UK

Polity Press.
350 Main Street
Malden, MA 02148, USA

ISBN 0 7456 3110 X
ISBN 0 7456 3111 8 (paperback)

A catalogue record for this book is available from the British Library.

Typeset in 10.75 on 11 pt Times New Roman by TechBooks, India

For further information on Polity, visit our website: www.polity.co.uk

Contents

Acknowledgements

For critical discussions and other support I thank Stefan Gosepath, Marcus Otto, Walter Pfannkuche, Holmer Steinfath and Bernhard Thöle: our Berlin colloquium made the beginning of this book significantly easier for me. The completion of the book was greatly helped by the supportive and stimulating atmosphere in Amsterdam, both in the Faculty of Philosophy and in the Amsterdam School for Cultural Analysis: for this I thank in particular Veit Bader, Govert den Hartogh and Hent de Vries.

Along this at times rather arduous path other friends too have helped me with advice, criticism and discussions: for this many thanks go to Martina Herrmann, Dunja Jaber, Christoph Menke and Herlinde Pauer-Studer. I owe a special debt of gratitude to Martin Löw-Beer, who at the end commented on the manuscript in its entirety and in the process pointed out a series of problems to me, and to Stefan Gosepath, who time and again read the various versions of the manuscript and made friendly and critical comments on it.

A conference on privacies in Amsterdam helped me enormously to put my thoughts together: I am very grateful to the participants, above all to Anita Allen, Moira Gatens, Axel Honneth and Nicola Lacey, for their contributions and discussions.

Bernhard Peters argued with me always with patience even though without always managing to convince me. I am deeply grateful to him for his support and advice and, above all, for his encouragement at the right time.

Finally, I should like to thank Rupert Glasgow for his meticulous and sympathetic translation and for his interest in really getting the meaning right, and the Wissenschaftskolleg at Berlin for providing perfect working conditions while I read my way through the translation of the book.

Beate Rössler

1 Introduction

The question of whom I live with is a private affair, and so is what I think about my colleagues at work. My diary is private, as is part of my correspondence. It is a private matter how I dress, which church I go to, and what profession I choose. My house and home is my private sphere, in other words my dwelling too. The question of where I send my child to school is a private one, and when I'm sitting with a friend in a café, though this may be a public place, it is a private affair.

This is an incomplete list of the things we describe using the complex predicate 'private'. Yet 'private' is not only a complex predicate, but also one which, depending on the context in which it is used, may have a directly evaluative or prescriptive character. This comes to light not only when we rebuff someone with the remark that something is none of their business or is a private matter, but also in complaints to the effect that privacy is under threat from the new information technologies, from the latest possibilities for eavesdropping on people, watching them, filming them, etc. Privacy is here typically referred to as something worth protecting that should be normatively respected. Even complaints about the 'blurring of boundaries' between the public and private spheres through the 'privatization' of the public appeal to an implicit evaluation not only of the public sphere but also of privacy as a realm worthy of protection.

What interests me in this book are the fundamental questions: why do we value privacy? And why should we value privacy? What I try to show is that we value privacy for the sake of our autonomy. In liberal societies, privacy has the function of permitting and protecting an autonomous life.

When I speak of privacy and the protection of privacy, etc., in what follows, what I mean by this is the protection of the privacy of individual persons. I am concerned, in other words, with a theory of individual privacy. What is private and what is worth protecting about the privacy of private enterprise or the privacy of institutions (such as the Catholic Church) will here at most play only a marginal role. And when I talk of privacy in what follows, I am not simultaneously referring to the public sphere. I shall be treating the other side of this 'great dichotomy' as a 'residual category' without any more precise structure, though where necessary I shall go into the interplay and interaction of the private and the public.[1]

This introductory chapter is intended to provide an overview of the subject, its background, and some of the questions involved. By the end of this introduction it should be clear what the ensuing path looks like and where it will be leading.

1 Discourses on privacy

Theories of privacy – theories of the change it has undergone, the threat it faces, the function it fulfils – are to be found in widely differing and often wholly separate discourses, each approaching the problem from a different angle, referring to different histories of privacy, and focusing on different aspects of the term's meaning. Here I intend to give only a brief sketch of these discourses. One way or another, they will come up in greater detail in the course of the following chapters.

Privacy is a prominent topic in sociological and philosophical theories of the *public sphere*. It is here understood both as the realm of intimacy and the sphere traditionally assigned to the family household.[2] This approach also includes such theories as the one set forth by Richard Sennett, since with his concept of the 'tyranny of intimacy' he is more interested in a theory of public life and its decline (through the incursion of intimacy) than in a normative theory of privacy.[3] In such theories of the public sphere, privacy is by and large thought of merely as a residual category – designated 'the private home' or the 'realm of intimacy' and not further differentiated – since the focus is on the development and modernization of the public realm and its present-day structures and functions. Privacy is also made a theme in this way in theories of civilization, such as the work of Norbert Elias, where civilizing processes affect the privatization of what were formerly public social practices and where these processes come to bear upon the regulation of private life itself.[4] In this first discourse, the spotlight is thus above all on changes in the boundary between the private and the public and transformations in the public or domestic realm, on civilizing processes as processes of privatization, and modernizing processes as processes of de-privatization.[5] Also included are the sorts of diagnostic approaches (not all of them sociological in orientation) that are concerned in general with a diagnosis of the present in terms of the private sphere (most often its decline) and identify the loss of clear dividing lines, the blurring of boundaries between private and public, as a pathology of late modern societies. Here too, however, there is in the main no direct interest in a normative theory of privacy, which is instead taken as a starting-point for cultural criticism of a more general nature.[6]

Likewise primarily sociological in orientation, a further sort of discourse focuses on privacy on its own account, and in particular the realm of the 'private family'. This type of discourse is interested in the changes undergone by the family as the traditional stronghold of private life.[7] Privacy is here considered in its classic sense as the realm of domestic life, of the family and of intimacy, a realm that in spite of its modifications, functional shifts, spatial reconfigurations, and the recasting of roles, has been preserved in its fundamental significance from antiquity to the present day.[8]

These thematic treatments of privacy have been greatly influenced by a form of discourse that, though also historical or diagnostic in orientation, is predominantly critical, that is the discourse of feminist theory.[9] This theoretical current has influenced the interpretations and conceptualizations of privacy in contemporary social debates more than any other. A political and philosophical discussion of the problematic nature of the public and the private has been going on in feminist theory ever since the 1960s, and it is here, much more than in the other discourses I have mentioned, that the *relations between* the two realms or spheres have been reflected upon. The diverse and heterogeneous feminist critique of the traditional distinction between private and public spheres has become interesting and influential in particular because it highlights deep-rooted ambivalences in the differentiation between the public and the private realm, as well as the repressive nature of this split. The history of private life is here told in a different way from the discourses referred to above, namely as the history of the banishment of certain persons and certain themes to the realm of privacy, as the history of an unjust social system and as the history of the emancipation from this.[10]

Quite independently of these challenges to the notion of privacy, the latest processes of modernization have seen the emergence of a new sort of discourse, one concerned with privacy of information. Its origins can be traced back to the end of the nineteenth century, when the spread of the yellow press in conjunction with the popularization of photography for the first time turned informational privacy, particularly of American public figures, into a legal and theoretical theme.[11] Yet it is only since the 1950s and 1960s that it has become a major public issue, as advancements in computer technology have encouraged an increased interest on the part of government bureaucracies in gathering and processing information. Examples of this sort of discourse range from the first major studies by Edward Shils and Alan Westin through to the more recent scenarios of a panoptic society and its dangers.[12]

A further discourse to be mentioned here is the *legal* discourse concerning the right to privacy, which responds to these other approaches to the subject in various ways but nonetheless remains independent of them. In the United States, these discussions of the right to privacy have become influential in legal theory ever since the end of the nineteenth century, when the first attempts were made by American jurisprudence to derive such a right from the Constitution.[13] In Germany, by contrast, discussions of the right to privacy often take place under a different rubric and in a different context: the inviolability of the home and the protection of personhood.[14] There are clear cultural differences in the legislation here, implying a culturally different coding of the interest in privacy. I shall return to this point in greater detail shortly.

Finally, there is a *philosophical discourse* on the subject of privacy. Various positions from feminist theory, theories of the public sphere and the definitions of informational privacy converge in this discourse, which since the 1960s has come to produce an independent body of philosophical literature centred upon a precise delineation of the definition and function of privacy.[15] Drawing in a variety of ways on the other discourses on privacy, this literature has been interested first and foremost in the conceptual assumptions that these other discourses tacitly take for granted, seeking to use precise definitions to establish in precise terms the functions of privacy within liberal societies. A further branch of this philosophical discourse, one that is nonetheless largely independent of these analyses, can be made out in the various liberal conceptualizations of privacy that can be traced through history from Thomas Hobbes via John Stuart Mill to Richard Rorty.[16] These approaches all connect the concept of privacy in functional terms with the concept of freedom, but often remain underdetermined with regard to the exact meaning of privacy and its specific relation to freedom.[17]

This brief survey of the various treatments of privacy shows that recent interest in reconceptualizing it is due to three distinct historical processes: first, the intrusion of intimacy into the public realm through previously private themes that have turned public, as well as shifts in notions of individuality and authenticity; secondly, radical changes in the relation between the sexes and the concomitant reconfiguration of the private sphere; and thirdly, recent developments in information technologies capable of threatening the protection of personal privacy in completely new ways. This survey also shows that there is not *one* history of privacy, and that the history of privacy may include more than what counts as 'private' at any particular time.[18] Finally, it brings to light the conventional nature of the separation between public and private life. Of course, there are many points of overlap between these diverse discourses and theoretical approaches, especially where feminist criticism, the sociological or diagnostic approach and theories of the public sphere are concerned. The treatment of informational privacy, however, almost always runs parallel to and independent of these other discourses. In the following chapters, I shall refer to all these discourses on privacy in varying measure, for in attempting a theory of privacy and its value I am concerned with as many as possible, if not all, of the problematic aspects of the term.

2 Privacy: conceptual clarifications

These various discourses concerned with the concept of privacy all presuppose a certain *meaning* of the concept, albeit for the most part not explicitly. I should therefore like to devote some attention to a more precise clarification of the concept, for only once the meaning of the concept and its definition are resolved can the function and value of privacy be discussed in more precise terms. First of all, therefore, I shall try to delineate the meaning of the concept of privacy in its full range. Following this, I want briefly to discuss some *definitions* that for the most part refer to a particular aspect of the meaning.[19] I shall then propose a definition that seeks to do justice to the range of the concept's meaning. Against this background I then intend to take the further step of briefly presenting the different normative suggestions concerning the function and value of privacy and sketching the idea of the value of privacy that will be elucidated in the following chapters.

Let us return once more to the semantics of the word 'private'.[20] For a start, 'private' should be distinguished from 'intimate'. What is intimate is also private, but not vice versa. 'Intimacy' has mainly erotic or sexual connotations, connotations of proximity and vulnerability that also – but not only – have to do with exposure of one's own body. It forms a nucleus of what one calls and wants to keep private, but for this very reason is not identical with privacy, which incorporates more than just the realm of intimacy. Secondly, 'private' must be distinguished from 'secret'. What is private can be secret, but is not necessarily so, as in the case, for example, of the thoroughly public private matter of how a person dresses. What is secret can be private, but is not necessarily so, as when, for example, one speaks of state secrets.[21] In this case, we thus find semantic overlaps that occur when privacy is dependent upon something being completely hidden or concealed, in other words upon a secret, as with secret diaries or also secret ballots.[22] Indeed, secrecy can even help clarify the semantic contrast between private and public, for everything that is not private is public, but what is public can still be secret, as when political meetings are secret but not private. Here, of course, the different aspects of the meaning of 'public' in the sense of 'concerning everybody' and 'accessible to everybody' also have a part to play.[23]

Let us now turn in more detail to the semantic field of privacy itself. The predicate 'private', as we have already seen above, is a complex one, which we ascribe to actions, situations, states of mind, places and objects.[24] Witness, once again, the diversity of the examples named at the outset.[25] In everyday language, there are two distinct semantic models underlying the various uses of 'private' and 'public'. The first is an 'onion' model, allowing one to distinguish between different layers of privacy. The centre of the onion is the realm of personal or bodily intimacy and privacy (including one's private diary, for example), as opposed to which everything else is regarded as 'public'. Then comes a second layer comprising the classic realm of privacy, that is the family (or other intimate relationships). As opposed to the family, the outside world of society and the state then constitutes the public realm. If we go a stage further, then it is society at large – the realm of economic structures or public civil society – that counts as ‘private’ with respect to intervention by the state, thus forming yet another realm of privacy in the face of the public realm of the state and its possible interference.[26] The second model in everyday usage lies at right angles to the first, for this time the term ‘private’ is predicated of actions or decisions that we may take or carry out no matter where we happen to be. Going to church is thus just as much a private matter as comments that I may make in public but as a private person. In this second sense, the concept of privacy describes a protected sphere or dimension of action and responsibility, where individuals can act in a way that is independent of decisions and influences from the public realm of state institutions and society at large. The second model lies at right angles to the first because it cannot be described in spatial terms but only in terms of dimensions of action and responsibility, dimensions of interest and concern.[27]

If we now seek to systematize the diverse uses of the concept in conjunction with the two semantic models in order to do justice to its whole range of meaning, then the different aspects of its meaning, I want to suggest, can be classified into three basic types. We use the term ‘private’ to refer firstly to modes of action and conduct, secondly to a certain knowledge, and thirdly to spaces. The question of whether I attend church, and if so which one, thus refers to a private mode of action (in public), as does the question of which school I send my child to or what clothes I wear on the streets.[28] Private knowledge or information can denote not only medical data and what I think about my colleagues at work, but also, for example, the question of whom I live with.[29] Private spaces are of course dwellings or rooms.[30] Expressions such as ‘private life’ and ‘the private sphere’ are to be understood, then, as hypostasizations or summaries of different aspects of these basic meanings. This classification of meaning thus seeks to integrate the various uses of the term as well as the perspectives of the two models. Of course, there are overlaps between the three basic meanings. Private ‘knowledge’, for instance, is also protected within private spaces.

So far, however, we have only systematized the *meaning* of the concept ‘private’. This does not in itself provide us with a clear definition of the term. A closer look at the various proposals for a definition of privacy found in the literature, especially the philosophical literature, reveals that they are almost all interested only in specific aspects of the concept’s meaning,[31] which can be arranged in short into five categories. First there are definitions of privacy that designate as private whatever ‘naturally’ falls within the sphere of the household, of reproduction, of the biological necessities.[32] Everything that takes place outside the (private) household, by contrast, is public. ‘Private’ is here accordingly understood only in its spatial meaning and as it were naturalized, so what is to count as private and what as public is established naturally and thus once and for all. As we know, Hannah Arendt still defined the concept of privacy in such terms.[33] For the time being, I shall limit myself to asserting that such a definition is not only too narrow (doing justice to too few aspects of its meaning), but also essentializes the term implausibly. I shall return to argue the point at a later stage.[34] There is another definition of the concept that has become influential in the literature. The right to privacy here means the 'right to be left alone'.[35] This very general definition of the term by Justices Warren and Brandeis prepared the field not only for detailed legal discussions but also for efforts to define it in philosophy, yet it is too general to be conceived as the starting point for a normative theory of privacy.[36] For one thing, the right to be left alone can be described just as well as a negative civil liberty. A distinction between rights to freedom and rights to privacy cannot be drawn with such a broadly based definition.

A more specific approach nonetheless associated with the claim to provide a general definition of privacy is the third category, which seeks to define privacy in terms of access to or the inaccessibility of a person. Ruth Gavison here provides a classic formulation: 'An individual enjoys perfect privacy when he is completely inaccessible to others.'[37] Anita Allen's definition is couched in similar terms: 'Personal privacy is a condition of inaccessibility of the person, his or her mental states, or information about the person to the senses or surveillance devices of others.'[38] Although the attempt to define privacy in terms of 'access' seems to be a valid approach, however, it remains incomplete if it is not joined by another factor, that of control. A crevasse into which I have fallen is clearly not 'private', even though it does comply with the condition of 'inaccessibility' proposed by Gavison and Allen.[39] If a state of isolation, seclusion or secrecy is enforced and not freely chosen, in other words if the person in question has no control over it, then one would not describe it as 'private'.[40]

On the other hand, there are also approaches – making up the fourth group of proposed definitions – that take the idea of control as their very starting point, that is control over specific areas of privacy. Here for a start we find those theories that define privacy as control over information. Such is the case with the influential definition by Westin: 'Privacy is the claim of individuals, groups, or institutions to determine for themselves when, how and to what extent information about them is communicated to others.'[41] Similar to Westin's definition is the one provided by Charles Fried, for whom privacy is 'the control we have over information about ourselves'.[42] However, this control can be understood in very broad terms. Iris Young thus writes: 'The Private [is] what the individual chooses to withdraw from public view.'[43] Control is here conceived as a retreat from visibility to the public eye. Finally, the notion of control appears in one further context, where privacy is defined in terms of concepts of closeness and intimacy, as exemplified by Julie Inness: 'Privacy is the state of the agent having control over a realm of intimacy, which contains her decisions about intimate access to herself (including intimate informational access) and her decisions about her own intimate actions.'[44]

What all these various approaches based on the concept of control have in common is that they each only posit one particular aspect of control and thus describe the concept of privacy too narrowly: as the control of information, as protection from the merely 'public view', as located only in contexts of intimacy. This means that there are crucial dimensions of the concept, as laid out above, that are left out of account in each of these definitions. This is not the case in the final group of proposed definitions, for here we find theories of privacy that aim both at a general meaning of the term and at a specific definition. Sisela Bok, for example, defines privacy as 'the condition of being protected from unwanted access by others – either physical access, personal information or attention. Claims to privacy are claims to control access.'[45] Privacy is here defined as a condition in which one is protected in various respects from undesired intrusions by other people. Even if the notion of a 'condition' here seems an inappropriate restriction (for one's home is not a condition), such a broadly based definition still seems most likely to cover the whole range of meaning of the concept of privacy.[46]

In accordance with such broadly based theories, I now want to propose the following definition of privacy: Something counts as private if one can oneself control the access to this 'something'.[47] Conversely, the protection of privacy means protection against unwanted access by other people. The term 'access' can here have both the direct, concrete, physical meaning, as when I demand to be able myself to control the access to my home, but it can also be meant *metaphorically*. This metaphorical sense refers both to the control I have over who has what access to knowledge about me, such as who knows which (relevant) data about me, and the control I have over which people have 'access' in the form of the ability to interfere or intervene when it comes to decisions that are relevant to me. The weight of this definition lies with the ideas of control and of unwanted access, and not, therefore, with the idea of a separation between the particular individual on the one hand and a public realm of all other people on the other. The spatial metaphor or the metaphor of a realm is here only one aspect too. Moreover, the concept of 'control' also brings to light the inherent normative moment, for the term 'private' is not normally used in a purely descriptive manner, but always has prescriptive elements. The word 'can' must thus also be understood in the sense of 'can and/or should and/or may'. Not always when I can *in fact* control the access to 'something' is this 'something' also 'private' (as when, for example, I have stolen someone else's diary), and vice versa.

To provide a brief demonstration of the plausibility of this definition in terms of control of access, I now wish to look at some of the various uses of the term. Take a private room: this room is private if I can control access to it, if I can evade the observation and control of other people. Take data or information about me: here too it is reasonable to say that this is private if I can and/or should control access to it. The words 'and/or' are relevant here because I cannot of course always *in fact* control access, but the normative element in 'should' makes it clear that for the legitimate circulation of this information (whether medical data or simply prattle and gossip) my assent really should be necessary. Access is here thus used in a metaphorical sense. This is even clearer in the following case, which again concerns protection against unwanted access in a figurative sense, this time control over the 'access to me' in the sense of possibilities of *objecting to* my behaviour. Such protection is demanded and expected for actions that we describe as private, such as the question of what clothes I wear on the street or what church I attend. Protection against 'unwanted access' must here be understood metaphorically as protection against possibilities of objection or interference from others when it comes to certain private decisions, actions, or ways of behaving or living.

These *dimensions* of privacy, defined in this way as possibilities for exercising control over 'access', can now be interpreted as three ways of describing the normativity of privacy. I speak of *decisional* privacy when we claim the right to protection from unwanted access in the sense of unwanted interference or of heteronomy in our decisions and actions. I speak of *informational* privacy when people claim the right to protection against unwanted access in the sense of interference in personal data about themselves, in other words access to information about them that they have no desire to see in the wrong hands.[48] And I speak of *local* privacy in a completely non-metaphorical sense when we claim the right to protection against the admission of other people to spaces or areas. Violations of a person's privacy can be defined, therefore, in these three ways: as illicit interference in one's actions, as illicit surveillance, as illicit intrusions in rooms or dwellings.[49]

Such a definition of privacy must be understood as conventional. Nothing belongs 'by nature' to the realm of the private. The dividing line between what is to be regarded as public and what as private is a constructed one and has not been laid down once and for all. In liberal societies, the boundaries themselves are open to discussion and thus also the relationship between the two 'realms'. Even so, such societies have certain conventionally defined realms that are considered private at a culturally very deeply ingrained level, realms of 'prescribed' privacy, which have to do in particular with the bodily functions and in general with the exposure of one's own body.[50]

Against this background of meaning and definition, I now want to take the one final step of briefly touching upon the question that will become a focus of attention in what follows, 'why do we value privacy?', and in so doing conclude for the time being our overview of the debates about the concept of privacy. This question too is given many different answers in the literature, answers that refer to its intrinsic value, to the constitutive protection of intimate relationships, or to the protection of personhood. And there is a range of approaches that establish a connection – of varying degrees of closeness – between the concepts of privacy and freedom.[51] I shall deal with the various problems associated with these approaches in detail below. Here I only want to outline what is to follow. What I shall try to explain is that we regard privacy as valuable because we regard autonomy as valuable, and because autonomy can only be lived out in all its aspects and articulated in all its senses with the help of the conditions of privacy and by means of rights and claims to privacy. If the *telos* of freedom is conceived as being able to lead an autonomous life, then spelling out the conditions for such an autonomous life brings to light that civil liberties alone are not sufficient for the protection of autonomy, but that autonomy is reliant upon these civil liberties being substantialized in rights and claims regarding the protection of privacy. A person's autonomy can be violated or impaired in ways that do not directly bear upon the civil liberties themselves, and it is because of this possibility that people are dependent in their autonomy upon the protection of privacy.

3 The framework of liberal democracy

The theory of privacy with which we will be dealing in what follows is grounded within a particular political and philosophical framework, namely liberalism. For liberalism, the distinction between a public and a private realm is not just any old distinction but a constitutive one, for this separation expresses the notion – fundamental to liberalism – of the protection of individual freedom and the autonomy of persons in the face of inadmissible interference or regulations on the part of the state.[52] With these reflections on the concept and the theory of privacy, my aim is also to make a contribution to the self-understanding of liberalism and the internal make-up of liberal democracy. For this reason, I want to draw a rough outline of the sort of liberalism and liberal democracy that will form the background to what follows.

The current theories of liberalism or liberal democracy can be described as a 'family'.[53] But the question is then what characterizes the family, what are the prominent squabbles within the family, and who does not belong (entirely) to *this* family and why not. I shall trace these points very briefly and in the process attempt to sketch the concept of an egalitarian liberalism presupposed in the following chapters.[54]

Liberty, equality, neutrality of the state, and democracy can unquestionably be identified as the four basic pillars of any liberal theory.[55] *Within* the family there are arguments firstly about which of these pillars forms the essential foundation for liberal theory, and above all which of the first two characteristics, liberty or equality, takes first place in the list of liberal priorities. This question is in turn connected in a general sense with various strategies for grounding a liberal theory.

Let us take a brief look at the four pillars in more detail, firstly at liberty. All liberal theories in equal measure assert the precedence of a particular set of basic individual rights as *individual civil liberties*.[56] In essence, the type of rights at issue here has not changed since Hobbes or at least since Locke, Kant, Constant and Mill, even if the area of application has.[57] Irrespective of whether one takes Immanuel Kant's classical formulation or John Stuart Mill's, the fundamental idea of negative civil liberties is basically the same, that is that individual rights are necessary to protect the (modern) idea of autonomy and freedom in the face of inadmissible intrusions from the state and society in general. If the idea of individual freedom is that we each in our own way pursue our own particular notion of the good, this does not in itself necessarily tell us anything when it comes to spelling out the meaning of the concept of freedom in concrete terms: both the characterization of the fundamental idea and the list of civil liberties are sufficiently general to incorporate competing substantializations of the concept. Borderline cases occur where the concept of individual freedom is bounded by communitarian aims.[58] Further below I shall delineate a richer and more concrete concept of freedom – freedom as autonomy. For this preliminary characterization of liberalism, however, this is not yet necessary.[59]

Let us now turn, therefore, to equality. With respect to the problem of equality, two levels can be distinguished. On a first level, equality denotes something akin to Ronald Dworkin's fundamental principle that all persons be treated as equals. This much is accepted by every liberal theory.[60] Over and above this, however, a stronger, more controversial postulate of equality can be described, which seems nonetheless to follow from this first one.[61] Depending on how strongly the first is interpreted, there are two paths that can be taken. In the first case, the concept of equality can be taken as one's starting point – 'liberalism based on equality'[62] – and liberties, rights and the neutrality of the state understood as ways of securing and realizing this original idea. As we know, this path is the one taken by Dworkin.[63] The other approach takes the idea of individual liberties as the basis for liberalism, yet then sets a limit to this principle in the form of the first principle of equality. The idea here is that *formally* securing (equal) liberties alone is not sufficient to meet the demands of the principle of equality. As we know, this path is the one taken by John Rawls and Jürgen Habermas. Indeed, this is how Rawls grounds the principle of the equal 'worth of liberty' in conjunction with what he terms the difference principle,[64] while for Habermas it is social rights that have the corresponding function of securing substantially equal liberties as opposed to a purely formal equality of liberties. In Dworkin, by contrast, the postulate of equality determines liberal theory through the idea of equality of resources right from the outset.[65]

It might be said, therefore, that the differences within the liberal camp refer to differences regarding strategies for grounding the theory but not necessarily regarding the consequences for liberal politics. I here want to underline the point – in the form of an affirmation rather than a substantiation – that it is precisely because of the equal importance granted by liberal thought to freedom and equality that the relation between the two must be understood not as one of rivalry but rather as mutual elucidation. In this spirit, Jeremy Waldron writes that 'a commitment to equal freedom is not a compromise between freedom and equality. What "equality" does in that formula is to pin down the form of our commitment to freedom; and what "freedom" does is to indicate what it is that we are concerned to equalize.'[66] This is of course still too general to be able to give an exact answer to the question 'equality of what?' But it provides a starting point for considering aspects in which the concepts can be compared. Feminist theory is also able to take up this idea of equal liberties, precisely because such an idea does not posit a patriarchal, gender-specific concept of 'equality'.[67]

The third idea of liberalism follows from the first two: the principle of the *neutrality* of the state, in other words the principle of the separation between generally valid state regulations open to consent on the one hand and the particular individuals' ideas of the good on the other.[68] The distinction between private and public realms of life here finds its liberal *locus classicus*,[69] for only when the state keeps out of 'private affairs' can the plurality of life-projects that follows from the idea of individual freedom genuinely be safeguarded. An initial distinction can here be drawn in broad terms between procedural neutrality on the one hand and neutrality of aims on the other.[70] It can then be claimed that while procedural neutrality, at least in a weak sense of the term, can be guaranteed in a liberal state, the neutrality of its objectives remains problematic. We can, it is true, follow Rawls in arguing against explicit support for individual (or common) notions of the good.[71] Yet the goals of the liberal state are still not neutral, firstly because they must always exclude certain anti-liberal ideas, and secondly because they always support collective ideas of the good determined by the cultural and historical situation of the state and its constitution. This is a point made by both communitarian and feminist criticism.[72] This insight means that even in a liberal state that is in this sense weakly neutral there must be argument both about the interpretation of its neutrality and about the necessity and contents of collective ideas of the good.[73] Yet such an insight is not without its consequences, for argument of this sort can only be liberal – in the sense of upholding equal liberties – if it does not always follow rules that as such prevent neutrality.

Let us turn, therefore, to the last of the four principles, the principle of democracy. The liberal guarantee of individual basic rights is valid in principle for three classes of rights – negative rights, social rights, and rights of political participation – as a result of which *political* liberty, or political participation, is secured at the same time as *individual* liberty.[74] This idea too is undisputed within the field of liberal political theories. The only thing open to dispute is to what extent the rights of political participation are to be seen as foundational.[75] What is important in our context, however, is the equal status of the two classes of rights and thus also the equal importance attached to securing equal individual and political liberties in a liberal democracy. A further point of dispute here is how the democratic procedures are to be described more fully and which form of democratic participation is to be posited.[76] One final point of dispute is how the concept of representation is to be defined and in what way it is suitable for in turn calling into question the neutrality of liberal democracy.[77]

Such is the framework within which the following reflections are situated. In the process, I assume a concept of egalitarian liberalism with all the consequences that this has for a theory of democracy or democratic citizenship, and where the question of privacy directly touches upon these assumptions I shall return to them with arguments.[78] Yet the outline of the liberal family that I have sketched implies limits to it as well: libertarian positions such as the one espoused by Robert Nozick, whose weighting of freedom and equality greatly favours the former at the expense of the latter, would not belong to *this* family.[79] Problematic borderline cases include communitarian ideas such as those propounded by Michael Sandel, republican approaches such as Arendt's and deconstructive positions such as Judith Butler's.[80] All of these, for different reasons, lie outside the liberal family merely in terms of their self-understanding. The fact that there are also good reasons based on the liberal principles outlined above for describing them at least as problematic cases is a point to which I shall return below. But always from the one perspective – the question of privacy and its value.

4 Cultural differences: autonomy and authenticity

My interest in the present study is a *normative* conception of privacy in and for modern liberal societies. One of the reasons that this needs to be underlined is that the cultural differences in the coding of privacy, which exist even within the spectrum of the Western liberal democracies, will not be given specific treatment but play at most a marginal role. Because of this empirical and thematic restriction, however, I should here like to look at least briefly at the cultural differences in this coding as they come to light – in an exemplary and simplified form – between Germany and the US. This is worthwhile for the additional reason that looking at what is considered particularly worthy of protection or remarkable about privacy will provide us with a preliminary notion of the different sides of a liberal conception of privacy.

As regards cultural differences between Western and non-Western societies in terms of the coding of privacy, a great deal can be learnt from anthropology and ethnology.[81] In contrast, there are surprisingly few comparative studies that focus on the differing cultural interpretations of privacy within the spectrum of modern liberal Western societies.[82] To illustrate the different ways privacy is evaluated in the United States and Germany, it makes sense to take a look at the differences in some prominent legal cases. In the United States, the accent concerning what counts as private and thus as worthy of protection is on the 'right to be left alone',[83] a right to be left in peace by the state or public society in the most important matters of one's personhood in order to be able to make decisions and act in accordance with one's own wishes. The most important and best-known legal verdict in this context is the legalization of abortion of 1973. In a famous formulation, this ruling says that the 'right to privacy' is 'broad enough to encompass a woman's decision whether or not to terminate her pregnancy'.[84] Even though it was and still is a matter of controversy precisely which constitutional law the right to privacy – which is not itself mentioned in the Constitution – is derived from, and even though the ruling on abortion itself remains every bit as controversial as ever, not only in court, what is beyond dispute is that the US Supreme Court here recognizes a general right to privacy, which means at heart that when it comes to decisions and actions that fundamentally concern one's individual personhood the state must keep its distance. The autonomy of persons in their decisions and actions is here coupled with a concept of privacy, 'decisional privacy', that is hardly customary in a German context. In Germany and Europe by contrast, it is inconceivable that a right to terminate a pregnancy be grounded upon a right to privacy. The concept of privacy plays virtually no part in these discussions.[85]

In Germany, the accent in the public – legal and social – discussions about privacy lies elsewhere. The paradigm for the debates here, as we know, is the *Grosser Lauschangriff* (The Great Bugging Operation), in other words the question of whether the state is allowed to monitor what its members say and do, and if so, to what extent. If privacy is under threat in Germany, then the accent is not so much on freedom from in*trusions* into one's decisions and actions as on freedom from in*spections* of one's daily life. Protection of the private sphere is thus called for when people see themselves as threatened in their day-to-day selfhood, as occurs when they consider themselves vulnerable to possible voyeurs, whether state snoopers or individual peeping Toms. This difference in the way privacy is coded in the United States and in Germany (or Europe) comes to light not only, for example, in the differences in the way private spaces are protected from observation,[86] but is also manifest in the jurisprudence concerning data protection, which is completely different in Europe and the US. There is no law in the United States that would correspond to the strict European Union directive on the protection of informational data.[87]

This difference can be further illustrated by the distinct jurisprudence with respect to the *Recht am Bild* ('the right over pictures of oneself'), for such a right exemplifies the significance of the protection of privacy in the public realm. Not surprisingly, and with logical rigour, the German Federal Supreme Court has conceded such a right over pictures of oneself, while a parallel suit in the US was unsuccessful. I shall here briefly cite the two verdicts, first the German one:

> The plaintiff is the joint proprietor of a brewery in K. He is an amateur jockey, who takes part in horse shows. The defendant is the manufacturer of a pharmaceutical preparation which in the minds of broad segments of the population also serves to heighten sexual potency. For the marketing of this product in Germany, including K. among other places, she distributed a poster with the illustration of a show rider. The poster was based on an original photo of the plaintiff, taken by the press publisher

> S. at a horse show. The plaintiff had not granted his consent for the use of his picture.[88]

It is well known that the Federal Supreme Court found for the plaintiff. The publication of the picture, it ruled, constituted a 'violation of the right over pictures of oneself':

> what is inadmissible about the unauthorized publication of pictures by a third party is that in this way the person depicted is deprived of the freedom to deal with this item from his individual sphere on the basis of his own resolution.[89]

In a parallel case in the United States, the court ruled exactly the opposite:[90]

> A couple was shocked to find a picture of their family in *Omni* magazine illustrating an article on research involving caffeine-aided fertilization. The article was entitled 'Caffeine and Fast Sperm'. Accompanying the story was a photo of the couple and their six children with the caption 'Want a big family? [. . .]' The couple sued for invasion of privacy. They [. . .] argued that their picture was not reasonably related to the subject.[91]

Complaining that the picture of their family of eight bore no relation to the content of the article, artificial insemination, the plaintiffs' suit was closely analogous to the case of the German 'amateur jockey'. In this instance, however, the ruling went against them.

Not only these particularly patent differences in the verdicts on the right over pictures of oneself, but also the aforementioned differences in jurisprudence on informational privacy and the termination of pregnancy, along with the accompanying social debates, can be read as different expressions of what is valuable about privacy: privacy in the sense of control over the authenticity of our self-presentations versus privacy in the sense of the protection of autonomous actions and decisions. Yet the two notions – that is both that privacy protects us from interventions in what we wish to do, and that it protects us from being monitored in what we say or do or restricted in the control of our self-presentations – can be conceived as different contextualizations or aspects of what is nonetheless one and the same idea. Underlying both is a liberal ideal, the ideal of being able to lead a self-determined, autonomous, authentic life, a life of one's own. Autonomy and authenticity as ideals that depend upon conditions of privacy for fulfilment are not to be interpreted as alternatives, therefore, but as two sides of the same coin. Accordingly, in the following chapters I do not intend to treat this cultural difference as a competition, but rather as distinct weightings given to the same liberal idea. The concern will thus not, or only marginally, be with questions of legislation, but primarily with the normative question of why we value privacy in all these aspects. Although the discussions are influenced in particular by US jurisprudence, I shall only be interested in this in so far as it is relevant to the normative philosophical question.

5 A comment on the method

The theme of privacy is located at the interface of political philosophy and social philosophy.[92] On the one hand it is questions concerning the theory of justice that are at issue here, and on the other hand questions about a rewarding life for a person in all her social relations. If the individual freedom of persons is dependent upon the protection of privacy, this refers to the justice of a society: privacy must be protected in the same way for all people. And if this privacy makes it possible for people to lead a life of individual autonomy, this means that such autonomy is dependent upon the protection of privacy in *social* relations and practices, not only with respect to the state and not solely through state or legal regulations. This, at least, is what the following chapters will try to show.

The approaches to the problem from the perspective of the theory of justice take up the liberal tradition from Locke, Kant and Mill through to Rawls, Habermas and Okin. The concept of privacy developed in this approach is consequently a normative one, and is thus the product, it can be said, of a *constructive* procedure.[93] Of course, such a procedure refers (loosely) to social configurations, yet the formation of its concepts is owed first and foremost not to these but to its normative grounds. The theme of privacy involves questions concerning not only the theory of justice, however, but also social philosophy, for privacy has to do with the social conditions under which subjects lead their lives. An analysis of these conditions always entails looking at the social norms, conventions, and ways of life present in liberal societies, each of which determines what is to count as private and what as public and in what way privacy is respected. If such conventions, norms and ways of life are also interpreted and described in terms of greater or lesser success or more or less favourable outcomes, then this means always seeking to develop the normative core from within these very conventions, norms and ways of life as well. Such a procedure can therefore be termed reconstructive. Reconstructive procedures may thus inform the normative concept, the constructive element, but in the end they will always have to withstand its judgement.

The critical reconstruction of existing social norms necessarily includes, however, a historical or genealogical moment as well. When this study attempts, for example, to explain feminist criticism in terms of the history of privacy as the domestic realm and thus expose the repressive element in such traditions, the genealogy of the concept cannot be dispensed with. Yet this does not mean that one cannot hold to the sense of such dichotomies as the distinction between private and public. Viewing them as historical or social constructs does not in itself point to their conceptual impossibility, normative inadequacy or social dysfunctionality.[94] As is natural, the following chapters thus apply various weightings in this respect. If the discussion of the normative connection between freedom and privacy centres on constructive procedures, the chapters on the specific dimensions of privacy will tend rather to proceed in a reconstructive, explanatory manner.

Methods in social philosophy are always problematic, because on the one hand they cannot commit themselves to forming purely normative, foundational concepts, while on the other hand they do not want to pursue conventional, sociological empiricism either. To illustrate modern experiences and assumptions, I shall occasionally turn to literary texts instead of empirical material, but these in a way have the same function. The method applied in the following study thus comprises diverse elements, which are intended to complement one another in such a way as to produce an adequate theory of the value of privacy.

6 Privacy and autonomy: the line of argument

Having circumscribed and situated the thematic background and the liberal-democratic framework and methodology, I now want to sketch the course taken by the following chapters. I shall start with a conceptual and historical clarification of the concept of privacy from the perspective of the theory of justice (chapter 2), in other words with the ambivalences and inconsistencies of the traditional liberal concept of privacy and its feminist critique. The aim of this first step is to rid the concept of privacy of its gender-specific connotations and thus clear the way to develop a theory of privacy and its value with a concept that is normatively adequate and free from contradictions.

The second step serves then to clarify the concepts of freedom and autonomy (chapter 3). If the hypothesis is that there is a functional correlation between privacy and freedom, then it is necessary to clarify what freedom we are talking about. The concept of freedom that I wish to elucidate defines the core of modern freedom as individual autonomy. A person is autonomous if she can ask herself the question what sort of person she wants to be, how she wants to live, and if she can then live in this way. Such personal autonomy, it will then be further explained, is determined on the one hand by subjective abilities, while on the other hand external conditions are necessary for its success. Following these clarifications of the concept of autonomy, I then want to ask what the value of privacy consists in and elucidate in greater detail the conceptual and normative connection between freedom, autonomy and privacy.

Only against this background will it then be possible to take a more precise look at the individual dimensions of privacy, dimensions that have already been distinguished above and will be substantiated and explained in more detail in the ensuing chapters (chapters 4–6). The dimension of *decisional* privacy serves to secure the scope for a subject to make decisions and take action in all his social relations. The dimension of *informational* privacy serves to secure a horizon of expectations regarding what others know about him that is necessary for his autonomy. The dimension of *local* privacy serves to protect the possibilities for spatial withdrawal upon which a subject is dependent for the sake of his autonomy. In each of these chapters, the aim is to show what the value of privacy inheres in and in what way the violation of these dimensions of privacy also entails a violation of the individual autonomy of the subject. What should become clear, therefore, is not only why we value privacy but also why we *ought to* value it. In the last chapter (chapter 7), privacy is looked at once more from a different perspective: from its points of interface with the public world. In the process, I want first to point up the ambivalences connected with the diverse ways in which privacy is treated or 'staged' in the public domain. Secondly, however, my intention is to give the question of interfaces a further, very different twist in order to ask about the *identity* of the public and the private person, about the meaning of such identity, about the need for it.

In the background to all these themes, however, there is one further one. If the protection of privacy is necessary for an autonomous life, and if an autonomous life is at least a necessary (though not a sufficient) condition for a life that is good or rewarding, then the protection of privacy is necessary for a rewarding life. This theme, a rewarding life, will nonetheless remain in the background, only coming to the fore now and again.

2 Equal Freedom, Equal Privacy: On the Critique of the Liberal Tradition

1 Head or heart: contradictions in the liberal concept of privacy

Midway through Dorothy Sayers' novel *Gaudy Night*, the protagonist Harriet Vane, a successful writer and Oxford graduate who has fallen for the celebrated Lord Peter Wimsey, torn between the ecstasies and agonies of love and poetry, enters into a discussion with the eminent don Miss de Vine on the 'difficulty of combining intellectual and emotional interests'. This difficulty, suggests Miss de Vine, does not 'affect women only; it affects men as well. But when men put their public lives before their private lives, it causes less outcry than when a woman does the same thing, because women put up with neglect better than men, having been brought up to expect it.' To which Harriet replies, 'But suppose one doesn't quite know which one wants to put first. Suppose (...) one is cursed with both a heart and a brain?'[1]

The heart and the head, feeling and intellect, women and men, private and public life: these parallels with all their connotations are among the classic features of the self-understanding and self-description of liberal societies.[2] To the realm of privacy belong feelings, home and hearth, emotional care for the male members of society as well as the raising of the children, while reason, 'brains' and professional life, by contrast, characterize the (male) public realm. Sayers here formulated – in 1935 – a dilemma of modern civil society that rests on this society's division into a pre-political sphere regarded as having nothing to do with political matters and as completely separate from political life,[3] and a public and political sphere where social life in its true sense runs its course. It is a dilemma inherent in the notion that one can only ever lead the one life or the other, and that traditionally a 'private' life is the one mapped out for women. At the same time, the domestic, private realm comes to acquire a twofold significance in the evaluative semantics of civil societies. On the one hand, this domestic sphere, including the family, is valued and prized as the realm that is sheltered from the demands of a hostile world, where love and affection prevail instead of competition and the pursuit of profit, and which provides a haven both from the hard laws of the economy and the implacable rules of politics. Yet alongside this interpretation, there exists another version, a negative one, which unambiguously associates the private sphere with 'women' and the public sphere with 'men' and characterizes the private as inferior in relation to the public, just as nature is inferior in relation to culture.[4] The subtext to this use of the concepts is that the family and the private realm are lower in value because it is the public sphere in which the relevant decisions are taken, where social responsibility is exercised, and where independence from the demands of nature and reproduction holds sway.[5] Even the traditional liberal differentiation between private and public thus displays an imbalance that is coded in gender-specific terms and works to the detriment of women, in so far as this coding of the spheres confines them to the household and reproaches them for their insuperable dependence upon nature.

On the other hand, however, the *practical core* of the liberal separation of private and public was and continues to be the idea that there must be realms or *dimensions* of life (the metaphor of a clearly demarcated domain is thoroughly misleading) that can be left to be shaped by the individual person and where the state should consequently refrain from using its opportunities for intervention. Indeed, the history of liberalism has been characterized from the very outset by the fact that this separation is not clear-cut but controversial and has constantly been open to renegotiation. The core of this conception of a protected private sphere is famously expressed, for example, in the notion of freedom of worship. The liberal understanding of the neutrality of the state shows itself in the fact that just such 'private matters' are none of its business. The liberal state accordingly distinguishes in general between realms that are to be regulated publicly and unregulated realms that are free from state activity.[6] What is to count as public and what as private is subject to historical changes and is clearly a matter of political processes and decisions. Such a distinction between private and public realms is thus fundamental to the social structure of modern societies and is part of the vocabulary taken for granted in their self-descriptions.

Alongside this concept of liberal privacy, however, there continues to exist the concept of the private family and household, and it is the latter that is essentially bound up with a fundamental feature of modern societies' hierarchical structure, that is the gender-specific division of labour. The liberal concept of privacy is thus fundamentally contradictory. On the one hand, it is equated with the freedom to lead one's life in accordance with one's own preferences and criteria of the good, and it is in this sense that Mill, for example, speaks of 'the liberty of private life'.[7] 'Private' is thus the term applied to certain dimensions of life to the extent that freedom in one's way of living, guaranteed by the liberal state, can here find expression and is protected in a whole variety of ways. Yet on the other hand, it is also the term applied to a realm that is delimited in its content and coded in gender-specific terms, a realm traditionally devoted to the family, to reproduction, child-raising and serving the emotional and other needs of the family, a realm of 'nature' and thus also of women. The two aspects, therefore, the dimensions of individual freedom no less than the female sphere of the family and care, are subsumed within one and the same concept, privacy.

Ever since Hobbes and Locke, liberal theory has thus been confronted with a genuine and pressing problem. For while it has provided grounds to justify the equality of all human beings and proposed establishing equal rights to individual freedom for all a state's citizens, it has at the same time limited these equal rights to adult men. And this has occurred because the distinction between a private, domestic, pre-political realm and a public, political realm is simultaneously a distinction between the realms of women and of men and for this very reason fails to open up *equal* spaces of freedom for both. The dilemma posed by Harriet Vane thus fundamentally contradicts the very idea of liberalism from Locke through to Rawls, for liberalism has been concerned to secure and guarantee equal rights to individual freedom for every member of society, equal liberties in the way one leads one's life and takes up the diverse options possible in a particular society, without fixing in advance *how* these options are to be taken up. Of course, liberalism does not guarantee every freedom. Even in a genuinely liberal-democratic society, one that as far as possible does justice to its normative foundations, problems and dilemmas may clearly still arise from the incompatibility of certain options or liberties, and these may bear directly upon the question of a good or rewarding life for an individual.[8] Yet such dilemmas would at least no longer be gender specific, and for this reason they would not have to be resolved in the way that Harriet Vane believed necessary, with women responsible for the private realm of the heart and men for the public domain of reason.

A first sketch of the problems has thus emerged. In what follows, I shall first provide further elucidation of this twofold liberal concept of privacy and then describe in greater detail the various aspects of the feminist critique of it (section 2). Following this, it will make sense to take a more exhaustive look at the theories expounded in certain classics of liberal thought (section 3), before in section 4 giving a more precise account of the concept of 'equality' or 'equal freedom' that we will have been presupposing in our account. The fifth and final section will elucidate once again the idea of equal freedom and privacy for all.

Let us start, therefore, by taking a closer look at the liberal concept of privacy. On the one hand this includes a *quasi-natural* concept of privacy that is clearly coded in gender-specific terms, and on the other hand it contains a *legal-conventional* concept. This is legal-conventional in character because it is founded on individual civil rights and liberties, and the question of how these rights are to be interpreted – where exactly the boundary is to be drawn between private and public concerns, that is which concerns are of public interest and which are not – is a matter of consent or convention, at best consent that has been democratically legitimated. This concept then also incorporates the sense of privacy and the private sphere that we use when we say that something is a 'private matter' and thus 'no one else's business'. And it is *this* concept of liberal privacy alone that can provide the basis for a convincing normative reinterpretation of the term that takes into account the feminist criticism and that can encompass the protection of one's house or flat as well. This legal-conventional meaning of the term should be categorically distinguished in liberal theory from the other meaning of privacy, the quasi-natural one.[9] Here privacy signifies the sphere in which 'domestic labour' takes place along with the general 'relations work' of attending to the emotional and physical needs of the citizens of the liberal-democratic state. And we have already seen that for just this reason the private sphere in civil society has been both extolled as a place of rest, a haven of peace and loving care, and reviled as a place governed *only* by women and nature. This concept is categorically different (that is different in a systematic sense, not in historical terms) from the legal-conventional one because the question, for example, of religious freedom as a 'private matter' on the one hand and the association of women with the 'private' task of raising children on the other clearly have nothing to do with one another.[10]

The significance of privacy as the sphere of the household, the family and women naturally has a history that predates liberalism, and this sort of separation and evaluation of the private sphere and its gender-specific connotations can be found in one form or another throughout Western political philosophy. In this sense, they are not restricted to liberal theory, but are known to find their classic articulation in Aristotle.[11] It is for this reason too that such strangely contradictory *evaluations* of privacy are to be found in liberal theory. For if Aristotle's conception and modern conceptions that follow an Aristotelian line[12] see the private domain as one of necessity, restriction, confinement and subjection imposed by the (unpleasant) laws of nature and reproduction, this interpretation and evaluation, though preserved in liberalism, is joined not only by the positive connotation of privacy as a refuge, but also by an entirely different interpretation and evaluation of privacy, diametrically opposed to the Aristotelian one, as the dimension of individual freedom, which is not found in Aristotle because for him it was the *public* realm that was the realm of (political) freedom. In modern liberal conceptions, therefore, the Aristotelian idea enters into a strange coalition with the genuinely *liberal* differentiation between private freedom and public control.

My hypothesis is that the inequality in the spaces for freedom enjoyed by women and men is closely bound up with one aspect of the traditional liberal distinction between private and public. If in liberal theory (as in liberal societies) women and men are granted different opportunities for leading a life of individual freedom, this does not simply represent an inequality in the opportunities for laying claim to rights that are formally equal for all, in other words a social inequality that could be described without appealing to the distinction between *private* and *public*. Rather, the inequality in freedom is an effect of precisely this misinterpreted separation between the two realms. If equality of freedom is to prevail, however, then this must be everywhere and for everyone in the same way, and this means two things. 'For everyone in the same way' means that the private sphere of the household must not be understood as a 'naturally' established realm to which women are assigned by nature in such a way that they cannot choose freely from among society's various options concerning how to lead their lives. And 'everywhere' means that even the realm traditionally known as private, the realm of reproduction and the raising of children, the realm of intimacy and familiarity, should be arranged in such a way that here too individual liberties can be experienced by all equally and women are not allocated certain tasks simply by virtue of their sex. The conclusion of this argument is thus that the liberal distinction between private and public needs to be reinterpreted if it is not to be inconsistent with the idea of equality in freedom. I shall return to these hypotheses at the end of this chapter.

In what follows, therefore, I view the separation between a private and a public sphere from the perspective of justice, because my concern is what it means for liberalism to secure equality of freedom. Accordingly, I argue against a certain aspect of the liberal distinction between privacy and the public without thereby wanting to give up the systematic idea of this distinction. By taking this tack, however, my objective in this chapter is a dual one, for I also argue against those feminist theories that would abandon the distinction between private and public entirely.[13] I start from the assumption that the difficulties associated with the liberal distinction between a public and a private sphere are not so categorical that the distinction becomes problematic *in principle*. This also means that protecting the privacy of intimate relationships such as the family is not in itself worthy of criticism, but the question is rather how both elements – the protection of intimacy *and* the more general protection of individual liberties as dimensions of private life – are compatible with the liberal postulate of equality when this calls for a critique of the *gender-specific coding* of the concepts of 'public' and 'private'.

2 The feminist critique

We have started by drawing a systematic distinction between the two meanings of the liberal concept of privacy. It is the traditional meaning, the quasi-natural one, that lies at the heart of the feminist critique of the liberal distinction between *private* and *public*, even though the feminist theories themselves have not always made a precise separation of the two aspects of the concept. Let us now, therefore, take a closer look at this feminist critique and the different stages of its development. In doing so, it makes sense to distinguish between various rounds in the debate on the concept of privacy. The preliminary round can be described as first of all providing a fundamental critique of the distinction between public and private in itself, based on the following, twofold grounds. First, it was said, the assignment of women to the realm of privacy entailed their exclusion from 'public', social and political life and – symbolically at least[14] – from the realm of gainful employment, while the work of reproduction, of looking after family and children, was shown to be socially irrelevant in that it was unpaid. As it was, the private household had only ever had a repressive function and significance for women, and the idea that 'my home is my castle' had never applied for them.[15] Secondly, it was argued, it was mistaken to believe that the private realm of the family was an idyllic realm free from repressions and the social structures of power and domination. This was wrong because, on the one hand, even 'public' regulations were *constantly* reaching into and organizing the realm of the family (for instance in the general structure of gainful employment, but also, more specifically, the laws concerning divorce and social welfare etc.),[16] while on the other hand it was precisely 'public' regulations that *failed* to reach into the private realm *sufficiently*.[17] Strictly speaking, of course, there is no realm beyond the state. The repressive family is always dominated by more general social structures.

This sort of critique of the gender-specific coding of the two spheres frequently rejected in principle the separation of a private – and that meant pre-political – realm from a public, political one. Feminists argued that what liberalism had regarded as private (in the quasi-natural sense) and non-political, above all the organization of society's reproduction and thus the question of the patriarchal order, needed to be explicitly politicized. The separation between private and public accordingly had to be not just reorganized but completely dispensed with, for otherwise it would be impossible to overcome the discriminatory and repressive assignment of women to the realm of the household, reproduction and nature.[18] As a consequence, this first round of the discussion frequently resulted in a radical critique of the distinction, with the realm of privacy being understood as obsolete, having only been conceived as a way of suppressing and discriminating against women anyway. This led to claims that feminist inquiry had 'dismissed such dichotomies as ideological' because women felt unable to live with the clash between the 'logics' of the two realms, as was recently asserted by Elisabeth Klaus.[19] Such diagnoses were often accompanied by a fundamental theoretical critique of liberalism and social contract models in general, since these were all assumed to be based on some sort of separation between a pre-political, quasi-natural realm, to which women, children, the household, care and reproduction were assigned, and a political or public realm, to which gainful employment, political activity in general, and the exercise of civil liberties all belonged.[20]

This type of feminist critique of the liberal concept of privacy focused exclusively on the aspect of the concept's meaning that I have referred to as the quasi-natural one, leaving the legal-conventional aspect out of account. The objective of the critique at this point was to show the ideological construction of the sphere of privacy as the sphere to which women were assigned 'by nature'. It should be realized, however, that this anti-ideological line of argument and the fundamental critique of the realm of privacy – in other words the proposed abandonment of the distinction between the spheres – at the same time entails the loss of the legal-conventional aspect of the concept, an aspect that finds expression in the idea of private freedoms and that insists on the equal necessity and significance of a private sphere for each and every member of society, that is a sphere that is free from the possibility of interference and intervention on the part of the state and that would also encompass – albeit without the gender-specific coding – the protection of one's home and family.

To grasp the need for a new conceptualization of privacy that also takes into account the feminist critique, a more differentiated second round of the discussion was necessary.[21] Only thus could it become clear that the feminist critique of the aspect of the meaning of 'privacy' associated with women, nature and reproduction need not and should not simultaneously mean a critique of privacy as such. This emerges in the political theory of thinkers such as Jean Cohen and Anita Allen.[22] These writers understand the essential importance for feminist political theory of developing a concept of privacy that on the one hand does justice to the situation and needs of women without falling into the old ideological trap of assigning women to the supposedly 'natural' private realm, and on the other hand – as a 'redescription of the private sphere' – establishes a normative conception of equal protection of privacy for women and men alike. In the United States, the discussion of this new concept of privacy was supported and fostered by Supreme Court decisions regarding the termination of pregnancy, in that the grounds for women being granted the right to abortion involved an appeal to the 'right to privacy'.[23] The right to the 'privacy of one's body' was of particular significance for feminist theory because it was above all this kind of privacy that women had previously not been entitled to claim, or at least not on equal terms with men.[24] The general idea of this particular feminist theory of privacy is that social discrimination can also (and must) be eradicated by guaranteeing equal rights to privacy, in this way salvaging the liberal core of privacy without retaining its connotations of a gender-based hierarchy. However, this 'redescription' of the private sphere has in turn met with further feminist criticism, which has come from two directions that I should briefly like to mention. In this dispute, the radical critique put forward by Catherine MacKinnon has featured prominently.[25] For MacKinnon, the appeal to juridical or moral rights to privacy is but a further manifestation of the attempt to push women back into an ideologically constituted realm of privacy defined as the non-political or pre-political, and only ever concede them rights in so far as they are seen as different or deviant.[26] What such a concept of privacy does, according to MacKinnon, is precisely to fail to call the sexual hierarchy into question, and instead simply preserve social power structures that find expression in the correlation of women with the private and men with the public.[27] The second form of criticism has come on the one hand from communitarians and on the other from the proponents of what is known as maternal thinking. While the former focus their critique on the right to privacy because of its dependence upon the liberal concept of autonomy (as in the case of Mary Ann Glendon),[28] the critique propounded by such theorists as Jean Bethke Elshtain and Sara Ruddick[29] is based on the defence of the classic realm of *family* privacy as the space where the 'feminine' virtues indispensable for the well-being of society as a whole (virtues such as motherliness, care, responsibility in relationships) are developed. The objective of feminist theory and practice, they argue, must consequently be a revaluation of these virtues in society so as to ensure that equal value is given to the situations and qualities of both men and women, not a 'new' interpretation of privacy.

I do not here wish to pursue any further either of these critiques, both of which, in their different ways, deal only with the quasi-natural concept of privacy and for this reason alone are inadequate.[30] For the time being, I would like instead to reiterate that, viewed from a liberal-democratic feminist perspective, the main issue is not the complete renunciation of a liberal concept of privacy, but rather how an *appropriate* conception of privacy can be developed from within liberalism. Of course, this then in turn bears upon the question of what such a conception might mean for the traditional structures of the family. The belief that liberal theory is fundamentally incompatible with feminist criticism, therefore, is a misconception that arises from a failure to distinguish sufficiently between the two different uses of the concept of privacy in liberal theory.

A feminist conception of privacy and its foundation must start out from premises radically other than appeals to a 'natural' sphere, however this may be defined. In order to guarantee the spirit of individual freedom, it must begin from the liberal concept of *equality of freedoms* and thus from the normative liberal postulate that all people have an *equal* political and social claim to the protection of private spaces and the private dimensions of their life. Such an approach would mean that the old stumbling block of the liberal distinction between private and public, with the gender-specific division of labour that accompanies the distinction and is sanctioned by it, would be cast aside and overcome, since from the outset an egalitarian approach would be adopted in the definition of privacy, and associated with this there would no longer be a difference in the allocation of social roles for women and men. Such a concept of privacy and such a foundation for the concept is precisely what I am aiming for. The distinction remains a constituent element of liberalism, yet it must be interpreted differently, as the coming chapters will show more clearly.

One might object to this feminist critique of the contradictory liberal concept of privacy that it is trivial, at least at first sight, for no theorist of liberalism, or at least no contemporary one, would contest the idea of equal rights and liberties in principle, including the notions of equal substantial opportunities within all areas of life (and thus also the domestic realm) and equal rights to privacy. No such theorist would want to claim that women belonged at home and that privacy must be coded in gender-specific terms. Nevertheless, liberal theory from Locke to Rawls and from Mill to Rorty has done nothing to prevent or resolve the contradiction it contains, or even to face up to it.[31] The gender-specific connotations have been not only accepted, but also given a theoretical underpinning, as happened with Locke, even though there can clearly be no genuine liberal argument for classifying its concepts in this way. First, therefore, I want to take a step backwards once again and with a short discussion of some of the classics of liberal thought show to what extent criticism of the liberal concept of privacy is justified. Following this, the concepts of equality and of equal freedom that I employ here will be discussed more fully.

3 Three classics of liberal thought: Locke, Mill and Rawls

In what follows, therefore, it should be clear that my concern is to demonstrate the *twofold* meaning of the liberal concept of privacy in the classics of liberal thought. In the course of this discussion of classic liberal texts, it will be seen that *one* of the reasons for the inability of liberal theory to measure up to its normative idea of equal protection of freedom for all persons, and thus also to conceptualize the issue of justness in the relation between the sexes, resides in its failure to reflect adequately on the organization of the traditional realm of privacy. Of course, the organization and conceptualization of the public domain and domestic privacy should by no means be seen and understood as independent of one another. It is only because traditional liberal theory confines the task of caring for the male members of society to the private sphere of the household, to be done by women, that it can conceive of the public sphere as unencumbered by these problems, and that it can – as Locke does – portray the men who conclude the social contract as disembodied individuals free of needs, so to speak, who may look after their 'private' interests – property and possessions – or the public welfare, but not the necessities of day-to-day care.[32] Should one then wish to find out where and how the relation between the sexes has been implicitly or explicitly treated in liberal theories, this in practice means looking into what has been written about the family. It proves fruitful, in other words, to investigate the status attributed to the family in the various theories, for the only seemingly fortuitous association between the relation of the sexes and the family entails something that is clearly not at all fortuitous, the association of women with the private sphere and the tendency to restrict the equality of freedom granted to women as subjects. From the way in which the family is conceived it is possible to gain insights not only into the theorist's stance on the relation between the sexes, but also how the twofold connotations of privacy described above are aligned. If the focus in what follows is on Locke, Mill and Rawls, this is because in their different ways the three of them are paradigmatic for the liberal tradition: for liberal social-contract theory (in the case of Locke) and for the utilitarian tradition (in the case of Mill), while in the figure of Rawls the discussion surely centres on the one theorist of liberalism who has influenced more than any other the political philosophy of the second half of the twentieth century onwards.

John Locke's *Second Treatise of Government* is the standard reference text in which social contract theory provides the grounds for liberal-democratic societies. It is also the standard reference text for the feminist critique of these very grounds, for as the radical critic Carole Pateman was first to show,[33] there are two sets of relationships that run counter to Locke's grounding of the social contract in natural law: the relationship between the men making the contract, in so far as it is only men doing so, and the relationship between man and wife, in so far as this is based ultimately on the natural inferiority of the woman with respect to the man.[34]

Arguing against Sir Robert Filmer, Locke makes a decisive move that on the one hand facilitates the liberal grounding of the social contract, but on the other also allows him to disregard the consequences of grounding the contract in natural law as far as the relation between the sexes is concerned: he makes a separation between conjugal, domestic power and political power. It is for this reason that in the *First Treatise* he argues with Filmer not about the legitimacy of paternal power but its area of application. If the

> words here spoke[n] to Eve [concerning her duty to subjection] must needs be understood as a law to bind her and all other women to subjection, it can be no other subjection than what every wife owes her husband. [. . .] If therefore these words give any power to Adam, it can be only a conjugal power, not political, the power that every husband hath to order the things of private concernment in his family, as proprietor of the goods and land there, and to have his will take place before that of his wife in all things of their common concernment.[35]

Now by comparison with Filmer this distinction between conjugal and political power at first sounds like a radical liberalization, for Locke is speaking not of natural but of conjugal power, something described more fully in the *Second Treatise* as the 'conjugal society [. . .] made by a voluntary compact between man and woman'.[36] Yet Locke is not consistent, as even the *First Treatise* leads us to suspect, since ultimately conjugal power is not rigorously based on a voluntary contract either, but on the natural superiority of the man: 'The husband and wife [. . .] will unavoidably sometimes have different wills too; it therefore being necessary, that the last determination, i.e. the rule, should be placed somewhere, it naturally falls to the man's share, as the abler and the stronger.'[37]

Locke thus ends up overlooking the contradiction between domestic, patriarchal power and the egalitarian grounding of civil liberties in the

Second Treatise. This comes to light most clearly in paragraphs 86 and 87.[38] The first of these opens: 'Let us therefore consider a master of a family with all these subordinate relations of wife, children, servants and slaves united under the domestic rule of a family.' But the start of the following paragraph then runs: 'Man [is] born, as has been proved, with a title to perfect freedom, and an uncontrolled enjoyment of all the rights and privileges of the law of nature, equally with any other man, or number of men in the world.' It is evident that the 'man' of this paragraph really does refer to men and not women, that is to the parties to what has been called the 'fraternal contract', and admission to civil society by means of this contract, in exchange for which every man gives up his natural liberty, is a construction that thus only applies to men.[39]

There are two different levels, therefore, on which Locke finds himself entangled in contradiction. At the level of the state of nature, for a start, the *natural* right to complete freedom, which is equal for all, is opposed by the *natural* inferiority of the woman with respect to the man. And at the level of civil society, the natural power of the paterfamilias is opposed by the guarantee – secured by contract – of equal individual civil liberties for all. On both levels, as a result, equal rights to freedom 'for all' come into conflict with the inferiority of woman in relation to man. As far as the organization of civil society is concerned, this means that the reason women do not enjoy equal civil rights is that they are naturally allocated their place in the family.[40] And the family, as 'the first society',[41] as it were forms a 'natural' relic within civil society and is completely unaffected by the nature of this society as a 'political society', since it remains what it always has been and is not held to be part of the 'body politic' anyway. This of course does not alter the fact that this very separation is a notably 'political' one and in functional terms too must be seen in connection with the organization of the body politic.[42]

In particular, this gender-specific separation between a private, domestic sphere and a public, political one means that all the work of the reproductive realm lies in women's hands. As Locke construes the social contract, political organization depends upon the tasks of child-raising and caring for the 'political fraternity' taking place within the private sphere, the realm of the family, and being carried out by persons whose job is limited to precisely this, that is by women. After all, the parties to the contract as such are nothing more than that, parties to the contract, and in this capacity they have neither natural needs nor a pre-political childhood: they are 'disembodied individuals'.[43] This brings to light, however, not only the contradiction between the grounding of equal freedoms in natural law and the legal protection accorded civil liberties in a civil society, on the one hand, and the natural inferiority of the woman, on the other. It also shows that Locke fails to grasp – at least as a problem – the twofold connotations of privacy as both a domestic sphere and a realm of individual freedom protected by the social contract, allowing both meanings to persist side by side unresolved.[44] These two ideas of what is to be regarded as private are nothing to do with one another in normative terms. But only once this has been clarified is the way clear to outlining a conception of privacy that overcomes this twofold coding and its inconsistencies.

The liberalism of John Stuart Mill is another example of the contradictory treatment of the concept and social function of privacy in liberal theory. In no other theory is there such a clear-cut distinction between private freedom and public regulation as in Mill.[45] The whole text of *On Liberty* is a justification[46] for the idea that individual liberty, as something private, must be set against public laws, both moral and juridical in nature, and that liberalism consists in nothing other than securing the greatest possible scope for individual liberty. Mill's distinction between 'all that portion of a person's life and conduct which affects only himself' and 'that part of the conduct of an individual which concerns other people'[47] is a classic expression of the liberal idea of individual civil liberties. In the 'modern world', Mill argues, 'the regulation of every part of private conduct by public authority'[48] is no longer possible or tenable: the greater the public interference, the more the individual is hampered in the liberty of his private life.[49] Just as clear in Mill's essay on liberty is that this right to liberty and thus freedom of action and speech – or, to put it more emphatically, the freedom to realize oneself – must apply for all adult members of society. Here at any rate, Mill omits to mention that this distinction between a private and a public realm should also coexist with gender-specific connotations to the effect that his concept of liberty only pertains to men. Indeed, his liberal, emancipatory impetus leads him naturally to appeal for this concept of liberty for all human beings as human beings, thus dividing society clearly into a private realm of free individuals on the one hand and a public realm in which individuals are subject to the rules of morality and law on the other.

If we look at the *family*, however, in other words if we understand the private realm in its traditional sense as the *domestic sphere*, then it becomes manifest that for Mill too the idea of equal liberties and political rights for women and men need by no means necessarily be accompanied by the idea that an *equal* measure of liberty be available to women. On the contrary, Mill continues quite naturally to consign women to their place in the realm that must now be described as domestic or private and that manifests the negative, gender-specific form of privacy:

> Like a man when he chooses a profession, so, when a woman marries, it may in general be understood that she makes choice of the management of a household, and the bringing up of a family, as the first call upon her exertions [. . .]; and that she renounces, not all other objects and occupations, but all which are not consistent with the requirement of this.[50]

Only for women does the privacy of family life conflict with the privacy of individual freedom. The unproblematic union of the two elements, the domestic role and the dimension of individual liberty (which, though private, is also lived out in the realm of public society), is something reserved for men. There thus exists a contradiction between the conception of private freedom in *On Liberty* and the designation of privacy as the realm for which women are responsible as women. The double reading of privacy remains – and with it the question of how the contradiction can be resolved and the liberal proposal of equal liberties for men *and* women actually be put into practice in a liberal society.

Mill is here only exemplifying what other liberals imply in similar fashion: that although women and men are equal in terms of the basic liberal idea and although in accordance with this idea they are strictly speaking also granted equal civil liberties and rights of political participation, this very freedom to lead their life as they wish is only granted them once they have dispatched their household duties. Yet light can also be shed on the other side of the Mill quotation, showing the way in which the private and the public realm are far from independent of one another but on the contrary intrinsically bound up with one other. For 'the man' can only pursue his profession and other interests, that is his private liberty, and can consequently only engage in the social, public sphere, if and when the work in the private, domestic realm is taken care of, in other words if and when the tasks not only of raising the children but also 'maintaining' the family – and not least providing the emotional care – have been secured. And this is precisely what lies in the hands of the women. To this extent, the liberal idea of observing private (in the sense of individual or subjective) liberties really depends upon the guaranteed organization of domestic privacy. The non-domestic domain (the social, public, economic or political sphere) can only function as it functions provided that there is a guarantee that the private realm will relieve the burden as necessary for it to function in this way. Conversely, this of course also means that if men and women are indeed to enjoy equal scope for individual, private liberties, this requires a reorganization of the separation between domestic privacy and the social sphere.[51]

In Locke and Mill, therefore, we have seen that a contradiction exists between the liberal idea of securing individual liberties for all persons equally on the one hand and the social organization based on the separation between the public domain and domestic privacy on the other. Now John Rawls's *A Theory of Justice* has in itself already become a classic of liberal thought. For this reason, I shall here start by discussing *A Theory of Justice*, even though twenty years on Rawls himself made revisionary comments concerning the standing of the family within the theory of justice. I shall return to look at these more exhaustively at a later point.[52] What emerges is that Rawls's *A Theory of Justice* is thoroughly ambivalent in its treatment of the relation between the sexes.[53] On the one hand, he explicitly holds the family to be one of the fundamental institutions of society, which must accordingly be structured in accordance with his two principles of justice.[54] Rawls consistently seems to take it for granted that gender is a morally irrelevant quality in the sense that it has no part to play in the question of the just distribution of rights, liberties, opportunities and other goods, even though he does not expressly mention this in his description of the conditions of what he terms 'the original position'.[55]

On the other hand, the family – and thus implicitly the relation between the sexes – becomes an explicit theme at three points in *A Theory of Justice*. One is in dealing with the problem of equality of opportunity for persons who come from differing family backgrounds.[56] Another is in the discussion of obligations towards future generations: in order to motivate the persons in the original position to have this sort of interest in their children and, where relevant, their grandchildren, it must be assumed, according to Rawls, that they are 'heads of families'.[57] And finally the family also appears when Rawls looks at the development of the sense of justice essential to his theory of justice.[58] At none of the points in *A Theory of Justice* where Rawls implicitly or explicitly refers to the family in this way does he appear to do justice to his own claim that the family too must be structured in accordance with the principles of justice: 'heads of families', at least, are clearly always men. As when he touches upon the issue of equality of opportunity for people who may be handicapped in varying measure by their family origins, Rawls here avoids posing the question in terms of the relation between the sexes. This means that in looking at the problem of equality of family opportunity, he focuses exclusively on inequalities of interfamily opportunity without examining intrafamily opportunity,[59] and so fails to go any deeper into the problem that girls and women – as well as boys and men – are in practical terms assigned roles that fundamentally influence their capacity to avail themselves of the diverse options within society.[60]

This becomes particularly clear in the third part of *A Theory of Justice,* where Rawls describes the moral development on which the formation of a sense of justice is based.[61] Here he appeals simply to the image of the traditional nuclear family, where mothers and fathers, daughters and sons, are evidently allocated distinct roles and tasks even though the family, as a basic social institution, ought in fact to be organized in accordance with the principles of justice. The text runs: 'As the child becomes older he is taught the standards of conduct suitable for one in his station. The virtues of a good son or a good daughter are explained, or at least conveyed by parental expectations as shown in their approvals and disapprovals.'[62] One would naturally like to know more about what the virtues in each case are and why they apparently differ according to gender. It is passages like these that foster the impression that Rawls has failed to pay enough attention to the structures within the family and their connection with structural injustices within society.

It might of course be objected that differences in the allocation of roles are not unjust in themselves and that it is therefore not necessarily unjust if women, *because they are women*, have certain social tasks and men, *because they are men*, have others. However, a liberal theory in particular would need arguments to support such a position, arguments showing firstly that women and men were naturally bound to observe their respective functions, and secondly that this sort of natural role allocation need not contradict the autonomy of persons, that is that the persons in question can actually rationally want these roles to fall to them. Neither argument seems especially promising, and they are not mentioned by Rawls anyway. It is thus in every respect the classic image of the family that is portrayed by Rawls, one that is characterized by anything other than the justness of its structures. For if one is guided, as Rawls is, by a concept of justice based on the 'equal worth' of liberties,[63] it is patently obvious that phenomena such as the gender-specific division of labour, the so-called 'double burden' borne by women, and the assignment of 'housework' and 'care' to a sphere of responsibility that is predominantly, if not exclusively, women's, are anything but conducive to a state of affairs in which women and men – either inside or outside the family – enjoy an equal worth of freedom.

Rawls is no more able than Locke or Mill to bring to fruition the proposal of equal liberties for all as long as he clings to a traditional conception of domestic privacy, incorporating a household with a male head of the family and different virtues for girls and boys. The guarantee of civil liberties and the stipulation of the difference principle may be intended to secure equal rights and liberties and equal opportunities for observing these rights and liberties. Yet this conception only makes complete sense as a liberal one if it is understood as providing *all* members of society with the opportunity to devise and pursue their own, individual, *private* life-plan – a life-plan that is 'private' precisely in the legal-conventional sense and not the 'natural' one.

With this inadequate construction of privacy, Rawls, Locke and Mill can be taken as paradigmatic for the liberal tradition and for contemporary liberal theory. It would be possible to trace similar structures of reflection in Hobbes as a pre-liberal thinker, in Kant as a classic liberal philosopher or in Rousseau as a republican liberal,[64] but this would serve little purpose. Yet it is surely neither necessary nor appropriate to seek to give up liberalism as such on account of this fault in its theory. The arguments against the gender-specific connotations and the gender-specific contents with which the concept of privacy is 'filled' do not speak against the concept itself, nor by any means against the idea that there should be such things as the protection of one's household, one's dwelling, one's intimate relations. What they speak against is simply the one particular, extremely influential interpretation and symbolic 'filling' of the concept. And the clarification of this concept, against and without its traditional connotations centred upon the idea of domestic privacy as the 'woman's realm', will surely have repercussions not only for the normative understanding of the concept of privacy itself, but also for the question of the organization of families and the gender-specific division of labour in general. Resolving these questions, however, will be the task of later chapters.

4 Equality and difference between the sexes

Throughout the chapter so far and particularly during the discussion of the texts by Locke, Mill and Rawls, a crucial assumption has informed the argument. This assumption is that it is normatively correct for feminist theory and the feminist critique of liberal theories to be guided by a norm of 'equality', a norm that proposes the equality of all persons and *a fortiori* the equality of the sexes within society. When it comes to interpreting the concept of equality and asking what is meant by the equality of the sexes, however, it is well known that recent years and decades have seen fierce debate in feminist theory under the rubric 'equality versus difference'. For this reason, I wish to make it clear in what sense I am here speaking of 'equality' and 'difference', in what respects I am considering the two terms. In fact, two objections may be made to a concept of privacy founded upon the idea of *equal* rights and liberties: first, that it is centred upon a (false) idea of androgyny, and secondly, that it is taken in by what is actually a 'male' norm of equality. So if the critique of a traditional liberal concept of privacy is to proceed via the concept of equal liberties, then in these respects at least the concept of equality is in need of clarification.

Parenthesis: On the debate over equality and difference

Especially in the early years of feminist theory, the debate over equality versus difference was a bitter one. Deborah Rhode describes the dilemma in the following terms: 'feminists generally have taken two approaches, both of which remain critical in contemporary debates over difference. One strategy has been to deny the extent or essential nature of differences between men and women. A second approach has been to celebrate difference – to embrace characteristics historically associated with women and demand their equal social recognition.'[65] The fundamental issue here is whether sexual difference can be understood and normatively conceptualized without at the same time seeing this difference as negative discrimination. If so, how is this to be achieved? What would a society look like in which justice also prevails in the relation between the sexes? Can a 'plea for equality' and the 'assertion of sexual difference' be formulated simultaneously?[66]

To clarify the different stances within the feminist discussion, I shall again distinguish various rounds in this debate over equality and difference.[67] In the first round of the contention, the two positions can still be described in comparatively schematic terms: the cultivation and celebration of female qualities and 'female difference' on the one hand, and the orientation towards equality (with men) on the other.[68] In political theory, those who proposed the equality of the sexes sought to eliminate social discrimination against women by *alignment* with the 'normal biographies' of men, with the result that demands for equality were limited in principle to extending the normal biography of men to women as well.[69] This meant setting their sights above all on the equal distribution of gainful employment, accompanied by a thoroughgoing critique of the gender-specific division of labour. The positions of difference, by contrast, insisted on the distinctness of the sexes and thus also on the distinctness of their social roles, and appealed for these to be given equal value in society – in other words, for a specific revaluation of the family and the tasks performed in the traditional private realm.[70] The alignment of the fronts was roughly the same, however, in all the disciplines. The position of difference was in general reproached (by the theorists of equality) for an essentialism that turned the 'female' qualities or 'female' thought – whatever exactly that was supposed to be – into something absolute and ontologically fixed, while the position of equality was found reprehensible (by the theorists of difference) for being centred upon an ideal of equality that only appeared to be humanistic and was in fact 'male' in orientation. A parallel was frequently drawn, indeed, between this confrontation and the opposition between French and Italian feminism on the one hand and Anglo-American feminism on the other.[71]

The polarizing opposition of the first round brings it home that this sort of schematization, which is no longer interested in arguments, is not enough. The second, more differentiated round of discussions can be described for a start as a critical reflection on the weaknesses of an oversimple schema of equality and difference. This second round accordingly begins with a critique of both positions. The thetic opposition between 'female' difference and 'male-oriented' equality, it was held, not only takes us up a theoretical blind alley, but also fails to achieve what this sort of theoretical conceptualization and its practical implementation really ought to be aiming for, which is to transcend *any* model of simple opposition that tends to tie women down to a fixed essence, instead pursuing an independent construction of diversified sexual identities.

The pitch of the debate has thus shifted significantly over the last few years, for in all of the above-mentioned areas there have been the most diverse attempts at mediation. At the forefront is no longer an opposition between difference and equality, but the question of how to get beyond this fruitless and simplistic confrontation.[72] To describe the *constructive* aspect of this second round, therefore, we might say that two distinct strands of the critique targeting the theorists of simple equality have emerged. The opposition here is no longer simply between the positions of equality and difference, but rather the debate is now concerned with how to conceptualize the difference of the sexes – which manifests itself also in the distinct situations in which women live – *without at the same time* relinquishing the idea of equal rights and liberties for women and men alike.[73]

The first form of this differentiated critique of the concept of equality that refrains from appealing to essentializing positions of difference is found most notably in MacKinnon, for whom any analysis of the actual structures of power and dominance prevalent in a patriarchal society cannot be oriented towards the 'equality' of the sexes. The concept of equality necessarily takes the situation and needs of 'the man' as the norm defining equality, as against which the situation and needs of women are always conceived as 'other' and thus as inferior or deviant. The use of the concept always falls into the trap of a patriarchal definition of what can and must count as equality and the ways in which one must thus subordinate oneself to a dominant equality. Instead of this, MacKinnon argues, the issue must be to criticize in the most fundamental terms the liberal idea of equality and the neutrality of the liberal state, as well as the underlying concept of justice, yet without thereby coming out in favour of an essentialization and ontologization of female qualities.[74] The analysis of structures of power and dominance must therefore form the heart of feminist theorizing, and not the superficial focus on a concept of equality that can only conceive of difference as deviance,[75] for which 'equal' means 'equal to the man', and everything specific to female needs and biographies is seen as different and thus 'unequal': 'No woman', MacKinnon writes, 'had a voice in the design of the legal institutions that rule the social order under which women, as well as men, live.'[76]

The second form of the more differentiated critique of the concept of equality no longer holds to the 'celebration of difference' either. However, it starts from different assumptions. It asserts, for example, that the old schema of equality and difference cannot be analysed exclusively in terms of power and dominance, for in this case a radical critique of the 'male' concept of equality can only be accomplished by alleging the victimization of women (which is the reproach against MacKinnon).[77] It claims, furthermore, that this schema can be transcended precisely through the legal and social acknowledgement of differences in the situations in which women live, since the male paradigm of what is to count as equal will be constantly undermined if women insist that they may possibly need *other* rights in order to attain *equal* liberties (this goes for the question of abortion, quota systems in the labour market, divorce law or the demand for day nurseries). In this way, the liberal idea of equality is not called into question *in its entirety*, but used to secure 'equal' – that is equivalent – rights and liberties for women too.

If the controversy surrounding the concept of equality is described in these terms, however, then it emerges that the different positions in this second round are not necessarily mutually exclusive. The discussions centre upon the problems of how to conceptualize what is in effect a 'new equality', one that no longer takes its bearings implicitly or explicitly from a gender-based hierarchy, that avoids reinforcing the gender-specific division of labour (through a revaluation of 'difference'), and that consequently seeks to design justice even between the sexes without perpetuating old, hierarchical dichotomies. The crux of the matter then becomes how discrimination against women can be eliminated in legal and social terms and how the different situations in which women live can be 'acknowledged' without consolidating these discriminations and different conditions. The differences between these approaches can indeed be grasped in Mendus's description of the new controversy: 'The crucial debate in contemporary feminism is the debate between those who urge that sex should become irrelevant and those who believe that sex should not provide the basis for inequality. Neither of these strategies involves rejecting equality. Rather, the dispute is about how equality is to be attained.'[78]

This dispute continues to be at the hub of feminist political theory, yet over the last few years there has emerged an increasingly fierce and increasingly controversial *third round* in the debate over equality versus difference. At the fore is no longer the argument over the conception of a 'new equality', but the argument about how to deal appropriately with the indisputable differences *between* women, in other words who is actually meant by 'women'. The two ways of formulating the question – the second and the third rounds – are not mutually exclusive. On the contrary, we shall see shortly that they can be mutually complementary. Even so, the perspective on the issue of equality and difference is significantly divergent.

There are two reasons for this inquiry into the differences between women and into a collective subject called 'woman', as for the uncertainty that underlies it. Both of them have had a decisive influence on the theoretical developments of recent years. First, there is the 'discovery' of difference among women, in other words the discovery that to speak of *the* collective subject woman, who is completely homogeneous not only with respect to her qualities but also her interests and needs, is not such a straightforward matter. The different contexts in which women live, the different interests connected with these contexts, different ethnic origins and sexual orientations, all these differences *between* women have increasingly come to the fore and led to a modification and 'pluralization' of feminism, and along with this a 'critique of the innocence of the category woman'.[79]

The second reason for the shift in the controversy over difference and equality lies in the increasing critique of the dichotomy between biological *sex* and cultural or social *gender*. Though this distinction had been conceived initially as an emancipatory step precisely because it was intended to show the independence of culturally formed 'female' qualities from the biological, anatomical sex, it became increasingly apparent that the binary notion of biological sex was still accompanied by culturally coded hierarchies. Historical studies, such as the ones carried out by Thomas Laqueur and Barbara Duden, empirical investigations into processes of socialization, as well as philosophical studies in the cultural construction of biological sex[80] led to the recognition that binary sexuality too was a cultural formation and its relevance culturally constructed. This critique sought to prove that even the apparently natural facts of sex are produced discursively in the service of political and social discourses of power, and in so doing it showed that biological sex itself is still a *gendered category*. Even the conceptions and conceptualizations of the biological, anatomical body, it was said, were not 'naturally given', but the products of historical and sociocultural interpretations. Prominent among these critics has been Judith Butler,[81] surely the most radical in her claim that the idea of binary sexuality is a purely cultural formation and 'sex' a discursive construct. This need not mean that biological differences are denied. However, it may lead to the realization that the critique of gender difference is at the same time bound up with a critique of the *significance* of the binary notion of biological sex and of the simple opposition between men and women that is a structural feature of societies.

The critique that invokes the differences between women has been dubbed post-colonial, while the one drawing attention to the discursive construction of sex has been called postmodern.[82] They frequently appear together, yet between them they end up forming a contradiction, for while the post-colonial critique as it were ratifies identity to the extent that it insists on the differences between women as well as the diversity of cultures and tends to celebrate such differences, the postmodern critique calls for precisely the opposite, referring to the character not only of sexual identity but of *any* identity as transitory, discursively constructed and thus liable to deconstruction. Both critiques, however, express legitimate points. For it cannot be denied that differences in the conditions in which women live may have consequences that bear upon their diverse (political) interests, and nor can the dividing line between biological sex and social gender be drawn straightforwardly enough to make it unnecessary at least to reflect on the meaning that is socially ascribed to biological sex.

The two approaches become problematic, however, when they claim to be able to dispense entirely with any conceptualization of what is to be understood by the securing of *equal civil rights and liberties* for women and men, and how one would describe the structures of a just society free of any gender-based hierarchy. After all, they claim, it is no longer possible to speak either of 'equality' or of 'women' as such, and any such focus on the concept of 'women' or 'the rights of the individual' is always associated with the generation of repressive structures.[83] They become problematic, in other words, when they lose all sight of the question of a (new) 'equality of the sexes'. This is problematic first for systematic normative reasons: if one wants to hold to a political theory and practice grounded in principle upon the idea (essential to democratic constitutional states) of inviolable, equal, individual civil liberties and rights of political participation, then one must obviously also hold to an idea of equality, for without this the talk of equal rights can clearly not be substantiated.[84] It is problematic secondly because both the 'postmodern' and the 'post-colonial' approaches themselves make implicit use of just such a concept of equality, which they never explicate. Both approaches assume not only that their feminist critiques of categories such as 'women' or 'identity' can be sited within the sociopolitical framework of liberal democracies, but also that they are compatible with the genuinely concomitant ideas of civil liberties, emancipation movements, distributive justice, etc. And this is obviously only possible if one is guided by an (inexplicit) underlying concept of equality, with the help of which the target, the basic structure of existing injustices (with regard to 'women' or to the constitution of 'identities'), can be formulated.

At this point we should once again remind ourselves of the initial reason for our interest in this discussion of equality and difference, which was to inquire into the possibility of a tenable concept of 'equal liberties' and to develop such a concept, since in what follows it will be brought into play to ground a liberal concept of privacy. In the process of further defending this concept of equal freedom against such criticism, therefore, I want to take up the concept of a 'new equality' described above, now no longer centred upon the controversy between difference and equality, but on the question of 'how equality is to be attained'.[85] It is clearly more promising to integrate the critical approaches into a conception that holds to the idea of equality with regard to rights and liberties. And if the objective is the normative one of securing equal spaces for freedom for both sexes, both aspects – the problem of differences *between* women on the one hand and the assumption of a collective subject 'woman' presupposing homogeneous interests and experiences on the other – can be taken up together. On the one hand, it is correct and appropriate to speak of a collective subject 'woman' to the extent that there are actual and potential experiences of discrimination that may affect all women simply as women. On the other hand, given the completely different worlds in which they live, their different biographies and opportunities, women are also exposed to differences in the specific type of restriction on their liberties (as well as in the factors that may make liberties feasible) and may thus pursue diverse interests and develop diverse needs. Efforts to spell out what justice between the sexes means and how differences due primarily to the social situation but possibly also to the biology of women can be 'recognized' without at the same time being consolidated or essentialized must accordingly be sensitive to the different background conditions in each particular case, as well as to forms of discrimination that are structural in nature. When in what follows I speak of the 'equality of the sexes', therefore, this is meant in the sense of such equality with regard to rights and liberties, that is in the sense of equality in the worth of freedom, going beyond a purely formal concern with equal rights.

We can now also see how this concept of equal liberties refers back to the question of an appropriate liberal concept of privacy viewed from the perspective of a *theory of justice*. For if, as I have tried to show, it is normatively correct to hold to a concept of 'equality of the sexes' that is centred upon the idea of equal freedoms for both sexes, and if the gender-specific coding of the twofold traditional liberal concept of privacy necessarily entails an *un*equal distribution of spaces for social freedom, then it is clear that a redescription of the liberal concept of privacy is a necessary – though of course not sufficient – condition for a conception of equal freedoms for women and men. The point of departure must be the legal-conventional meaning of the concept of privacy. Implemented as a norm, this will then have repercussions on how the privacy of the domestic sphere is interpreted. This is something to which the following chapters will return.

5 Equal freedom, equal privacy

It has become clear so far that the concept of privacy in traditional liberal theory has two significantly different semantic components, a 'legal-conventional' one and a 'natural' one, and that only the first of these is justifiable and (as we shall shortly see in detail) normatively tenable in terms of liberal theory itself. Secondly, we have seen that feminist criticism, or at least some of it, is unconvincing and unfounded in its claims that a critique of the concept of privacy as the realm of women necessarily entails having to give up the very distinction between private and public. Consequently, it has emerged that this distinction should be held on to in the face of such criticism, including a positive concept of privacy that needs to be redescribed in new terms. Finally, we have seen that the concept of 'equality of the sexes', which I take to be presupposed by feminist criticism, refers to the equality of rights and liberties, is centred upon the 'worth' of freedom and to this extent cannot be misunderstood as an androcentric concept.

In conclusion, I should now like to take up another perspective on the problem of the connection between equal freedoms and the constitution of privacy. It is a perspective that focuses in particular on the entanglements and interdependencies between the private sphere and public society, interdependencies that manifest the structural inequality in the 'worth of liberty' for women and men, and that contribute inherently to the symbolic reproduction of the relation between the sexes. These interdependencies come to light when one asks where the power to define what counts as private and what as public is located and who is protected by the conventions that constitute the boundary between the two spheres. One then comes across the phenomenon, for example, that even in social or public contexts women find it difficult to cast off the connotation that they 'really' or at least 'partly' belong in the private sphere (in its 'natural' sense as the realm of the household and care), and that they cannot dissociate themselves, at least not completely, from the responsibilities of caring for others.[86] Conversely, of course, social power structures, assumptions and relations of dominance do not simply stop at the gates to the family. Not only is the family itself not an unlegislated area, but institutions such as the marriage contract regulate the supposedly 'pre-political' conditions in an eminently 'political' manner.[87]

However, the fact that the power of these conventions is typically directed against women is further shown by the way in which the rules governing privacy in its other, legal-conventional sense also function. The right to privacy – as a right to be left in peace, a right to the protection of one's personhood – is clearly coded in gender-specific terms in such a way that in cases of conflict men are granted protection of their privacy far more generously than women. This has been shown in exemplary fashion by Nancy Fraser in her study of the now classic case of Clarence Thomas's hearing prior to his appointment as associate justice of the US Supreme Court and the accusations of sexual harassment made against him by Anita Hill. The way in which a man's insistence that his behaviour towards women was private and had nothing to do with the trustworthiness of his public person here prevailed over a woman's inability to keep her own private life out of the public discussion (that is the de-privatization of Anita Hill's life as against the privatization of Clarence Thomas's behaviour) clearly showed how the conventions for protecting privacy are able to reproduce power relations and inequalities in the worth of liberty.[88] It is not only the different roles actually assigned to the two sexes and the different social spaces to which they are assigned that contribute to this tendency, but also the gender-specific definitions of what can count as private and worth protecting in each particular case.

Such conventions, role assignments and repressive structures are called into question in equal measure by feminist criticism, which queries all relations, even intimate and private ones (structurally, as types), and seeks to analyse their character as an impediment to freedom. For nothing is private in itself: the concept of privacy must be understood as a conventional and not a natural one. But all individuals need the protection of privacy equally in order to be able to lead a life of freedom and live within intimate relationships: the function of privacy is to protect freedom. Such a reinterpretation of privacy, however, would entail a different model of society. It would mean a different concept of work as a result of the critique of the concept of (private) *house*work, a different (not gender-specific) distribution of labour, the neutralization of gender roles, an end to the association of women with the private sphere, and the renunciation of the gender-based hierarchy implicit in the differentiation between private and public. Equal private 'spaces', equal opportunities for being on one's own, equal scope for private decision-making would have to be guaranteed equally for all individuals. A different model of society means, then, that the 'equal worth of liberty' should be conceived as 'equal scope for liberty'. Even though this involves focusing upon the concept of *equal* rights, these rights – being historically contingent and therefore open to revision – may be *different* in order to secure an equal, that is equivalent, scope for women to be free.[89]

If one is aiming, therefore, to realize the idea of equal spaces for women and men to be free, seeking to abandon the association of privacy as the domain of women while nonetheless maintaining a liberal concept of privacy, then it follows at least tentatively from the connection between individual freedom and liberal privacy (a connection taken for granted so far without being further explained or grounded) that there are particular dimensions of such (equal) freedom that should be protected by means of privacy, dimensions or realms that seem to be indispensable for the autonomy of the individual. These would presumably include particular areas of action and responsibility as well as private spaces and intimate relationships. The conclusion of the reflections so far, however, is above all negative. Up to now, we have addressed only what it is about the twofold concept of privacy that is false or misleading – false or misleading, that is, from within a liberal perspective. Why exactly privacy is worth valuing and how privacy and freedom form a connection remain to be seen. The question of how to specify a concept of privacy that is acceptable from a normative perspective is likewise still open. These issues, and with them a constructive reinterpretation of privacy, will be the theme of the next chapter.

3 Freedom, Privacy and Autonomy

1 Introduction

The close conceptual and normative connection between the ideas of freedom and privacy has come to light on various occasions so far and has been taken for granted throughout, yet it has not been presented and grounded in greater detail. This is now the task of the following chapter. It will be concerned first of all, that is, with the concept of freedom and then with the question of what the connection is between freedom and privacy. During the brief discussion of the concept of liberalism, we saw at the outset that a defining characteristic of liberal societies is that they provide their citizens with possibilities for living their life in accordance with their own particular ideas of the individual good. This, one might say, is the spirit and the origin of modern societies. The crux of this idea is thus the freedom of the individual. If we now enquire more closely into this concept of individual freedom, then we are enquiring into what it means to say that a person is free to be able to live her life in a way that is good or rewarding for her. This seems to be at any rate the core of the modern idea of freedom. What follows is concerned first of all, therefore, with a normative conception of what should be meant by freedom. At issue is a concept of individual freedom that shows that a concept of this sort implies not only certain conditions of autonomous action but also a certain practical relationship to one's own actions and thus to one's own selfhood. If we ask what it means for a person to be free, we are simultaneously asking what it means for a person to be free to live her life, in other words what it means for a person to be able to live her life *autonomously*. The normative core of this understanding of freedom is formed by the possibility of asking oneself the 'practical question', that is asking oneself how one would like to live and what sort of a person one would like to be. This is the one thesis that this chapter is aiming to ground and elucidate.

In the introductory chapter, a definition of privacy was given, together with a normative concept of what is worth protecting as private in liberal societies: privacy as control over access by others and thus as protection against unwanted access from other people, this access being defined both as actual physical admission (to spaces) and as metaphorical access to one's personhood, in the sense of access to information on the one hand and in the sense of possibilities for intruding and intervening in a person's behaviour on the other. Accordingly, what we understand by private can be divided into the following three aspects or dimensions: privacy of place, privacy of information control, and privacy of decision or action. What the chapter that follows now *also* seeks to show is that privacy in liberal societies is valued and needed for the sake of individual liberty and autonomy, that is for the sake of both freedom from interventions on the part of the state or other persons *and* the freedom to develop a 'life plan', the freedom for each individual to fulfil himself, and thus ultimately for the sake of a life that is rewarding. I shall be seeking, therefore, to ground and explain the fact that we value (certain forms of) privacy for people in liberal-democratic societies because without the protection of privacy it is not possible to make sense of the idea of individual freedom and autonomy that is basic and central to liberal democracies.

Accordingly, the task of the following sections is to spell out in more precise terms firstly the concept of freedom and autonomy and then the relation of this to the concept of privacy. Bearing this in mind, I want to begin by elucidating various aspects of the concept of freedom with a view to gradually unfolding the concept in concrete terms and drawing a distinction between the concepts of freedom in general and freedom in the sense of autonomy (sections 2 and 3). The starting-point here is a general and formal definition of the concept, a three-pronged definition in terms of a free *person* (section 2a), who is free from *obstacles* (section 2b) so as to be able to select *options* (section 2c). Yet explicating the separate elements of this general concept of freedom does not in itself provide a sufficient definition of what is understood by a person being free to act. Although in a broad sense of the word one might say that persons are 'free' if they simply have the abilities and opportunities to choose what they do and how they wish to act, in a more substantial sense 'free' does not just refer to any old choice, but only to one that can be grounded and is executed in a certain way, that is an *autonomous* choice. In a next step (section 3) I shall thus seek to clarify what autonomy ought to mean in this context and how this concept is connected to the concept of freedom. Only then, in a further step (section 4), will it be possible to discuss in general the question of why we value privacy, and finally, in a concluding step of this chapter, to ground the hypothesis that we value privacy for the sake of freedom: it is at this point that the precise connection between freedom, autonomy and privacy will come to light (section 5).

2 A general concept of freedom

The classic general and formal analysis proposed by Gerald MacCallum can be regarded as a comparatively unproblematic starting-point for a definition of the concept of freedom that aims ultimately to provide a normative conception of the term. According to MacCallum, freedom can be defined as follows:

> Whenever the freedom of some agent or agents is in question, it is always freedom from some constraint or restriction on, interference with, or barrier to doing, not doing, becoming, or not becoming something. Such freedom is thus always *of* something (an agent or agents), *from* something, *to* do, not do, become or not become something; it is a triadic relation. Taking the format '*x* is (is not) free from *y* to do (not do, become, not become) *z*', *x* ranges over agents, *y* ranges over such 'preventing conditions' as constraints, restrictions, interferences, and barriers, and *z* ranges over actions or conditions of character and circumstance.[1]

Taking this conceptual triad as a starting-point has two advantages. The first is that the concept of freedom is conceived from the outset as relational, since a person is not free in some absolute sense, but always with respect to possible obstacles or possible options for action.[2] However, this reference to MacCallum's proposed conceptual formalization need not mean that one shares MacCallum's view that discussion of the nature and conception of freedom can be reduced to discussion of what an agent, an obstacle or an aim or option is. The interpretation and analysis of the individual relational terms and the connection between them together produce a particular normative conception of the concept of freedom that must differ from others and must be set off against them using reasoned argument. MacCallum's approach does not necessarily, therefore, constitute a reduction in the points of dispute, but is a plausible proposal for a systematic analysis of the necessary elements of a conception of freedom. A second advantage consists in the fact that this formal definition really is formal in the sense of normative neutrality or value-neutrality, yet is nonetheless complete in its inclusion of all the necessary elements. It only acquires a normative component once the elements themselves are explicated and specified in concrete terms in their relation to one another. In what follows, I shall briefly look in turn into these three determinants of the concept of freedom. These will clearly be the first steps in our approach to a normative conception of the term.[3]

(a) What are we meaningfully asking about when we ask what it means to say that a person is free or was free to act? The claim that a person is or was free to act evidently means that she could also act differently or that she could have acted differently. The meaning of 'could' here under discussion contrasts not with 'necessity' but rather with 'inability':[4] if we ask what it means to say that a person could have acted differently, we are asking about certain abilities that are prerequisites for this, but not about whether – for causal or whatever sorts of reasons – she necessarily had to act in this way. It may be objected, however, that the issue here is – or at least ought to be – not so much freedom of action as freedom of will.

To say that a person is free (to act) means for a start that she *could have willed or wanted otherwise* too. Yet what does 'willing' mean here? Again, the concept of 'willing' must be conceived not in contrast to necessity, but as an ability. One must have this ability to will something to be able to be understood as 'free' – 'willing' not in the rudimentary sense in which we can also speak of 'willing' in animals, but in a more substantial sense that implies an awareness of the willing. This accordingly entails the presence of certain mental abilities that permit a person to possess and employ concepts such as choice, decision, action, consequences, etc.[5] A person possesses such mental abilities, therefore, if she is in a position to form intentions, devise plans, weigh up alternative courses of action, and in general – at least at a rudimentary level – to give reasons for her actions (to herself or others) and to differentiate between aims as well as between the appropriate means of achieving them. Such a concept of the mental requisites – being able to will – for a person's action to be free goes further than the mere concept of freedom, for a person may also be called 'free' in this sense when she is not free to *act*, in other words when external obstacles are put in the way of her actions.[6] Yet this is only apparently a contradiction. A genuine contradiction would only arise if it were impossible to distinguish between the free person, freedom from obstacles, and freedom for options, in other words if the concept of freedom were not divided into these three separate elements by way of analysis.

These mental abilities are taken into account first and foremost to ensure that persons are in general in a position to form intentions and devise and follow plans, that is have a certain minimum measure of practical rationality. The concept of the freedom of the 'chooser'[7] and the idea of practical rationality here also imply, at least in rudimentary terms, the ability to distinguish between important and less important options, to form hierarchies and priorities among options, and to distinguish between ends and means when it comes to attaining selected targets.[8] One cannot, therefore, speak of a free subject without at least a basic ability to engage in processes of deliberation. If a person possesses nothing akin to concepts of choice, rational selection (at least in a broad sense of the term) and relevance, the idea of a free subject makes no sense.[9]

So far, therefore, we have seen that the question of what it means to be free to be able to act refers us to the question of what it means to be able to will (otherwise). Yet two elucidations are still necessary at this point. First, we must rule out the possibility of a person's freedom being limited or precluded by internal obstacles such as drugs, hypnosis or compulsive behaviour.[10] If a person is in this way prevented from actually being able to decide between two alternative courses of action, one can no longer really talk of her having the necessary mental prerequisites to be able to behave freely. Persons under hypnosis, for example, are precisely that, namely under hypnosis, and to this extent unfree. Secondly, it is important to see that as regards this first determinant of what it means to say that a person is or was free to act, the ascription of the requisite mental abilities should be understood as a *threshold* concept, not a *gradual* concept.[11] If we applied the concept as a gradual one, it would make sense to distinguish between various *degrees* of the ability, in other words to say of people that they have to a greater or lesser degree the ability to do this or that. And this 'greater or lesser degree' would then also become the criterion for saying of a person that she was better or worse at putting this ability into effect. In order to be able to attribute freedom to individuals or persons *in the first place*, however, they only need to possess *fundamental mental abilities*. If they do (if they have crossed this 'threshold'), they count as free, irrespective of how wisely or unwisely, prudently or imprudently, competently or incompetently, rationally or irrationally they may lead their life and choose between options. The first step towards defining the concept of freedom, where the aim is to determine the preconditions relating to the subject's abilities in order to be able to speak of a 'free subject' in general, can and need thus be nothing more than to cite the basic preconditions of rationality which make it possible to attribute free actions to persons in the first place.

(b) Let us now briefly turn to the problem of the obstacles to freedom. As we know, there are influential conceptions of individual liberty that define this exclusively in terms of the absence of obstacles, as was the case with Hobbes, for whom complete liberty was simply the complete absence of obstacles.[12] Nevertheless, it makes more sense to distinguish between different forms of obstacle in order to see more exactly whether there are certain obstacles we have reason to say make us unfree – and if so, what these are – and whether there are others in spite of which we can still be called free. To be able to identify obstacles to freedom as such, it makes sense to start by drawing a distinction between a lack *of freedom* and a lack *of (human) abilities* to do something.[13] This distinction is not trivial, since we cannot, for example, meaningfully describe the human inability to fly without aid as an obstacle to freedom or a restriction on liberty and we should not, therefore, refer to contingencies lying outside the scope of human influence in these terms.[14] It can then be concluded that we only call something a restriction or obstacle to freedom if it lies within the sphere of human influence, or if people could change it if they wanted to.

There is one aspect of this general outline of possible limitations on freedom, however, that I should like to elucidate more closely, that is the question of the conceptual distinction between a 'lack of freedom' and a 'lack of opportunity'. There is, for example, a patent difference between the freedom to travel (or the civil right one has to travel freely) and my lack of opportunity because my car has broken down or I have broken my leg. In conceptual terms, a clear difference in principle can be ascertained. On the other hand, however, it is frequently not really clear how best to describe particular cases, whether as restrictions on freedom in the sense of *obstacles*, that is a 'lack of freedom from', or as a 'lack of opportunity', as a restriction on options, a restriction of the 'freedom to. . . '. Let us take one example. If a country's statistics show that poor people are ill and disabled noticeably more often than rich people because the health system is organized in such a way that rich people can afford better medical care, it is evident that the rich here enjoy a greater measure and a different scope for freedom than the poor. What is open to question is whether the difference in possibilities individuals have for doing things is best described as an obstacle to the particular individuals' freedom to do things or as a lack of opportunity, of 'freedom to. . . ', as options lacking or not open to the poor. An unequal distribution of resources obviously leads to an unequal scope for freedom. But this is not all, for the lack of material resources may also constitute a restriction in the scope of one's freedom in the very fundamental sense that the more one has to worry about mere survival, the less scope one has for designing a 'life plan'. This probably means that it only makes sense to talk of individual freedom against a background exempt from existential poverty.[15] Both the unequal distribution of material resources and privation in general make it clear that in this context a distinction between obstacles to freedom of action on the one hand and opportunities to act on the other hand, that is the distinction between 'freedom from' and 'freedom to', is not a clear-cut one. It is not always possible, in other words, to draw an unambiguous boundary between what Berlin famously called 'freedom from chains' and 'open doors'.[16]

The question of the difference between obstacles and opportunities thus brings us to the third element of MacCallum's analytical triad, the 'options'.

(c) The absence of obstacles on its own does not yet say anything, or at least not enough, about the actual freedom of a person. To be able to look at this freedom, it is thus necessary to ask what options are available. As Berlin formulates it: 'Freedom ultimately depends not on whether I wish to walk at all, or how far, but on how many doors are open, how open they are, upon their relative importance in my life.'[17] It is important to secure a range of options because an action cannot be called free if the agent did not have sufficiently different possibilities from which to choose a particular one.[18] In the passage just cited, Berlin addresses three points relevant in this context: the number of different doors, how open they are, and how important they each are to me.

If there are no alternatives, for a start, then no choice can be made – this much is obvious. Yet absurd or insignificant alternatives are excluded from consideration or at any rate fail to broaden the scope of one's freedom in any substantial way.[19] Benn and Weinstein nonetheless claim that it is always better to have more alternatives than fewer, because every further alternative increases the degree of individual freedom.[20] But this seems implausible, since the alternatives or options must be sufficiently different (the same sort of ice cream five times over is no true choice) and sufficiently important to a person.[21]

Berlin's second point alerts us to the fact that the mere existence of possibilities or alternatives by no means guarantees that they can also be realized and to this extent actually broaden the person's freedom. 'How open' the doors are, how attainable and liveable the options are, is clearly decisive in determining the scope of one's freedom. At this point we again run into the distinction between a lack of freedom and a lack of opportunity, which can this time be illustrated in different terms. For it is not only big differences in disposable wealth that can produce greatly varying opportunities for realizing guaranteed liberties. They are frequently also produced by symbolically constructed differences, such as the discrepancies between gender roles.[22]

Finally we come to the last question, concerning the relative importance of the options for action in my life. The availability of options in liberal societies should be oriented towards permitting the citizens of these societies a rich life – rich in the sense of the possible pursuit of substantial life-projects – in other words a rich life that permits and supports the independent pursuit of self-determined goals. This idea of 'freedom to' expresses the fact that freedom can also be limited if the possibilities available for leading one's life and choosing between alternatives are such that in themselves they preclude any genuinely rich life.

What we have achieved so far, then, is a gradual delineation of the concept of freedom, one which, though not entirely uncontroversial, is still rather general and excessively broad. Although it goes beyond Hobbes's definition of the concept as simply the 'absence of obstacles', also incorporating a description of the free person and a specific conception of options in its analysis, part of the reason it remains too general is that it does not yet tell us anything about the conception of freedom in the modern age, and because it is thus not yet possible to answer the question of what exactly we mean by individual freedom and why we value this particular freedom in modern liberal societies. And this brings us to the connection between a general concept of freedom and a concept of freedom as autonomy.

3 Freedom and autonomy

Why should the concept of autonomy be any more substantial than the concept of freedom as elucidated up till now? The consideration here is that we would not really describe persons as free if they made their choices 'only' freely, arbitrarily, without reason, acting as though in the pure freedom of the 'chooser',[23] without at the same time also being determined or grounded by a certain attitude towards themselves and towards their possible options.[24] One must be free to be able to be autonomous, but not every free action is an autonomous one, and we expect people to choose, act, behave and live not only 'freely' but also autonomously.[25] The reason that we demand or, to put it more weakly, expect autonomy from persons in their actions and – more fundamentally – life-projects appears to lie in the fact that a life lived autonomously seems 'more valuable' than a merely free life. Only a life lived autonomously, such is the underlying idea, can also be a rewarding life.[26] A life lived autonomously is first of all one for which we can give ourselves (good) reasons. A person who took even important decisions without the least reflection, without asking herself how she would 'really' like to live, would not be called unfree, but presumably not autonomous either. This is precisely the difference I am interested in here. At issue, then, is a concept of autonomy that implies a certain attitude to oneself and with this a certain relation to choice and options, and that recognizes that not every choice is autonomous simply by virtue of being a choice – it must be as good as possible too, that is it must be founded in the correct way.

The aim in what follows is to explain in more concrete terms the considerations sketched above. First, I want to show that with the help of the concept of autonomy the normative core of the modern understanding of freedom can be described. Specifically, this is (the possibility of) asking the 'practical question', or the question of what sort of person one would like to be and how one would like to live. The idea is that to do justice to its normative core, the understanding of freedom includes more than just the idea of choosing in general. It incorporates autonomy too. The question of what such autonomy is and what it consists of forms the more detailed part of this section. Only at the end of the chapter is it my intention to show that a concept of freedom understood in this way as autonomy requires certain conditions of privacy.

This concept of freedom as autonomy is a modern one because only with the modern, individualistic concept of freedom are people free to live as they themselves want. The tradition here is the classic liberal one of Kant and Mill: 'The only freedom which deserves the name, is that of pursuing our own good in our own way,' as Mill famously put it.[27] The freedom to strive after our own good means first that without freedom our own good would not be achieved. Yet if the *telos* of such freedom is our own good, the mode in which this good is pursued is through autonomy. Finding one's own good in one's 'own way' – or at least searching for it – seems to mean that without autonomy individual felicity is not possible or available. A non-autonomous life would in this sense not be a rewarding life, for without this form of self-determination we would fail precisely to achieve our *own* good as our own.

This concept of freedom in the sense of autonomy can now be explicated with the aid of Ernst Tugendhat's reflections on the concept of self-determination and the 'practical question'.[28] Summarizing his theory in a nutshell, Tugendhat writes: 'We are "free" in the sense of "self-determined" [. . .] when we act on the basis of explicit or implicit reflection in which the practical question is posed [. . .] in its fundamental sense.'[29]

Firstly, therefore, the heart of the modern understanding of freedom is conceived as the possibility of asking oneself the 'practical question'. This relates to how I want to live, what sort of person I want to be, and how I should best strive for my own good in my own way.[30] The possibility of asking oneself the practical question is here grounded in the possibility of holding an attitude to oneself in general. If we did not have the opportunity to adopt a position with respect to our desires and actions, we would be unable to ask how we wanted to live, and we would be unable, *a fortiori*, to ask how we wanted to lead a self-determined life that is a rewarding one for us.

The above-cited 'fundamental question' of one's practical self-relationship is described by Tugendhat as the possibility we have 'to distance ourselves somehow from our desires as well as from the roles in which we find ourselves and the norms by which we are guided, and to ask ourselves: what am I myself in all this? what is it that I myself want?' The fact of the matter is, he says, that 'in all one's deeds and wants one somehow always adopts an attitude to oneself too, and this attitude to oneself is updated in special fashion when one reflectively asks: am I being myself in what I do there? what is it that I myself want?'[31] From the possibility of this attitude towards oneself, in other words, there results the possibility of behaving reflectively with respect to one's own life: autonomy or self-determination can accordingly be described as a certain relationship of the person to *what* she chooses and to *how* she chooses it, that is to the *object* and the *mode* of her choice. Tugendhat thus establishes that it is not just any old action or any old choice that is free in this sense of self-determined, but one that *I* have chosen in a reflected decision on whether this (this option, this life) is really what I want, and whether this is really the way I want to live. When I speak of autonomy, I am consequently not referring to *moral* autonomy in the sense in which the concept is often still used following Kant,[32] but *personal* autonomy in the sense of general personal self-determination concerning how I want to lead my life.[33] The moral respect for a person's autonomy is what makes it possible for people to lead an autonomous life in the first place, and for this reason individual personal autonomy is always dependent upon and bound up within an intersubjective network where (moral) norms such as respect, fairness and tolerance are acknowledged. Yet this does not mean that the concept of autonomy should therefore be identified with the concept of moral autonomy.

Tugendhat draws a plausible distinction between situations in which fundamental, vital issues are at stake and other situations where this is not so: 'When does the question have a fundamental sense?' he asks. 'Surely when we are not questioning individual actions out of consideration for something else, but are calling into question our activity, and this means our life, as a whole. [. . .] The practical question is in fact not posed in fundamental terms when circumstances that I can change are taken for granted.'[34] With this reference to the practical question in its fundamental sense, however, Tugendhat is not only making a distinction between situations, actions and choices that are more important with regard to our life as a whole and those that are less so. The distinction concerns the mode of asking to the extent that the question is only posed fundamentally if I am actually trying to act and to live *as far as possible* in a self-determined way, and this means taking nothing for granted that could possibly be changed or altered through my self-determination.[35] Of course, the limits to personal autonomy also reside in the type of unalterable circumstances that may substantially restrict the field within which genuinely autonomous decisions are possible. Yet even a generally sceptical perspective on these circumstances (sceptical in the sense that unalterable circumstances are assumed to be relatively numerous in a person's life, as with the determinant influence of one's cultural or social origins) cannot avoid establishing conditions of autonomy, as there will still be scope for autonomy even for the sceptic (or realist).[36]

Just as circumstances must be understood to be alterable for the practical question to be asked, there are no criteria for its content that can always be taken as given, for otherwise responsibility for the choice would no longer be 'mine', but would be 'shifted' on to those criteria.[37] On the other hand, however, one would not be 'seriously' asking the practical question if one were unable to distinguish between those circumstances that can meaningfully be said to be at one's disposal and those that cannot. Wisely, Tugendhat does not here play the radical existentialist. It is not a question of completely reinventing oneself over and over or radically calling into question one's whole life, but rather – in a way that relates to one's situation and requires constant updating[38] – considering or reflecting upon whether the way in which one lives, behaves towards others, and interprets oneself in certain contexts is really the way one wants to live, behave and interpret oneself. Yet this also means taking seriously the question of how one has understood oneself so far, that is how one wants to conceive or interpret one's own life-story in the context of new situations.

Individual freedom thus permits a certain attitude to oneself. It permits – and demands – a form of self-determination and reflection on who one would like to be, what sort of person one wants to understand oneself as, what sort of life the good one is for oneself. This of course does not mean that every free decision or choice should be understood as a decision about one's whole life, but that the core and *telos* of this freedom is to be able to ask oneself how one would like to live and take one's decisions from this perspective, as well as to be actually able to live in accordance with the decisions taken in this way. The idea is that to be 'free' in this sense means to choose how we want to live, how we want to be.[39]

To be able to ask oneself the practical question and to live accordingly is thus to be autonomous. This does not yet throw sufficient light upon the concept of autonomy itself, however, and the aim of the following section is consequently to elucidate the concept by specifying and explaining its central features as necessary and sufficient conditions. By autonomy I here understand a quality belonging to persons, and, derivatively, I also speak of autonomous desires and actions and an autonomous life.[40] To be able to say of someone that she actually leads an autonomous life requires an interplay of objective and subjective conditions, conditions that include certain rights, modes of behaviour and social structures, etc., in other words general social conditions that go beyond the abilities and attitudes of the subject. My concern in what follows, however, is firstly just with the concept of autonomy that can be conceived as a quality of persons. Three conditions can here be distinguished for attributing autonomy to a person.[41]

Authenticity and identification

To describe a person as self-determined, we expect her desires and actions to be authentically hers, in the sense that she can in principle identify with her desires and actions as her own. This is the idea I here want to set out. If a person is to see herself as autonomous, then she must be able and in a position to *reflect* on certain desires and, on the basis of such reflections, to accept, reject or modify them. At issue here, then, are the components of a subjective, critical ability. As we know, this idea stems from Harry Frankfurt's conception that persons are constituted by the ability to form what he calls 'second-order volitions', that is the ability to deliberate and decide what first-order desires they would like to possess and to be moved to action by their decision.[42] Corresponding to Frankfurt's concept of a *person* is the definition of *autonomy* by Gerald Dworkin, who writes that an autonomous desire or action is one with which the agent can actually identify.

> A person is autonomous if he identifies with his desires, goals, and values, and such identification is not itself influenced in ways which make the process of identification in some way alien to the individual.[43]

Leaving aside for the moment the second half of the remark, which qualifies the process of identification, the first component of Dworkin's definition of autonomy claims that a person is autonomous if her desires – and the actions that result from desires – are actually her own, that is if, one might say, they are authentically hers. Yet this notion of identification requires further elucidation.[44] First, the act of identification must be understood to be *evaluative* and not merely *confirmatory*, for the goal of such identification is to be able to choose between different desires, possible modes of behaviour and ways of life in such a way that an autonomous decision is the result. If the person were guided exclusively by convention and the preferences of others in her actions, without making an evaluation of her own, she would not be called autonomous. And if she were simply able to accept and identify with any desire whatsoever, she would be dependent upon the desires that might arise and would possibly come into conflict with the idea of self-determination on this account. Although she would indeed be authentic in one sense of the word (that is in the sense that she would identify with her own desires as her own), she would not be authentic in the sense that the authenticity of a desire or action must be based upon a critical process of identification to be a condition for its autonomy.

This brings us to the second problem with the concept of identification, which is the question of the *reasons* a person has for identifying with certain desires as her own and rejecting others if she wants to act autonomously or understand herself as an autonomous person. *Prima facie* one would say that the only convincing reasons are ones that make the person appear rational to herself and to others.[45] But what can 'rational' mean in this context? It would clearly be inappropriate to bind autonomy to a strong notion of rationality. If one has one's own good reasons for identifying with and acting upon such-and-such a desire, these reasons need not also appear sensible or sound to everyone else. After (at least hypothetical) reflection, I must be willing and in a position to accept a desire or (retrospectively) an action for myself, that is to accept it as well founded for myself and in this sense *as my own*. But this does not mean that third parties will necessarily understand it as well founded in the same way. The process of reflection and identification will always incorporate personal feelings, obligations, memories and biographical influences that as such need not appear equally sensible or convincing to everyone. In considering what reasons might be good ones for a person to identify with and act upon certain desires and reject others, a crucial role is thus played by the sorts of factors that go to make up each individual's life-story, the biographical background of the person as a whole, and her self-understanding, that is that bear precisely upon the question of what sort of person she wants to be.[46]

A helpful distinction has here been proposed by Richard Lindley[47] between *authorship* and *acceptability*. A person is autonomous in the sense of having *her own good reasons* if she is able to understand herself as the author of an action. But this need not simultaneously mean that other people accept these reasons too: general (potential) acceptance is here not a test for rationality in the sense of an action being well founded. Nonetheless, even given a slight uncoupling of rationality and autonomy, what remains is that the person should not lose her *orientation towards the truth* in the process of identification, as otherwise it would no longer be possible to distinguish between the person's own good reasons ('authorship') on the one hand, and a descent into wishful thinking, illusions and self-deception on the other. To this extent, the concept of authorship alone is of course too weak. 'Orientation towards the truth' here means that the person must be guided by true opinions about the world and thus also by true opinions about her relations to other persons (relations which almost always underlie the conflicts of desires within a person), and finally by true, valid opinions about herself, her own abilities and her own history. This may presuppose or set in motion a process of self-enlightenment, which in this sense is then necessary for the person's autonomy. Indeed, such self-enlightenment in avoiding deceptions and self-deceptions is clearly as relevant as it is difficult in determining a person's autonomy. A person is never completely transparent to herself anyway, yet her autonomy as a whole is not jeopardized on account of this. Even though the issue of self-transparency may in a certain sense represent a limit to one's possible self-determination, it does not for this reason cease to make sense to speak of autonomy within these limits.[48]

A notoriously controversial aspect of the concept of identification is also the matter of when – under what conditions – we would say that the act, or process, of identification has actually come to an end. Can one not, goes the question, iterate the figure of identification with first-order desires on the second, reflective level, and so forth to the nth level?[49] It is certainly reasonable not to want to rule out on conceptual terms the possibility that the results of processes of reflection might as such be called into question once again, that is to assume that there may be higher-order levels of reflection.[50] But it is certainly just as reasonable to hold that this process of reflection and ever new identification is brought to an end when the person – in so far as she can be called autonomous – has as it were gone through as many aspects and levels of her self-understanding as possible (if not all) and reaches a point where she can identify with a desire or action as a whole person, even though this may be heavy-heartedly rather than wholeheartedly. It can be seen that one aspect of what it means to be autonomous is to be in a position to reflect even on ambivalences in such a way that though these may often enough lead to a questioning of the results of reflection they do not result in an inability to act. To this extent, the idea of identification shows both that it may in certain circumstances make sense to iterate reflections *and* that a distinctive feature of autonomy may be to bring this process to a practical end for pragmatic reasons and perhaps in spite of not being entirely sure of oneself.

These thoughts on the concepts of reflection and authentic identification do not of course mean, however, that autonomy consists in constantly having to ask oneself whether one's current desires, actions and behaviour are authentic. This component of the concept of autonomy can only plausibly hold that authentic identification must be *hypothetically* possible:[51] if I were now to reflect on whether I really want to do this, whether I am really behind this action, whether I really want to understand myself as the sort of person who does such-and-such a thing, then the answer would either have to be 'yes' or produce a change in the course of my actions. Of course, such reflections in an autonomous person on her own behaviour and life themselves form a part of this person's behaviour and life, yet it is neither possible nor necessary to pinpoint *exactly* how frequently such reflections must take place for us to be able actually to call the person autonomous.

However, these elucidations of the first component of the concept of autonomy remain incomplete without one final step being taken. During the explanation of the concepts of authenticity, reflection and identification so far, the impression may have been given that this first component of the concept of autonomy could be understood as an entirely solipsistic process, as though it was in isolation and without – or possibly even in opposition to – everyone else that the person necessarily reflected on what she wanted to do or how she wanted to live. This is of course not so. Intersubjectivity is *in general* intrinsic to the process of autonomy in various respects regarding both the genesis of autonomy and the question of what aims and projects a person is able and wants to pursue. We shall presently look at both aspects more closely. Viewing the moment of intersubjectivity specifically with the problem of authenticity in mind, what emerges is that such intersubjectivity becomes relevant in particular in situations where concrete conflicts between desires, actions or decisions arise for a person, for the processes of deliberation then necessary are also, typically, intersubjective. Together with others, confronting their expectations and opinions, people consider what they themselves 'really' want and what sort of person they see themselves as. Yet this reference to the intersubjective dimension of the process of reflection on decisions, conflicts or ways of life is relevant for a further reason. When we typically discuss conflictive situations or deliberate on fundamental issues in our life within close relationships or among friends, we interpret ourselves in the light of the reactions and interpretations of these others as well. The authenticity of such self-interpretation, and with this an autonomous life, thus also depends in these respects upon the *authentic* reaction and interpretation of those others. Accordingly, the conditions of authenticity (and autonomy) are also external, and the aforementioned relation of autonomy to truth thus acquires a second meaning.[52]

This first component of the concept of autonomy can thus now be called the *component of authenticity* or the structural component. Accordingly, I do not consider the ideas of autonomy and authenticity to be in competition with one another, but understand authenticity as a condition for autonomy in that a person, a desire or an action, if not in this sense authentic, cannot be called autonomous either.

Parenthesis: On the concept of authenticity

In recent years, however, there has been quite varied discussion on the relationship between autonomy and authenticity, in which authenticity has been understood as the antagonist of autonomy. Two distinct versions of such a model can be differentiated here: an *intersubjective* one, where the conceptions oriented either towards autonomy or towards authenticity are understood as different conceptions of positive freedom; and an *intrasubjective* one, where these conceptions are viewed as different orientations of the subject. The reference here is to *two* versions of *a single* model because they each represent only different weightings within the one understanding of a fundamental opposition between autonomy and authenticity.[53]

It is Charles Taylor who has most influentially championed this idea of authenticity in the sense of an independent, normative conception of positive freedom.[54] The term 'authenticity' is here used in such a way that an inauthentic life would be one which had failed to realize a 'true' core of the self,[55] and one's life would thus have to be called failed, misspent or inauthentic if one had not recognized its true purpose or had thoughtlessly disregarded it. This notion of authenticity stands in opposition to or in competition with the conception of autonomy to the extent that autonomy is understood as moral autonomy and the idea of the authentic, good life is able to counter such – formal and universalistic – conceptions of autonomy and rationality. The reason for this is that the idea of authenticity refers to individualized identities, whereas the idea of autonomy is oriented towards what is common to all.[56]

The second version of this oppositional model is concerned, by contrast, with an orientation *within* the subject, in other words an intrasubjective conflict, that is a possible conflict between the ethical and the moral orientation of the subject.[57] Alessandro Ferrara, for example, thus defines the concept of authenticity in explicit opposition to the concept of autonomy.[58] Authenticity for him is an *ethical* concept, in contrast to the *moral* concept of autonomy. As sincerity regarding oneself, authenticity essentially denotes an attitude towards one's *true self* that may on occasion come into conflict with autonomously chosen principles of morality and rationality. In such a conflict, authentic behaviour is not what would correspond to the autonomously chosen moral principles but what does justice to the truth of one's own particular self:

> Authentic conduct has the quality of being somehow connected with, and expressive of, the core of the actor's personality. It brings into play the actor's uniquely personal, as opposed to culturally or socially shared, identity. If I am insensitive to my deepest needs, if I betray them, or if I inscribe my action into a life-plan which in turn fails to fit who I am, then I may act [. . .] inauthentically.[59]

Authenticity is here a quality that may be attributed to a subject in greater or lesser measure according to whether he succeeds in giving expression to his 'true self', his deepest needs, in realizing himself, in unfolding himself, if need be even contrary to his underlying moral convictions and thus also in opposition to his autonomy. If the subject behaves inauthentically, then he fails to realize possibilities that were actually available to him, since – as in the first version of the model – every subject in principle has a true core, which he may either develop or fail to develop. The opposition between autonomy and authenticity can thus also be given a further definition, for autonomy consists in the ability oneself to choose rational, moral principles and to behave in accordance with them, whereas we are authentic when we reflect on our own individual selfhood, basing our behaviour on this irrespective of whether it corresponds to those principles.[60]

Yet both versions of authenticity, both approaches to the meaning of the concept, seem to be problematic. This is because both of them (necessarily) narrow the concept of autonomy out of all proportion and in the process hypostasize the concept of authenticity just as disproportionately. As regards the first version of the model, this means that autonomy is narrowed to *moral* autonomy, authenticity is tied to the idea of a hypostasized true self (a rational, moral, autonomous life, by contrast, would be a life that is alienated from this 'true' self), and it is only because of this conceptually unconvincing opposition (for who 'determines' what is authentic and what is not? is the self piloted or driven, so to speak?) that it can come to such a division or separation of autonomy and authenticity in the first place.[61] This is even clearer with the second version of the concept of authenticity. A theory such as Ferrara's has to restrict the concept of autonomy to generating solely moral principles. Only by doing so does Ferrara obtain the possibility of contrasting a concept of authenticity with that of autonomy in such a way that the former alone is made responsible for ethical questions of the good life, for self-realization and individualization. It is unclear why this should be so, why in certain situations a moral perspective in the subject might not also be authentic.[62] And why it cannot conversely be regarded as a sign of personal autonomy, indeed its constitutive feature, for a person to be in a position to weigh up different orientations and perspectives in the subject. Would it not rather be permitting a significant element of heteronomy to claim that the authentic perspective of the subject is one that might, or indeed had to, contradict the autonomous perspective? Finally, this conception of authenticity leaves it quite unclear how a conflict between the two perspectives can even be described without positing self-determination as the highest *authority staging the conflict* and thus as a prioritized concept. For these reasons, it seems more plausible to accept the perspective of the subject's self-determination as – in the hierarchy of possible perspectives[63] – the 'highest' or deciding one, which tries to bring other possible perspectives into line with one another or integrate them, without thereby positing that the autonomous perspective is to be equated with a rationalistic, moral one.

As against these versions of the concept of authenticity, therefore, it is a fundamentally different concept that I have used so far and shall use in what follows, for the authenticity of a desire, an action or a person as an explicatory condition is tied to the concept of autonomy. Autonomy only works if the person also, in the sense described above, acts authentically, in other words if she can identify with her desires and actions, in the sense described above.

However, there are two objections that can be raised to defend the *contrast* drawn between the two concepts against this conception of autonomy-as-authenticity. The first objection claims that it is perfectly possible and makes perfectly good sense to describe someone as leading an autonomous but nonetheless inauthentic life, yet this manner of speaking and this idea cannot be explicated by the model of autonomy-as-authenticity. Especially in literature, runs the objection, we find figures who lead an autonomous life – one that is self-determined, self-chosen – that is nonetheless not the one they would have actually wanted to lead, in which they could have lived out their desires more genuinely, more authentically, more completely, more contentedly, could have satisfied a greater number and diversity of needs, and would have been more likely – or at least had a chance – to realize themselves. Every case of renunciation must be described in such terms, for renunciation (of a love, of an artistic vocation) is the abdication of a (more) authentic way of life, which is, or at least can be, nonetheless founded on a perfectly autonomous decision.[64]

The question now, of course, is how such cases are best described – described in such a way that none of the range, wealth or depth of the phenomenon itself is lost and yet the explicatory concepts are consistent and plausible. Even without entering into details, however, it is not going too far to say that conflicts between desires, between obligations, between projected ways of life, are by no means excluded from the model of autonomy-as-authenticity. What would be said here is that the decision about how to live, which desires to identify with, which goals to allow to guide one's actions, which 'project' to pursue, can be an immensely difficult one, where completely different and incompatible desires have to be weighed up, different self-images compete with one another, and biographical features – as well as affective commitments and obligations, the nature of which may not even be clear in the first place – can be evaluated and interpreted in different ways. Yet once the person has brought herself to make a decision, to choose a way of life, then at least – if the decision-making process was at least roughly autonomous – this is *her* decision, one that she identifies with and is authentic. The *reasons* for choosing the other possibility, the reasons for realizing oneself in a different way, for leading a different life, continue to exist and are not rendered obsolete by the decision.[65] Yet this does not in itself mean that it would have been this other life that was the authentic one. Such a description only follows if one believes firstly that autonomy must be understood as moral, secondly that priority must always be granted to the moral perspective, and thirdly, making the first two conditions possible, that a precise separation of the ethical (authentic) and the moral (autonomous) perspectives can always be made in the first place. However, in phenomenal terms a separation of this sort is frequently difficult.[66]

Yet what about the perhaps rather infrequent, but intuitively plausible notion of 'failing to realize oneself'? Does this not presuppose a somehow authentic self, which – either in spite or because of one's autonomy – one may fail to recognize, fail to realize? This brings us straight to the second objection. Here the claim is that the theory of autonomy and identification also presupposes a 'self' or an 'I' that identifies or otherwise with desires, that on occasion may thus even identify with a false desire, not the true or correct one (unless this is ruled out on purely conceptual grounds), and that so fails to realize the authentic self. Now for a start this is certainly a valid warning that any conception of autonomy must not be naive with respect to the theory of the self it presupposes. Yet it can be argued, first, that one may fail to realize oneself even in the model of autonomy-as-authenticity, as when one acts or lives in a manner that is not as autonomous as it might have been – out of self-deception or conformity with conventions. The idea of 'failing to realize oneself' could also be expressed in the awareness that one is unhappy with the decisions one has taken, that one is not (has not become) the person one thought one had chosen to be. All this is certainly possible. Decisions are well known to have implications that are not always foreseeable, and contingencies frequently determine one's own life more than one might wish. Yet this does not mean, secondly, that such a conception of autonomy cannot, within limits, be neutral with respect to a theory of the self. How this theory is described more exactly is clearly, within two limiting points, not laid down in advance. These limiting points are set on the one hand by the fact that at least a certain unity of the self must be posited if autonomous decisions are taken, and on the other hand by the fact that the theory of a core – a core which it is just a matter of discovering, which alone describes a true self, and in only one way – must be understood to be unsuitable in phenomenal and normative terms in the model of autonomy-as-authenticity. Yet within these limits it makes sense to speak of self-invention or self-discovery, of conflicts of the self, of a permanent process that never comes to an end (one must keep on asking oneself anew how one would like to live), and even of 'finding one's self' as the person one would like to live as.[67]

The genesis of desires and autonomy as habitus

If we now turn first to the specific question of how *individual* desires and actions come about or are developed, and then to the general question of how we learn to develop autonomy as part of our *habitus*, of the disposition or make-up of our personality, and to see and value ourselves as autonomous, we come to the *historical* component in the concept of autonomy. At issue here is a vertical line, so to speak, rather than a horizontal one as with the first aspect we discussed. To start with, I intend to return to Gerald Dworkin's definition of the concept of autonomy and its second condition, which is that the process of identification should take place in a manner that is 'procedurally independent', in other words not itself subject to manipulations or non-reflective influences:

> A person is autonomous if he identifies with his desires, goals, and values, and such identification is not itself influenced in ways which make the process of identification in some way alien to the individual. Spelling out the conditions of procedural independence involves distinguishing

> those ways of influencing people's reflective and critical faculties which subvert them from those which promote and improve them.[68]

What is meant by this? The problem is that the way a person identifies with a desire, even though it may fulfil the requirements of authenticity, does not necessarily tell us whether the desire itself did not perhaps come about as a product of manipulation – in which case even authentic identification with it cannot show the person in question in a genuinely autonomous light. For this very reason, for a desire or action to be authentic, reflection on its genesis is necessary, first with respect to the person's individual capacity for developing a non-manipulative relationship towards herself. Reflection on the question of which desire a person wants to identify with and act upon thus also comes to include the question of how the person interprets the genesis of this desire *with regard to herself*, what interests, preferences, relations it was based on, in other words what subjective context it was formed in. Reflection on the genesis of desires in this sense is thus intended to prevent as far as possible self-deceptions and manipulations. I referred above to the orientation towards truth and the concomitant self-enlightenment that are required for our concept of autonomy. Given the problems associated with the genesis of desires, this requirement now acquires a further significance.

Secondly, however, reflection on the genesis of a desire is necessary, as feminist criticism in particular has pointed out, with respect to the *external* conditions that gave rise to it.[69] Autonomy in a person necessitates non-manipulative outward circumstances allowing that person to build upon forms of recognition in intersubjective relations that are intrinsic to the development of a non-manipulative self-relationship. This can again be conceived as a normative proposal regarding the reflecting person (to distance herself as far as possible from manipulative outward conditions), but also regarding the social conditions in which she lives. A non-autonomous life in this *external* sense would thus be one that is lived under conditions that (necessarily) bring the person to form systematically false opinions – at least in certain respects – about her possibilities, actions, goals, desires and expectations, that is conditions of systematic repression, manipulation and deception. The fact that (structurally) non-egalitarian conditions may in this sense result in a lack of autonomy is something that has been pointed out, for example, by Phil Benson.[70] Manipulation in the sense of the conscious or structural deception of a person about who she is or could be (for instance, about what constitutes a realistic evaluation of her abilities and motives) may on the one hand be an aspect of general social conditions, as is the case, for example, with the (patriarchal, and therefore structurally non-egalitarian) society in which we live. Yet it may also be an aspect of our intimate relations if manipulations or deceptions take place within them.[71]

Indeed, this condition of the 'right' or appropriate genesis or history of a desire may prove an extremely demanding one if the term 'non-manipulative' is interpreted in a very strong sense. The upshot in practice would be that it was impossible, for women at least, to be genuinely autonomous, because they grow up and live in conditions that still deny them equal forms of recognition and that force them (and men too, incidentally) into stereotypical role patterns in contradiction with an autonomous life.[72] The degree of autonomy that can be attributed to individuals as members of groups in this respect is certainly something extremely hard to measure, and it is difficult likewise to tread the fine line between paternalism on the one hand and naivety or abstraction on the other. From a purely normative perspective, it is enough to insist that the conditions for the development or genesis of desires should be such that authentic identification with them is at any rate not systematically or structurally prevented, in other words that there must at least not be any directly intended manipulations or repressions at play in the development of these desires, convictions and self-images. This may in certain circumstances even mean, moreover, that we accept a desire or approve certain ways of acting or behaving even once we have understood that they came about as a product of manipulation. We may see and recognize this and still want to consider ourselves the sort of person who behaves in such and such a way or is so and so in nature.[73] For the rest, a person is always autonomous to a greater or lesser degree, never ideal and never wholly so. Autonomy is a *gradual* concept, and for this very reason too it makes sense as a normative concept in empirical contexts.[74]

This reference to the external conditions of an autonomous life has yet one further aspect, for – as also emerged above – an intersubjective moment is constitutive in the development of individual autonomy, in certain respects at least. Persons are dependent upon forms of intersubjective communication conveying to them self-respect, self-esteem and the sense that their own personhood and needs are taken seriously. They are dependent, in other words, upon the value of autonomy in themselves and others being conveyed to them. It is thus not paradoxical to ask how autonomy is learnt or acquired. This is the general question of how autonomy is acquired as part of our habitus, as a stance to be valued.[75] For only if autonomy is valued as it were habitually or dispositionally by oneself and others is it also possible to see oneself on the whole as an autonomous person and to act autonomously in individual situations – and this is precisely why the reference to the intersubjective and social conditions under which autonomy is *learnt* is constitutive in this context.[76]

Goals and projects

Up to now, we have implicitly assumed a further factor, which will now be explicated as the third element in the equation. This is the fact that to be called autonomous, a person must have a certain understanding of herself, namely as someone who is able and in a position to form goals and design projects, and then also pursue these goals and projects, and who can also reflect on just this. If the core of the modern idea of freedom consists in being able oneself to decide about one's life (within limits), and if freedom must thus be conceived as autonomy, this means that the ability to *get involved in goals and projects* in the first place and the ability to commit oneself to these goals and projects are the conditions for being able to consider oneself an autonomous person. Self-determination only seems to make sense if one has (deep) projects, meaning that one can pursue priorities in such a way that one would give up other things for them, can convince oneself and others of them, etc.[77] This can be further clarified with the help of a well-known passage from Isaiah Berlin explicating the concept of autonomy in general: 'I wish my life and decisions to depend on myself, not on external forces of whatever kind. I wish to be the instrument of my own, not other men's acts of will. I wish to be a subject, not an object [. . .] I wish to be somebody, not nobody [. . .] deciding, not being decided for [. . .] as if I were a thing [. . .] incapable of conceiving goals and policies of my own and realizing them.'[78] This passage is frequently cited, for it seems to contain at heart all the relevant elements of the concept of autonomy. What interests me here are the factors 'deciding' and 'conceiving goals and policies of my own and realizing them', which Berlin encapsulates in the notion of wanting to be 'somebody, not nobody', for in this way Berlin is equating the ability to form and pursue goals and projects with the development of one's practical identity – one's identity in the sense that one understands oneself (in a variety of contexts and aspects) as *somebody* who pursues such and such a project, that is as *somebody* at all.[79]

It is just this form of self-understanding in a person,[80] over a period of time and in important aspects of life, that can be called autonomy. This means having an idea or understanding of oneself – of the way one lives (within limits, but in important respects nonetheless) and the way one behaves (within limits, but in important respects nonetheless) – as willed by oneself or at least accepted by oneself. And it thus also means having a self-understanding that involves not simply being at the mercy of the opinions, expectations or demands of other people (a family, social group or society) or of the circumstances of one's life without a will of one's own. It entails a self-understanding, in other words, in which projects and goals are not just present on an intellectual plane but must also be pursued in practice. This does not necessarily tell us anything about the moral value of such projects themselves, but only about the relation of the person to them, even if in fact the only sorts of goals and projects pursued by persons are those also regarded as valuable by (certain) others. Goals and projects need not be conceived here as perfectionist or as moral. Both may apply, and typically do, yet this is not itself inherent in the concept of autonomy.

Two further observations still remain to be made. The first concerns the problem of the formation of hierarchies and priorities among the subject's projects and goals. Frequently an internal obstacle to a person's autonomy is that clear priorities cannot be established among one's projects and goals, which may be difficult to compare or even incommensurable.[81] This often gives the subject the sensation of a lack of self-determination with respect to his own life. Indeed, the creation of priorities among the projects, goals and commitments in a person's life can certainly be a complicated matter and may well only be accomplished with a heavy heart. On top of this, the very question of what is – subjectively – feasible as a target or project ('conceiving goals') is itself frequently a difficult (or courageous) decision for a person to make. Yet the only thing this can mean is that autonomy is on occasion difficult to attain. It would be mistaken and neither necessary in phenomenal terms nor appropriate in normative terms to describe these problems as limits to autonomy in principle.

Secondly, it must be realized that the offer or range of options, goals, projects and ways of life available to a person is of course always determined (among other things) by specific cultural assumptions and by the social context, which thus always have a determining influence upon what sort of person one wants to see oneself as and how one wants to live. Yet this awareness of the way in which our life is interwoven with our social and cultural background does not mean that we cannot in turn free ourselves from it, albeit with great difficulty and at a high individual cost. If a person views herself as autonomous, then she will also be capable of reflecting upon the way she is situated in cultural, social and intimate contexts and seeing how moral concepts, commitments and dependencies contribute to determine her identity and make her life valuable, and to what extent they (always) form part of her goals and projects. This does not mean that such dependencies are *prior* to autonomy. Yet it does mean that these sorts of bonds will always enter into the autonomous person's reflections, precisely because they can be experienced as valuable as well as repressive. If a person sees herself as someone who pursues goals and projects and who regards the question of how she wants to live – and thus also the question of what projects she pursues – as fundamental for a rewarding life, this entails that the person in question must also be in a position to change her projects or goals fundamentally if she comes to realize that she has been pursuing false goals or living inauthentically, or if she wishes to 'redescribe' her situation or life for other reasons. The practical question can be posed in very radical fashion. This is illustrated, for example, by 'renegade literature', which shows not – as Sandel would claim – that a person who tries to break with her 'constitutive attachments' must be viewed as shallow and unprincipled, but on the contrary that she has the strength of character to reflect on her projects and her life in such a way that she can break with them if she understands them as unsuccessful.[82]

So where do we now stand? So far I have tried to show that a general definition of the concept of freedom is not enough to grasp what is meant by the normative core of modern individual freedom, for by this we mean asking ourselves the question of how we want to live and then also being able to lead this life – in other words autonomy. I have tried to show just how such a concept of autonomy must be spelled out more precisely by analysing the three (necessary and sufficient) conditions for this. To ask oneself the 'practical question' in the way described above thus means to ask oneself how one is to behave in certain situations, in the face of certain desires, in the light of one's own history and in the light of the convictions that are important to one. And this then means asking oneself which of one's conflicting desires or convictions one wants to identify with, how to assess specific desires or preferences in their genesis, and what fundamental life-projects (are to) play a part in the appraisal and assessment of this identification. To this extent, the three components in the concept of autonomy simply spell out the more generally formulated, underlying normative idea that an autonomous person is one who asks herself the 'practical question' and attempts also to live accordingly.

Before now moving on to the next section, I should briefly like to make two explanatory comments. The first concerns the 'strength' of this concept of autonomy with regard to the possible conceptions of freedom in a liberal democracy. If a distinction can be drawn between negative civil liberties, which make it possible or necessary to be autonomous, and positive conceptions of freedom, which always want to see in freedom the realization of a particular goal (that is to characterize *freedom to* in a quite specific substantial and not merely formal way), then a concept of autonomy that goes beyond the arbitrary freedom of pure caprice can be characterized as substantial on account of the self-reflexive relation in the free person, but not as a positive concept. What cannot be given or detailed are substantial particulars concerning the success or failure of such an autonomous life in the sense of the *right* options that must be chosen, the *correct* projects that must be pursued, particulars of the sort provided by positive conceptions of freedom. This concept of autonomy, therefore, is still a formal one.[83] This also means that I consider it unfortunate to call such a concept 'ethical autonomy', for this implies there must be an opposition between ethical and moral autonomy. The question of what sort of person one wants to be, how one wants to live, is thus not reduced to the ethical but always incorporates a moral perspective as well.

The second comment refers to the connection between an autonomous and a good or rewarding life. Even though the central claim regarding the link between autonomy and privacy that I am concerned with in this study does not depend upon this other link between autonomy and a life that is good (for one might find the idea convincing that privacy is valued and needed for the sake of a person's autonomy, without considering plausible the further thesis that only an autonomous life can also be a rewarding life), I want at least briefly to elucidate which direction an argument would have to take.

Why, therefore, should autonomy be given such special status? By way of argument, we can start by citing Raz's sober observation that the value of autonomy is part of the self-evident description of our life and culture: 'The value of personal autonomy is a fact of life. Since we live in a society whose social forms are to a considerable extent based on individual choice, and since our options are limited by what is available in our society, we can prosper in it only if we can be successfully autonomous.'[84] The link between autonomy and a rewarding life, as Raz also points out, has to do with the value of autonomy in a particular culture, that is in the liberal modern age. This is the first qualifying remark, which limits the claim being made about the connection between autonomy and a rewarding life. In *this* cultural context though, such is the claim, this connection applies, normatively and without qualification. Yet such an idea of an autonomous and rewarding life, in this culture, does not in itself mean that a specific way of leading one's life is stipulated. As will become clearer below, autonomy announces the form of a life, but not its content.

The second qualifying remark highlights that autonomy is not a sufficient condition, but at most a necessary condition for a rewarding life, and that a rewarding life – as the concept is to be understood here – is not to be equated with a happy life.[85] The reason it is not a sufficient condition is that my self-determination (say, the pursuit of certain goals and projects, alone or with others) may fail for reasons that are not in my hands. Plans may go awry or have unforeseeable consequences, unexpected occurrences may thwart the projects I have developed, expectations may prove to be unfounded, etc.[86] And the reason a self-determined life need not be a happy one is that, quite independently of my self-determined plans, contingencies (may) influence or shape my life so decisively that although one can still speak of self-determination (with respect to one's own life-projects) it may no longer be possible to speak of happiness. Children may fall ill, loved ones may die, relationships may come to grief, one may have accidents or be made redundant. Self-determination offers no protection against unhappiness and misfortune.

Yet despite these contingencies and these limits to self-determination, and despite the realization that a person's autonomy for the most part finds expression not in 'life plans' but in individual, specific goals and projects that may be revisable, fallible or unwise – despite all these considerations, it is clearly part of our self-understanding that we value deciding our life for ourselves and deem autonomy essential and indispensable for a rewarding life.[87]

4 Why do we value privacy?

What is it about privacy that we value? Why do we attribute a value to it at all, and why do we find it so difficult to conceive of living in a society without privacy? In what follows, I wish to discuss various answers to this question and then substantiate how the fact that we value privacy is a function of the fact that we value freedom or autonomy. This thus connects once again with the general question of the relation between freedom and privacy. In systematic terms, we can start by distinguishing fundamentally between two distinct groups of answers to the question of what the value of privacy inheres in: those that reduce the value of privacy to another value or to several other values, and those that do not, i.e. that claim that it is an irreducible fact that we value privacy. Within this second group, we can then draw a further distinction between 'intrinsic' and 'functional' explanations. Intrinsic approaches regard the value of privacy as grounded within privacy itself, while functional approaches – though describing privacy as not further reducible in its significance – see its value, the reason we value it, as nonetheless grounded in a norm or value other than privacy itself.[88]

Reductive conceptions try to show that any apparent interest in privacy, right to privacy, or genuine value of privacy only at first sight represents an interest, right or value of *privacy* and can in fact be reduced to other interests, rights or moral concepts.[89] Ferdinand Schoeman[90] calls these approaches sceptical rather than reductive, because they are sceptical with respect to the possibility of grounding a (moral or juridical) right to privacy, as well as with respect to the possibility of describing the phenomenon of privacy in a unified and distinct way in the first place.[91] A prominent and controversial advocate of this sort of reductive or sceptical position is Judith Jarvis Thomson.[92] Thomson's starting point is that it is completely unclear what a (moral or juridical) 'right to privacy' is supposed to consist in, as the familiar phenomena are too heterogeneous and the familiar definitions unable to do justice to this heterogeneity. Her thesis is that in every single concrete or applied case what is known as the right to privacy proves in fact to be another right already in existence, in other words that rights to privacy can in each particular case be reduced to other rights, in particular rights over the person and property rights.[93] Her method is to describe a variety of heterogeneous examples of a supposed right to privacy and in each case try to show that one would do just as well – if not better in most cases – to speak of some other right instead of the right to privacy.

Yet there are three arguments that speak against Thomson's theory of reduction. The first is that she finds herself forced to refer to some strange rights, since every single case of a right previously described as a right to privacy must be described as *another* right, for example as a right not to be looked at. Thomas Scanlon thus writes, '[a]s far as I can see I have no such general rights to begin with. I have an *interest* in not being looked at when I wish not to be, and I may have a similar interest with respect to certain objects. But rights directly corresponding to these interests would be too broad to form part of a workable system.'[94] Even if not only juridical but also moral rights were meant here, Scanlon would be right in his criticism of Thomson. A general desire, an interest or simply a feeling of unease cannot meaningfully be reformulated as rights in Thomson's sense. Secondly, Thomson cannot explain why it is that in spite of her reductive proposals we still find it intuitively plausible to give the predicate 'private' an independent meaning that, though perhaps heterogeneous, is nonetheless not reducible. The reductive approach results in us no longer being able to interpret what that extra something is that makes such good sense in everyday speech and that we clearly understand when we refer to or describe an infringement of our privacy. When we say, for example, that something is no business of other people (or of the government) or is a private matter, this manner of speaking clearly indicates that underlying the term 'private' is a value that need not perhaps be described as intrinsic (this would be the contradictory position to Thomson's) but at least as functional. Thirdly, Thomson seems rather rash in her claim that there is no unified meaning underlying the predicate 'private'.[95] She is too quick and too sweeping in her dismissal of the possibility that there might be a unified definition of the various uses of the term and that it might thus also be reasonable to assume that underlying the various uses and applications of the right to privacy there is a unified interest or an orientation towards a unified value. By way of argument, it is enough here to point out that such plausible approaches do exist. Thomson does not refute them individually, but mistakenly relies on the examples she gives being convincing as synecdoche.

Reductive approaches such as Thomson's are thus not genuinely plausible even if they attempt, as Thomson does, to give precise explanations of individual uses of the concept of privacy. Yet the term evidently signifies more than reductive answers are able to convey and explain. *Intrinsic approaches*, by contrast, seek to show that we attribute value to our private sphere or to private dimensions of our life intrinsically and irreducibly, in other words that we value privacy purely and simply for its own sake. These approaches are frequently difficult to distinguish from functional ones, because it is not always completely clear whether privacy is being valued for the sake of another good or for its own sake.

An example is offered by Scanlon, for whom realms of privacy are always 'conventionally defined' and obtain in their own right, that is they cannot be marked out by means of other rights or claims. Scanlon's concern is to show precisely that we value privacy as such, irrespective of how it is determined in a particular case (that is in particular societies or from a particular perspective). '[O]ur zone of privacy could be defined in many different ways; what matters most is that *some* system of limits to observation should be generally understood and observed.'[96] Scanlon insists on the *conventionality* and to a certain extent also the arbitrariness of these limits in order to be able to show that something we call 'privacy' is *irreducibly* violated if, for example, we are observed against our will, or strangers read our letters, etc. The fact that such limits exist – however varied they may turn out to be – is for Scanlon an indication that the value of privacy must be declared to be intrinsic.

Now it is certainly true, as Scanlon writes, that we regard it as a violation of our privacy if people observe us or eavesdrop on us against our will or without our knowledge (regardless, moreover, of where this occurs, whether at home or on the streets). Social space is clearly traversed by this conventionally defined line that separates private from public, and we value the realms or dimensions delimited in this way first and foremost simply for their own sake. Scanlon's approach, like other intrinsic ones, has the indisputable advantage that it takes seriously the *intuition* that privacy is an irreducibly valuable phenomenon. An example here is the case of a person being observed without her knowledge (and against what is assumed to be her will) and without her ever discovering or noticing what is going on. Here one would clearly say that the privacy of this person has been infringed, even though she herself is not conscious of this and never will be.[97]

Yet even if we claim that such realms or dimensions of privacy are intrinsically valuable, this does not in itself mean that we do not also value them for a function they fulfil. Intrinsic and functional approaches are not mutually exclusive,[98] for it *also* makes sense to ask *why* we value privacy, what it is that would be lost if we were to lose our privacy. Intrinsic explanations are in themselves perfectly plausible, yet they are unable to satisfy this deeper explanatory need.[99]

It is *functional theories* that take this further step.[100] Indeed, most of the definitions and explanations of privacy to be found in the literature are 'functional' or can at least be interpreted as such. These functional approaches in turn differ from one another fundamentally according to the 'function' in terms of which privacy is valued,[101] whether this be the protection of intimacy, the protection of a delimited space where individuals can do what they want, the protection of a realm where persons can be 'left alone', the possibility of 'self-disclosure' (of opening oneself only in the way and to the people one has oneself chosen when it comes to revealing things one regards as fundamental to one's own identity), or the possibility of self-invention that relies upon the protection of private dimensions of one's life. Others conceive privacy as functionally connected to the constitution and fostering of intimate relationships, the protection and development of individual personhood, or the respect for persons and regard for their inviolability.

In systematic terms, these very different approaches can be assigned to two broad groups: those theories that relate the functional value of privacy to the protection of (intimate) *relationships*, and those that relate it to the protection of (various aspects of) *individual personhood*.[102] I want briefly to discuss these approaches with the aid of examples in order to show why it is in principle correct and appropriate to pursue functional answers, and also – even though I regard both approaches based on functional explanations as insufficient – in order then to follow these functional explanations further.

The work of Julie Inness[103] is a good example of a functional grounding of privacy, which, although it also takes up the concept of autonomy (and in this sense is individual-oriented too), then proceeds to centre exclusively upon the protection of relations. Inness seeks to show that the reason we value privacy or private dimensions and realms is that they protect the aspect of our autonomy that finds expression in relations of friendship and love: 'Privacy protects our autonomy with respect to our expression of love, care and liking.'[104] Yet there is a series of counterarguments to Inness's and other, comparable positions. For a start, privacy protects the autonomy of relations even when 'love, care and liking' are not involved, or at least not in an interesting, substantial sense, and this is also to be desired. A relation can be intimate without this entailing that the other person is particularly loved. One's relation with a prostitute is also an intimate, private one and as such worthy of protection. Further, such an explanation is unable to account for many uses of the predicate that nonetheless seem indispensable and essential to the meaning of privacy, such as the fact that information about a serious illness I might have must not fall into the wrong hands, since it is a private affair, or the fact that we consider what I write in my diary to be absolutely no business of anyone else, an utterly private matter. Clearly neither of these examples has anything to do with the intimacy of relations.[105] The heterogeneity in the use of the term 'private' is thus homogenized by the idea that everything we call private must refer to intimacy: 'What unites these apparently disparate areas [of privacy] is the common denominator of intimacy.'[106] Yet even functional explanations should not disregard central aspects of the idea of privacy.

A second example is provided by a theory that places the protection not of relations but of the person herself at the centre of its explanation of why we need and value privacy. Like Schoeman and Benn,[107] Jean Cohen[108] takes the heart of the idea of privacy to be the protection of the inviolability of the person. She accordingly conceives privacy as necessary in various aspects and dimensions, which are nonetheless all ultimately grounded in the basic value of the inviolacy and thus the identity of the person. She distinguishes between relational privacy, bodily integrity or privacy, decisional autonomy and the 'territories of the self',[109] all of which are to be brought together and protected by a 'general right to privacy'.[110] The individual aspects and fields of privacy are for their part traced back to the fundamental need to protect the inviolability of the person, which underlies and justifies them. Cohen's theory, along with Benn's conception that privacy is necessary to be able to recognize 'respect for persons' and Fried's thesis that privacy is necessary for people to have the freedom to define themselves as themselves,[111] all seek in their own characteristic but analogous ways to develop a fundamental idea regarding the value of privacy. And I shall take up such approaches as Cohen's or Benn's when I attempt to show that the functional value of privacy is related to the concept of autonomy.

What I find problematic are the notions both that privacy relates to the protection of the inviolability of the person and that it relates to the protection of 'respect for persons'. This is not because I believe that the two ideas do not have an important part to play in explaining why privacy is and should be valued, but because neither of them is able to do justice to *all* the key aspects of privacy, and if the claim is that they provide a general theory of (individual) privacy this is precisely what they should be able to do. Above all, however, I regard these theories as problematic because both Benn and Cohen become reductive in their approaches. In Cohen, for example, it is no longer clear why special rights or claims to privacy or conventions of privacy should be needed or called for, since they can evidently also be described as rights or (moral or conventional) claims to protect the individual *freedom* or the *inviolability* of persons.[112] Rights to privacy then turn into rights to freedom or civil liberties. That in particular cases it is no longer clear where the difference between the rights in question is actually supposed to lie comes to light in passages such as this: 'One needs *privacy* (*autonomy* and *inviolability of the personality*) within, as well as for, intimate relationships, the home, and communicative interaction.'[113] Apart from the plausibility of the basic idea expressed, it remains completely unclear how the equation of privacy with autonomy and the inviolability of personhood is to be understood, for if the terms are equated thus as different ways of stating the same thing, then there is no further need for a separate theory of privacy. In this case, the independence of (the value of) privacy is no longer in evidence. The arguments against reductive theories of privacy, however, have already been made clear above.

5 Privacy and autonomy

I now wish to return to and take up the liberal concept of privacy set out in the introduction, according to which something is regarded as private if one can oneself control the access to this 'something'. The protection of privacy then denotes protection from undesired access by others. On the one hand, 'access' must here have its direct, concrete or physical meaning, exemplified in a person's right to be able to control access or admission to her room or home. On the other hand, however, there is also a metaphorical access over which people demand to have control. This concerns who has access to which knowledge about the person, in other words who knows what (relevant) data about her, and it also concerns who has access in the form of opportunities to intervene or intrude in decisions relevant to the person herself or in actions not directly concerning others. There are three dimensions of privacy that are thus distinguished: local privacy, informational privacy and decisional privacy. A definition such as this is centred upon the basic idea of control, and not, therefore, upon the separation between a particular individual on the one hand and a public sphere comprising everyone else on the other. This also means that privacy as a place only constitutes one aspect within the whole spectrum of the term's meaning. With the concept of 'being able to control', moreover, a definition such as this gives expression to an inherent normative moment, for *being able to control* must be understood as *being allowed* or *supposed* to control. Rights to privacy are thus rights to be able to control access by others, and if need be rule out such access entirely, not have to take it into account at all. The control in question can also be understood, moreover, as democratic control or democratically legitimated control, as where data protection is concerned. In this case, the person has control because access to these data is secured and controlled democratically (that is in principle also by her). Conventions, it must again be pointed out, here of course play a crucial part – conventions we typically fall back upon as long as explanations of privacy are *unproblematic*. If privacy is called into question, however, then so are they, and the appeal to convention itself is no longer enough.

The thesis I am concerned with is that the true realization of freedom, that is a life led autonomously, is only possible in conditions where privacy is protected. As a condition for autonomous decisions and the ensuing autonomous life and behaviour (a life of 'projects'), there are certain forms of one's practical self-relationship – reflections on conflicting desires and self-images, on the genesis of desires etc. – that can only be successfully developed if there are protected private realms and dimensions in one's life. Conversely, this means that we need and value (symbolic and literal) private spaces not only because we regard them intrinsically or simply as valuable, but also because in these (symbolic and literal) spaces and dimensions we want to develop, design and exercise our autonomy. This then also includes us wanting and being able to decide for ourselves when we want to be alone, when with certain other people, and when it does not matter whom we are with. These spaces and dimensions are again for the most part conventionally defined, but their normative end finds expression in the protection of autonomy. Whenever this normative reference point is at variance with a particular (historically) established definition, conflicts can typically arise concerning, for example, the 'natural privacy' of the household. For this reason, it also makes sense to say that nothing is *in itself* private. In liberal democracies, it must always be possible to question the boundary between the private and the non-private, because the concept of privacy may also be associated with repressive functions.[114]

The idea, therefore, is that the concept of privacy demarcates for the individual realms or dimensions that he needs in order to be able to enjoy the individual freedom exacted and legally safeguarded in modern societies. Indeed, such realms or dimensions of privacy substantialize the liberties that are secured, because the mere securing of freedom – despite the 'intricate complex of rights and duties' that characterizes such liberties[115] – does not in itself necessarily entail that the *conditions* are secured for us to be able to enjoy these liberties as we really want to. With the protection of privacy, therefore, freedom and autonomy are protected in a quite specific, irreducible manner. The separation between 'private' and 'public' regulates our behaviour in a way different from and supplementary to the dividing line between 'free' and 'unfree'. For why is it that we do not want to be observed or eavesdropped on, whether alone or with friends?

Why do we like having 'a room of our own'? Why do we want it to be in our hands what our colleagues know about our private life? Because all of this – in different ways in each specific case (different ways to which the following chapters will return) – would encroach upon our autonomy. To be able to ask oneself authentically who one is and how one would like to live, it is clearly necessary to have possibilities for withdrawing from the gaze of other people. To be able to conceive, develop and pursue goals, it is necessary to have dimensions in one's life that are free from the objections or control of other people. To be able to develop authentic plans, to design or define oneself through one's dealings with 'specified others', one's expectations with respect to other people's knowledge about oneself must not be mistaken.[116] If we consider the *telos* of freedom to be autonomy and thus the possibility of asking oneself what sort of person one wants to be and how one wants to live, and if civil liberties guarantee just this (within the well-known limits), it is clear that – when it comes to the question of how one would like to live – violations of privacy *restrict or tie a person down* in a way that contradicts the spirit of the civil liberties demanded and secured, but that for a variety of reasons is not or cannot be prevented by the civil liberties themselves.

We started by delimiting what is referred to as 'private' with the help of the concept of control, and we then claimed that we value this possibility of privacy because in various respects we want to be autonomous and because without various dimensions of privacy autonomy cannot work. In substantial terms, the connection between privacy and autonomy exists, therefore, because it is only through such 'spaces' marked out by the borderline between private and public that the design, development and exercise of (certain aspects of) autonomy become possible. To the question 'autonomy in what respect?' the reply would have to be that privacy protects autonomy in those respects in which the exercise of autonomy is dependent upon my control of the 'access' of others to me, to my person, to my (reflections on) decisions, and to information about me. And these (symbolic) spaces cannot be demarcated other than with the help of the normative distinction between what is to count as private and what as public, since the difference between 'free' and 'unfree' alone is not sufficient for the purpose of these demarcations.

However, the connection thus described and grounded between the concepts of privacy and autonomy can be fundamentally queried on two accounts. Firstly, one may again seek to call into question the sense of the relation between autonomy and privacy, and secondly one may be sceptical with respect to the claim that it is these – and only these – three dimensions of privacy that are necessary for autonomy to be successful.[117]

In putting forward this claim regarding the connection between autonomy and privacy, must we simultaneously make the claim that the more autonomous a person is, the more private (symbolic) spaces she has at her disposal? Or conversely, that the more private (symbolic) spaces are available to a person, the more autonomous she is? What about if she consciously and deliberately gives up certain aspects of her privacy? Is she thereby giving up aspects of her autonomy as well? Can she autonomously make up her mind to give up her privacy completely without at the same time giving up her autonomy? It depends of course on what aspects of privacy are affected, but in principle there is no reason why the idea cannot be reformulated in such a way as to affirm that when (aspects of) privacy are given up, so too are (aspects of) autonomy. If, for example, we on principle make no distinctions in what we say about ourselves and whom we say it to, or if we indiscriminately allow anyone to see inside our private dwelling,[118] or if we delegate the decision about whom we would like to live with to our parents (or anyone else), in all these respects the renunciation of privacy, the renunciation of the 'control of access' to our own personhood, at the same time entails – symbolically or literally – a renunciation of certain fundamental aspects of our autonomy.

Yet caution is due in describing the cases involved here. When John Lennon and Yoko Ono give up the privacy of their sex life in the Amsterdam Hilton as an act of political dissent, they may (for a time) be renouncing their privacy, yet such a *temporary* renunciation motivated by a political programme need not be described as a renunciation of autonomy. On the contrary, it might sooner be conceived as an articulation of autonomy in the face of specific social norms. Another example is provided by Avishai Margalit, who describes how a woman sunbathing in her underwear in a park is thought to be indecent, but not other women doing the same thing in their bikinis, the justification being that underwear is *private* and has no business on show in public.[119] The behaviour of the incriminated person can clearly not be described as a renunciation of autonomy (on account of this renunciation of privacy), because not every convention protecting privacy aims to protect the autonomy of the persons concerned. Rather, it is a relatively trivial case of the sometimes painful cultural and historical changes in the conventional boundary between private and public domains. Yet this example can also illustrate another point, which is that the conventions for protecting privacy may always have to do with the other side of the boundary as well, the protection of the public. This particular scene can also be interpreted in such terms that it is not the woman and her privacy or autonomy that are at issue, but the protection of the other people involved ('the public'), who in their scope for freedom in turn depend upon others keeping to (meaningful) limits of privacy. This aspect of the conventions thus in no sense conflicts with the characterization of privacy that I am undertaking.[120] Such examples show that not every renunciation of privacy need be described as a renunciation of autonomy, but not that fundamentally private dimensions of life need not be available if autonomy is to be enjoyed. For this reason too, as Margalit for one has pointed out, totalitarian states prohibit their citizens as far as possible from having private 'spaces' at their disposal, for in so doing they forbid them the individual autonomy known to be potentially dangerous.[121]

The second objection expresses a more sceptical consideration. Why should it be these three, and only these three, dimensions of privacy that we depend upon when it comes to an autonomous life? This objection is made not from the perspective of privacy (which would be concerned with whether what we call *private* ought not to be systematized in completely different terms), but focuses upon the problem of whether *autonomy* might not be dependent upon other dimensions or aspects of privacy for its success, or perhaps might not be dependent upon all three but only on one of them. In other words, why these three in particular? Even though it will not be until the following chapters that a precise answer is given regarding each of the individual dimensions, here I at least want to give a schematic account of the principles involved. For what these different dimensions of privacy are meant to protect is autonomy with respect to certain aspects of my relationship *to myself*, to *specified other people*, and to *unspecified other people*. The idea, therefore, is that the diverse relations that we may have as persons are in each case – and in each case differently – dependent upon the protection of privacy for it to be possible to structure them as autonomous. The protection of 'a room of my own', *one* aspect of the local dimension of privacy, is something I need because otherwise – to name one reason among others – I lack the opportunity to be undisturbed in my behaviour towards myself. The protection of my relations of friendship or intimacy, *one* aspect of the informational dimension of privacy, is something I need because otherwise – to name one reason among others – I lack the opportunity to be undisturbed in my behaviour towards other people (of my own choosing). And protection from strangers, *one* aspect of the decisional dimension of privacy, is something I need because otherwise – to name one reason among others – I lack the opportunity to be undisturbed by these strangers in my behaviour (in my public behaviour too). All three dimensions of privacy also have other key aspects and justifications. But from the perspective of the concept of autonomy, this tripartite structure can be understood precisely in terms of this threefold protection.

In all these aspects of privacy, it is possible to distinguish between those realms, dimensions, rights and claims guaranteed by a liberal constitutional state by means of legal entitlements (to privacy), and those rights or claims that we can invoke and regulate only on moral grounds or on the basis of mere conventions. One can thus draw a distinction between legal, moral and purely conventional claims to privacy. The claim to the privacy of my flat is a clear case of a legal right, albeit of course one that is morally grounded. The claim to the privacy of my room – a claim I make with respect to the other members of my family – is a moral one, which cannot meaningfully be imposed by law. And the claim that the size of my salary is a private matter is purely conventional: while in Germany the subject is viewed to all intents and purposes as a private taboo, in the United States it has virtually no significance as a private issue. These are of course differences that can in turn be queried and are in need of explanation. But they are also indications firstly of the different ways in which a person's autonomy can be affected, and secondly of the different cultural codings in which the relationship of autonomy and privacy finds expression.

This has up to now only been a general argument about the functional connection of privacy and autonomy. The following chapters will show in detail how the various dimensions of privacy – decisional, informational and local – can be conceived in their relation to the concept of autonomy and what their content and their function is in each case. The question will thus be what privacy has to do with autonomy in each context, how violations of privacy would at the same time be violations or infringements of autonomy, and in what way an appeal must be made to the concept of autonomy in order to ground each of the claims to privacy. Above I briefly showed (or at least claimed) that in the modern age we cannot imagine a rewarding life without freedom, and that meant without autonomy. If this connection between autonomy and privacy is correct, what the following chapters can now show too (however indirectly this may be) is how the individual dimensions of privacy are bound up with the idea of a rewarding life.

THE THREE DIMENSIONS OF PRIVACY

4 Decisional Privacy: Scope for Action and Decisions

1 Private matters and freedom for decisions

Expressions such as 'religion is a private matter' or even such as 'that's my private decision, it's none of your business' manifest a sense of privacy that can clearly be reduced neither to an informational aspect (concerning what other persons know about me, or what they are allowed or supposed to know) nor a local aspect (in the sense that my flat is private). The notion of a 'private matter' expresses a dimension of the meaning of privacy that refers not to the enclosure of a space or the seclusion of inaccessible knowledge, but to what may even be a positively 'public' private life. We have seen that 'privacy' is called for when one is entitled to control of (symbolic or literal) access. With regard to decisional privacy and the conventions and norms supposed to protect it, this clearly means *prima facie* that there is, or should be, a form of privacy protection ensuring that we may with good reason tell other people that such-and-such a matter is none of their business, that is ensuring that there are dimensions to our life to which we ourselves can control the symbolic access of others in the form of objections and interventions of the most various sorts. Such protection can be considered to cover certain forms of behaviour in public, as well as questions of lifestyle and more fundamental decisions and actions, such as the issue of what church one goes to or what one studies, the broad life-projects that a person pursues: in other words, ways of acting, behaving and living, and general goals and projects. In all these respects, it seems not only meaningful but also enlightening for a person to react to attempted objections on the part of others by pointing out that this is nobody else's business and that it is ultimately 'a private matter'. The more significant such decisions, actions or ways of life are to people, the greater the tendency seems to be to understand and declare them to be private. This also means that no further explanations are owed to other people concerning these decisions or modes of behaviour.

In fact, the concept of 'decisional privacy' is inappropriate on two accounts: first because at issue is the privacy not only of decisions but also of actions, modes of behaviour and ways of life; secondly because its constitution – if not its meaning – goes back to a tradition of American jurisprudence that grounds reproductive liberties (such as the right to contraception or the right to abortion) in a right to decisional privacy, a tradition that in fact expresses a confusion of rights to freedom or civil liberties with rights to privacy, as I shall attempt to show below. If I nonetheless hold to this concept, then this is not merely because it is employed in the literature,[1] but also because with it other traditions of greater explanatory value, such as Mill's essay on liberty, can easily be taken up and in this way the subject itself explained.[2]

In what follows, I want to start (in this first section) by elucidating more precisely what is meant by decisional privacy. Decisional privacy and its protection establishes a space for manoeuvre in social action that is necessary for individual autonomy. To this extent, as I also hope to explain, the concept of decisional privacy lies at right angles to the distinction between negative and positive freedom and grants a different perspective on that between ethics and morality. At the same time, I shall also add to this first section a brief parenthesis on how the right to decisional privacy was used to ground the right to terminate a pregnancy, in the ruling of the US Supreme Court in the *Roe v. Wade* case (see p. 93). This ruling has not only decisively influenced the juridical literature, but also dominates many of the stances taken by philosophy and political theory with regard to ideas of decisional privacy, which frequently follow this legal discourse in taking it for granted that 'reproductive rights' must be conceived as *rights to privacy*. Doubts concerning such a strategy for grounding the right to abortion will be elucidated in the course of this parenthesis. Following this first explanation of the problems involved, the aim is then to specify them further in two more steps. On account of its functional connection to the concept of autonomy, (decisional) privacy cannot be understood as a realm or space granted, conceded or permitted to subjects by society, but must be conceived in stronger terms as a claim or right of individuals. This is taken up in the analysis of communitarian critiques in section 2 below. At the same time, decisional privacy continues to refer to a concept of individual *autonomy*, examined in the analysis of feminist criticism in section 3. In one final step, in section 4, I shall then once more justify the concepts of decisional privacy and individual autonomy thus obtained as liberal ones in a brief analysis of competing conceptions of freedom.

The uses of the word 'private' described at the beginning of this book refer to civil liberties, for (negative) civil liberties guarantee (within the well-known limits of liberal democracy) one's choice of a way of life, one's selection of a companion and the right (within the limits of liberal democracy) to act and behave as and where one wants. Yet these liberties are dependent upon a social space in which they can be lived out unhindered, that is on the protection of decisional privacy. Gavison describes this aspect of the concept when she points out that 'privacy thus prevents interference, pressures to conform, ridicule, punishment, unfavorable decisions, and other forms of hostile reactions. To the extent that privacy does this, it functions to promote liberty of action, removing the unpleasant consequences of certain actions and thus increasing the liberty to perform them.'[3] A person should thus be entitled to decisional privacy in all relations. This privacy is intrinsic to her self-determined life, in a variety of ways, in a variety of respects, in all her social relations. This is the form of privacy being claimed by a daughter when she tells her parents not to meddle in her choice of friends, or by the purchaser of a porn magazine to protect himself against disrespectful comments from the shopkeeper.[4] This is the privacy that is being defended by a person who takes exception to discussions of her private life at work, and that is claimed by someone whose flamboyant clothes attract unwanted comments, or by a homosexual couple seeking to protect themselves against objections to their way of life from relatives, friends or unspecified others. All these actions, decisions and ways of life have their basis in civil liberties, and these liberties are in turn of course always protected by a network of rights and obligations. Yet they are also dependent upon the *specific* protection of the private person in social space so that they can be enjoyed without the objections, comments or judgements of others. Rights or claims to *privacy* thus substantialize and facilitate rights to *freedom* or civil liberties. These (moral) rights and claims to privacy are for the most part (though not necessarily) non-juridical, finding expression in conventions beyond which it is felt to be an encroachment[5] when a person meddles in someone else's life. Such conventions, I wish to claim, derive their normative validity from the fact that they protect a person's attempts to lead a self-determined life. (Juridical) *civil liberties* in the face of the state or other people are not enough actually to generate and guarantee the social contexts in which this sort of self-determined life can be lived. Accordingly, these liberties must be substantialized and in this way the social contexts secured through rights and claims to privacy (which may be juridical too if need be).

At this point, the relation between civil liberties and decisional privacy can be further clarified by casting a brief glance at the work of John Stuart Mill (as well as Richard Rorty, who employs similar categories), for as we know, Mill's version of the distinction between private liberty and public regulation has proved particularly influential.[6] Like Rorty, however, Mill in fact seems to be reducing privacy to freedom, and what I should first like to show here is how these claims to privacy go beyond negative civil liberties and cannot be identified with them. Then I shall also look at what can nonetheless be learnt from Mill's separation of the two spheres.

In Mill's tract 'On Liberty' we find the famous passage: 'But there is a sphere of action in which society, as distinguished from the individual, has, if any, only an indirect interest; comprehending all that portion of a person's life and conduct which affects only himself, or if it also affects others, only with their free, voluntary, and undeceived consent and participation.' Mill's principle is that in the modern world 'the regulation of every part of private conduct by public authority' is no longer possible or justifiable, either by the public authority of legislation or by social morality. The 'interference of the public with purely personal conduct', according to Mill, hampers the individual in 'the liberty of private life', and thus conflicts fundamentally with the notion of modern liberalism.[7] Conversely, this means – and this is the normative principle – that the freedom of a person's private life must be respected and regarded precisely in so far as other people are not 'affected'. A sidelong glance at Rorty shows that it is this very distinction between *private* and *public* that his own conception takes up: 'This book', writes Rorty, 'tries to show how things look if we drop the demand for a theory which unifies the public and private, and are content to treat the demands of self-creation and of human solidarity as equally valid, yet forever incommensurable.'[8] As with Mill, for Rorty the separation between the private and the public sphere is a separation between the public realm of liberal justice on the one hand, where civil liberties are secured and social justice or, as Rorty says, peace and prosperity are ensured as far as possible, and the private domain on the other hand, where each individual's freedom in his way of life is realized as self-creation.

The basic idea in both Mill and Rorty is thus the same.[9] Both of them are concerned with dimensions of action or areas of life that can be lived out without interference from others and without having to justify oneself to anyone else. Without naming it so, therefore, both of them are also writing about the issue of *decisional* privacy (and neither of them is thus concerned with privacy as a place). For both of them, moreover, the function of the separation of public and private is to create the freedom for individual self-fulfilment. It soon comes to light, of course, that in both cases this separation between the public ('unfree') and private ('free') realms is conceived too schematically and too simplistically, for if privacy is *identified* with freedom, it is no longer clear what remains to be explained by the concept of 'privacy' beyond what is 'individual', in what sense 'private freedom' is supposed to be more than or different from 'individual freedom', and why privacy cannot be reduced to freedom. It is this unresolved connection between freedom and privacy that finds expression in the implausible formulation of Mill's principle that one is free or private if others are not 'affected'. It does not even really seem to be Mill's idea that is formulated so crudely in this principle of freedom.

Indeed, in direct opposition to the radical formulation of Mill's principle, one learns from him that it is *precisely because* others can always be affected by my actions, ventures and projects that they are obliged to withdraw behind the limits imposed by respect for decisional privacy. Contrary to his original formulation of the principle, this is something Mill himself seems to see. He thus writes: 'the principle requires liberty of tastes and pursuits; of framing the plan of our life to suit our own character; of doing as we like, subject to such consequences as may follow: without impediment from our fellow-creatures, so long as what we do does not harm them, even though they should think our conduct *foolish, perverse, or wrong*.'[10] This is where the true, convincing side of Mill's theory shows itself, that is in the notion that we do not owe people explanations or reasons for all our decisions, modes of behaviour and ways of life, but on the contrary should be able to expect restraint, reserve and indifference from others when it comes to actions that may indeed – more or less directly – affect them but that are nonetheless not immediately 'their business'. In so doing, however, Mill himself is implicitly drawing a distinction between civil liberties and the possibilities for making use of them, for if anyone were to describe my behaviour in public or even within my circle of friends as 'foolish', this would not be a direct violation of my liberty. I need not necessarily pay any attention to such a person. Yet what would, in certain circumstances, be violated is my (decisional) privacy, the opportunity for me to behave or live *unhampered* as I wish in social space. In such a conflict, one would appeal not to principles of liberty but of privacy.

There is in fact another point that we can learn by reading Mill against the grain. This is that the reference to social space necessary for individual autonomy is not in turn necessarily associated with a strong concept of positive freedom. The freedom that is the true freedom both for Mill and Rorty, that is the freedom for experimental self-fulfilment, is just one among the range of possible substantializations of that autonomy. The distinction between freedom and (decisional) privacy is not a distinction between freedom and one specific mode of its utilization. Even though the idea of experimental freedom is particularly suitable for referring to the need to protect (decisional) privacy in social space, for defending private experimentation against public convention, for demanding public restraint with regard to private passions, conceptions of freedom or autonomy that are less radical, less experimental, less centred upon ideas of self-creation also refer to the difference between civil liberties and claims to privacy, that is to the need to give a concrete, substantial form to these liberties in the protection of the private person.

Accordingly, the idea of decisional privacy lies at right angles to the distinction between negative and positive freedom.[11] The concept of autonomy that I have attempted to develop – one that concretizes the concept of freedom – does not in itself have its own specific positive idea of the autonomous life inscribed into it, for such inscriptions, whether oriented towards experimental self-fulfilment or rational life-plans, always in turn appeal to a concept of individual autonomy that thus lies beyond, indeed must lie beyond, the inscription.[12] We shall see in greater detail shortly, however, that not every more substantial conception of (positive) freedom is compatible with this.[13] What is relevant here is that the concept of autonomy and its various inscriptions are always bound up with a claim to protection and respect for decisional privacy too. The difference between claims to freedom as autonomy and claims to privacy is not the result of a particular conception of positive freedom, but antecedes any such conception. What, therefore, has come to light thus far? The protection of decisional privacy is necessary so that freedoms in social space and with respect to other individuals in society can be enjoyed in such a way that modes of action, ways of life and projects can be pursued without undesired interference from others. Restraint, inattention, reserve and indifference – as forms of respect for this decisional privacy – are expected from others when it comes to the private aspects of the life a person leads in public. One must here of course distinguish very different aspects of decisional privacy according to their social context, but the argument underlying the claim to protection of such privacy remains structurally the same. If one understands a person's self-determination and autonomy to consist in her right to be the author of her own biography (within the limits described above[14]), among other things this must mean that in social contexts her life should not be subject to commentary and interpretation – or, more strongly, to influence – from other people to whom she does not wish to grant this sort of interpretative sovereignty over her life. Sovereignty over the interpretations and decisions of one's own life is made possible by conventions that guarantee that contexts are differentiated according to the degree of interference, commentary or influence possible in each case. Within the various social contexts, therefore, there are various forms of distancing oneself. Given the tension between one's subjection to cultural, social and biographical circumstances on the one hand and the attempt nonetheless to lead a self-determined life on the other, if need be asserting oneself against the conceptions, expectations and assumptions bound up with those various sets of circumstances, the individual person is dependent on access to the sort of distance that can be guaranteed in the protection of decisional privacy. It is true, of course, that various forms of intersubjectivity are what make autonomy possible in the first place.[15] Yet such relations can only have this function if a person is repeatedly able to distance herself within them. Otherwise, autonomy would be the last thing they made possible. And they can only have this function if they incorporate conventions or rules pertaining to interference and the pressure to justify decisions and behaviour, that is, if there are various guarantees of private 'spaces' or 'vanishing points' within them.

Let us now take a closer look, therefore, at these different social contexts and the various aspects of the protection of privacy.[16] For a start, we can specify distinct groups of *addressees* targeted by claims to privacy. These may be intimates or loved ones, friends, acquaintances with whom we are not necessarily friends, and finally anonymous third parties. Depending in part on what knowledge the individuals concerned have about one another,[17] these relationships bear on different aspects of a person's autonomy and life. Accordingly, these groups of addressees also prefigure the *aspects* of the claims that may be at issue. In our intimate dealings with our partner, parents or children, our claims to privacy have to do with other actions, decisions, modes of behaviour or ways of life than when we are dealing with non-intimate friends, and in our dealings with these the concern is different from the case of more distant social contexts. Without going into a more precise typology of social relations here, one might say that each of these relationships is constituted through different aspects of a person's life, and that in each of these relationships privacy is called for with a view to protecting those aspects that can be understood as non-essential to the relationship and therefore not relevant to it. What is here to count as relevant or otherwise is on the one hand a matter of convention, but on the other hand also has to do with making a self-determined life possible (and this, in turn, is the normative viewpoint when it comes to assessing the legitimacy of the conventions of privacy). One's choice of friends might thus be declared a private matter with respect to one's parents. How one spends one's holidays might be deemed private in a professional context, ways of dressing would be private with respect to anonymous third parties, and how one raises one's children with respect to friends, to name but a few examples. Each of these matters is not directly relevant to the particular relationship itself, which is constituted in each case through other aspects of the person's life, though of course the boundaries involved may always be open to dispute.

The different addressees are associated not only with different *aspects* of the protection of decisional privacy, however, but also with various *articulations of respect* for the person's privacy. If this respect can in general be designated 'restraint' (a concept I shall elucidate in greater detail shortly), one might say that this restraint is articulated in various manners characteristic of the various relations. While we in general expect parents to show a well-meaning and caring form of what is nonetheless still restraint towards their children, and the same is expected from one's partner or friends, when it comes to anonymous third parties we look for pure indifference and in professional or social contexts reserve or inattention (with respect to certain themes or aspects of the person's life). In all social relations, the idea of a self-determined way of life thus implies a borderline that demarcates an area from which any interference can be repelled. This is not just a matter of objections and comments regarded as negative, moreover, but also of positive interference and approval. Privacy can be violated not only by derogatory remarks, but also when a person makes positive comments on someone else's clothing (or appearance), for the right to freedom from interference and attention may also mean that approval is not wanted either. My privacy may thus be infringed by acquaintances expressing their approval of the way I treat my partner or by a stranger at the supermarket check-out praising the way I bring up my children. Both commentaries may rightly be felt to constitute a disturbing interference in private modes of action and behaviour.

To denote the various articulations of the respect for a person's decisional privacy, I have so far used terms such as restraint, reserve, indifference and inattention, terms that are employed in particular in theories of the public sphere to describe the distance necessary for social, and especially urban, coexistence.[18] In his analysis of the conditions of individual life in the modern city, for example, Georg Simmel famously developed such concepts of reserve. The situations envisaged by Simmel in which reserve and indifference are called for are ones marked by 'the throng of the city', which is what gives the concept of indifference its overtones of cultural criticism.[19] Elsewhere Simmel also speaks of forms of distance and withdrawal 'without which it would not be possible to lead this sort of life at all',[20] where 'this sort of life' can be interpreted as meaning the life of modern individual autonomy, dependent as this can be upon such forms of distance and withdrawal in all social contexts.[21] Where Simmel refers to indifference and reserve in one's anonymous relations, the analogous term in Thomas Nagel is 'civility'. Nagel describes this as a characteristic feature of liberal societies. An attitude of civility towards one another on the part of liberal subjects, as in social encounters between strangers, is intrinsic to what he terms liberal culture, where an 'element of restraint' towards others proves indispensable in all social relations on account of the plurality of life-projects that people have.[22] Accordingly, one should differentiate clearly between the various articulations of restraint. While the term can be used in general to describe the range of attitudes based on respect for decisional privacy, the differences between indifference, reserve, inattention and well-meaning restraint characterize the distinct social relations within which subjects live. The restraint shown by parents towards the decisions of their children is thus a different kind of restraint from what is shown by colleagues at work towards one another's private affairs or among the anonymous travellers on the tube or subway, yet restraint is still what it is in one form or another. This also means that in social contexts – whether conversations at work or small talk with acquaintances – people have certain modes of behaviour or ways of life that are 'private' and as such not available for discussion or comment, even though they may be common knowledge to all involved and to this extent public in nature. This form of civil distance is not merely an inane or empty convention of politeness. The point of it is to ensure that persons have the symbolic space in which they can lead a life that is independent and if need be runs counter to convention or collective modes of thought. Interference may disturb such a way of life, even in the form merely of unwanted commentary.

This civil distance, termed civility by Nagel, also refers to the fact that revealing private details about oneself in the wrong context and with no sense of distance likewise disturbs other people in their scope for freedom, for those involved find themselves compelled to confront issues and problems they – rightly – want nothing to do with. It is only thanks to this sort of distance that social space permits the plurality of self-determined life-projects and forms of conduct, and both these factors are required: respect for the privacy of others on the one hand, and on the other the subjective ability to keep within these invisible boundaries in one's own self-presentation too. This gives rise to typical conflicts. For if privacy is conceived as functionally related to the protection of individual autonomy, then the dimension of decisional privacy entails a tension that results from the interplay of claims to privacy with public society at large. The idea is that the conflicts and tensions arising from living one's private life in the public, social domain are in a certain sense counteracted by the indifference and restraint to which we have referred. Of course, the conventions that counteract such tensions are never fixed once and for all, but must constantly be reconfirmed and reaccepted, and this only happens successfully if they do justice to their normative purpose, which is to ensure the protection of (equal) scope for action available to individuals.[23]

The symbolic sanctuary of decisional privacy is intended to ensure that the person as a whole is able to live a life of freedom undisturbed. It accordingly makes sense to describe decisional privacy as *bodily privacy* too, for a person's privacy may be violated not only when objections are raised to her way of life, but also when unwanted comments are made about her body. An example of this would be the violation of a woman's privacy when she is molested by remarks directed at her on the street, irrespective of whether these remarks are pejorative or supposedly well-intentioned in nature.[24] The reason for the displeasure felt and articulated by women in such cases can be explicated in terms of the violation of their decisional privacy. The woman is compelled to subject herself to commentaries from third parties although she is entitled to privacy and distance even in public spaces, and what is violated, therefore, is a form of bodily autonomy. Here again, it is clear that where conventions are criticized – as with the 'conventions' (for this is exactly what they are felt to be) of sexual harassment with which women take issue – the underlying normative principle being appealed to is the principle of respect for persons, that is respect for their autonomy as individuals, and in this case for their bodily autonomy.[25] What also becomes clear once more is that the borderlines between what is to count as public and what as private are often coded in hierarchically gender-specific terms that grant the sexes different opportunities for self-presentation in public space.[26] Again, of course, this sort of claim to privacy in turn generates typical conflicts. For while not every comment can fall back upon the right to freedom of speech, it is also true that not every comment can be repulsed on the grounds that it constitutes a violation of decisional privacy. When such conflicts arise, however, they must be hammered out in public as structural conflicts, for which liberal societies surely have no other possible solution than such a public process.[27]

Restraint, reserve or even indifference is thus the attitude required in the face of the claims of decisional privacy, and with the help of these concepts we can now also draw a distinction with respect to one further concept, a concept that might actually have been thought to be the most fitting one here, namely *tolerance*.[28] After all, Mill too speaks in this context of tolerance,[29] and restraint is certainly one possible description of how tolerant behaviour manifests itself. In fact, it is customary to understand a characteristic feature of the requirements and problems of tolerance to be that the term has validity with respect not simply to individuals, but to individuals considered as members of political, religious or cultural groups or factions.[30] For this reason, it is typical to speak of tolerance towards people with different political views. In the context with which we are concerned here, however, this is at most *one* aspect among several, for decisional privacy has to do above all with the individual person *as an individual*, with her various aspects in relation to everyone else, in other words with the individual person and her individual projects, ways of life, ideas and manners of conduct, etc. Such indifference must then have validity in *all* social contexts, including *within* the sort of group that as a group demands tolerance from others. Indifference or restraint with regard to decisional privacy is necessary even in the smallest group, relationship or family. Nor is it usual to speak of tolerance towards eccentric individuals. More essential to the notion of tolerance are political contexts of group differentiation.[31] Yet differences between the terms relate above all to the *attitude* itself, for tolerance is always called for in situations where the behaviour or way of life of others meets with my disapproval, opposition or antipathy, this indeed being the origin of the paradox of tolerance.[32] Restraint or indifference with respect to the privacy of others, by contrast, is something that is called for utterly irrespective of whether or not one approves of the conduct in question: even praise can exert an uncalled-for influence on decisions, even assent can be unwanted, even encouragement can be out of place. This is why the reference to Simmel's notion of indifference or reserve proves so useful, for this is frequently the only attitude that genuinely respects the privacy of persons, having to do with inattention in the strict sense of the word rather than the combination of attention plus forbearance that is implied by tolerance. From the man who wolf-whistles at a woman on the street, it is not tolerance but indifference that is expected. And as for the conversation taking place at the table next to ours in a café, we should not be paying attention to it and tolerating it, but simply not paying any attention to it in the first place.[33]

So where do we stand now? It has emerged that the respect for decisional privacy entails a marking of limits to the interpretations, objections and influence from other people that might impede or restrict a person in her behaviour and way of life or, more generally, in her individual autonomy. Only thus is it possible to open up the social space for individual actions, decisions and modes of conduct that is intrinsic to liberal plurality in the pursuit and implementation of aims and projects. Forms of distance may thus be called for in all of a person's relations. One might also put it that a person may be required to provide possible justifications for her own behaviour and way of life in her various relations only (at most) in certain respects. Yet if a person's claim to decisional privacy can also be described in key respects as the freedom from obligations of self-justification,[34] then this dimension of privacy – privacy in one's decisions and actions – can be elucidated once more from a further perspective. The question now is how radically a person can make the claim that her own life, her own projects, and her own life-story are a private matter with respect to others. How radically can she insist on distance in such matters?

The context in which this question is usually posed and discussed in practical philosophy is in reflections on the distinction between ethics and morality,[35] a distinction that seeks to clarify and explain the different sorts of reasons that should play a part in justifying an action in distinct contexts and in the light of distinct problems. As regards the issue of decisional privacy and the need for a person to provide a justification for modes of conduct or ways of life, therefore, it seems reasonable to turn to the distinction between ethics and morality precisely in so far as this distinction is based on a differentiation of actions and problems in terms of the distinct sorts of reasons and justifications that can be given for them.

In attempting to separate ethics and morality in this way, we can distinguish three factors that define a problem as either ethical or moral in nature.[36] First there is the question of whom it concerns, secondly the question of to whom the reasons have to be given, and finally the question of what form these reasons take. To put it schematically, a problem can be said to be ethical in nature if I am the only one it concerns, and moral if others are involved. Ethically, I am required to give justifications (in the event of conflicts) only to 'ethical others', in other words only within my personal relations, whereas in the case of moral problems such reasons in principle have to be given to all others. The reason in question is ethical if it can be viewed as good purely from the partial perspective of the first person, while justifications for moral problems (necessarily) refer to the *impartial* perspective common to all other people.[37] Ethical problems are the sort of problem concerned exclusively with the question of my own (good) life, while unambiguously moral, 'irreducibly intersubjective' problems are the sort, for example, concerned with justice in distribution.

From the standpoint of privacy, one might start by looking into the very basic and general question of whether this distinction between ethics and morality can be meaningfully applied to the idea of private life-projects. It might be claimed, for example, that life-projects always integrate a whole range of distinct perspectives that subjects can adopt towards themselves. Ethical designs are fragile arrangements in which commitments – towards friends, colleagues, relatives, parents and children – are always implicated too, commitments that are closely bound up with one's expectations and where it is frequently not even all that clear to what extent they really are moral duties or perhaps supererogatory obligations to oneself or simply just agreements that it would not be too difficult to renege on. In a nutshell, a characteristic feature of private life-projects is that ethical and moral problems are inextricably intertwined within them. But for the time being I shall leave this as a bald assertion and return to it at a different point and from a different perspective.[38]

More relevant in the present context of decisional privacy is another point. This is the question of how strongly the claim can be made – even within the ethical context of individual self-fulfilment – that ethical projects, decisions and goals should be identified and justified to the 'ethical others', in other words to friends, partners and parents, etc. What can the term 'private' mean in terms of a possible refusal to provide explanations and justifications in one's relation with specific others and with others in general? Far-reaching in its implications is the stance taken by Jürgen Habermas, for whom there is, so to speak, no social space exempt from justifications. According to Habermas,

> the self-critical appropriation and reflexive continuation of my life history would have to remain a non-binding or even an indeterminate idea as long as I could not encounter myself before the eyes of all, i.e., before the forum of an unlimited communication community. Here 'myself' means: my existence as a whole – in the full concretion and breadth of the life contexts and formative processes that shape identity.[39]

Ethical self-fulfilment must be able to identify and justify itself in the eyes of everyone else (for what else can the verb 'encounter' here mean?), and this concerns not only certain synchronic aspects of my life such as specific decisions or modes of behaviour, but my whole life considered diachronically, my life-story as a whole. But what does Habermas mean by 'before the eyes of all'? The point of his argument is that individual, ethical life-projects should always be located at some point on an intersubjective 'scale of values', for otherwise the self-esteem or identity of the person concerned would be unable to establish itself in the first place. Accordingly, it is necessary to seek the recognition of all others possible. This becomes clear in another passage from the same text:

> Whoever judges and acts morally must be capable of anticipating the *agreement* of an *unlimited* communication community, and whoever realizes himself in a responsibly accepted life history must be capable of anticipating *recognition* from this *unlimited* community. Accordingly, an identity that always remains mine, namely, my self-understanding as an autonomously acting and individuated being, can stabilize itself only if I find recognition as a person, and as this person.[40]

Habermas is surely right in his basic proposal that ethical self-fulfilment is always embedded within a cultural framework, for the life-plans developed by a particular person are at least in origin always dependent upon what is offered by an intersubjectively shared culture, and the cultivation of meaningful individual projects is possible only in the context of a shared cultural horizon, shared cultural assumptions, etc.[41] This means, moreover, that the evaluative framework within which identities are formed must be broad enough, so to speak, to ensure that it does not exclude possible life-projects improperly. It seems doubtful, however, whether Habermas's reference to an '*unlimited* communication community' is necessary here. Significantly, the metaphor 'before the eyes of all' is one that plays with the relationship of private and public, for this makes it clear on the contrary that the individuality of life-projects depends vitally on *not* having to be designed, disclosed and decided 'before the eyes of all', not even hypothetically so. In fact, it should be clarified first of all what is meant here by 'recognition', for the more the concept implies positive evaluation, the less tenable it becomes. Indeed, in ethical questions there is no need for a person either to expect or actually to receive this sort of positive evaluation from *all* others. Post-conventional identity, it might be claimed against Habermas, proves itself precisely in the ability to distinguish between those situations where the consent of all is required, those where acceptance is required only from certain relevant individuals of my own choosing (and indifference from most people), and those where I have to negotiate with myself alone about what is important to me. In the process of searching for a self-determined ethical life-project, a person may in certain situations want specifically to assert herself against prevailing social and cultural assumptions and thus disappoint the expectations of 'the eyes of all' or at least almost all. In this case, however, the concept of recognition is either vacuous or obsolete.

Later, indeed, Habermas himself modifies this claim that ethical endorsement should be sought 'before the eyes of *all*',[42] and individual self-fulfilment comes to be viewed as reliant only on recognition from the 'ethical others', not all others. Recognition from the ethical others remains essential, however, because it is the encounter with these others, with their recognition and their criticism, that brings into play the points of view that make the individual endorsement of ethical self-realization possible. This modification in the demands of ethical justification certainly seems reasonable, just as it seems reasonable to suggest that in their ethical projects people are typically dependent upon recognition – at least in the sense of positive evaluation – from ethical others of their own choosing. What appears problematic, however, is that this form of recognition of ethical projects is viewed from the perspective of a *pressure* to justify oneself, such that the person *has to* identify, ground and justify these ethical projects, albeit only to the ethical others.

However, the intersubjective discursivity of ethical projects – the fact that it must be possible to articulate them in a common language – should not be confused with justifying them in an intersubjective context. Although Habermas does here limit the area or dimensions in which the subject has to justify himself to others, it is my contention that the demand for justification is still too strong. This comes to light for example when Maeve Cooke, following Habermas, writes: 'In marking off certain dimensions of individual identity as essentially private, it [i.e. what Cooke regards as the misguided notion of privacy] implies that in these areas the critical judgment of others is not even in principle relevant with regard to the validity of the individual's assignment of meaning and value.'[43] If this is to be anything more than a terminological point (for it only makes sense to speak of 'meaning and value' in intersubjective contexts anyway, and ethical reflections, in so far as they are reflections and thus linguistic in nature, are always articulated in a common language), then the implication of Cooke's affirmation – that there is in principle no area of a person's life in which the judgement of others is not relevant – strikes me as problematic both in phenomenal and in normative terms. In phenomenal terms, each person surely has an essentially private domain that includes, at the least, the chaotic realm of thoughts and contradictory sensations, unrealized life-projects and unfulfilled desires, a thoroughly private disorder to which she may nonetheless attach 'meaning' and 'value', specifically in terms of her autonomy and authenticity.[44] One's daily life, one's everyday biography is clearly contingent upon the creative reserves of privacy, which – for the sake of their creativity – must elude any judgement from others and which nonetheless have meaning and value in subjective terms. In attempting – in one's encounter with others and if necessary even in opposition to them – to find one's *own* interpretation of one's own life, these reserves of privacy form a refuge and a vanishing-point. As *interpretations*, they are couched in language and to this extent intersubjective. As *one's own* interpretations, they are nonetheless able to elude the judgement of others (completely). The way in which a person deals with her life-*story* may also be private in this sense. How she copes with breaches in her biography, for example, or how she looks upon her memories of previous periods in her life may be a private matter to her in the sense that she no longer wants to expose it to the critical judgement of other people. Leaving aside for now the issue of how strong a concept of personal identity is at stake,[45] in other words, the person may consider that the path she has (previously) taken to become who she is no longer needs to be recognized by others or justified to them, indeed not even to what might be called an internalized *forum externum*. The inner chaos and the depths of one's private memories all contribute towards one's life-story as a whole, and thus also to one's autonomy and authenticity. Assuming responsibility for one's own past life, however, can mean precisely that it is able to stay private in the strictest sense of the word, which is that it is 'no one else's business'.

Taking this into account, the normative moment can be made even clearer, since it is specifically for the sake of a person's autonomy and authenticity that the difference between recognition and control must always be strictly manifest. Having to give reasons for one's actions in the context of ethical self-fulfilment only makes sense as a way of making autonomy possible provided that it does not lead to restrictions through (ethical) others. Certain ideas for autonomous projects become conceivable precisely when subjects are able to refer back to fundamentally private dimensions of their life, not by trial involving real or imagined judgements from other people but resolutely independently or even in opposition to them. Too strong a notion of recognition or consent from others (even just ethical others) results in a reduced notion of privacy. Yet an essential reason for the value attached to privacy is that it applies with respect to all possible others and that such strictly private aspects of myself form a part of my self-understanding as an autonomous person, albeit an autonomous person with a non-linear life-story.

Let us recapitulate. I started by defining decisional privacy as an individual subject's scope for action in all his social relations, a space for taking action and making decisions in which individual life-projects can be devised, developed and safeguarded. In the process, various forms of restraint or indifference came to light as the appropriate attitudes in the face of the decisional privacy of others. A key aspect of decisional privacy was here shown to be the question of to whom an individual should give which sort of justification for his decisions, actions or ways of life. This was what made an analysis of the connection between ethics and morality necessary. It emerged that it must be possible for decisional privacy to be understood in a very strong sense of the term for the sake of the autonomy and authenticity of individual subjects.

The aim of the following parenthesis is to elucidate how the concept of decisional privacy has been employed in the relevant rulings pronounced by the United States Supreme Court, as the use of the term in this context has been decisive in its influence upon the way the concept has been understood in recent Anglo-American philosophy and political theory.

Parenthesis: Abortion and the right to decisional privacy (*Roe v. Wade*)

Ronald Dworkin has described *Roe v. Wade* as 'undoubtedly the best-known case the United States Supreme Court has ever decided'.[46] Similar comments can be found in countless other articles, showing the sheer extent of the discussions sparked off by the ruling in United States society.[47] As the explanation formulated by Justice Blackmun famously put it, 'this right of privacy [. . .] is broad enough to encompass a woman's decision whether or not to terminate her pregnancy.'[48]

Put succinctly, the argument advanced by the Supreme Court was that the right of privacy, though not explicitly set down in the US Constitution, was at least implicitly contained in it.[49] This right is fundamental, and can only be restricted if the state has compelling interests to do so. In the question of abortion, such interests may pertain above all to the life of the foetus or the health of the woman. Nonetheless, the life of the foetus is not considered relevant in this sense during the first trimester, and the right to privacy is therefore broad enough to incorporate the woman's decision to terminate her pregnancy. In other words, the US Constitution grants women a right to abortion in the first trimester based on a right to privacy that embraces their reproductive autonomy. This applies to every woman, irrespective of her family situation.

The ruling in *Roe v. Wade* had been preceded and prefigured by two others, *Griswold v. Connecticut* and *Eisenstadt v. Baird*.[50] In the first of these, the Supreme Court declared unconstitutional a state law prohibiting the sale of contraceptives to married couples, while in the second the ruling was extended to include the unmarried. Justice Brennan's explanation contained the now famous sentence: 'The *right to privacy* gives an *individual*, married or single, the right to be free from unwarranted governmental intrusion into matters so fundamentally affecting a person *as the decision whether to bear or beget a child.*'[51] Regardless of anything else it might be, therefore, the right to privacy is a right that incorporates and safeguards reproductive liberties. Privacy is interpreted as a reinforcement of the liberties covered by constitutional law, a reinforcement that pertains to those of a person's decisions that fundamentally concern her personhood or, in different terms, the realm of her sexuality.[52] This is the link that leads directly from the idea that the right to privacy secures one's right to use contraceptives to the idea that the same right secures one's right to terminate a pregnancy. On the basis of this connection between (decisional) privacy and sexuality, Supreme Court jurisprudence has since extended the right to decisional privacy to cover four areas, and along with the use of contraception and the right to abortion, decisional privacy now grounds the right to interracial marriage and the use of pornography.[53] As we know, the right to engage in homosexual practices continues not to be included within its scope (*Bowers v. Hardwick*, 1986).[54]

Particularly in the case of *Roe v. Wade*, the Supreme Court ruling has triggered not only fierce debate in society at large but also a flood of academic literature on the topic. Indeed, the verdict was and continues to be highly controversial in a whole variety of respects. If we focus solely on the use of the right to privacy as a foundation (and leaving aside the more general question of the legitimacy of abortion in the first place), the ruling can be seen to have provoked, on a first level, fundamental legal and hermeneutical discussion concerning the correct interpretation of the Constitution in general.[55] On a second level, there was argument about whether such a right to privacy is to be found in the Constitution, in other words about the correct way of interpreting it in this concrete instance. And thirdly, countless articles were written on the issue of whether, even if the Constitution does in principle provide for a right to privacy, this right is applicable to the case of abortion.[56]

Above all, however, the decision has spawned a whole series of articles in the feminist literature ranging from disapproval to influential expressions of assent.[57] The latter have welcomed the *Roe v. Wade* verdict not only for lifting controls on abortion, but also for grounding this verdict in a right to privacy,[58] and the ruling has as a result come to exert a considerable influence on feminist philosophy and political science in general, not just in the United States. Much of the philosophical and in general the non-juridical literature, not only what is feminist in orientation, has ceased to query the justification given by the Supreme Court, but seems to take it for granted as the norm, a tendency with decisive implications for the analysis of the concept of privacy (not only decisional privacy) in philosophy and political theory. I regard this as an unfortunate development.

In what follows, I am *not* concerned with the question of the moral legitimacy of abortion. Nor is my concern with the hermeneutical and juridical problem of interpreting the US Constitution or the correct legal foundation for the right to terminate a pregnancy. My concern is exclusively with the limited normative and philosophical problem of whether the right to privacy can and should play a part in grounding the right to abortion.

For a start, we can distinguish here between two sorts of criticism levelled at the Supreme Court verdict, both of which call into question the connection between privacy and abortion. On the one hand there are communitarian critiques and on the other certain feminist standpoints. Exemplified in the work of Mary Ann Glendon, Michael Sandel and Amitai Etzioni,[59] communitarian critiques claim that the Supreme Court ruling exhibits an atomistic concept of privacy and autonomy that can do justice neither to the actual relationships in which persons, that is women, are always implicated, nor to a normative notion of the good life. Moreover, it is argued, this approach necessarily leaves out of account the genuine moral conflict in cases of abortion, which is the conflict between the foetus and the woman. The crux of the argument is that when it comes to abortion, appealing to the concept of privacy is normatively inappropriate because the liberal concept of autonomy upon which it is based is untenable. The communitarian critique of the Supreme Court verdict is thus embedded within a broader framework, namely the basic dispute over the connection between a concept of individual autonomy and a general concept of privacy. The critique, in other words, is interested not so much in the verdict itself as in its liberal presuppositions. I take this to be mistaken. Given its broader framework, however, it makes more sense to examine the critique not only in the context of *Roe v. Wade*, but in more general and more fundamental terms. But I shall save this for the following section.

The feminist critique exemplified by MacKinnon, which likewise challenges the connection between privacy and abortion, adopts a different tack. In very general terms, for MacKinnon the Supreme Court's appeal to the right to privacy represents just another expression of the idea that women should be pushed back into an ideologically constituted realm of privacy defined as the non-political or the pre-political, only ever conceding them rights in so far as they are considered different or deviant. If the right to terminate a pregnancy under given social conditions is conceived as a right to privacy, says MacKinnon, what this does is not call into question the gender-based hierarchical order, but simply further consolidate the social power structures manifest precisely in the correlation between women and privacy on the one hand and men and the public sphere on the other. MacKinnon's claim, in other words, is that the liberal concept of privacy is so implacably repressive that it cannot be used to ground women's rights of self-determination.[60] In her eyes, liberal talk of a right to privacy is thus but a cover for actual relations of power and dominance and can do nothing to guarantee women control over their bodies in legal terms. Yet even though it must be admitted that a great many emancipatory changes will indeed be required before it is possible to speak of a feminist reinterpretation of such terms as privacy, I nonetheless regard MacKinnon's approach here as misguided, for there is no obvious reason why one must have such a pessimistic view of the concept of privacy as she does. I have attempted above to show in what way a reconceptualization of privacy is possible and apposite.[61] What is surprising in MacKinnon is above all that she completely omits to look into other dimensions and components of the term, indeed just those dimensions that could be taken up in an emancipatory spirit. MacKinnon's critique falls short to the extent that she targets an unreasonably narrow concept of privacy and is thus unable to challenge the connection between the right to privacy and the right to abortion as radically or as cogently as possible.[62]

Neither the communitarian nor MacKinnon's feminist line of criticism, therefore, seems to be viable. Starting from a *reductive critique* of the Supreme Court decision, I shall now attempt to show in what way the connection it established between the right to privacy and the right to abortion really does appear problematic. The claim of this reductive critique is that the appeal to privacy is unnecessary, and in fact represents a detour in the argument, since reproductive rights should be able to be grounded as civil liberties. This is the purport of the argument put forward, for example, by Ruth Gavison.[63] Like other jurists, Gavison holds that in the course of the case the concept of privacy comes to be needlessly and unduly watered down: limits to the state's ability to intrude upon a person's liberty to make up her own mind in questions of contraception and abortion can be grounded sufficiently in the notion of individual freedom and autonomy, without it being necessary to appeal to special rights to privacy. In a similar spirit, John Hart Ely notes that in fact 'the court provides no account of why it thinks privacy is involved.'[64]

This criticism of the Supreme Court's justification for its decision is bolstered firstly by the terminological imprecision of the authors who come out in favour of this justification. Frequently it remains uncertain exactly how the relation between decisional privacy and freedom or autonomy should be defined. In an article by Anita Allen, for example, we read: 'Decisional [. . .] privacy signifies the ability to make one's own decisions, free from governmental or other unwanted interference.'[65] The same applies to Cohen, who refers both to 'decisional autonomy' and to 'decisional privacy (autonomy)'.[66] What is unclear is how to define the relation between decisional privacy and autonomy in such a way that the concept of privacy does not become redundant or obsolete through its identification with autonomy. For one can then ask what is actually lost by deleting the appeal to the right to privacy? It is evident that in such cases what is called for – and directly so – is freedom from restrictions, freedom in the sense of individual self-determination with respect to one's own body.[67] In this way, a direct connection can then be established between civil liberties as rights to freedom and the right to abortion.[68] The second point is that it is counterintuitive to describe the (possible) conflict in the case of abortion as a conflict between the privacy of the woman and the right of the state to interfere. It seems plausible to describe the conflict not as being between privacy and the state, but between the woman's right to self-determination and the duty of the state, if need be, to protect the foetus. What would be violated if the state – acting in the interest of the foetus – were to make abortion illegal would clearly not, first and foremost, be the privacy of the woman, but her right to bodily self-determination, her bodily integrity. By contrast with this, her privacy seems secondary.[69]

Now it may of course be claimed that the reason for the Supreme Court's appeal to the right to privacy to ground the right to abortion was that it had already used the same right to ground 'reproductive liberties' (that is access to contraceptives first for married couples and then also unmarried couples) in cases *prior to Roe v. Wade* (*Griswold v. Connecticut* and *Eisenstadt v. Baird*).[70] If the justification is held to be tenable in these cases, then why should the same right to privacy not also be used to legitimize abortion? What is the difference? Yet in the case of access to contraceptives, as well as homosexual practices,[71] what is at issue is a self-determined sex life, and – to be self-determined – this is indeed dependent upon the protection given by privacy, the privacy of spaces and the privacy of information. In the following chapters we shall see how people rely on possibilities for withdrawing from company, for escaping from the gaze of anyone else, in particular where their sexuality, their intimacy and pure corporeality are concerned. However, dimensions of *decisional* privacy do not seem relevant here.[72] This is something that Sandel involuntarily makes clear when he writes with respect to the *Griswold* verdict: 'The Court vindicated privacy not for the sake of letting people lead their sexual lives as they choose, but rather for the sake of affirming and protecting the social institution of marriage.'[73] Yet this, of course, is a communitarian misconception, for regardless of what the grounds for the Supreme Court's verdict actually were,[74] in normative terms it is quite correct to claim that in granting access to contraceptives the issue is *not* the protection of marriage but a self-determined sex life. In liberal democracies, individuals clearly have such a right to a self-determined sex life, and this right rules out contraceptives only being made available to certain persons. A liberal-democratic state is one that is neutral with respect to individual ideas of the good,[75] and accordingly, in such fundamental matters as the individual's sex life it cannot lay down precepts that would be tantamount to a collective idea of the good. It is every bit as correct, therefore, to claim that the right to privacy is intrinsic to a self-determined sex life. For in order to be able to lead 'sexual lives as they choose', individuals rely on dimensions of informational and local privacy – irrespective of whether they are married or not. In liberal societies, the protection of marriage is one thing, sex life another, and the two cannot necessarily be related.

From a normative perspective, therefore, there is good reason to believe that both in *Griswold v. Connecticut* and *Eisenstadt v. Baird* the Supreme Court's appeal to the right to privacy in making and justifying its decisions was an appropriate one, but that this justification was not applicable to *Roe v. Wade*. As we shall see more closely in the following chapters, relationships can only flourish and their intimacy endure if they enjoy the protection afforded by privacy from all unwanted people, whether the state or individual persons. When it comes to abortion, however, the situation is rather different, for what is at stake here are not relationships, sexual or otherwise, but the legitimacy of a woman's right to self-determination, her right to make her own decisions about her own body and her own life. The conflicts involved in this case and the rights in question can clearly be fully described, explicated and grounded without any appeal to privacy, whatever the dimension. This does not mean that the concept of decisional privacy has become superfluous. It simply plays no part in *this* context.

2 Decisional privacy and autonomy (1): the communitarian critique

In general it is the connection between (decisional) privacy and autonomy that is called into question by authors from the communitarian tradition. The reason for this is that privacy is here conceived not as a realm or dimension of individual freedom, that is functionally related to the individual self, but as a realm or dimension of life concerned with specific *practices* also relevant to the community at large, which must accordingly be understood not as a realm to which the individual has a claim qua autonomous being, but as one conceded to the individual as a member of the community. This is the theory in a nutshell. I now wish to examine more closely how it is argued in detail, focusing paradigmatically on the work of two theorists who deal explicitly with the concept of privacy, Michael Sandel and Amitai Etzioni.[76]

Both Sandel and Etzioni write what amounts to a history of the decline of the concept of privacy in the United States, as exemplified in Supreme Court jurisprudence. While Sandel's argument against the ideas expressed in this jurisprudence is based upon a specific concept of the self or person, Etzioni argues from the point of view of the community in general. It is a story of decline because the two of them distinguish between an 'old', 'traditional', 'substantive' form of privacy and a 'new', 'voluntarist', individualistic privacy that cannot be brought into line either with the real concept of privacy or with constitutional tradition.[77]

Sandel writes: 'Where the contemporary right of privacy is the right to engage in certain conduct without government restraint, the traditional version is the right to keep certain personal facts from public view.'[78] For him, the 'traditional' use of the concept is the one that refers to the seclusion of the household, to the protection of personal things from the public gaze, while the 'new' idea, by contrast, is that privacy includes certain modes of behaviour in so far as these are shielded from the intervention of the state or society. Yet this very contrast shows that seclusion from the public gaze does not cover all 'conduct', but that only very specific modes of conduct or practices are to be protected. This is made even clearer by the previously cited text commenting on the *Griswold* ruling: 'The justification for the right was not voluntarist but based on a substantial moral judgment; the Court vindicated privacy not for the sake of letting people lead *their sexual lives as they choose*, but rather for the sake of affirming and protecting the social *institution of marriage*.'[79] Not all conduct, not all aspects of the sex life chosen by an individual come under the protection of the private sphere, but the practice and institution of marriage does. This is how Sandel interprets the Supreme Court decision, and for him, as for Etzioni, the decline of privacy in Supreme Court jurisprudence thus only starts *after* this verdict, that is with the verdict that made contraceptives freely available to every single person.[80] The old form of privacy, it might be said, thus incorporates the local dimension and the informational dimension, neither of which, however, is seen by Sandel or Etzioni as having anything to do with the protection of freedom and autonomy. What is new for Sandel is decisional privacy, which indeed cannot be conceived except as functionally related to the protection of freedom and autonomy. To this extent, however, Sandel and Etzioni alike are targeting not only the Supreme Court jurisprudence in the matter of reproductive liberties, but in principle any association of privacy with autonomy. I should now like to look more closely at this point.

For Sandel, it is above all the non-voluntary relations of an individual that should be protected by privacy, in other words family or intimate relations, and religious or communal relations. From the outset, he thus takes issue with the sort of concept of privacy that is centred solely upon the individual person and her solitary decisions.[81] Accordingly, Sandel's critique of the 'new' concept of privacy cannot be separated from his critique of the liberal theory of the concept of a person, or indeed from his critique of the conception of the neutrality of the liberal state. His critique as it were bundles these aspects together again.[82] The liberal state, so runs his well-known argument, is not neutral anyway, nor is it even possible for it to be so, but its putative neutrality always comes attached with a certain voluntaristic, atomistic notion of the self and the person, of choice and individual autonomy, which – precisely because it refuses to be oriented by certain communal practices and values – instead turns against these practices and values. Yet this is disastrous in its consequences, because the constitution of the self, even the liberal self, its formation and development, is *always* intrinsically dependent upon such cultural practices and values. For Sandel, the voluntaristic conception of privacy that the Supreme Court has read into the Constitution – against its spirit – epitomizes the dire state of this relationship between self and state.[83]

The reason that Sandel's argument is problematic is not his insistence on the individual person's intrinsic implication in relations. The fact that the self is relationally constituted (and for this very reason also reliant upon forms of privacy of one's own choosing) and the extent to which this must be conceptualized in political theory as well are lessons that were learnt by (early) liberal theory from communitarian as well as feminist criticism.[84] Nor is Sandel's argument necessarily problematic on account of his critique of conceptions of the neutrality of the liberal state, at least not if this critique is interpreted (in a weak sense) to mean that every state always has certain predetermined cultural specifications, is inevitably 'permeated by ethics',[85] and that this finds expression not only in the constitution but also in the jurisprudence and administration in general and must be reflected on and criticized as such. Sandel's argument becomes problematic when he wants to use the protection of a person's privacy to protect not their privacy but certain highly valued practices that individuals pursue in private. In other words, it is problematic when he avails himself of a concept of privacy that is not formal ('formal' in the sense in which the liberal state is only able to take an interest and assume responsibility for the formal conditions of a good or rewarding life), but that seeks to suggest to the individual that such conditions are substantial in nature, in this way giving precedence to the value of these practices over the value of the individual person's ability to decide, that is over her autonomy.

Only thus is he able to apply the line of argument used by the Supreme Court in *Griswold v. Connecticut* to the case of *Bowers v. Hardwick* and criticize the Court's verdict in the latter case. For Sandel, the *Griswold* decision protected the sanctity of marriage (and for this reason alone protected the privacy of persons), and to the extent that homosexual relations are 'similar to marriage' – if they prove valuable in this sense – they are entitled in similar terms to the protection of privacy. Yet this is only because the practice protected in this way has an *intrinsic value*. Sandel is consciously employing a substantial, as opposed to a formal, concept of privacy. This approach is controversial in liberal societies, however, because in such societies people want to experience the substantial conceptions of their good life, that is the practices they value, not as a *regulation* but as an *offer*.[86] On account of this opposition between substantial and formal or 'voluntarist' conceptions and the classification of privacy into supposedly old and supposedly new forms (a classification based solely upon one particular view of constitutional interpretation), Sandel is from the very outset unable to see the importance of decisional privacy in the context not of reproductive liberties but of 'old' uses of the term to the effect that religion is a private affair or such-and-such a matter is private and thus nobody's business. This is something Sandel is unable to see except as an aspect of informational or local privacy, dimensions that for him nonetheless always incorporate *communal* practices too. Yet as I attempted to show in the introductory section, this is an abbreviated, reduced understanding of what has been meant by references to the decision-making and action-taking dimensions of privacy probably since the seventeenth century and certainly the nineteenth century (to this extent it is relatively 'old') and of what in normative terms should be meant by such references in liberal societies.

The communitarian impetus of Sandel's reflections is only made genuinely clear, however, when he is read in conjunction with Etzioni – even if Sandel is the much more astute theorist and it might appear somewhat unfair to place him in such a context.[87] Simply in terms of the fundamental normative question he is asking, Etzioni makes no bones about where he stands with respect to the liberal approach. The question he poses is not why we value privacy, but how much privacy a society can allow its members: 'how much and what kinds of conduct are legitimately exempted from social scrutiny?' Privacy, he writes, is 'a societal license'.[88] In this respect, Etzioni diverges radically from a liberal perspective, for to exempt or except something from social control naturally implies instigating the control that makes exceptions of the exceptions in the first place. Although Etzioni, like Sandel, argues against the 'new' (decisional) and in favour of the 'old' (informational) privacy,[89] likewise basing his case on a variety of uses and practices associated with the term and a variety of verdicts returned by the Supreme Court,[90] his *real* argument is a different one that no longer has much to do with the distinction between informational and decisional privacy, but is concerned instead with the clash between the idea of individual freedom and the idea of a strong community.

Etzioni shows unequivocally that such a conception of privacy entails a model of society that differs radically from the liberal. Communitarians, he writes,

> hold that important social formulations of the good can be left to private choices – provided there is sufficient communal scrutiny! [. . .] [T]he community [. . .] relies on subtle social fostering of prosocial conduct by such means as communal recognition, approbation and censure. These processes require the scrutiny of some behaviour, not by police or secret agents, but by friends, neighbours, and fellow members of voluntary associations.[91]

If privacy is defined from the very beginning as a societal licence, then from this communal viewpoint it is only logical that no importance be attached to dimensions of privacy as possibilities for individual autonomy. The categories only permit this sort of autonomous aspiration to freedom as something always subordinate to the community as a whole. For Etzioni as for Sandel, therefore, possible conflicts are not the sort that arise between the distinct aspirations to freedom of individual persons and thus their distinct claims to privacy, decisional or otherwise. Rather, the only conflicts that are analysed as such are those taking place (or capable of taking place) between the individual's aspiration to freedom on the one hand and the interests of the community on the other. And in these conflicts, at least from Etzioni's point of view, it is always the community that wins.[92]

These references to Etzioni in conjunction with Sandel should make it clear that the connection drawn between privacy and valuable social practices on the basis of the relational condition of the subject is not possible without the concept of a community that controls individual privacy (and if need be steps in to take measures against it), even though such a strong concept of community is not the actual goal of Sandel's argument (as it is with Etzioni).[93] In this sense, Etzioni shows particularly clearly what we must expect in normative terms if the subject's self-willed aspiration to autonomy is not itself granted an independent space or dimensions through and with the protection of privacy. As a normative claim, privacy is conceded, permitted or granted by the community (for social practices), but it is no longer something to which one is entitled in opposition to this. The analysis of the problem of privacy in communitarian criticism again brings to light, therefore, the extent to which this criticism falls short of the normative self-understanding of the modern subject, who seeks privacy precisely in so far as he stands apart, in certain respects at least, from communal practices held as valuable. In fact, Sandel is not consistent in the matter. After all, it was certainly only through people appealing to their decisional privacy (in private and public alike) in opposition to the common practice (of heterosexuality) that those very homosexual practices that he has himself defended became possible in the first place. Even while acknowledging that the culturally subversive moment of homosexual relations is limited, it is patent that openly homosexual relations naturally *also* constitute a change in conventional practices. And it is just this that is not only permitted but also guaranteed by the modern idea of liberty itself, with the consequence that practices are always *recognized* as something that can change and be changed.[94] Or to put it the other way round, only in so far as subjects are entitled to decisional privacy are they able to recognize existing practices in a creative and self-accountable way. Given the tension between on the one hand being situated and rooted within a cultural context and on the other hand striving to lead their own life, to live and also interpret their own experiences, if necessary in opposition to the values and assumptions of the community at large, individual subjects are reliant upon ways of acquiring distance that find expression in the protection of decisional privacy as the protection of their autonomy.

3 Decisional privacy and autonomy (2): the feminist critique

As we have seen, communitarian theorists such as Sandel and Etzioni criticize the idea of decisional privacy fundamentally in conjunction with the liberal concept of autonomy. A number of feminist theorists subject the concept of autonomy to criticism in similar fashion. In the following discussion of aspects of this critique, the aim is above all to ascertain how the connection between decisional privacy and autonomy can be further elucidated. I shall of course be taking up the concept of autonomy developed above and testing once more whether it can stand up to certain critical objections.[95]

Right from its beginnings, feminist theory has given voice to a very radical critique of the concept of autonomy. Alison Jaggar, to take but one example, described 'the ideal of autonomy as characteristically masculine'.[96] This critique focused throughout on the same points.[97] The autonomous subject of liberal thought, it claimed, was male, autogenetic, atomistic, individualistic, self-interested, fixated on dominance and obsessed with power; it was unable to take into account relations of care, indeed interpersonal relations in general, and overlooked not just that autonomous subjects are only formed *within* relations but that for many people reality does not consist in being independent and separate from others but dependent and joined together.[98] This critique of the concepts of autonomy and the subject was frequently accompanied by a fundamental scepticism as to whether such concepts served any purpose or were of any benefit at all to feminist philosophy.[99]

It is possible, however, to make out a second round in these discussions, which has learned and profited from the first round and seeks to turn the critical rejection of the terms into a more discriminating reinterpretation of them. This time, the attempt is made to use the concepts of autonomy and the subject to benefit feminist theory. These critical approaches try to provide a richer definition of the self, the subject and its autonomy by conceiving the autonomous subject as something that is always already implicated within commitments and bonds, determined by feelings and attachments, caught up in partialities that make up its self-image, constituted by a body that forms part of its self-understanding, and rooted in a cultural context that shapes its formation. Such approaches seek to develop correspondingly diverse conceptions of autonomy that always already incorporate the subject's bonds, commitments and corporeality, the power of feelings to open up the world, as well as cultural contexts and family and emotional backgrounds.[100] In so doing, however, they no longer see themselves as targeting the concept of the autonomous subject *in principle*. Frequently, the reason for this interest in a reinterpretation of the concept of autonomy is the realization that for feminist theories that see themselves as contributing to political theory within a liberal-democratic framework, however critical or revisionary this contribution may be, there is no way round concepts like the subject, autonomy, individual rights, freedom, etc.

Present discussions are shaped by the continuation of these critical approaches and their integration. The focus, it might be said, is upon the question of the *relationality* in the concept of the autonomous subject.[101] The term 'relationality' here refers not only to the *learning* of autonomy in relations, or to living autonomously *within* relations, that is to the relationality of contexts. Rather, it is understood as *constitutive*, as intrinsic to the concept of autonomy itself, as inscribed within it. Particularly radical are the stances here adopted by Jennifer Nedelsky or Virginia Held, who propose, for example, that the concept of autonomy be reconceptualized on the model of the mother–child relation.[102]

However, this perpetuation of critical approaches within liberal political theory (in the narrower sense of the term) only represents one side of the debate, for the relationality of the subject and of autonomy is also invoked – in radical fashion and using different conceptual categories – in another line of discourse, that is in postmodernist criticism.[103] When Wendy Brown describes the autonomous subject in its liberal conception as free-moving, unencumbered by family commitments, self-sufficient and pursuing only its own interests and concerns, there are strong echoes of the radical criticism of the early days of feminism, yet the spotlight is now on the concept of relationality or connection rather than on dependence upon others. Brown aims to articulate 'a formulation of autonomy in the context of connection', replacing 'permanent hierarchies of dependence with mutual, partial, or contingent dependencies'.[104] In so doing, however, she applies a different theoretical vocabulary, one that insists on the discursive constitution of the (autonomous) subject and that in principle objects to conceptual dichotomies on account of their exclusionary character. This is made clear by Butler:

> The subject is constituted through an exclusion and differentiation, perhaps a repression, that is subsequently concealed, covered by the effect of autonomy. In this sense, autonomy is the logical consequence of a disavowed dependency, which is to say that the autonomous subject can maintain the illusion of its autonomy insofar as it covers over the break out of which it is constituted.[105]

Butler too is unwilling to relinquish the term, yet the conception for which she is gunning is so strongly relational that it is open to question whether it still makes sense to talk of autonomy.

What interests me here is the problem of whether the notion of relational autonomy needs to be understood as running counter to the concept of autonomy set out above and to the idea of decisional privacy, which calls for privacy in *all* of the subject's social relations, or on the contrary whether the idea of decisional privacy (and the concept of autonomy it protects) might for its part determine possible limits to relational autonomy. From the standpoints I have just described, 'relational autonomy' must be conceived in opposition to the concept of autonomy that I sketched in chapter 3, because for these standpoints the relationality is inscribed into the concept itself and understood as intrinsic to it. By contrast, my view is that relationality is relevant in two respects and in two contexts. This difference between a substantially relational and a procedurally relational concept of autonomy now calls for a brief elucidation.[106]

First, it is indisputable that autonomy is something that is learned in social relations, in the first place in intimate relations, where the aim is for dependent children to grow by degrees into independent persons not only endowed with self-confidence, self-respect and self-esteem, but also as a result able to see themselves as autonomous persons. While it is true that for the cultivation of autonomy as a *habitus* people are dependent upon successful intimate relationships, upon loving recognition from others, and upon external conditions that make (achieving) autonomy possible, this means neither that they must understand their autonomy *in opposition to* bonds and commitments, nor that autonomy need be described as relational *in conceptual terms*.[107] What it does mean, however, is that repressive forms of socialization, which lead to self-images of dependence and inferiority, can unambiguously be understood as an impediment to autonomy. Relationality may have two sides. It may be conceived and practised as a condition for the possibility of autonomy on the one hand, but also as an obstacle to a person's autonomy.

Secondly, autonomous people will typically find themselves in *relational living contexts*: most of us live within relationships with friends or loved ones, etc., and a person can think of herself as autonomous if she is competent and in a position to decide – alone and with others – how she would like to lead her life and what sort of person she wants to see herself as. This means that she is competent to make up her own mind about the relational context of her actions, to decide *whom* she wants to live with and in *what* sort of relationship, *which* commitments she is willing to enter into, and *what* wholly individual projects she wishes to pursue. At this point, the central moments of autonomy that I pinpointed above become crucial.[108] Independent and full reflection on one's own situation and the search for one's authentic needs, desires, convictions and objectives can on occasion help free an individual from manipulative relations. Projects may fall through, relationships go wrong, and a person is autonomous if and when she is able to break free from such projects and break away from such relationships. This point seems particularly important from a feminist perspective, for to recognize non-egalitarian relations and – autonomously – dissociate oneself from dependencies or insist on independence may well prove emancipative in effect.[109] From the point of view of privacy, moreover, the insistence on individual autonomy is of especial relevance to women because ascriptions of 'natural' privacy – that is the ascription of certain roles and thus the prescription of a certain way of life, or at least of significant moments of a certain way of life, such as bringing up children – are still so dominant that insistence of this sort could liberate them from ascriptions and assumptions rooted in a gender-based hierarchy. This is just where the postulate of decisional privacy may prove effective, for in all her relations a woman must be entitled to this privacy and this scope for making decisions and taking action when she asks herself, for herself, the question of how she wants to live her life.

To this extent, a non-relational concept of autonomy and of the dimensions of privacy that protect it[110] strikes me not only as conceptually consistent but also normatively apposite in the face of the circumstances in which women live, where women in general tend to be encouraged to see themselves not as independent but as dependent and are thus deprived of an equal right to ask themselves the question of how to lead their own life.[111] It is just this difference between a relational and a non-relational concept that gives a person the possibility of breaking with the bonds that have tied her. This of course is something that may be done in an irresponsible fashion. Yet autonomous decisions too remain open to criticism: they are not always morally right, and in certain circumstances where there are conflicts of interest they have to be weighed up against one another. But inscribing the moment of relationality into the concept of autonomy would be of no help in resolving this sort of conflict either.

4 What sort of freedom is protected by privacy?

This clarification of decisional privacy has also made it possible once more to clarify the concept of autonomy. This has emerged in the course of the previous sections, where we have looked at the various social contexts of decisional privacy, its role in communities, its role in relationships. The insistence on the individual's free space in all social relations does not entail that the autonomous person is conceived as disconnected from all relations, but it does mean that she is able to distance herself from and also within relationships, is entitled to restraint in all these relationships, and that she is reliant on such restraint.

Accordingly, we can here take up the sketch of the liberal-democratic framework that was drafted in the introduction. Having seen the various aspects of decisional privacy in social space, it can now be made clearer why certain positions – such as the standpoint taken up by Sandel – are problematic borderline cases, and what sort of 'family' of theories it more exactly is. The concept of autonomy, as the previous chapter showed, is not so substantial that it necessarily implies *specific* conceptions of a rewarding life, that is that it entails a prejudgement with respect to positive conceptions of freedom.[112] Even the sort of conception of freedom that would explicate individual freedom not by using a strong concept of autonomy (on a first level) but by appealing to notions such as perfectibility, self-realization or experimentality remains conditional upon some concept of autonomy if it intends to make any use of the concept of *individual* freedom.[113] To this extent, one might thus say that this conception of autonomy and the privacy associated with it remains neutral with respect to the possibilities for a rewarding, autonomous life. Taking up the threefold differentiation that I suggested above,[114] a distinction may be drawn firstly between negative liberties, which permit one and require one to be autonomous, secondly a concept of autonomy that posits a reflexive relationship on the part of the free person without simultaneously proposing a positive concept of the substantial conditions for the failure or success of such an autonomous life, and finally those conceptions of freedom that along with freedom always want to see its objective realized (positively). In this way, it becomes clear that the concept of autonomy and (decisional) privacy we are tracing here seeks to explicate the second of the three categories.

Even so, not every conception of freedom and privacy that would place itself within a liberal framework is compatible with this combination of autonomy and privacy. Indeed, an inadequate concept of privacy may point to a misleading concept of freedom, and vice versa. To explain this point, I now wish to discuss one particular conception that helps elucidate what I mean both by an inadequate concept of privacy and by an inadequate concept of freedom. This is Hannah Arendt's outline of the connection in *The Human Condition*,[115] a work that seems to rule out the very possibility of decisional privacy in conceptual terms and that thus helps clarify once more how privacy and freedom are connected with one another and refer to one another. Following this, I shall close by cautiously suggesting the conclusions to be drawn from this conception of privacy for conceptualizing the relationship between the private dimensions of the subject's life and his public engagement as a citizen.

Hannah Arendt is well known to have been a prominent critic of the modern difference between 'private' and 'public'.[116] In her history of the decline of public life, she describes the distinction between private and public domains, between the private and public dimensions and functions in life, in thoroughly Aristotelian terms as the distinction between the private sphere of necessity and the public sphere of freedom. In Aristotle, the private domain is the domain of the household, 'the sphere where the necessities of life, of individual survival as well as of continuity of the species, were taken care of and guaranteed'.[117] The private realm is thus the one in which, as the living beings that we are, all of us are equal, at least to the extent that we all have to comply with biological necessity.[118] By contrast with this, the public realm alone is where individual differences can express themselves:

> Thc public realm [. . .] was reserved for individuality; it was the only place where men could show who they really and inexchangeably were. [. . .] Excellence itself, *arete* as the Greeks, *virtus* as the Romans would have called it, has always been assigned to the public realm, where one could excel, could distinguish oneself from all others. Every activity performed in public can attain an excellence never matched in privacy.[119]

The reason Arendt's history is one of decline is that with 'the rise of the social' this distinction has become impossible and the different functions have become indistinguishable: 'both the public and private sphere of life are gone, the public because it has become a function of the private and the private because it has become the only common concern left.'[120] What has been lost, therefore, is the true function both of privacy and of public life: this is the lesson we can learn from the Greeks. And along with this distinction what is also lost is the possibility of a clear-cut distinction between the different activities, and with this, so it seems, the very possibility of political freedom itself.[121]

In what follows, I should now like to make a few critical remarks concerning Arendt's conception. To start with, it should be pointed out that Arendt interprets the separation of the spheres in 'natural' terms and uses a 'natural' concept of privacy. Nature is private, and culture public, as the Aristotelian tradition famously has it.[122] Accordingly, she is bound to be oblivious to the character and meaning of privacy that is defined *conventionally* and need not have any sort of *natural* connotations. Accompanying this in Arendt is an unreasonably strict and essentialist social ontology of the activities assigned to each of the two realms: 'If we look at these things, regardless of where we find them in any given civilization, we shall see that each human activity points to its proper location in the world.'[123] The distinction she draws between labour, work and action allocates each of these categories its natural place in the social world. Yet this seems problematic not only in empirical but above all in normative terms, for in this case the question can no longer be asked whether everything that has its 'natural' place in the sphere of the household actually has its – normatively – right place there. I have already attempted to show why this may prove problematic from the perspective of a society that is liberal and just.[124]

In other passages, however, Arendt distinguishes what is a thoroughly modern concept of privacy from the ancient, Aristotelian one. The modern concept refers to the protection of intimacy and sees itself in strict opposition both to the social and the political realms.[125] Yet it remains unclear what relation this bears to the ancient concept of privacy, which Arendt clearly sets apart as normative. The features of privacy that she designates 'non-privative' also seem to imply a modern concept of privacy,[126] for here she specifies that a completely public life must be understood as superficial and a retreat into privacy as indispensable. But this is modern only at first sight. Arendt's real point is that there are human subjects who have not understood, so to speak, that some activities are dependent upon privacy and others upon the public realm, that these subjects thus lack the subjective capacity to assign their activities – which always have an *objective* localization – to their proper realm, and that such people appear incapable of genuine depth.[127]

The inadequacy of Arendt's categories comes to light most clearly, however, in their connection with the concept of freedom. Although Arendt draws a distinction between private and public analogous to the natural separation of nature and culture, she at the same time understands this natural separation as a functional one, its function being to keep the public realm free of processes or activities (or, historically, people) that might disrupt the freedom.[128] Yet this separation blinds her to the fact that what is ostensibly private always plays a part in the public sphere: that women are women, for example;[129] that people in public are unable to abstract from such 'private' characteristics; and not only that classifications of what belongs in the 'private household' and what in public may at any time also become a public issue, but that furthermore such discourse is actually necessary to make it possible for all persons to participate equally in public life.[130] Arendt does not really seem to be interested in these problems. Moreover, with such a definition of privacy she is unable to describe the dimensions of privacy that people rely upon for the sake of their freedom in the public realm too, such as decisional privacy. The meaning or value of the privacy of seclusion, by contrast, can for its part only be developed with a concept of individual freedom or autonomy that is able to grasp such dimensions of seclusion as an intrinsic aspect of itself or, to put it differently, that is able to conceive the retreat into privacy as a condition for successful self-presentation in public.[131] A reduced concept of freedom goes hand in hand with a reduced concept of privacy.

One might, however, go one cautious step further than this critique of Arendt, for its insistence on the value of privacy as protection for individual autonomy cannot mean that the political dimensions of individual freedom are as it were lost or replaced. The question is whether a specific conception of the relationship between an autonomous person and her political and public life could be grounded from this perspective, in other words whether the insistence on the value of privacy sets limits to the political dimension of individual freedom. If this were the case, it would mean that such a conception of privacy would have implications for the theory of democracy.

This I regard, however, as going too far. This conception of autonomy and privacy does not lay down in advance how positive versions of freedom and a rewarding life are to be described, but only formulates a framework. Nor is it possible for problems from the theory of the public sphere and the theory of democracy to be solved from *this* perspective *alone*. Even so, it is perhaps possible to indicate boundary points within which, viewed from the perspective of privacy, theoretical reflections on the public sphere and democracy would have to establish themselves. We can then outline a countermodel to Arendt's model that is nonetheless analogously untenable. As one such model, I shall briefly cite Edward Shils:

> Democracy requires the occasional political participation of most of its citizenry some of the time, and a moderate and dim perceptiveness – as if from the corner of the eye – the rest of the time. It could not function if politics and the state of the order were always on everyone's mind. If most men, most of the time, regarded themselves as their brother-citizens' keepers, freedom, which flourishes in the indifference of privacy, would be abolished.[132]

Shils is right to insist here on the freedom of privacy as freedom that is dependent upon the protection of privacy. Yet the contrast he posits between looking out of 'the corner of one's eye' and being one's 'brother-citizens' keeper' does not seem an apt one, for political engagement in a democracy is of course not to be equated with neighbourly control. In the second half of the cited passage, Shils adopts a Millian perspective that opposes private freedom to public control as *social* control, yet in the first half of the passage he inadmissibly identifies *political* engagement with social control and in disavowing the latter, he disavows the former.

Yet Shils thus seems unable to pay sufficient attention to the interplay of private freedom and public – social, political – space either, clearly underestimating the role played by democratic public society in the question of what is legitimately to count as private freedom and what is not. After all, private freedom is something that people live out in public space too. In order for it to be possible for everyone to enjoy this freedom in equal measure, therefore, it is necessary not only for the appropriate forms of indifference to be exercised, but also for the traditional domestic sphere to be organized in a way that prevents freedom from being 'unequally distributed' simply because the organizations and institutions themselves are unjust.[133] For this very reason a model along the lines proposed by Shils would be insufficient, since it fails to take into account public discussion and the engagement this calls for concerning how and where the boundaries between public and private are to be drawn. Particularly from a perspective that insists on the value of privacy, one must thus describe freedom in other terms than simply its sense of privacy. As these brief references show, both models seem imbalanced from the point of view of (decisional) privacy. For a precise answer to the question of what sort of freedom is protected by privacy, these reflections can thus be no more than hints, because any such answer would necessitate a theory of the public sphere too. But this is not the place for such a theory.[134]

5 Informational Privacy: Limits to Knowledge

1 Expectations: what do other people know about me?

Why do we generally regard it as improper, impolite, immoral or even illegal when other people without our knowledge (or even with our knowledge) and against our will observe us, eavesdrop on us, or even film us or tap our phone calls, whether this takes place at home, in the office, on the streets or in a café? Why do we feel upset, shamed, injured, scarred, insecure or manipulated once we realize what has happened? Why do we find it injurious when medical data concerning us is passed on to third parties, and why is it unpleasant to be the object of gossip? Why is it wrong for enterprises to pass on personal data or for close friends to pass on information about us they only know by virtue of being a close friend?

Such questions illustrate the scope and complexity of the theme of informational privacy and possible violations of it. If privacy in general means being able to control 'access' to one's own personhood, then – as we saw earlier – this must in one respect be understood and interpreted as control over what other people can *know* about oneself. This, roughly speaking, is what I should like to elucidate here under the rubric of 'informational privacy'. At heart, what is at issue here is who knows what about a person and how they know it, in other words control of the information relating to that person. 'Control' here refers to the fact that it is in many respects in a person's hands – and in other respects she can at least guess – what others know about her in any particular instance, that she can thus make well-founded assumptions concerning what the people or institutions she deals with know about her, and that in accordance with these assumptions and expectations she may also possess corresponding possibilities for penalizing or at least criticizing infractions.[1]

In fact, for numerous theorists (once again)[2] the dimension of informational privacy represents the true, or at least the central, dimension of privacy. Charles Fried is representative when he describes privacy as 'the control we have over information about ourselves'.[3] And in similar terms, Alan Westin has produced what is now regarded as the classic definition. Privacy, he wrote, is 'the claim of individuals, groups or institutions to determine for themselves when, how, and to what extent information about them is communicated to others'.[4] The question now, therefore, is why it is considered that we have a universal right – which varies with the context in its particulars – or at least a well-founded claim not to be observed or eavesdropped upon against our will and/or without our knowledge (irrespective of where we happen to be at that moment, that is leaving aside for now the question of the privacy of our dwelling).[5] It is why we do not want information about us to be circulated against our will or without our knowledge, and why we do not want to be deceived about whom we give information to about ourselves and what happens to such information. Moreover, all this applies to all the relations that a person may have, that is her relations not only to 'unspecified third parties', institutions or the state, but also to friends.[6] The reason why people see such violations of informational privacy as forms of damage or alienation is not simply that they find them downright unpleasant, shaming or injurious and accordingly repulse them (although this is part of it too), but also and above all that these violations of informational privacy always at the same time result in violations of the conditions for autonomy. Individual autonomy is dependent upon informational privacy.

In what follows, I should now like first of all (in this first section) to mark out in more detail the general framework within which the issue of informational privacy has to be discussed, and in the process set out, in quite general terms to begin with, a thesis concerning the connection between informational privacy and autonomy. In the second section, I shall analyse more closely the particular meaning of informational privacy that is regarded as the genuine one in discussions of data protection and the police state. At issue here, therefore, is the protection of information in the face of 'unspecified others', for the group of people able to do the observing, eavesdropping, deceiving or controlling in this context is in principle open and may be completely unknown to the person to be protected. The third section will then focus on the protection of information in the face of a second class of people, that is people who are in principle familiar to the person to be protected. It is concerned, in other words, with the protection of informational privacy in the face of 'specified others'. I should like to show that in protecting informational privacy in both these respects – and protecting very different types of 'personal information' in the two cases – what is also at stake is the possibility of various aspects of individual autonomy. In the fourth section, I shall sum up once more by clarifying the connection between the protection of knowledge, expectations and autonomy.

To describe the field covered by informational privacy, a distinction must be drawn for a start between various ways in which it can be violated. The first can be called the 'paradigmatic case' for the simple reason that it is the most obvious and is regarded as the classic case. This is the case of a person who is observed or eavesdropped upon without her knowledge and against her will: it is the case of the voyeur. A second possibility is the case where, though a person is *aware* that she is being watched or listened to or that data about her are being passed on, this happens against her will or at least without her consent: such is the case, for example, when a list of subscribers to a particular magazine is passed on to other enterprises.[7] A third possibility is the case of a person who is aware that she is being in some way observed, but this does not necessarily happen against her will, and she puts up with it, as it were, because other things that she receives in return are more important to her, as might occur with open video surveillance in shops. The second and third cases, it might be said, are thus derivative with respect to the paradigmatic case. But all three represent situations in which a person is monitored in word or deed, or possibly deceived about the transmission of data, by an in principle *unspecified third party*. If the circle of people involved is restricted somewhat, a further case can be described, in which a person is deceived about the 'transmission of data' in the sense that personal information she has *herself disclosed* is passed on to others against her will (and with or without her knowledge), as happens with gossip among acquaintances or even within a close circle of friends.

In all these cases, what is at stake, in various ways, is control over what other people know about me and who those others are to whom I give information about myself. The loss of such control in each case requires a distinct description and in each case will have different repercussions that vary in their seriousness accordingly. Let us now look more closely, therefore, at what is actually being violated when informational privacy is violated. If informational privacy consists in a person in principle being able to control or at least know or estimate who has what information about her, then a violation of informational privacy consists for a start in the person no longer having this control. What is decisive, however, is that this means that her *expectations* concerning the knowledge others have about her prove to be false, are disappointed or come to nothing. Accordingly, I should like to suggest that violations of informational privacy be understood and interpreted in general as false or disappointed *expectations*, where these expectations concern knowledge and thus also a particular attitude or approach taken towards the person by her interaction or communication partners. A specific feature of violations of informational privacy, in other words, is that they have to do with expectations and assumptions regarding what other people or institutions know about the person, how they acquired their knowledge, and thus *what relation* they bear to that person *on the basis of this knowledge*. This may also refer to the situation of a person who is not expecting or assuming any contact with anybody, though she is in fact being observed by people who consequently know more about her than she expects (as is the case with someone being watched by a peeping Tom or by the 'abstract others' of hidden video surveillance). So it is not simply that the 'data record' of the person is damaged, but the person herself is violated in her knowledge, for there is something that *she does not know* that *other people do*. As a consequence, her expectations regarding the way other people behave towards her and her expectations regarding whom she is actually dealing with or whom she is actually facing in her interactions are based on false presuppositions.

My hypothesis, therefore, is firstly that the loss of control entailed by violations of informational privacy implies a disruption of the (in various ways) well-founded, normative (i.e. not merely cognitive) horizons of expectations that a person has regarding the knowledge that others may justifiably or legitimately have about her, horizons of expectations that are necessary for the exercise of autonomy. But what is the relevance here of the concepts of freedom and autonomy? If a person is observed, eavesdropped on or talked about, she is not ostensibly being impeded in any respect relevant to the question of her civil liberties. At first sight at least, she is not being restricted in her freedom at all. Why should I no longer do what I want to do simply because other people are watching me or listening to me do it? And why should the transmission of 'data' – if this is not associated with some sort of actual restriction – pose any threat to my freedom, especially if I am not even aware of it and may never even learn of it?

To illustrate this connection between autonomy and the control of information, let us briefly look at some examples, firstly at an example of the paradigmatic case, the case of the voyeur:

> 'Want to eavesdrop?' I whispered impulsively to Rennie. 'Come on, it's great. See the animals in their natural habitat.' Rennie looked shocked. 'What for?' 'You mean you never spy on people when they're alone? It's wonderful! Come on, be a sneak! [...]' [...] Reluctantly she came over to the window and peeped beside me. It is indeed the grossest of injustices to observe a person who believes himself to be alone. Joe Morgan, back from his Boy Scout meeting, had evidently intended to do some reading, for there were books lying open on the writing table and on the floor beside the bookcase. But Joe wasn't reading. He was standing in the exact center of the bare room, fully dressed, smartly executing military commands. About face! Right dress! 'Ten-shun! Parade set! He saluted briskly, his cheeks blown out and his tongue extended, and then proceeded to cavort about the room [...]. I watched entranced by his performance, for I cannot say that in my strangest moments (and a bachelor has strange ones) I have surpassed him.[8]

This example can of course be interpreted in many different ways,[9] but what concerns me here is simply the point that Joe Morgan's behaviour is essentially determined by his expectation or assumption that nobody *sees* him and nobody *knows* of the way he behaves, the show he puts on. Only because this is what he expects does he behave in this way, and if he knew of the people observing him his reaction would be shame, fury, anger, etc., and of course the painful sense that had he known of them beforehand he would have behaved differently. From this moment on, moreover, his interaction with his friends (and observers) is disrupted, at least in the sense that his expectations regarding what they know about him are false. And this means also that one aspect of his capacity for self-determination has been critically violated.

I should like to elucidate the same point, or at least a closely parallel one, with another example, this time from the public sphere (though likewise a paradigmatic case), the case of hidden video surveillance of public places. When we go out on the streets to do the shopping, we do so of course expecting to be seen by other people, to come into contact with other people. We expect and put up with the fact that other people will take in or notice how we look today, what we are wearing. We expect that we may well bump into acquaintances or get into conversation with complete strangers at the check-out. We have expectations, in other words, concerning a particular circle of (in principle) unfamiliar people whom we might meet, and we have expectations concerning how these people will behave towards us, namely with (in principle) a certain distance, and without making comments. But we do not expect our being seen and noticed in this way to be recorded on film and thus converted into something that can be reproduced and shown in public irrespective of time and place, that can be analysed, passed on and controlled. If we knew of such observation, we would possibly behave differently or at any rate act *in the awareness that* we were being filmed. And as in the first example, this difference shows that one can and should characterize violations of informational privacy as violations of autonomy even when the person in question never finds out that she has been observed or filmed. After all, her behaviour took place 'under false conditions'. It was *apparently self-determined* behaviour, but it was only apparently so because the assumptions made by the person were false.

A third example concerns the transmission of data by computer, say, the transmission of medical data. If my employer for example, with the help of experts, gains access to data (from my doctor or insurance company) that provide information about my medical history, he is not only violating the assumption I make that besides the people I have personally informed my medical data are known only to my doctor and possibly my insurance company, but he is in the process also restricting the capacity I have to behave in a self-determined manner, the control I have over my self-presentation, and the authenticity of my behaviour in such professional contexts. This is at any rate the case if I find out about the deception. But even if I merely presume that such deception has taken place or can no longer take it for granted that such transmission does not take place, my capacity for self-determined behaviour may be hugely reduced as a consequence.

For the fourth and final example, there is no need to bring up the latest technologies. Regardless of the context and possibly also of the intentions of the gossipmongers themselves, gossip and idle chatter about people likewise constitute a violation of informational privacy. In this case, the 'data' in question are typically the sort that are felt to be especially important to the person, above all from a first-person perspective, and the context is limited to 'specified others', others with whom one is acquainted. If I have told a friend something about myself that is important to me and that I do not want other people to learn about under any circumstances (say, because I would find it embarrassing), then it is clearly a violation of informational privacy if my friend passes on this information. And it is not only my expectations regarding his behaviour or the 'state of his knowledge' about me that come to nothing in such a situation (for what he knows about me is the fact that other people know these stories about me too), but also my expectations regarding the knowledge of those other people. Yet this engenders inauthentic forms of interaction between people, for those involved are in an important respect not the people they present themselves as being, and the relation they bear to the deceived person is different from what she assumes it to be.[10] Her control over the knowledge others have of her is illusory. Her expectations, though justified, have been let down.

These examples can now, I believe, illustrate a more far-reaching hypothesis. This is that the reason the protection of informational privacy matters so much to people is that it is an intrinsic part of their self-understanding as autonomous individuals (within familiar limits) to have *control over their self-presentation*, that is control of how they want to present or stage themselves, to whom they want to do so and in which contexts, control over how they want to see themselves and how they want to be seen. By means of the information that they give other people about themselves or that they know other people have always had about them, individuals simultaneously regulate the range of very diverse social relations within which they live.[11] Without this form of self-determined control over what one allows to be known about oneself and by whom – without this form of 'controlled self-disclosure' – the self-chosen diversity in one's relations would not be possible. Nor, therefore, would self-determined, context-dependent, authentic behaviour towards others, or the variety of self-chosen forms of interaction with others, of communication and reflection on self-chosen problems and issues, graded, as it were, according to the relation in question. Nor would it be possible to find an answer *authentically* to the question of how one wants to live.[12]

The very moment the deceived person becomes aware of the situation, the presence of observers, the knowledge of unexpected third parties, or the deception on the part of actual communication partners always results in a change or shift in perspective. And it is just such an involuntary shift in perspective from the first to the third person that prevents self-determined, authentic behaviour, that is that prevents one from actually doing what one would like to or acting as one wants to, without consideration for others or at any rate with consideration only for those 'others' whose presence one is aware of and whose perspective one knows.[13] Even when a case is paradigmatic in the sense described above that the person being observed or deceived is completely unaware of this observation or deception, we can still say that the person is impaired in her self-determination on the basis of the *false assumptions* on which she is acting. This applies *a fortiori* when she is unsure whether or not she is being deceived (watched or listened to, etc.), that is when she can no longer be sure of her expectations regarding what others know and whether they are present.

In appealing to the concepts of freedom and autonomy in my explanations here, I am also taking up theories of the sort expounded by Westin, Benn, Fried and even by the German Federal Constitutional Court. These theories all see a close connection between the violation of informational privacy and the possibility of individual freedom.[14] Stanley Benn, for example, thus describes[15] how the presence of other people or the fact that they are observing us compels us to take into consideration the very fact that others are present or that we are being observed. Respecting a person's privacy thus involves accepting that one's own behaviour may influence other people's actions in ways that are not desired.[16] As we shall see shortly, it is not just a matter of the quantitative participation of people, but also their qualitative involvement, for the expectations I have regarding who is present also refer to the way in which those who are present are *involved* in my affairs. One's expectations thus relate crucially to the way in which particular standpoints are involved in a communication or their degree of involvement, and these crucially influence how the person acts, the way she sees herself and presents herself. Respect for a person's privacy is respect for her as an autonomous subject.[17] In order to be able to behave in a self-determined way, as Benn points out, we must in general believe ourselves justified in assuming that we are not being observed, eavesdropped on, or deceived with respect to the transmission of data, the presence of other people, or what the people who are present know about us and 'who' they therefore are 'for us'. Accordingly, the derivative cases in which people *know* about the violation of their informational privacy may in turn also help explain the truly paradigmatic case, where people lack this knowledge. What happens openly in the derivative cases also occurs in the paradigmatic case, where there is a reduction in autonomy because the person is deceived about who is present or who knows what. By the same token, it is no use people *knowing* that they are being observed if they do not *want* to be observed – for in this case it is the very fact that they (have to) adapt themselves to being observed that prevents them from acting in a way that is self-determined and authentic.[18] Analysing the field of informational privacy in this way, it becomes clear that what is involved here are not only issues such as the 'bugging operation' carried out by a state on its citizens, but deceptions that are in principle possible in any relation in which a person lives.

This whole fabric of controlled self-presentation and self-disclosure, of control over the knowledge that other people have and the knowledge that they either show or do not show, is of course regulated by convention. The legitimacy of these expectations regarding the behaviour and knowledge of my interaction partners rests on the validity of social conventions and norms, which regulate – in ways that may vary greatly with the culture[19] – what counts as worthy of protection and as intimate, what is viewed as a legitimate shield or zone protecting a person from public attention or control, in other words what is to be subject to individual information control and what is not. These expectations are regulated, therefore, by a complex, but nonetheless stable fabric of social norms and conventions within which we operate and can control the various relations in which we live.

Such conventions or social rules, which here mark out dividing lines between public and private, can be understood as the expression of a normative principle guaranteeing not only negative liberties but also positive possibilities for living out these liberties unchecked, for enjoying them authentically. These conventions thus ultimately have to be validated in terms of this principle guaranteeing and facilitating individual autonomy.[20] This validation or verification of the normative foundations of such conventions comes to the fore when the conventions are called into question or criticized, or when they have become dysfunctional or restrictive. It also becomes relevant, however, when methods are discovered or fields developed that in their technological innovation transcend the established concepts and applications of private and public. Phenomena such as 'webcammers' (people who install in their home a camera that transmits its moving pictures directly onto the internet), the CCTV or video surveillance of shops, or the protection of privacy on the internet are all very new developments, for which there are still no conventions. In interpreting the concept of privacy in the context of these technological developments, therefore, normative principles must be explicitly appealed to.[21] The social and legal norms here must not just be a matter of form but also *effective* enough for me to be able to assume that my rights to informational privacy are in principle guaranteed, for autonomy can be threatened by the very fact that I no longer feel able to count on the self-evident *assumption* that these expectations are justified.

This brings to a conclusion our preliminary survey of the issue of informational privacy. There are clearly a range of cases involved, with a range of moral claims that vary greatly in strength and a range of consequences that vary greatly in the way they impair my autonomy and damage my identity.[22] But only by describing the problem in such broad terms is it possible to conceive and analyse the various aspects of informational privacy with reference to the different relations in which people live.[23] Adopting this rather unorthodox perspective still allows us to look at the now classic problems of informational privacy such as data protection, yet it means that these problems will not be a focal point but appear as just one element in the whole domain within which informational privacy may be violated. The problems arising with the new technologies and the associated possibilities for surveillance of course go beyond the realm of *individual* information control and extend to the sorts of *democratically delegated, state* control that people (must be able to) rely upon for the protection of their informational privacy.[24]

In what follows, I want to look more closely into the various aspects of the issue of informational privacy, investigating the question of what 'information' is actually involved and at the ways and contexts in which it is infringed. I shall proceed in two stages. Starting out from a first-person perspective, my concern is firstly the protection of informational privacy with respect to 'unspecified others' (in section 2) and then this protection with respect to 'specified others' (in section 3). The division I make, therefore, is not primarily in terms of how bad, serious or malicious the different methods of eavesdropping, observing, controlling or deceiving are, but the different circles of people who may infringe the individual's informational privacy and who may be pursuing different interests accordingly.[25] By proceeding in this way from completely anonymous relationships to intimate relationships in our analysis of the protection or infringement of informational privacy, it is also possible to explicate the difference in the quality of these relations. In the process, the intention is also to bring to light the extent to which the various ways of infringing informational privacy express different aspects of the connection between informational privacy on the one hand and individual freedom and autonomy and in particular the authenticity of self-determined behaviour on the other.[26]

2 Informational privacy and unspecified others: the panopticon

Alarming accounts of the 'end of privacy' and the Orwellian police state are a constant feature of today's media, a regular theme in the news stories of the daily papers, background reports in the weeklies or the endless production of new books.[27] And this tendency shows no sign of stopping, if only because new ways of acquiring, storing, processing, transmitting and selling information about people are constantly being discovered. The tapping of telephones, CCTV and video surveillance of shops and public spaces, 'tracing' on the internet, data transmission between firms or insurance companies, or the audiovisual supervision of houses and flats are no longer unusual phenomena, but seem to have become more or less commonplace. Even those fairly hardened to the subject are likely to feel a certain disquiet when they read up on the relevant literature, for these visions of a panoptic society can no longer be dismissed as pure science fiction.[28] If all the technical possibilities for surveillance and observation are put together, the project of the 'visible human' does not seem so far-fetched.[29]

Of course, life in social contexts always entails a certain degree of social observation and control. The problem is how – in spite of the developments in the new information technologies in the twentieth century – we can preserve enough 'normality' to ensure that our concepts of autonomy and a non-controlled life do not lose their meaning completely (as would happen, for example, if we were simply to get used to permanent CCTV surveillance). The new technologies are making *new categories* of observation, control and social transparency possible. I am not claiming that things have already reached this stage for 'us',[30] and I shall not be looking in any great detail either at individual cases or at the general range of technical possibilities and the dangers they represent. This has already been done in full and highly informatively by others.[31] My goal here is the modest one of again taking a step back and asking why the various forms of observation and data transmission in fact constitute a problem and, if they can be considered dangerous, why this is so. I am concerned above all, that is, with clarifying in more detail the concepts involved and investigating the implications of the 'end of privacy' being heralded by some. The frame of reference is formed by the reflections expounded in the first section on the connection between knowledge, expectations and autonomy and thus the question of what infringements of informational privacy may actually involve. In what follows, I seek to elaborate this frame of reference in more concrete terms by looking at the problems of a panoptic society.

The fundamental point here is that the new information technologies may be problematic on the one hand because people are as it were being 'de-privatized' against their will and the *protection* of privacy is in jeopardy,[32] and on the other hand because people are becoming more and more willing of their own accord to reduce or 'negotiate' their private sphere, the dimensions of their privacy, in return for other goods. The reason this can or should be considered a problem is that both a deliberate and a non-deliberate reduction in the protection of informational privacy may result in certain forms and dimensions of self-determined and authentic behaviour not only becoming substantially less practicable, but also being conceived as less relevant, less crucial, less intrinsic to a rewarding life. This would also entail a change in people's *self-understanding* to the extent that in important aspects of their lives people would be renouncing the chance to be unobserved, unidentifiable, inaccessible and protected in their informational self-determination. This affects not only the idea of a rewarding, self-determined life, however, but also the idea of liberal democracy itself, which is dependent upon autonomous subjects who are aware of and who value their autonomy.

This is a rather roughly sketched hypothesis. I should like to explain and ground it somewhat more fully in what follows, starting with a brief look at the history of nightmare visions of the end of privacy in (Jeremy Bentham and) Michel Foucault as a way of putting the issue of informational privacy into context once more. Then I shall take the first step of classifying the problems: the data that are actually involved, the methods used, the persons and institutions concerned, the contexts and the motives (for observation and for data transmission). Only then will it be possible to take a second step that allows us to see more exactly the *conflicts* involved in the issue of the panoptic society, the normative principle in terms of which the conflicts can be described and resolved and ambivalences cleared up, and the interests that are in conflict.

It is Bentham's image of the panoptic prison[33] that first served Foucault as a metaphor for the processes of discipline characteristic of modern societies in general and that is now being brought into play to illustrate the new transparency of the information society.[34] As is well known, the panopticon was Bentham's idea and plan for a prison in which countless inmates could be almost effortlessly controlled by a single supervisor. Foucault describes it in the following terms:

> We know the principle on which [Bentham's panopticon] was based: at the periphery, an annular building; at the centre, a tower; this tower is pierced with wide windows that open onto the inner side of the ring; the peripheric building is divided into cells, each of which extends the whole width of the building; they have two windows, one on the inside, corresponding to the windows of the tower; the other, on the outside, allows the light to cross the cell from one end to the other. All that is needed, then, is to place a supervisor in a central tower and to shut up in each cell a madman, a patient, a condemned man, a worker or a schoolboy. By the effect of backlighting, one can observe from the tower, standing out precisely against the light, the small captive shadows in the cells of the periphery.[35]

Foucault then proceeds to apply this image of the prison to society as a whole:

> But the Panopticon must not be understood as a dream building: it is the diagram of a mechanism of power reduced to its ideal form; its functioning, abstracted from any obstacle, resistance or friction, must be represented as a pure architectural and optical system: it is in fact a figure of political technology that may and must be detached from any specific use.[36]

It is not Foucault's theory of law and morality that is of concern here, nor is it his relentless view of the disciplinary practices and power structures of modern societies in general. Foucault is interesting in this context because his image of 'mechanisms of observation' that increase 'the ability to penetrate into men's behaviour', of 'the automatic functioning of power'[37] in the panopticon, can be taken and applied to the question of what is problematic about the threat to informational privacy. In short, the problem is clearly that one can be constantly observed as a matter of course, that one can be constantly identified as a particular person as a matter of course, and thus also controlled, if necessary constantly and as a matter of course. In spite of what Foucault says, moreover, what is involved here is not the observation, control and identification of an Orwellian police state, but possibilities in principle available to everyone towards everyone else: the shop owner towards his customers, parents towards their babysitter, insurance companies towards their members, hackers towards all other internet users. This power to infringe informational privacy, in other words, may be a thoroughly egalitarian power, an egalitarian power that makes it difficult here to talk any longer in terms of those who exclude and those who are excluded. It is also a form of power that need not even be used in order to be effective, let alone used with the aim of harming others. Curiosity alone, for example, is in principle a relatively innocuous motive. The point above all is the effect of these possibilities, that is the fact that in principle one *can* be seen, traced, described and thus controlled. Bentham describes with splendid clarity the state of mind produced in the panopticon's inmates by being subject to constant observation. It is 'the sentiment of an invisible omnipresence'.[38]

In terms of the fabric of knowledge, expectations and self-determined behaviour we looked at above, this means that if I must *always* expect other people to know more[39] about me than I should be able to and would want to expect according to the established, traditional conventions and conceptions, my behaviour can *always* be attuned to this in advance. Such a violation of informational privacy thus *always* entails a shift of perspective, compelling me to adopt a perspective towards myself and my behaviour that – for reasons that may vary with the context – I do not want to adopt or that I used not to want to adopt but have now become accustomed to adopting, constantly and as a matter of course.

This, it is said, is the danger. But what are the data, the methods, the mechanisms, contexts and motives involved? In what follows, I want briefly to go into these questions in more detail so as then to be able to describe more clearly the sort of conflicts that arise and the various sorts of interests involved, in other words whether Foucault's impending panopticon is necessarily a suitable description of the situation. When it comes to determining what data are to count as 'personal' and thus as 'worthy of protection', the definition established by the European Union directive of 1995 has come to be influential in all public (European) debates on the protection of informational privacy:

> For the purposes of this Directive, 'personal data' shall mean any information relating to an identified or identifiable natural person ('data subject'); an identifiable person is one who can be identified, directly or indirectly, in particular by reference to an identification number or to one or more factors specific to his physical, physiological, mental, economic, cultural or social identity.[40]

As Ploeg, for example, has made clear,[41] however, this definition of personal data should not be understood in essentialist terms but as merely contextual in nature, for such data do not make sense as such (the number of my passport is just a number), but only when placed in a context such that the relevant person can if necessary be identified. Data only become personal when provided with a method of verification. The problem with this sort of data is thus that they *can* identify persons precisely. This is made clearer by the sophisticated typology set out by Oscar Gandy Jr, as well as Reg Whitaker, who distinguish eleven categories of data to be regarded as worthy of protection,[42] including personal data (birth certificate, driving licence, passport, etc.), financial data, insurance data, data concerning hobbies and leisure activities, employment status, training, legal data, etc. These categories are relevant, according to Gandy, because all the data concerned can be ascertained, stored and transmitted, and can serve to identify a person or assign (sensitive) data to a specific person. The context in which the data are collected and stored is again clearly relevant. Identifications can be made possible, for example, simply by bringing together two data records. In assessing what should be permissible or possible (a point to which we shall return in more detail shortly), one must thus constantly appeal to concepts such as 'likely' or '(good) sense' (asking how likely data-matching is to occur, or which data does it make sense to use in a particular set). The answers to this sort of question are not as such laid down in advance.[43] A violation of informational privacy thus takes place when data so defined find their way into the wrong hands.

On the other hand, however, the category of 'personal data worth protecting' must also include such data that can be related to persons already identified. This has been a central guideline in the relevant jurisprudence in the United States since Warren and Brandeis,[44] for whom possible violations of informational privacy include firstly 'intrusion upon a person's seclusion, solitude or private affairs', then 'public disclosure of private, embarrassing facts', 'public disclosure of a private person in a false light', and finally 'appropriation, for one's own advantage, of another's name, image, or other mark that is an aspect of that person's identity'.[45] In addition, Warren and Brandeis mention the defence of 'personal writings and all other personal productions [. . .] against publication in any form', counting 'sentiments' and 'thoughts' as expressions that deserve (legal) protection in the same way as written expressions.[46] It is interesting to contrast their classification with the one proposed by Gandy et al. and possibly combine the two of them. In this way, it emerges that the two perspectives are both necessary to cover the whole range of possible data that must be defined as 'personal' and potentially worthy of protection. The protection of persons already identified and the protection of persons potentially identifiable must be treated alike as themes of informational privacy.

Accordingly, I want to propose a slightly changed typology and distinguish the following categories of data that – in the appropriate context – must be considered to belong to the realm of a person's informational privacy and as worthy of protection. To start out from the most fundamental level possible, we should mention the privacy of thoughts and mental states,[47] of feelings and views in general. The importance of such data for one's identity or personality can be established simply by introspection. What is important to a person, what she thinks of as especially intimate and private, is also a matter of her own choice and can be generalized and objectivized only within limits. The relevance of this point for the normative principle to come will become apparent shortly.[48] Among all the other reasons for protecting this aspect of privacy, one that must be mentioned is that we would live in utter chaos if it were indeed permanently possible to know or find out everything about everyone else and if we were always totally transparent to one another.

A second group of data would be all those described above – as in the European Union directive or in the writings of Gandy and others – as 'personal data' in the context of the new information technologies, data that can be used not only to identify one person among all possible others, but also to ascertain a person's preferences, traits and habits. At issue here is the broad spectrum of computer-based data, including (for example) data concerning a person's 'browser behaviour',[49] as well as traditional data such as personal records (diaries), letters and documents, etc.

As a third category of data worthy of protection, one should count everything (legitimately) done by a person within her own home.[50] Life on one's own and in family relations will be dealt with in greater detail below. Here the point I wish to make is simply that these modes of behaviour form an important set of data that can be referred to as informational in so far as people have an interest in ensuring that unspecified others do not 'know' anything about them. In their typology, Warren and Brandeis focused above all on the private person in public contexts, and Gandy, for example, is concerned (exclusively) with data associated with the new information technologies. But data relating to one's private life at home should also be included within the category of data that are personal and for this reason worthy of protection.

Finally, one must distinguish a fourth group of data that relates to activities and habits taking place outside the house and to the spatiotemporal facts about a person. Video and CCTV surveillance in public spaces and in shops is an example of this sort of data collection, which can make a person in principle identifiable and be used to help supervise and control people.

We have differentiated four groups of data, therefore, concerning persons both already identified and yet to be identified. The questions of when these data actually become 'personal' in nature or when legitimate data collection ceases to be so, as well as when data can be used to identify a person, refer us to the problem of the *context* in which data protection or the protection of informational privacy acquires significance. My passport number is not relevant in every context. Nor does it in every context represent an infringement of my informational privacy if someone knows of my preferences when surfing the internet. Problematic contexts cannot be described independently of the people or institutions that have an interest in possessing the data about a person, in observing or identifying her, etc. To ask about the context is thus to ask about what motives are involved and who it actually is that collects or passes on such data. As far as motives are concerned, it is surely curiosity that can be cited as the classic example (as with respect to the paradigmatic case). The voyeur is characterized by curiosity, and no less curious is the hacker. Even if curiosity constitutes a relatively innocuous motive in violations of informational privacy (and in fact tends to be regarded as a virtue anyway), the curious observer is still an observer and as such always produces an infringement of privacy, whether spying on a person without her knowledge or eavesdropping on her in a café. This is not so when it comes to a second factor that can today be described as a classic motive behind data collection, which is efficiency. The fact that state bureaucracy collects personal data, or that insurance companies, commercial enterprises and firms from the service sector do likewise, need not *prima facie* be associated with pernicious intentions but may be due to an interest in rationalization and efficiency that does not as such entail an infraction of informational privacy. Nor does the further motive of sheer financial profit as such constitute an intrusion into the private realm of a person. Both efficiency and profit may flip over into motives that are problematical, but neither is in itself harmful.[51] A motive clearly does become problematical, however, when it becomes a matter of control, against the will and/or without the knowledge of the person being controlled. Such is the case with the 'nannycams' or miniature cameras now being used to supervise babysitters.

Closely linked to the question of motives is the question of the interested parties, which can be answered comparatively simply in terms of the following categories. Along with arbitrary individuals (such as voyeurs and hackers) and non-arbitrary individuals (such as private employers or parents who have installed nannycams), it is on the one hand state institutions and on the other hand commercial enterprises that might have motives and opportunities to violate people's informational privacy.[52] Even the methods of infraction can here be summarized in brief (although other approaches may of course focus on these as the crucial factor[53]). A first distinction should be drawn between those methods that do not rely upon the assistance of technology and those that do, and this assistance can be further divided into traditional electronic devices and the new information technologies.

Having looked at the various data and at the various contexts, motives, methods and interested parties involved, it now becomes possible to take the second step of analysing more closely the *conflicts* that may arise in panoptic society. What is the normative principle in terms of which conflicts can be described and resolved and ambivalences clarified? What are the interests that may clash? If we attempt to start out, once more, from the most fundamental level possible, what comes to light is a point that has frequently gone unnoticed in present-day public discussion on the matter.[54] This is that the *onus* of justification and explanation lies primarily not with whoever wants to do the observing (etc.) but with those who do *not* want to be observed.[55] If one starts from the basic assumption that people have the right and the liberty to look at the world – out of curiosity – as and when they want to,[56] and to tell others that they do so as and when they want to, then any restriction upon this right and this liberty needs to be justified. This perspective brings it home that rights to privacy must be grounded in values just as basic as such liberty, that is likewise in the value of freedom or autonomy or in respect for persons, since otherwise there would be no reason for the 'restrained person' (to use Benn's term) to see why she is not allowed or not supposed to do what she would like to, namely look at the world as and when she wants.

Starting out from such basic assumptions, what also becomes clearer is that the protection of informational privacy cannot be a perfunctory matter, but – colliding as it does with an elementary right – must be grounded in just such elementary terms. (Otherwise there would be no conflicts, as it would always be possible for this protection to be overtrumped by the more basic right.) This conflict is primarily a conflict, therefore, between a 'wanting to know' and a 'wanting to hide', and the normative principle upon which this protection is grounded must start out from the idea of the autonomy of a person or of respect for her identity. It is only because it is necessary and possible for the interest in (informational) privacy to be grounded on such a basic level that it can, if need be, restrict or overtrump the 'freedom to look at the world' as well as the right to freedom of expression for all persons. In order now to characterize the principle of autonomy as foundational, we can at this point refer back to the reflections set out in the previous section on how and why a person's autonomy is dependent upon control of the knowledge others have of her and thus also upon a certain stability in the fabric of knowledge, expectations and control. In what follows, therefore, I want to sketch against this background the lines of conflict that might arise involving these aspects of informational privacy, with the (modest) aim not of proposing solutions to concrete problems, but of simply describing what these conflicts look like and what is at stake when they occur. Three perspectives should here be distinguished.

The first perspective focuses upon state institutions and the way they capture, collect and store personal data concerning individual people. In itself, there is nothing bad about this. On the contrary, as has frequently been pointed out,[57] the idea of individual rights and the possibility of making a whole variety of claims on the state naturally and necessarily entails the possibility that an individual might be identified and that the new information technologies might be used to do so. In this sense, it is also an expression of the endeavour to achieve equality among the citizens of a state. Efficiency and rationalization necessarily take bureaucratization and legal individualization, as it were, to a new technological plane. This gives rise to dangers that as such present problems, albeit in a different way from genuine conflicts. Such dangers come about when personal data are shifted from one context to another, permitting new classifications that are no longer harmless but may lead to discrimination against the persons thus classified. In this way, efficiency and rationalization may have a tendency to flip over into control.[58] Indeed, it is because of this threat arising from the misuse and improper 'de-anonymization' of data that offices such as data protection commissioner have been introduced and have proved to be necessary.[59] By contrast, actual *conflicts* come about when the state genuinely pursues other interests compared with the individual subject who aspires to liberty. This sort of conflict thus represents a collision between the public welfare sought by the state and the interests of the individual citizen, and is typified, for example, by the government's concern to guarantee safety in public spaces (with video surveillance), to protect the health of the population, or to fight terrorism.[60] Such security interests, which can also, of course, be described as serving to protect the freedom of the individual, clearly have to be taken seriously in a liberal democracy. A closer discussion of individual cases is called for in the matter.

Nonetheless, at the level of general normative principles, one can still ask how the two sides should be weighed up against one another and whereabouts the lines of conflict should run. Starting out from the idea that a liberal democracy guarantees *individual civil liberties* and from the assumption described above that autonomy is contingent upon a particular working fabric of knowledge, expectations and the ability to control one's self-presentation, it is clear that any weighing up of the issue must incorporate a series of questions such as the following. What aspects of a person's life would be affected by a restriction in informational self-determination? How likely would it be to result in an actual reduction in the person's freedom? To what extent would each individual's everyday life or day-to-day social practices (as opposed to exceptional situations) be affected by such state control of information? What weight, by contrast, should be given to the interests of public welfare? In what way does the identification of groups provoke and support discrimination against them? If we further bear in mind that the way state bureaucracy deals with the protection of individual informational privacy is an especially sensitive issue because in practice the dangers of bureaucratic control cannot be gainsaid, and that a special symbolic component is involved (not only, but also) on account of the associations with the Orwellian police state, it is plain how exceptionally difficult it is in this case to overtrump the individual's interests in freedom and protection, and how substantial the demands for the right to privacy in the face of the state prove to be. It was just such reflections that were cited as arguments against phone tapping in the course of the inquiry into the 'Great Bugging Operation' in Germany, and that led to the European Union directive on data protection being drafted and passed.[61]

The second perspective spotlights the financial interests that may be at stake in the issue of the violation and protection of informational privacy. Conflicts come about here between the different individual interests involved, both of which, moreover, can be formulated as interests in liberty. The problems confronting us here, as sketched out above, concern the 'de-anonymization' of (computer-based) data, the identification of persons in contexts in which they do not wish to be identified, the transmission of data to individuals or business enterprises[62] unbeknown to the person involved, the storing of 'browser behaviour', etc. The examples of 'data sale' – the main source of income for most internet (dotcom) companies – that can be read about in accounts of the situation in the United States are particularly shocking.[63] Given the different jurisprudence under the European Union directive, most such cases would not be possible in Europe, or at least not lawful. But the normative crux remains the same. The question is to what extent it is acceptable for one person's profit to be at the expense of another's de-anonymization. This starts, of course, with CCTV surveillance in shops. Once more, a balanced appraisal of the matter must include a number of questions: What aspects of a person's life are affected by such a restriction on her informational self-determination, and, more generally, what social practices? How likely is it to result in an actual reduction in the person's freedom? How far will the individual's everyday existence (as opposed to exceptional situations) be affected?[64]

When it comes to the broad field of the service sector as a whole, however, it is especially awkward to speak of conflicts and infringements of informational privacy because people are increasingly inclined to relinquish, negotiate or 'sell' their privacy of their own accord provided the benefits outweigh the costs. Accordingly, the *third* perspective focuses directly on what has been termed the 'participatory' panopticon.[65] Not only is everyone who surfs the internet, pays by credit card, or makes purchases through the net, etc., willingly giving up certain realms of their privacy on a daily basis. The routine installation of cookies is just one example here. But conversely, skills that are relatively easy to learn enable a person to intrude upon the privacy of others on the internet. Video surveillance too is clearly a double-edged sword. On the one hand, it is an obvious restriction of forms of controlled self-presentation. On the other hand, for example, it was a (private) video that happened to capture the images leading to the conviction of the policemen responsible for the beating of Rodney King in Los Angeles – a video that as such infringed the informational privacy of those involved, but that had undeniably positive effects as part of a democratic panopticon. This panopticon thus looks different from the one envisaged by Foucault. On the one hand, we frequently have rights and opportunities to insist on more privacy, yet fail to make use of these rights and opportunities. And on the other hand, we are not only victims, but also potential culprits. The fact that all we need is a computer or a video camera in order to turn into a culprit is shown, for example, by the aforementioned nannycams that are now perfectly run of the mill in the United States.

Yet these developments have their dangers. One of the effects of giving up private domains and being able to control the everyday privacy of others is that one becomes accustomed to regarding certain forms of privacy not only as no longer protected but also as no longer important. This applies potentially not just to all relations in which services involving computer-based data are used, but also, on account of (both private and public) video surveillance, to public spaces where one may either want or have to spend time. If it can in principle no longer be taken for granted that one has control over one's informational self-determination or that one is not (constantly) being observed, and if, as a result, one must (constantly) present oneself as though one were being observed, the result is a loss of autonomy in terms of the authenticity of one's behaviour, which is turned into behaviour *as if*, that is alienated behaviour. It is alienated behaviour, in other words, because it can no longer be guided by a self-determined diversity of relations, and because it is no longer owed to the person's own control of her self-presentations.

The dangers reside, therefore, on the one hand in the voluntary renunciation of informational privacy, and on the other hand in non-voluntary control. The horizons of a person's expectations with respect to the knowledge that others may justifiably and legitimately have about her, which are based on various factors depending on the various people or institutions concerned, may as a result be disrupted or prove to be false. Privacy – in the form of informational privacy – can thus be conceived as a protective shield allowing the individual to act towards all possible unspecified third parties, whether individual persons or institutions, in accordance with his expectations concerning the 'level of information' they each have.[66] Autonomy is dependent too upon external conditions of authenticity. If people are structurally and systematically mistaken in their expectations about what others (may) know about them and about the opportunities different people may have for obtaining information on them, or if they have to assume on a structural and systematic basis that they will be observed, supervised and controlled, this may also produce a change in their interpretation of what self-created, self-determined behaviour, or in other words autonomy, can be in the first place. In normative terms, this is of course highly problematic, not only because of the connection between autonomy, authenticity and a good or rewarding life, but also because liberal democracies are reliant upon subjects who are autonomous and who see themselves as such. From a purely strategic point of view,[67] indeed, liberal democracies necessarily have a substantial interest in ensuring that their citizens in turn have a substantial interest in self-determination, since they would otherwise be jeopardized in their very function. A possible loss of informational privacy thus appears to be directly relevant for public autonomy.

3 Informational privacy and specified others: collusions, friendships and intimate relations

So far I have described threats to the fabric of a person's expectations, knowledge and autonomy in her relations with unspecified others, in other words threats to individual self-determination connected above all with the new information technologies. I now want to ask the further question of what is implied by the protection of informational privacy when it comes to interaction at the closest level, that is how this protection is relevant for and within friendships and what informational privacy actually means in this context.

What I should like to show in the following is that even in one's relations with 'specified others' the protection of informational privacy is intrinsic to individual autonomy. This applies both to the privacy *of* relations and to privacy *within* relations. My intention is to start by looking in detail at theories that claim that the (true, exclusive) function of privacy is precisely to make intimate relations possible in the first place or to secure the very possibility of diversity in one's relations. The point here is that close, private relationships differ from more distant, public, professional ones in (among other things) how much and what sort of things people *know* about one another, and how much and what sort of things they *want to* know about one another.[68] Such theories of relational privacy do not necessarily see themselves as theories of informational privacy.[69] Yet their place in this account is here, because they are inherently concerned with defining the function of privacy in terms of the exchange of certain information, seeking to draw a precise distinction between public and private relations in terms of who knows what about a person. I wish to take up such theories of relational privacy, but also go beyond them in so far as they fail to take into account either the context or setting of intimate relations, or the more precise function of communication within these relations, that is to find out or test what form self-determined, authentic behaviour or a self-determined, authentic life might take, and what modes of self-presentation would be possible, desirable, authentic, etc. Essential for the process of autonomy to unfold and the practical question to be posed successfully are forms of intersubjective evaluation and deliberation that are unthinkable without the protection of privacy. This will become clearer shortly.

The first step will thus be to analyse more closely theories of relational privacy, and the second will be to focus in more detail upon the setting of such intimate relations and the form and function of communication within them. In a third and fourth step, I finally intend – with the help of Erving Goffman and Uwe Johnson – to discuss two distinct ways in which a person's informational privacy in her relations of friendship or intimacy may be disrupted or infringed and how such damage may simultaneously be understood as an impairment of her autonomy as an individual. The first case has to do with the protection of informational privacy within friendships, the second with such protection within love relationships.

Of the theorists of relational privacy, it has above all been James Rachels and Charles Fried[70] who have attempted to show that without the protection of privacy and the separation of public and private realms it would not be possible to have intimate relationships at all, or indeed relationships of diverse intensity in general. One of the ways of differentiating the relationships that people have is according to the degree of information or knowledge that people divulge about themselves. The point is that a person must in principle have control over what any other person finds out about her and how she does so, for the closer she lets anyone come to her, the more things she lets the other person know about her that are important aspects of her identity, the more she is willing to 'disclose herself', and the more vulnerable she becomes.[71] It is thus only because people are able and in a position either to withhold or divulge such information about themselves with respect to the rest of the world that they are capable of forming intimate relations in the first place. From this theory of relations it is then possible to derive a right to privacy, that is to the protection of informational privacy, since otherwise fundamental humans needs cannot be met. If it is an essential part of human nature to have friendships and intimate relationships, and if these relationships are constituted by the targeted and controlled diffusion of information, by selective self-disclosure, then a right to privacy is the result.[72]

Fried combines his initially plausible thesis that without the possibility of individual 'information control' the protection of private relations is unthinkable in purely logical terms with the claim that such information control is both a necessary and a sufficient condition for private, intimate relations to exist. Yet this thesis seems too strong, for the condition is not a sufficient one. On the one hand, the context or setting in which these forms of intimate communication take place appears to play a greater role than Fried maintains. And on the other hand, the 'exchange of information' that takes place within friendships or intimate relationships, that is the function and form of such communication, itself seems in need of explanation and interpretation. I intend to explicate both of these points in what follows.

Why is the context in which the 'exchange of information' takes place so important? Clearly, when a person divulges something intimate about herself this does not always in itself constitute a close or intimate relationship. One may also reveal such details about one's life to a psychoanalyst, for example, without this in itself making the relationship into a private or intimate friendship. Comparable cases may occur in other contexts, such as a chance encounter with strangers on a train, where a person may talk about very personal matters in the knowledge that she will never see them again. It is obviously not only the amount and significance of the information we reveal about ourselves that determines the degree of intimacy and closeness of a relationship.[73] The exchange of information of which Fried speaks is always dependent upon a setting characterized by affection or love, care or consideration, and a special form of interest. It is a context, that is, in which it can be assumed that the standpoints involved in the communication are not the dispassionate standpoints of detached observers, and that a caring interest thus exists between the people concerned rather than the indifference that exists between strangers.[74] In private relationships – to the extent that they are private – we act differently, present ourselves differently, 'rehearse' ourselves in a way that differs from what occurs in relationships with people with whom we are not on special or close terms. In this respect, the private sphere constitutes nothing less than a symbolic space in which, in our dealings with persons of our own 'choosing', we can 'invent ourselves' or at least act without protection. This protected space permits unprotected behaviour in the form of the unprotected divulgence of emotions, as well as unprotected self-abandon in bodily intimacy. These are dimensions of the self that can only find expression in the private sphere of intimacy and for which this private sphere alone is able to provide the context.[75] Against this background it is again possible to describe a fabric of knowledge, expectations, information and assumptions about what the other person knows about me, a social fabric, so to speak, on the level of one's intimate relationships. But this fabric is always found within a particular context of affection, care or commitment that exists between the people involved, and to this extent it cannot be described independently of this context.

The relational theory of privacy must accordingly be watered down substantially. Not every case of self-disclosure is an act of intimacy. Nonetheless, such self-disclosure – as a way of imparting one's self to others – can still cautiously be described as a necessary condition for intimate relations.[76] This gives us a both weaker and broader concept of relational privacy and brings us to the second of the above-mentioned amendments. This concerns the specific form of communication in friendships and intimate relations, and criticizes the notion that a mere 'exchange' of information is what takes place. The protection of the privacy of relations clearly has a further function that goes beyond a simple swapping of information, for such relations are the scene for processes of intersubjective confrontation that must be conceived as intrinsic to the identity and autonomy of those involved in them.

It is relatively uncontroversial to assume that the self or identity of a person is constituted dialogically, in the sense that for the development of her practical identity a person is reliant upon symbolic interactions with other people, which are what make the development of self-consciousness and a practical self-relationship possible in the first place.[77] This at the same time means that people depend upon relationships that convey the love and esteem essential to such development, for only in such relations can the self-confidence necessary for identities to flourish actually be attained. This further means, however, that a specific aspect of communication in these relations is in effect the intention of conveying this sort of self-confidence or self-esteem in such a way that autonomy is made possible: that is, part of one's practical identity comes to consist in seeing oneself as autonomous and as the sort of person who values having the opportunity and capacity for individual self-determination.[78]

Typically, however, such relations can only succeed within the protective sphere of privacy. This is because the forms of communication and of affective care specific to this context are accompanied by feelings and vulnerabilities in the persons involved that – as sketched above – could not even be articulated without the protection afforded by privacy. It is only thanks to this protection that it is possible for a person to make herself more vulnerable or behave more vulnerably in some relations than in others, and for her to decide for herself which particular relations these are to be.

Going one step further, it can be seen in general terms why it is so unconvincing when Fried talks simply of an 'exchange of information' in private relations. For it is clear that it is not just the private family in communication with children that has a specific function in terms of the development of identity, self-confidence and autonomy. And it is also clear that – both in intimate relations and in friendships in general – what is at stake is not merely the *formation* of a self or the *learning* of self-determination but rather the non-stop reappropriation of self-determination, a constant updating, that is autonomy as a *process*. As a rule, the disclosure of information to which Fried refers is not just any disclosure, but communication with 'significant others', that is specific people who matter to one, and (not only, but also) about questions concerning one's own practical identity. 'Information control', in the sense of independence in the regulation of one's relationships, is something that subjects typically want to have because in these intimate relationships they deliberate (not only, but also) about questions fundamental to their life. It is not just any old information that is involved, therefore, but a particular form of communication in which people depend upon affective recognition from specific others. This is because it is in the light of the reactions from these others that they deliberate upon what sort of person they are and what sort they want to be, how they want to live. It is in the light of interpretations by these others that they interpret themselves, their conflicts and their decisions. And it is in the light of the recognition from these others that they experience themselves and their own projects as valuable. In this particular interpretation of privacy, the relational theory thus makes a contribution that is relevant in normative terms. Clearly this dialogical dimension must not eclipse the *monological* component that must be provided by the subject if he truly wants to see himself as autonomous, possibly in circumstances when respect is denied him. Even so, one may still see the dialogical constitution of identity, self-consciousness and autonomy as a necessary condition for this dimension of the self, though not a sufficient one, since the autonomy of subjects goes beyond the recognition they receive.[79]

It is on the one hand the context, therefore, that must be taken into account to broaden the relational theory of privacy, and on the other the specific function and form of private, intimate communication. In this way the theory becomes tenable, and elucidates an important aspect of informational privacy. The categorical difference between private and public contexts and relationships is only possible on the basis of the individual person's control over information about herself, which exists within a social fabric where the person's interaction partners always respect her informational privacy in so far as they are aware of the effects of such reflexive (self-)interpretation. The protection afforded by informational privacy is thus a double one: it is protection *of* relations (for their constitution) and *within* relations (for their inner structure). With the aid of two examples, I now wish to take the further step of showing the ways in which the structure of informational privacy and thus also the autonomy of a person can be disrupted or damaged. The first example concerns an aspect of the structure of friendships in general, the second concerns an aspect of the structure of intimate relations. Both cases have to do with deception regarding the 'knowledge' that people impart about themselves and that they can (or have to) assume in the other person involved. By highlighting the ways it may be infringed, such deceit may thus cast further light upon the function of informational privacy.

The social competence that is generally taken for granted in a person includes not wanting to know certain things about other people, or pretending not to know certain things, or keeping to oneself certain intimate knowledge about them. We protect the informational privacy of our friends by not gossiping about them (and we fail to respect it by gossiping about them). Idle chatter or gossip[80] is of course a very manifold phenomenon. In certain forms, indeed, gossip is actually expected or desired in social relations, even within friendships, and it is an important medium for the flow of information.[81] In order now to illustrate the exact connection between gossip and infractions of informational privacy, I should like to make a brief detour via Erving Goffman's concept of collusion, which clarifies the status and the structure of communication within friendships.

As we know, Goffman uses the term 'collusion' to designate a configuration of individuals where two or more persons deceive a third party about their relation to each other (and to her): 'A "collusive net" or "collusive alignment" is a coalition aimed at one kind of control – the third party's definition of the situation.'[82] In a collusive net, that is, there are colluders on the one hand and on the other the 'excolluded' person, whose definition of the situation is secretly managed by the colluders.[83] Benign or not so benign, collusions thus amount to conspiracies by two or more persons against a third. Benign, socially acceptable collusions are those that regulate what is best seen and understood as private and what as public in certain social contexts.[84] As such, says Goffman, they are doubtless a 'desirable part of social life'. This sort of collusion is a basic component of the customary rules of politeness and friendship, and 'egos are preserved by it and faces saved by it' everywhere.[85] Social relations also live off the shifting nature of the collusions that take place, 'round-robin collusion' as Goffman calls it,[86] which means simply that there are changes in the coalitions existing within social groups: the same thing is not always said to all concerned, nor do all concerned always know what all other people 'really' think about them. As social conventions, collusions to this extent also entail that one is expected to stick to these ways of dealing with the information one has about other people, such conventions serving the purpose of creating free spaces in which to behave. Indeed, keeping to such forms of reserve[87] can be viewed as an important social competence enabling a person to negotiate the relevant borderlines between public and private, borderlines that are subtly differentiated in social terms and in many contexts difficult to see clearly. As the free space for self-determined behaviour constituted by such conventions, the fabric of expectations, knowledge and autonomy described at the outset here manifests itself in the form of (benign) collusions.

People normally take it for granted that the 'definitions of the situation' that they have themselves are in principle shared by others (within the bounds of what can be expected). A correspondence between such definitions is just as essential to the self-description and self-perception of the individual as to his description and perception of others.[88] Goffman refers to them as 'virtual definitions'. They form the common background for the individual and the community, a background against which the individual interprets himself and makes assumptions about the interpretations of others, assuming a common definition of the 'immediate social scene',[89] that is the context in which this takes place. In this way, the nexus of self-interpretations, interpretations by others, assumptions about the interpretations by others, and the definition of the situation can be described as a complex structure of reciprocal implications: 'The individual stakes out a self, comments on his having done so, and comments on his commenting, even while the others are taking the whole process into consideration in coming to their assessment of him, which consideration he then takes into consideration in revising his view of himself.'[90] Because the individual defines himself (in part) in the context of these social relationships of friendship, the way he sees himself is also based upon this complicated structure of implications.

Along with these normal variants of collusion, however, there are also cases where infringements are involved. The process of reciprocal interpretation of self and other follows specific social rules that are essential both to a successful relationship to others and a successful self-relationship. *Infringements* of these rules have repercussions for the entire nexus of recursively linked interpretations. As Goffman puts it, such 'rules of conduct are fundamental to definitions of a self', and violations can produce pathologies in these definitions. In such non-benign collusions, persons are intentionally deceived about the definition of the situation, information is deliberately withheld from them, or information about them is deliberately passed on against their will (and without their knowledge). In this way, the individual concerned is *excolluded*. Excollusion here implies 'falseness knowingly used as a basis for action', for the aim is to deceive the excolluded individual about the relation existing between the other persons and thus about the relation of these persons to him. Indeed, the 'personal relationship that an excolluded individual feels he has in regard to each of the colluders would be undercut if he discovered that they have a collusive relationship to one another in regard to him'.[91] This deceit concerning the *relations* involved is accompanied by deceit concerning the true *description of the situation*, for the objective of collusion is to leave the excolluded individual in the dark about the situation in which he lives, to mislead him with a description of the situation that does not correspond to the truth, that is to keep private something that should actually be public, shared and accessible. And such deception ultimately also entails deception in the person's *self*-interpretation.

Non-benign forms of gossip and idle chatter, it now becomes clear, produce exactly the same phenomenon, the excollusion of a person through a violation of the rules that regulate the nexus of relations, i.e. through a violation of the rules that determine that everyone knows (approximately and in important respects) what everyone else knows (approximately and in important respects) about the other relevant persons in question, and that there is a common definition of the situation that is similar in significant respects among the various participants. A substantial discrepancy between the person's own assumptions and other people's assumptions[92] entails – and this is the violation – a disruption in the social fabric of expectations and knowledge that provides the basis for a person's self-definition, for the authenticity of her interpretations of herself and of others and of her own relation to others. Collusions among friends can in this way damage the autonomy of the excolluded individual involved. This is not simply because in relationships with friends as well as in general terms a person seeks to keep control of her self-presentation, but also – to go a step further – because in confronting these relationships the person creates herself, defines herself, and interprets herself in the light of their interpretations, and in precisely these respects she can thus be hurt by such collusions. This applies both to situations in which the person finds out about the deception and realizes in retrospect that her actions have only *seemingly* been self-determined, and to those in which she never finds out. In this case, the reason her life is not a self-determined, authentic one is that she is mistaken in key facets in her assessment of her own behaviour and the behaviour of specific other people. Even so, these collusions and the infractions they may result in must clearly be graded in their gravity. There are configurations that are dramatic and those that are less so, there are relations that are close and those that are less so, and the assumptions of the excolluded individual that are defrauded may be relevant or less so for the person concerned.

If we now link Goffman back to what was said about the intersubjective constitution of the self, the philosophical relevance of both the relational theory of privacy and Goffman's analyses can be illustrated from a different angle. The point is that in private relations and close friendships we depend upon sincere, authentic recognition from others because it is in our confrontation with these others that we first develop plans, establish priorities and in general reflect on what sort of person we want to be, what sort of life we want to lead, and in this way constantly refashion our self.[93] We interpret ourselves in the light of their reactions and interpretations, and to this extent rely upon the authenticity of their interpretations in order to be able to form (authentic) preferences and make (authentic) choices ourselves. This being the case, non-benign collusions can mean that a *supposedly autonomous* life is *in fact* not so, in the sense that the conditions under which conflicts are resolved, options and projects formed and chosen, and self-descriptions formulated are not in fact what they are assumed or taken to be. The disruption or damage done to friendships by non-benign gossip or idle chatter – and thus the disruption or damage done to *privacy* – is at the same time disruption or damage inflicted upon a person's chances of leading a life that is autonomous, a life that for her is rewarding, self-determined (and not determined by others), and her *own*.

In one final step, I now want to show how one person's knowledge about another can be violated not only within friendships but also in intimate contexts, with effects that bear directly upon fundamental conditions of her autonomy. In this way, I shall complete the spectrum of possible infringements of informational privacy ranging in terms of those involved from completely unspecified, distant others to one's fully specified nearest and dearest. At issue now is the 'smallest group', in other words the intimate relationship. In what follows, I should like to illustrate this manner of infringing a person's privacy and impairing her chances of living an autonomous life with the help of a literary example, Uwe Johnson's 'Sketch of a Casualty'.[94] This is intended to show what it can mean to a person to lead or have led her life under false assumptions – with false beliefs – regarding her relationship to another person.

'Sketch of a Casualty' is a tale about the writer Joe Hinterhand, who, after twenty years spent – he believed – happily married, discovers that his wife has been 'deceiving and cheating him from the beginning' with another man (and not just any other man),[95] and for this reason kills her. The story tells how Hinterhand emigrates to England and the United States, forced to do so by the Nazi regime in Germany, while the other man involved is a member of the (Italian) Fascist party. The marital deceit and emotional betrayal thus also transcend Hinterhand's personal relationship and turn into a betrayal of his convictions and his work. What is interesting about Johnson's tale from the point of view of the violation of privacy and the way this can damage a person's autonomy, however, are not necessarily the mere facts of deception and murder, so much as Johnson's description of how the protagonist Hinterhand comes to see his life as devalued, his feelings as inauthentic, and his actions as not his own, indeed how his whole life strikes him as 'failed'[96] because in the most private, most intimate of his relations he has been betrayed and a rift has opened, that is because the specific privacy or intimacy of the relationship has not been respected.

The story is narrated once the events have run their course from the perspective of Hinterhand, who, having been convicted of murdering his wife, is released from prison after seven years 'for conducting himself in the desired manner'. Now he not so much lives as 'survives' in New York, in a flat that friends let him use and that is described as 'chance pinned down', that is no longer something he has himself chosen or wished for but mere 'chance', albeit something that stays. His 'needs' are reduced to those 'from former times': he has no present ones, nothing but 'living out' the time that is left for him to live. Hinterhand has lost or relinquished any sense of a self-determined life, a desired life-project. He no longer has plans for old age, for example, plans of the sort he used to share with his wife ('When we're old, though, you a bit fatter and me more wrinkled, we'll live . . . '). All ideas of the future, growing old, making plans, have themselves become absurd and superfluous. This loss of autonomy and the damage to his identity finds especially powerful expression in his loss of language: talking now 'with a thick German accent', Hinterhand has completely lost 'the North American intonation', even his handwriting is 'destroyed' and his signature no longer legible. His language has become mechanical, now only functioning automatically, and the only thing he is suited for any more is translating, in which he is 'highly regarded [. . .], accurate, punctual'.[97] Just as language is constitutive of one's (past) life, it is also an expression of the way it has been devalued.[98]

Yet it is not just the time subsequent to Hinterhand's discovery of the deception that is felt to be non-autonomous and damaged in this way. It is his life as a whole, 'everything about his life in those twenty years', that becomes 'untrue': 'like photos, the stocks of his memory had been stamped with the words: Untrue. False. Poisoned. Devalued. Invalid.'[99] The same goes for his recollections of 'mornings by the sea, [. . .] waking up while swimming, [. . .] devalued, poisoned, lost'.[100] Hinterhand's sense that all his past experiences, his entire past life, are devalued and untrue comes not only from having led a different life from the one he believed he was leading but also from thus being (or having been) a different person from the one he believed he was. Language here becomes a symbol in a different sense, for strictly speaking Hinterhand is himself an author, or in his own terms a part-author in that his wife too plays an essential part in his writing: 'she provided him with reality.' This part-authorship of his written works thus comes to coincide with the part-authorship of his own and their shared life. With the deceit, however, 'the validity of words' is abolished, the validity of his writings, the validity of his life. The 'legend of the Hinterhands', their symbiotic relationship, finds its symbol in this shared, failed authorship.[101]

A feature that may seem exaggerated in the case of Uwe Johnson or Joe Hinterhand[102] nonetheless expresses a point that is philosophically convincing in its substance. This is that in an intimate relationship with another person an act of self-creation always takes place as well. One is *provided with reality* about oneself, with an interpretation through the other, and this becomes part of an authentic understanding of how one wants to live and the sort of person one sees oneself as. One describes oneself and interprets oneself in and through the confrontation with the other and the recognition they bestow. A person's relationship to herself and to her own decisions and actions may thus appear in a different light according to how she interprets the relationships within which she lives and how others interpret their relationship with her. The way in which she leads her life as an autonomous life therefore seems anything but independent of the interpretations that she fashions of herself in the light of (how she sees) her relationship towards others and that others fashion of her in the light of her behaviour towards them. And it is for this reason too that the concept of privacy here takes on significance in the first place. For it is to the precise extent that such relations are private that this form of confrontation and self-creation is possible and that one trusts the authenticity of the standpoint involved. Only thus does one divulge such information about oneself, making oneself vulnerable as a whole person. A deception of the sort that comes Joe Hinterhand's way must be described as an infringement of informational privacy, because the structure of privacy is regulated through this fabric of knowledge, expectations and self-disclosure, because in this way even in the most intimate of contexts the shared description of the situation is regulated and guaranteed, and because when this is violated the autonomy of the person deceived is damaged too. Of course, even in these intimate contexts one can insist on the 'right to secrecy', again appealing to one's own autonomy. But beyond the limit of what can be expected, secrecy turns into deception, the sort of deception that may end up leading to a non-autonomous and failed life.[103]

I have tried to show that certain *external* conditions of authenticity are to an extent also intrinsic to a self-determined, authentic life.[104] It is these conditions that are at issue here, for a person's decisions about who she wants to be and how she wants to live may come to grief – and with them her life itself – if she is mistaken in her beliefs about who (intimate) others are, deluded in her assessment of the way they behave towards her.[105] Joe Hinterhand, as Johnson makes clear, has for twenty years lived his life under false conditions, and this is why it is untrue, false, poisoned, devalued and invalid. It also explains why it makes no sense to object that all this would not have applied if he had never found out about the deception. Of course, from his own, inner perspective this would indeed have made a crucial difference. Yet this sort of objection betrays a misunderstanding of what the concept of autonomy – and *a fortiori* the idea of a good or rewarding life – actually means. The fact is that in order to be able to see themselves as autonomous, people reject – indeed must reject – such deceptions in the fundamental matters of their lives.[106] Once again it is the derivative case, in which the person finds out about the infringement of her informational privacy, that throws light on what is termed the paradigmatic case, for it is the derivative case that first clarifies what is actually felt to be the infringement. A person's autonomy can be damaged, therefore, if she makes her decisions *only seemingly* in the light of the correct data, assumptions and opinions, that is if she in general leads and plans her life under conditions and in a manner that she has *only seemingly* chosen herself.

4 Expectations, knowledge, autonomy

> That all relations between human beings are based on the knowledge that one person has of the other – this is such a banally self-evident fact that it is not easy to think of the not at all self-evident nuances and calibrations of this knowledge and to what extent, as cause and as effect, they characterize what is special about each relationship.[107]

The 'banally self-evident fact' to which Simmel here refers forms the leitmotif, so to speak, that implicitly runs through the above reflections. The way in which the 'calibrations' of such knowledge, 'as cause and as effect', characterize each relationship in its own particular way is an equally central theme. Essentially, the question of informational privacy has to do with who knows what about a person and how they know it, that is it has to do with control of the information that concerns her. In explicating the connection between knowledge and relationships, the question was thus also how deceit about such 'calibrations' results in violations of informational privacy. Simmel is fully aware here that assumptions about this knowledge shape or 'characterize' all of a person's relationships, to specified others and to unspecified others alike. To the extent that the person, in her autonomy, relies upon her expectations about these 'calibrations' not being defrauded, however, they constitute external conditions, as it were, for her autonomy and authenticity. Only on the basis of the (fragile) stability of her fabric of expectations, knowledge, assumptions and selective self-disclosure is it possible for a person to exercise control over her self-presentation and thus, in a broader sense, to enjoy the possibility of a self-determined life.

This of course also means that a person can always insist on not imparting any 'knowledge' about herself, withdrawing entirely into a realm of informational privacy in all her relations. This brings me to my final point on informational privacy. In answer to the question posed in section 2 above concerning which 'data' we should be able to count as worthy of protection, the first set we distinguished comprised the mental states, thoughts and feelings of a person. Not only should what a person divulges not find its way into the wrong contexts, but what she never wants to divulge in the first place should remain precisely what it is – a private matter. The seclusion or secrecy into which she can here withdraw represents a limit to any social relationship in which she finds herself, for in all such relationships she is entitled to informational privacy of this order, and this ultimate control over her self-presentation constitutes the condition for her autonomy. This is on the one hand because the subjective chaos of thoughts, feelings, images, self-definitions and self-interpretations is constitutive in determining what discloses itself as essential to the person's life and how it does so. On the other hand it is because the question of what elements from this subjective chaos enter into the public, shared realm and how they do so bears directly upon her self-presentation in her various relationships and various contexts. This may lead to conflicts, not only of the sort that have just been described (in the previous section, viewed from the opposite point of view), in which a person lays claim to such privacy in the form of a concealment, but also the sort in which a person's silence in general results in differences or dissonances between her public self-presentation and her private thoughts and feelings, thus engendering problems of personal identity.[108]

Just how problematic these conflicts are, and how strong the particular claims to informational privacy must be considered, are a matter of the person's moral judgement. If there is a clash between different claims to privacy as claims to autonomy, one claim cannot simply prevail over the other, but the conflict is a moral one, and this can only be resolved as an individual case. Once again, moreover, it emerges that privacy is characterized by the inextricability of ethical and moral perspectives and problems. It is impossible to make a precise separation of the two factors here for the simple reason that ethical self-realization, itself conflictive, must take place within various moral contexts that are at times themselves in conflict, and it cannot genuinely be abstracted from these.

With these reflections, we can leave the realm of informational privacy and turn to the third dimension, which is local privacy. In one sense, this dimension can be conceived as a subcategory of informational privacy. Indeed, one of the main reasons people value (and need) a private home is that they do not want to be observed and that here of all places they seek to keep control of information. Yet we shall see that the case of local privacy and one's private life at home has its own functions, problems and lines of conflict that must be understood and interpreted using different categories from the protection of information.

6 Local Privacy: The Private Home

1 The refuge of privacy

The theme of local privacy brings us now to the dimension of privacy's meaning that continues to be considered the classic, traditional one, even if it is open to dispute whether this meaning of 'privacy' really does span all cultures and historical periods.[1] Yet in modern liberal societies this is where what is regarded as one's true private life is localized. At issue here, that is, is the privacy of the household, of one's flat or room, and thus the privacy of personal objects, which also form an inherent part of the privacy of these spaces. The sober term 'local privacy' thus diminishes the richness of what it designates, for the privacy of domestic life refers to more than just a simple spatial realm. In modern societies it denotes a realm of life and a way of life that is bound up with this realm and is intrinsically indebted to the existence of private spaces, however varied the concrete form this might take. In protected spaces we live – we are able to live – differently, doing different things, from when we are exposed to the gaze of anyone who happens to be looking (or are out in the open). Private life in private spaces follows different rules from life outside these spaces, and these different rules are what permit and promote a different relationship to oneself and a different relationship – different behaviour – towards others. We associate existential experiences with our private, domestic life, and even if (at least in this country) it is rare for life to begin and end at home any more, it continues to be our home to which we attribute the function of fundamentally protecting and fostering our life, our identity.[2] This, incidentally, in itself says nothing about the question of private *property*. A claim to the protection of private spaces on conventional or moral grounds by no means necessarily entails a claim of ownership. The question of private property is a question of the general distribution of property in a society. The protection of and the respect for the privacy of spaces is not contingent upon the ownership of these spaces, but only upon the ability to use them.[3]

The term 'local privacy', therefore, does indeed refer to an area, and the diversity of private life finds expression not only in the opportunity it presents for different modes of conduct towards oneself and (intimate) others, but also in the spatial arrangement itself. Spaces become private, that is, not only through the control I have over who can enter them and when, but also because I am able to arrange them in my own way, the objects within these spaces are ordered in a certain manner, and these objects are themselves specific ones: that is, the arrangement of the interior constitutes a meaning which is my very own, a private meaning.

Conceiving house and home as *private*, therefore, and everything and everyone not belonging to this realm as *public*, one theme that requires treatment is the way people live together in this place, that is the protection that a private place provides for relationships, for families. What then emerges is that in spite of the long tradition of this separation and the institution of private relationships and the family, the modifications characteristic of our present-day understanding of the term can be traced on the one hand to the emergence of liberalism and on the other hand to the emergence of the bourgeois family in the nineteenth century (at the latest). Liberalism gave rise to the idea of the equality of all (individual) human beings, while the bourgeois ethos gave rise to the family in the form in which we still know it today, at least as a normative ideal. And the two of them together gave rise to conflicts that are symptomatic of liberal democracies today.[4]

In looking at these conflicts, therefore, I am returning to tie up some of the loose ends that were left untied in chapter 2. There we saw that it is normatively inappropriate and under liberal premises unfeasible to adopt the traditional and conventional distinction between a private realm to which women are consigned and a public sphere belonging to men. We saw that this very distinction must be described and grounded in new terms if it is to carry conviction as a norm for a liberal perspective based on a belief in the equal worth of freedom for all members of liberal democracies. This chapter will also be concerned with this issue, that is with the question of how the functions, duties, activities and ways of life traditionally assigned to the realm of domestic privacy can be described and defined in such a way that one gender (and the other for that matter) is not from the outset tied down to certain roles, tasks and options in life. Expressed in different terms, the problem that is interesting from a normative standpoint is how to conceptualize privacy in a way that can do justice on the one hand to our relations based on care and love and on the other hand to the modern, liberal and post-traditional recognition of substantially equal rights to freedom and the proposal of a life of autonomy of equal value for all.

Yet private spaces are valued not only as a place for (family) relationships, but also as a place for solitude. At this point, the 'onion' model discussed in chapter 1, with its various layers of privacy, becomes relevant once more, for one may lay claim to privacy with respect to others even within spaces or relationships that already count as private, as when one asserts a right to privacy with respect to other people with whom one lives together privately.[5] Yet why should it matter to a person to have such a room to herself? In the following I shall try to show that without such an opportunity for being alone central aspects of what is to be understood by autonomy and an autonomous life are lost or at least *may* be lost,[6] that is possibilities for what I shall term 'self-invention' and 'self-presentation'. In the process, I shall be returning to themes that have already been discussed in the chapters on decisional and informational privacy, where it was shown that one of the essential conditions for freedom in liberal societies consists in being able to exercise control with regard both to the fundamental decisions in one's life and the information that others may have or are supposed to have about oneself. It will emerge below that the protection of private spaces is necessary for both these aspects, that is for protection from the interference of administrative regulations, and protection from the eyes of others in society. This is a point argued by Virginia Woolf,[7] who maintained that certain forms of a life of autonomy depend upon the right to have 'a room of one's own'.

The fact that in modern, liberal societies private spaces have to be protected and respected is one of the self-evident presuppositions in such societies. The aim of the following account, however, is to ask the more fundamental question of *why* this is the case, *why* we want and value private spaces in this way. It is also to enquire into the normative difficulties that are typically bound up with such a claim to privacy in liberal societies. In order to shed light on these problems, the first task (in section 2) is to look more closely into the nature of the connection between identity, autonomy and the protection of a 'room of one's own', and at why the possibility of being alone must be conceived as constitutive for the possibility of individual autonomy. Only in the following section 3 will the focus shift to look at how the protection of privacy may generate conflicts within intimate, family relationships, conflicts that are genuinely bound up with the normative assumptions of liberal democratic societies, and at how such conflicts can best be understood and resolved.

2 A room of one's own: self-invention, self-presentation and autonomy

When we say 'this is my room', we mean by this not only that we can determine who is and is not allowed to enter it and when. We also mean that in it we can do or not do just what we want, unobserved, undisturbed. And we mean that this room, just as it is, is mine, made for me, for my needs, my requirements, my habits, my history, my predilections and my interests. Accordingly, the terms 'privacy' and 'private room' refer to more than just the room. It is also the objects *within* the room that are private (and this need not only be one's diary), their presence within a private space giving them a private significance that must be respected and that can be violated by strangers in a very specific way. The objects in my home, in other words, acquire a symbolic component as an element of my own – private – identity, and they do so in part on account of the irreplaceability of the significance they have for me. This can be illustrated even by a child's bedroom, with its correspondence between the arrangement of the room and the needs and preferences of the child, between the child's body and the space of the room, that is the way the objects themselves and their layout are geared towards the size and the habits of the particular inhabitant.[8] This applies all the more in the case of adults, who express – or at least *can* express – their own individual life-story and their own particular identity through the arrangement of the room and the sort of objects that are in it. At this point, one only need recall Emmanuel Levinas's phenomenological analyses of 'the dwelling' and 'habitation', which show the way people may identify with their surroundings and consider them a significant part of themselves.[9] And it is precisely this quality of personal spaces to which Martin Heidegger attributes the character of 'inconspicuous familiarity'.[10] It is thus perfectly reasonable for the German Federal Constitutional Court to say, with respect to Article 13 of the German Constitution, that an intrusion upon the inviolacy of the dwelling regularly constitutes 'a serious intrusion upon the personal realm of the person concerned'. The 'protection of living spaces in the narrower sense of the term by constitutional law is thus in keeping with the fundamental precept of unconditional respect for the private sphere of the citizen [. . .] and is closely connected with the protection of the development of personality'.[11]

This is clearly a basic aspect of the normative grounds for protecting private spaces. At issue is a person's ability to make her home within a meaningful setting. Yet such protection means more than this. It guarantees the conditions for a person to test out ways of behaviour towards herself that can be understood as attempts at self-definition.[12] It is a matter of having the peace, so to speak, to develop one's relationship to oneself, being able to ask oneself on one's own account the practical question of how to lead one's life, having the chance to be alone, if necessary, to reflect on who one is and who one wants to be, independent of the judgement – whether positive or negative – of other people. For this reason too it can be said that central aspects of what we analysed and discussed above under the headings of decisional and informational privacy are reliant upon privacy of space. Specific aspects of what makes authentic behaviour and thus autonomy possible also relate to the protection of spaces.

We can here, however, pick out two distinct *aspects* of what is expressed by the idea of having the 'peace to develop one's relationship to oneself'. The first aspect can be termed 'self-presentation'. This refers to the different roles that people always seek to play in their different relationships and communications, the different ways in which they present a self. By the same token, it must be assumed that there are possibilities for being alone where this sort of self-presentation is unnecessary, indeed where the roles for such forms of self-presentation can be rehearsed, as it were. This does not in itself entail, however, that a person is only being authentic when she is not playing any sort of role in relation to others. The second aspect, 'self-invention', refers to the fact that processes of self-description, self-definition, self-discovery or indeed self-invention[13] – as processes of finding out how one would like to live and what sort of person one would like to see oneself as – are dependent upon a person bringing herself face to face with herself in conditions in which she can really be sure that she is protected from the eyes of anyone else. I shall now look more closely at these two aspects in turn, starting with self-invention.

What is lost when private spaces are no longer available to people? What is lost when the very idea of privacy is lost? The literary *locus classicus* for this sort of question and reflection continues to be George Orwell's *1984*.[14] With unsurpassable clarity, the novel portrays how a lack of privacy entails a lack of control over one's own life, a lack of autonomy. And with unsurpassable clarity, it thereby brings to light what it means for liberal-democratic societies to protect private space and private life. From the very outset, Orwell makes it plain that an intrinsic mark of totalitarian states is that they do not grant or permit any realms, spheres or dimensions of privacy, instead ensuring the total surveillance of the individual. No activity, no thought may remain uncontrolled, let alone, of course, the corner of a room. Accordingly, it signifies both liberation and opposition when Winston finds he has a tiny corner in his flat to himself, a corner into which the cameras of Big Brother are unable to reach and in which no one can observe or monitor him.[15] The opening sequence of *1984* deals not only with this 'unusual geography of the room',[16] but as it were 'privatizes' the scene even further, for in an out-of-the-way junk-shop – the upper floor of which will later provide him with the supposedly private hiding place for his supposedly clandestine life with Julia – Winston has found a diary, one with 'smooth creamy paper' and 'of a kind that had not been manufactured for at least forty years past'.[17] The corner of Winston's room that is out of range of observation and the chance to write his own diary represent two equally symbolic themes from the very outset of the novel, allowing Orwell to shed light on the internal structure of liberal societies. The issue here is not metaphysics, that is not freedom and truth and justice, but the *interior* that is necessary for these values and without which neither truth, freedom nor justice seem to be thinkable, feasible or liveable. Winston sits down in his corner and after long hesitation begins writing:

> Suddenly he began writing in sheer panic, only imperfectly aware of what he was setting down. His small but childish handwriting straggled up and down the page, shedding first its capital letters and finally even its full stops:
>
> *April 4th, 1984. Last night to the flicks. All war films. One very good one of a ship full of refugees being bombed somewhere in the Mediterranean. Audience much amused by shots of a great huge fat man trying to swim away with a helicopter after him, first you saw him wallowing along in the water like a porpoise, then you saw him through*

> *the helicopter gunsights, then he was full of holes and the sea round him turned pink and he sank as suddenly as though the holes had let in the water. audience shouting with laughter when he sank. then you saw a lifeboat full of children with a helicopter hovering over it. there was a middle-aged woman might have been a jewess sitting up in the bow with a little boy about three years old in her arms. little boy screaming with fright and hiding his head between her breasts as if he was trying to burrow right into her and the woman putting her arms round him and comforting him although she was blue with fright herself, all the time covering him up as much as possible as if she thought her arms could keep the bullets off him. then the helicopter planted a 20 kilo bomb in among them terrific flash and the boat went all to matchwood. then there was a wonderful shot of a child's arm going up up up right up into the air a helicopter with a camera in its nose must have followed it up and there was a lot of applause from the party seats but a woman down in the prole part of the house suddenly started kicking up a fuss and shouting they didnt oughter of showed it not in front of kids they didnt it aint right not in front of kids it aint until the police turned her turned her out i dont suppose anything happened to her nobody cares what the proles say typical prole reaction they never –*
>
> Winston stopped writing, partly because he was suffering from cramp. He did not know what had made him pour out this stream of rubbish. But the curious thing was that while he was doing so a totally different memory had clarified itself in his mind, to the point where he almost felt equal to writing it down. It was, he now realized, because of this other incident that he had suddenly decided to come home and begin the diary to-day.[18]

Winston writes *without feeling anyone's eyes upon him*, as though he were not being observed or controlled, not even by himself. And this is what makes the gruesome description possible, this almost unbearably dense, uninhibited flow of thoughts that nonetheless leads him exactly where he wants to be led – to the 'other incident', to his memory of the scene with O'Brien, their fleeting but decisive exchange of glances. Only thus does Winston succeed in describing what is important to him and *who he wants to be* – that is only by means of the sort of concentration, the sort of focused attention and brutal disinhibition that are conditional upon him having a space of his own, a space in which he is alone by himself and with no consideration for other people and their perspective. This opportunity to retreat in order to be able to discover/invent himself in a process of self-confrontation manifests itself in the momentum of his writing, which – more and more confused and staccato in style – brings Winston to the point he wants to reach, the memory he seeks to recall. In the singularly private activity of writing a diary, Orwell gives concrete form to Winston's process of finding himself as a process of finding what is essential to *him*, the way *he* wants to see himself, the things that give shape to life *for him*. In this way, privacy becomes a condition for self-definition and self-invention.[19]

Only in one more, decisive passage is there any further mention of Winston's diary. This occurs during his interrogation at the hands of O'Brien, who seeks to bring Winston to acknowledge that 'two plus two' can sometimes also make 'five'. O'Brien's point is that it is impossible to see reality other than through the eyes of the Party, to conceive truth in other terms than those laid down by the Party:

> 'That is the fact that you have got to relearn, Winston. It needs an act of self-destruction, an effort of the will. You must humble yourself before you can become sane.'
>
> He paused for a few moments, as though to allow what he had been saying to sink in.
>
> 'Do you remember', he went on, 'writing in your diary, "Freedom is the freedom to say that two plus two make four"?'[20]

Self-destruction is called for, because Winston has made the attempt to determine himself, to invent himself. His attempt began in the only way imaginable, with the diary, and for this reason O'Brien must now bring up Winston's diary as a way of making it clear just what is actually meant by self-destruction. Self-surrender, as O'Brien knows, is the diametrical opposite of self-invention, which is what Winston at least tried out when he started writing the diary. The totalitarian state is totalitarian not only to the extent that it prevents private spaces, but also in that it no longer even permits the privacy of thought: 'newspeak' is the attempt to control what can be spoken and thought in such a way that it is simply no longer possible to think certain thoughts or say certain sentences. The totality of the totalitarian state is absolute when privacy is no longer thinkable even in its most hidden corners, the heads of human beings. The protection of a person's dwelling in liberal societies is so fundamental and is laden with such symbolic significance because it symbolizes just this retreat from any form of control. Winston's diary can be viewed as an even more compact paradigm for this retreat, an expression of the striving for undisturbed privacy in the name of one's autonomy, which has its origins in a critical relationship to oneself, in self-discovery and self-assessment.[21]

Such scope for privacy is clearly also necessary *within* relationships. The need to withdraw may exist in relation to any other person, even intimate others, and its normative legitimacy obtains not only with respect to anonymous third parties. Fried makes this point when he writes: '[T]he most complete form of privacy is perhaps also the most basic, since it is necessary not only to our freedom to define our relations with others but also to our freedom to define ourselves.'[22] This freedom to define oneself, above all in the secluded intimacy of wholly uncontrolled thought, is exemplified by the first entry in Winston's diary.

This brings us to the other perspective on the need for people to be on their own, that is the second aspect of the function of local privacy in relation to individual autonomy. This is the aspect of *self-presentation*, which has to do with the need to take a break from role-playing, and the opportunity for 'making fools of ourselves'.[23] If one of the defining characteristics of social space is that various roles have to be played and various expectations fulfilled within it, private space by contrast proves to be what makes this public self-presentation possible, a space in which we can 'set aside the arms'[24] with which we have to defend ourselves in our various social relationships, in which we can relax and 'take our ease' in order to have self-control in the other, public realm. Even the way people dress shows naturally how they always seek to present themselves in a certain manner and in some contexts indeed have to do so. The awareness of having an effect on others and the fear of what this effect may be are among the constant and basic aspects of human self-perception.[25]

However, such an awareness, required by sociality, demands that there be realms in which this effort can be waived, and voice or expression given to aspects of one's personal, intimate life that – on the basis of their public self-presentation – people want to come to terms with by themselves.[26] The sociological analysis of this normative construction is provided by Erving Goffman. In his analysis of the 'presentation of self in everyday life',[27] he draws the well-known distinction between the 'front region' and the 'back region' or 'backstage': whereas on the stage itself particular forms of behaviour, particular performances, are intentionally and consciously acted out or put on, behind the scenes – in the private spaces – roles are rehearsed, invented, practised, rewritten, and put to one side for a break.

> A back region or backstage may be defined as a place, relative to a given performance, where the impression fostered by the performance is knowingly contradicted as a matter of course. There are, of course, many characteristic functions of such places. It is here that the capacity of a performance to express something beyond itself may be painstakingly fabricated; it is here that illusions and impressions are openly constructed. [. . .] Here the performer can relax; he can drop his front, forgo speaking his lines, and step out of character.[28]

Goffman does not, however, equate his distinction between the front and back regions with the distinction between public and private, presumably because for him privacy is synonymous with the private sphere in the form of the natural realm of the household, and he plausibly seeks to apply his distinction *within* this domestic sphere as well. Goffman is in this sense guided by the 'natural' interpretation of the distinction between public and private domains – on the one hand house and home, on the other hand anonymous others – and does not conceive the interrelation between the two as multidimensional, as I am here attempting to do. Yet Goffman's distinction can be correlated without difficulty with the separation between private and public, and to great explanatory effect at that, by employing (as I do) a concept of privacy that allows of diverse dimensions and thus permits the differentiation of various perspectives and realms *within* the sphere of domestic privacy itself. It then becomes clear how private spaces are relevant for Goffman's front region and the self-presentation that is necessary within it.

Goffman's distinction between the front region and backstage does not, however, entail any fundamental division between authentic and inauthentic behaviour. Indeed, it is perfectly feasible for a person to be acting or presenting herself more genuinely in one of her roles, so to speak, than when she is taking a break from them. Nor does such a systematic distinction simultaneously imply that in order to be able to tie all one's roles together within a *single* identity, something akin to a 'meta-role' is necessary, this 'meta-role' then also coinciding with the private, authentic one. What is implied is simply that in order to be able to act autonomously in the various roles that are socially and emotionally required of people, it is necessary for them to have the possibility of withdrawal – or perhaps a variety of 'withdrawals' – from these roles, in other words withdrawal from their presentations-for-others. In order to be able to be oneself in all one's roles, a region seems to be necessary, as Goffman shows, in which one can, as it were, effortlessly present oneself for oneself alone.

Of course, this idea of self-presentation further has not only a mental, but also a thoroughly physical side to it. It is also for the intimacy of our body that we need or seek to claim our own space, a controlled domain, a possibility for withdrawal, not just for the sake of being-alone-for-ourselves with our own thoughts.[29] Part of the reason that people time and again need a room or area of retreat all to themselves or at least wish to be unobserved is that they seek bodily seclusion. The role played by the body and its public presentation in this context has a substantial symbolic component, and is regulated by convention and coded in gender-specific terms.[30] That such a normative separation of realms may bring to the fore feelings such as shame is a point that has been made on many an occasion and in a great variety of ways.[31] Yet what also emerges is that the banishment of intimate corporeality to the realm of privacy may be evaluated not only negatively (as a banishment) but also positively to the extent that such a separation of one's private and one's public image can equally be understood as making individual self-determination possible. Self-presentation has a crucial bodily dimension in that people want to conceal their own body from the eyes of others and themselves control the presentation of their corporeality. This is not contradicted by the fact that the intimate, naked body belongs to the realm of conventionally *prescribed* privacy, which at first sight has nothing to do with the idea of autonomy or control given that the body is banished by convention, not hidden by choice. Indeed, prescribed privacy may perfectly well correlate with a person's desires to control her self-presentation. Over and above this, it protects the other side, so to speak, for one of the tasks of prescribed privacy is to protect public space – and thus also the (decisional) privacy of the other people involved – from an unnecessary excess of intimate, private details. Just how to interpret this 'unnecessary' is of course a question of culture, is coded in gender-specific terms and is possibly also a matter of the progress of civilization.[32]

I should now like to provide a further illustration of the way in which being looked at by others may threaten or infringe not only my privacy but also my autonomy. I shall do so with the help of Jean-Paul Sartre's reflections on the phenomenon of 'the look' (*le regard*) in *Being and Nothingness*, for reading these reflections against Sartre himself, they can be taken as an argument in favour of the possibility of withdrawing into privacy.[33] The look of the other, writes Sartre, 'represents an irreducible fact', yet at the same time it always pins us down and objectifies us. I grasp 'the Other's look' as the 'solidification and alienation of my own possibilities', forcing me into a very specific interpretation of my actions and modes of behaviour: 'Thus I, who in so far as I am my possibles, am what I am not and am not what I am – behold now I *am* somebody!'[34] Sartre's idea is that intersubjective relations are always at least partly determined by the way the presence of the Other in the look he directs at me deprives me very specifically of the possibility of creating myself in a self-determined manner, of interpreting and understanding myself independently. It is an idea that of course gains particular interest in the context of an enquiry into the normative grounds for protecting the private sphere, for just as I experience the Other's look as the 'death of my possibilities' and with it 'a subtle alienation of all my possibilities',[35] so it may conversely be posited that we could behave towards ourselves without such restrictions if we were protected from the look of Others.[36] 'With the Other's look', writes Sartre, 'the "situation" escapes me. To use an everyday expression which better expresses our thought, *I am no longer master of the situation*.'[37] Yet this is precisely what I want to be when I seek to bring myself face to face with myself, that is to behave reflectively towards myself in opposition to or at least independently of the judgement of others. This may either be in situations that have a fundamental bearing upon an outlook on life or a life-project, or where (as Sartre's analyses show) the opposition to the look of the Other has its origins more in the maintenance of a particular reputation or self-presentation.

Even concurring with the criticism that Sartre's conception of intersubjectivity is in general – and in particular in the chapter on 'the look' – false and misleading in its failure to account for the factor of recognition by the other that is essential to the subject,[38] it is still possible to acknowledge the element of truth in Sartre's theory, which resides in his recognition that intersubjective relations with the other always entail a restriction or exclusion of possibilities in one's behaviour towards oneself and one's self-interpretation. The flip side of the possibilities opened up in and through the look of the other and the constitution of subjectivity and individuality through one's relation to the other is that such a 'look' always pins one down, restricts or limits one, and is an invitation to correction. Yet Sartre's observations further elucidate another point, for the right to be 'private for oneself' goes beyond a right to *freedom* as a negative right. The look of the Other, even though it does not restrict me in my actual liberty (for it is only a look, after all, nothing more), may nonetheless limit me in my autonomy, in my striving to act in a way that is autonomous and authentic.[39]

Morally grounded claims to privacy go beyond morally grounded claims to liberty.

In private, therefore, subjects have possibilities for withdrawal that are necessary for *substantializing* the freedom guaranteed by liberalism but exist on the basis not of claims to freedom but claims to privacy. Assuming that civil liberties guarantee the freedom to do or not to do what one wants (within the bounds of liberal democracy), the appeal to the protection of one's privacy is necessary because before the eyes of others we may be 'free from' (that is exempt from actual restrictions), but nevertheless not possess the 'freedom to', in other words we may not be at liberty to do the things, to behave, in the way in which we wish to as autonomous subjects, and to enjoy the (symbolic) spaces necessary for us to be able to create ourselves accordingly.[40] The intrinsic connection between the availability of a protected, private *place* (or if need be its functional equivalent) and successful autonomy might be characterized, therefore, in terms of the fact that reliable private spaces are valued because they permit one to discover or invent a self without consideration for the standpoints or interests of others, to develop a relationship to oneself free from restrictions. To be able to escape from the view of others is clearly crucial to the success of autonomy. If a subject has the opportunity to be alone, by himself and unmolested by others, whenever he wants to, this is surely a decisive help when it comes to putting into practice successful forms of self-determination and working out what one thinks and wants, how one wishes to be and to live.[41]

This brings us back – not only implicitly, as up to now, but also explicitly so – to the various aspects of autonomy described in chapter 3. The forms of testing and discovering/inventing who one wants to be and what effect one wants to have are expressions or articulations of the processes of reflection upon one's desires and goals, questioning which of one's desires or actions are authentic and which self-descriptions and self-definitions are best suited to oneself.[42] Self-determination of this sort – asking oneself the 'practical question' – also, of course, takes place in a person's confrontation with 'significant others'. Why this is so and what function this has was seen in the last chapter. We have now, therefore, taken up the opposite perspective on the practical question as the search for one's self, and it is only the two perspectives together – the confrontation with others and the confrontation with oneself – that can produce a complete picture. If one does not wish to make the claim that the process of autonomy *is subsumed entirely* within one's confrontation with others and the recognition they bestow upon one, and thus also within one's responsibility towards others, then one must show that without possibilities for retreating into individual privacy this process of autonomy, that is the autonomous development of one's practical identity, is at the very least made considerably more difficult. Precisely because the presence of the other can always mean both things, constituting and at the same time pinning one down to certain possibilities, the protection of privacy is necessary in like measure for the autonomy of the *person-as-an-individual* and for the autonomy of the *person-in-relations*.[43] The insistence on the value of privacy for the solitary person is thus neither a solipsistic move nor inconsistent with the arguments put forth in the last chapter.

I should now like briefly to raise an objection to this conception of local privacy and autonomy.[44] This is that although a normative conception of local privacy is in principle meaningful and necessary, the idea that we need and value private spaces for our autonomy to be successful is too strong, both in normative and in empirical terms. In empirical terms, runs the objection, it can be shown that the character of rooms and their interior decor, as well of course as the use to which they are put, have in many respects changed decisively over the last few decades under the influence of the developments in the electronic media.[45] In most rooms it is no longer one's diary that is written, but the internet that is surfed or television watched, yet this has nothing to do with testing, learning or practising individual autonomy, for such activities, which are completely alienated, embody the exact opposite. At present, the much publicized culmination of this development are the people known as *webcammers*, who allow themselves to be filmed all day and all night in their home or in one of their rooms by video cameras that transmit the images directly on to the internet, of their own accord denying themselves or depriving themselves of the possibility of private spaces to withdraw into.[46] Even so, it cannot be claimed that such people are for this reason any less autonomous or lead their life any less autonomously. All these *empirical* developments, continues the argument, show simply that the *normative* coupling of local privacy and autonomy is too strong: people need such privacy simply in order to be alone, to do as they please – it is merely an aspect of individual freedom, without this being of special relevance to the testing out of *autonomy*.

This objection is certainly right in many respects. It is undeniable that the electronic media are exerting upon the perception of space and the use of private space an influence that is difficult to gauge in its scope. Yet this does not in itself clarify what such developments actually mean for the significance of privacy.[47] The first thing to be realized is that the phenomena of permanent television (to exaggerate a little) and so-called webcamming represent problems of the same sort and lie, as it were, at different points on the same scale, at least for the approach I am adopting. This scale measures the degree to which people duly appreciate and make good use of their privacy.[48] For a great variety of reasons, it is not especially attractive to spend a large part of one's life in front of the television or computer. Yet this aspect of a general theory of alienation and cultural critique is not my point here. My concern is more limited in scope, focusing on the objection that not only in empirical terms is private space not actually used for the sake of successful autonomy, but that even in normative terms this is an excessive requirement.[49] To counter this objection, I want to return to the reflections on the concept of autonomy from the last chapter. There we saw that the idea of autonomy is essential to a description of the core of individual freedom; that an autonomous life is one where the person asks herself the practical question concerning how she wants to live and what sort of person she wants to see herself as; and that this involves, among other things, reflection upon one's own desires and goals, upon one's own past, and upon previous and possible new self-definitions. If all this is so, then a person's solitary self-confrontation – the sort of confrontation that can be imagined taking place in the seclusion of a private room, a confrontation with her own history and with desires or self-images that may be in conflict, her deliberation upon *what* she wants and what her goals are, upon whether she does indeed want *anything*, whether she actually has goals – is certainly a precondition for autonomy to succeed. This does not mean that a person has to be ceaselessly reflecting upon herself in her private room in order to be autonomous. There are of course countless other things one does in private rooms that make one value such privacy. What it does mean, however, is that it typically forms part of one's self-understanding to seek the refuge of privacy for the sake of this confrontation with oneself. What form this confrontation actually takes is clearly a different matter: it does not have to be diary-writing. Yet what can be said, at least, is that activities that prevent such confrontation – to the extent that they are *intended to prevent* it, as may be the case with computer games and television – are inadequate in this sense and produce effects of self-alienation.[50]

This is not in itself sufficient for a cultural critique of the media and the way they are used. But it is sufficient to make it clear that when web-cammers, for example, deprive themselves of the opportunity to be alone by themselves, they are in the process also depriving themselves of these strategies for autonomy. On the other hand, it should be emphasized once more that changes in the perception of private realms by no means entail as such that people lose all sense of privacy. Even webcammers for the most part seem to attach importance to keeping certain places in their homes where they can be alone and no one can see them. And even webcammers seem to revel above all in being able to 'produce' or 'present' themselves in front of the cameras, and themselves having control over when the cameras are turned on and off.[51] Autonomy is a 'gradual' concept, and not one that can be operationalized. To this extent, certain standards can be specified, as I have tried to do, standards to which people typically conform if they legitimately describe themselves as autonomous. But this is all.[52]

3 Privacy and the family: love and justice

Up until now, our perspective upon the privacy of place has been exclusively the perspective of the individual person on her own. It has emerged that, regardless of whether people live in family relationships and what sort they live in, they need and value the possibility of privacy because it seems indispensable for the success of individual autonomy. In what follows, the aim is now to adopt the other perspective on local privacy, the perspective of persons in relations. The question now is what are the normative reasons that we value the privacy of spaces in the context of the possibility and realization of intimate relations. And what are the specific problems that arise here for the concept of privacy? What are the specific conflicts with which one is faced? We have already seen in the chapter on informational privacy why we need and value privacy for the possibility of intimate relations in general: only in privacy can feelings be given expression without protection, can intimacy, sexuality, and bodily and emotional self-abandon be lived out; only with the protection of privacy can persons make themselves vulnerable in their entirety. It is where people are at their most exposed in what they feel and express that they are most dependent upon the protection of privacy.

If we now ask more specifically why a secluded physical space is considered intrinsic to this sort of intimate or family relationship, what comes to light is that it is only in spaces, rooms, flats or houses that we are able to live relations as a *way of life*, relations in the sense of the joint organization of daily life, relations in the sense of a spatial institution. Family relations are traditionally and classically considered to embody these relationships, and it is the family that has been and still is the locus of privacy. Accordingly, it is the institution of the family that I intend to discuss once more in what follows.[53] In a quite pre-theoretical sense, the difference between private and public is owed in large measure to a social structure composed of families on the one hand and public life on the other, and since the nineteenth century at least the institution of the family has come to symbolize private space. A haven of repose, love and safety in the face of the frights and the indifference of business and legal relations – such is the common stylization of the difference between private and public. And of course, this is at the same time also a difference between women and men.

Even though these stylizations of the family are neither desirable in normative terms nor convincing in empirical terms, there is a reluctance to give up this image of the family entirely. As Max Horkheimer has expressed it, families pursue 'the growth and happiness of the other', giving rise to an opposition between them and 'hostile reality outside'.[54] These aspects of life, these spaces, should be private, in other words, because they are concerned with something different – our happiness and the happiness of others, love and care, intimacy rather than distance – and because this private life is (therefore) defined by our desire to lead it as we please and our unwillingness to let either the state or society at large meddle in it (even though such 'reality' need not necessarily be 'hostile' in nature). The theme of the family is thus of central importance in the analysis and discussion of local privacy, for it has to do with intimate, primary relations that would not be possible without the protection afforded by privacy. Part of the reason we want as far as possible to determine for ourselves how and with whom we live is that it is in these contexts and with these people that we talk about issues that concern our self-determination and our life as a whole. Furthermore, if we have children, it is in these contexts that we wish to show them by example what it means to be a self-determined human being and lead a good life.[55]

Yet before setting about a more detailed discussion of the topic, I should first like to clarify just what a 'family' is. This conceptual problem is of relevance because the traditional, classic nuclear family comprising man and wife and (only) biological children is increasingly waning in significance, while other forms of family life are gaining in number and social impact.[56] Yet it makes sense not only on empirical but also normative grounds to seek another definition of the family apart from the so-called traditional one, for there are no normative reasons (that do not contradict the basic tenets of liberal democracy) why single-parent families, homosexual families, families founded by divorcees (with or without children from previous marriages), families with adopted children and families without children should not also be called 'families'. We thus need as broad a definition as possible, one that does justice to all these forms of living together but that is nonetheless not so vague that it ceases to be useful (or is no longer in keeping with the ideas of Horkheimer cited above). Bearing this in mind, I should like to fall back on a definition of the family proposed by Iris Young:

> I define family as people who live together and/or share resources necessary to the means of life and comfort; who are committed to taking care of one another's physical and emotional needs to the best of their ability; who conceive themselves in a relatively long-term, if not permanent relationship; and who recognize themselves as a family. Families are the ones who care for you when you are sick, and for whom you care when they are sick. Family members are mutually obliged to remember one another's birthdays, they are the ones on whom we dump our troubles. Family entails commitment and obligation as well as comfort: family members make claims on one another that they do not make on others.[57]

Young appositely characterizes the family with the help of Wittgensteinian 'family resemblances', although such a definition, which centres first and foremost upon a perspective internal to (functioning) families, is too loose to be able to hold its own in legal contexts or in the context of communities that live only nominally as families. It can be assumed, however, that Young is not seeking a definition that is appropriate for legal purposes, but wants to describe a (normative) model that is adequate and broad enough from an empirical point of view and thus sufficient for the discussion of moral problems. With these reservations I regard Young's proposed definition as plausible, but would nonetheless like to give special prominence to three central characteristics: people form a family if they see themselves as being in an – as far as possible – permanent relationship, if they live in a shared household (or share the necessary resources), and if they themselves recognize themselves as a family. This self-recognition of the family then also entails those very obligations and considerations that we only feel to be legitimate if we are also prepared to describe ourselves as a part of the family.

Equipped with this working definition of the family, if we now turn our attention to the connection between privacy and the family, then the normative problem at issue here is as follows. On the one hand, we value and want the protection of privacy because it is only *within* and *on the basis of* such protection that in private we can live in the way we want to (within the known limits). Only thus can we have relationships as we want them, and enjoy the closeness, the intimacy and the caring for one another. Only thus can we raise our children in the way we believe correct, without being exposed to the supervisory view of public society or the state – even though there is of course a limit to how far one can (and must) free oneself from prevailing conventions regarding what form such a self-determined life is to take. On the other hand, however, the normative self-understanding of liberal democracy is based not only upon equality of opportunities, but also something stronger than this, that is the equal worth of freedom for all, the equal opportunity for leading an autonomous life, as was set out in greater detail in chapter 2. And this clearly means that the organization and institution of privacy must itself not be unjustly or unequally structured, at least not to the extent of producing disparities that manifest themselves as structural inequalities in the worth of freedom. (Here too I am picking up one of the loose ends from chapter 2.)

This conflict, which is specific to the family in liberal democracies, comes to expression in three different ways. *First*, it is a question of how far state and society are permitted to intervene in the private sphere in such a way that the freedom of the individual may possibly be restricted. At issue here is thus a specific, concrete instance of the conflict between liberty and equality, for it can be said that the claim to the protection of privacy for the sake of one's self-determination in intimate relations constitutes a postulate for liberty, while the claim to the equal worth of liberty and autonomy can be conceived as a postulate for equality. *Secondly*, it takes the form of a conflict between justice and love: everything that goes on in the private realm of the family takes place, and should take place, out of love, while public relations prove to be the sort based on law, respect and justice. *Thirdly*, the conflict expresses itself as the problem of what Habermas has called the 'juridification' of privacy, or the 'colonization of the life-world'[58] that threatens when free spaces in private life-worlds have to comply in ever greater measure with the constraints of the administrative system rather than follow their own inner rationality.[59]

It could here be objected, of course, that all these are problems of the *traditional* family, that especially in recent decades family life has been subject to fundamental changes, and therefore this diagnosis of the problem is no longer applicable. It is certainly true that family structures have changed. This reflects not only the increase in women who have a job, or at least a succession of temporary jobs, but also the growing number of nursery school places and the guarantee of a right to such a place. It reflects the disappearance of cross-generational family structures due to the increased mobility of the younger generation.[60] It reflects changes in life at home, not only on account of the television and computer, but also the microwave oven, coffee machine and the whole gamut of practical household appliances.[61] Yet all these changes, as far as one can tell, have not brought about a fundamental transformation of the normative problems. They may in certain respects have defused the conflicts or produced a shift in emphasis, but they have certainly not resolved them. To clarify this point, I should like briefly to remind the reader of why the reconstruction of the private family is in fact so important, and what such problems of justice and equality have to do with the family and privacy. In other words, I should like to call to mind in an abbreviated form what is claimed by feminist critics (among others) and why these claims are made.

First, the traditional liberal confusion between the natural and conventional understandings of the difference between 'private' and 'public' continues to result in women being naturally assigned to a role as the keeper of the household, with all the accompanying connotations as the one who cares for and feeds the family, is irrational, etc. These connotations of privacy make a crucial contribution to the symbolic reproduction of the gender order. *Secondly*, unjust conditions within the family also lead to general differences with respect to possibilities for taking chances and opportunities in society at large, that is for leading one's life autonomously. If one has less time for doing things outside the household, one does indeed do less. Representation in public is directly related to one's presence in private. *Thirdly*, the gender-based division of labour continues to mean not only that women, irrespective of whether they are in gainful employment, statistically do substantially more housework than men, but also that the labour market itself is still severely segregated according to gender. *Fourthly*, family work, housework, relations work, and the raising of children are regarded as women's work *and therefore* as inferior, as a socially less significant achievement: this logic has been shown by empirical investigations into the loss of status undergone by certain occupational groups when a greater number of women enter them, and vice versa.[62] *Finally*, the family is also a place where children are socialized. And among other things, it is through the images and structures of equality and inequality, power and powerlessness, closeness and distance experienced within the family that they are socialized and develop a sexual identity. To the extent that the family contributes to the development of sexual identities and these aspects of practical identity contribute to the reproduction of structural inequalities, the modes of socialization within families bear part of the responsibility for these very inequalities.[63]

All these points make it clear that social injustices can come about within families and on the basis of the families' internal structures. The normative question to be asked here specifically concerns the extent to which the requirements of justice can, should or must be understood as normative structures for families, without this depriving families of their true function and essence – relations based on love and centred upon happiness – and without thereby forfeiting the idea that private life can be lived free from (state or social) intervention. Is justice an alternative to love? Does juridification always pose a threat to private ways of life? Can we restrict individual liberties even here? Hardly surprisingly, in what follows I wish to argue that families need not regard the appeals of love and the requirements of justice as antagonistic: demands for justice, as demands for equality, cannot here be understood as an alternative to freedom, and juridifications as such do not represent a direct threat to the family, let alone grounds for its decline. To put us in a position to discuss the issue, one option is to turn to existing theoretical models that each give very different answers to these questions, that is models that evaluate freedom, law and love (the three forms of the conflict) and define the relation between them in distinct, if not antithetical manners. In the following account, I shall start by briefly presenting two such models, those proposed by Axel Honneth and John Rawls, which not only locate the origins of the conflict differently but accordingly seek to resolve it differently. Subsequently, I want to set forth a third model that draws upon a number of authors.

Honneth begins his critique of the family with a diagnosis of the problem. He sees the increasing autonomy of marriage and the family since the nineteenth century, which has served the 'institutionalization of a private sphere separate from society',[64] as the onset of a process of 'inner emotional disintegration' in the family. The family, claims Honneth, is today jeopardized above all by the rising mobility of lifestyles, the increase in options and opportunities,[65] and the dwindling influence of the gender-specific division of labour. These disintegrative tendencies deprive the traditional family of its ideological basis, leaving behind, as it were, a normative gap, a gap in its foundations. Honneth presents two possible solutions for dealing with this set of moral problems and the question of the integration of the family. To do so, he draws on Kant and Hegel, on a legal model on the one hand and an affective model on the other, that is one model that sees marriage and the family first and foremost as a relationship of mutual rights and duties and one that seeks to understand affective attachment alone as the form of recognition and of integration.[66] These two proposals thus differ in terms of the *structure* they regard as essential to communicative relations in families and the *source* of the moral attitude: 'according to the legal model, what can be called justice in the family is presented as a context-specific application of a general moral principle: what is to be considered just within the family is only those actions or attitudes that respect the moral autonomy of the partner.' Opposed to this Kantian paradigm is the Hegelian one: 'wherever in families rights that have a legal character are put forward by a member, the moral substance of familial life has already been destroyed. [. . .] What is crucial for the affective model is the notion that what constitutes the source of all moral attitudes in the family is not rational insight into rights and duties, but solely the feeling of attention and love.'[67]

We are dealing, therefore, with two different moral orientations. And the family is a locus where these two moral orientations can constantly collide with one another.[68] According to Honneth, however, what is specific and proper to families is solely action motivated by love and oriented towards meeting needs: 'Caring actions [. . .] lose their moral value in these relationships as soon as they are performed not out of the feeling of love but out of rational insight into a duty.' For Honneth as for Hegel, the threat to the family is that the love-based or affective model might as it were tip over into the legal model. Even in Honneth's model, however, conflicts of justice within the family can result in a Kantian orientation towards mutual rights and duties temporarily gaining the upper hand. But this will not destroy the family provided that the family members are able to 'translate rational insights back into affective attitudes'.[69]

Honneth is certainly right and justified in insisting on the family's special status with regard to its mode of integration, the motivations for action that predominate within it, and its internal structure. His model appears problematic for more specific reasons. Honneth localizes the 'disintegration' of families on the one hand in the tendency of family members to appeal to their rights or autonomy, and on the other hand in the decline of the traditional nuclear family in favour of other family structures.[70] Yet neither factor is immediately plausible. The fact that the traditional nuclear family is being superseded by other forms of relationship – and that this process is taking place not without a certain ambivalent sorrow among those who were themselves socialized in such nuclear families – is only to be lamented if one believes that certain of the functions that a family is supposed to fulfil can *only* be fulfilled in this traditional form of family.[71] But this is tenable neither in normative nor in empirical terms. Also, the question of whether it need be considered a sign of the disintegration of a family if the members of that family in their interaction and communication appeal to their rights, mutual responsibilities and autonomy seems to depend upon the concept of love or justice being presupposed in each particular case. I shall return to this point shortly. What clearly must be described as a threat to the integrity of families and as a disquieting symptom of disintegration – which is surely the objective of Honneth's account as well – are tendencies relating to the decline in the significance and function of the family, as when certain forms of affective recognition, of successful, protected and protective communication go missing, when unprotected conduct and particular forms of closeness and intimacy are no longer possible. Yet all this does not necessarily have anything to do with the two factors localized by Honneth. If the family is indeed losing its function in this way, the fact that family members stand up for their rights, it might be said, is something to be welcomed.

There is another aspect of Honneth's model that seems more problematic, however. This is the reference he makes to two alternative moral orientations, the first centred upon the needs of 'the other' and the second centred upon one's opposite as a legal subject.[72] It is not immediately clear why the two orientations should be in conflict in the family. Honneth too holds that families should in principle be just: it is simply that postulates of justice should not be involved when it comes to motivations for action; on the contrary, being guided by such postulates represents a moral loss within family relations.[73] Yet this is just what fails to convince. First, it is difficult to imagine that it can make sense to describe being guided by principles of *justice* as a moral *loss*, whether this has to do with personal attitudes and motivations or the postulate of justice in institutions (such as the family).[74] Secondly, a postulate of justice is explicitly and necessarily involved whenever – in subjective terms – there are conflicts between needs, which cannot be judged and resolved without recourse to a standard of justice.[75] It is certainly true that we treat members of our family differently from other people and in particular want to be treated differently by them too. It is true that the affective moment should always be present in such modes of action and behaviour. But it is hard to see why needs *and* autonomy, love *and* respect should not always be equally involved in moral issues within family relations. The affective standpoint cannot mean that justice within the family, mutual rights and duties, and respect for the autonomy of other family members are understood to be in any way dispensable. Rather, they are always intended by it *as well*.[76] That relationships based on love and closeness follow a logic other than the logic of justice cannot and need not mean that postulates of justice are as it were *replaced* when one is guided by needs. Nobody would wish to deny that such standards of justice within the family are in practice frequently difficult to meet, which can be attributed, among other things, to the uncompromising forms of (working) life outside the family. But such difficulties have no bearing on the correctness of the normative idea.

The question now is whether Rawls – with his markedly Kantian perspective – is able to provide alternatives or amendments to Honneth or even just cast a critical light upon his account. I should like, therefore, to return to Rawls's theory of the family. If I consulted Rawls above[77] in general terms as one of the classic liberal thinkers, this time I would like to treat him specifically as a political theorist with quite explicit views on the issue of justice within the family.[78] The requirements of political justice, he writes in his essay 'The Idea of Public Reason Revisited', place demands and essential restrictions upon social institutions by securing the fundamental rights and liberties for all members of society inside and outside these institutions. The idea is that no institution, including the family, can or may be structured in such a way as to deny its members the basic – politically just – rights or prevent them asserting these rights. No institution, including the family, may thus be unjust in the essential aspects of political justice. Rawls is here clearly referring to his two principles of justice, the first of which calls for an equal guarantee of equal basic liberties, while the second sets a limit to social and economic inequalities in the form of what he calls the 'difference principle'.[79] He thus writes:

> The family as part of this basic structure cannot violate these freedoms [i.e. the basic liberties secured by political justice]. Since wives are equally citizens with their husbands, they have all the same basic *rights, freedoms and opportunities* as their husbands; and this together with the correct application of the other principles of justice, suffices to secure their equality and independence.[80]

For the rest, Rawls also makes it clear that his distinction between political and non-political justice does not imply that there is a pre-political realm in which the principles of political justice do not hold sway. On the contrary, says Rawls, if one considers the social realm solely in terms of the range of application of political justice, there is no distinction at all between 'political' and 'non-political', 'public' and 'private', for these principles cover the entire social space and thus also place limits upon what is possible within the family. Everything else, however, must be left open, for according to Rawls the next step does indeed entail distinguishing between various principles of justice, namely between those that pertain to society generally and are applied to the structure of all its institutions, and those that regulate the 'internal life' of the particular institution or association itself and as such cannot be subject to political control – provided, of course, that they do not contravene political justice.[81] This comes to light in particular when Rawls compares the family with other 'private' institutions, such as the Catholic Church. One cannot, he says, prescribe the inner justice, the inner structure, of either of these institutions. All one can demand of either is the guarantee that they will not infringe the principles of political justice. The question of who is admitted to priesthood is no more a matter of political justice than the question of how we bring up our children (or of how we resolve conflicts within relationships, one should add). Providing appropriate conceptions of justice that are not political but can do justice to the internal life, the logic and rationality of the institution or association in question is not the task of a conception of political justice itself. What an appropriate conception would be is a separate, additional question that depends, Rawls writes, upon the nature and function of the institution, group or relation concerned.[82]

Yet the Rawlsian model too leaves fundamental questions unanswered. Can one equate the institution of the family with other private and voluntary associations and institutions in society? Can it be claimed, so to speak, that the difference between the Catholic Church, for example, and the family is just a matter of degree? Of course, the reason Rawls believes he must answer this question in the affirmative is that he regards as much liberal plurality as possible not only as normatively imperative, but also as most practicable for society. But in the process he seems to be underestimating the status and function of the family, which, unlike the

Catholic Church, is not a *voluntary* institution. Indeed, in his discussion of the neutrality and tolerance of the liberal state in *A Theory of Justice*, Rawls himself writes:

> The notion of a confessional state is rejected. Instead, particular associations may be freely organized as their members wish, and they may have their own internal life and discipline subject to the restriction that their members have a *real choice of whether to continue their affiliation*.[83]

Yet it seems quite inappropriate to maintain that members of a family – children, for example – have such a 'real choice'. Even if they do have the possibility of escaping from conditions that are inhuman, this seems to be a much more momentous and existential step than discontinuing one's affiliation with the Catholic Church (and as a result is hardly comparable with it). Moreover, even when one does leave a particular family, even as an adult, one generally finds a new one, and to this extent, unlike the Catholic Church, the family is without alternatives. Above all, however, there is the crucial fact that society too has a vital interest in the family, which still bears a great deal of the responsibility for the primary socialization of the future members of society and thus has a formative and very specific influence upon society to come.[84] The sort of work that is done within the family – housework, the upkeep of relationships, care – is a constituent part of the socialization and support people need and thus a constituent part of the operation of society as a whole. A society is reliant upon the existence and operation of families in a completely different way, therefore, from the existence (and operation) of, for example, the Catholic Church.

For all these reasons, society – and every single member of society, as a (potential) member of a family – must have a categorically *different* interest in the internal structure of the family from the interest it has in the internal structure of the Catholic Church. Yet if this is the case, the distinction between public and private or between political and non-political justice must be investigated once more in a different light. What remains unclear in Rawls is where exactly the boundary is drawn between the area in which political justice applies and the regulations specific to particular institutions, and who draws this boundary. When the passage cited above refers to 'the same basic rights, freedoms and opportunities', what does this mean? At what point can a restriction on freedoms and opportunities no longer simply be entrusted to the logic of the regulations within an institution? When does it call for the (possibly increased) application of political justice?[85] Of course, one cannot expect there to be a clear-cut answer to this question that Rawls has simply overlooked. This is not the problem. The problem is that the connection between justice within the family and opportunities in society is infinitely too far-reaching, complex and significant for the life of the persons involved for us to be able to compare even in approximate terms the self-understanding of the structure of families (what sort of institution it is and the implications of this), whether couched in first-person or in third-person terms, with that of the Catholic Church, for example.

So where do we stand now? The first thing to be underscored is that Rawls goes a step further than Honneth as far as the validity of justice is concerned, for neither in moral philosophical terms nor with respect to the integration of the family does he find it problematic to speak of the validity of principles of justice or of behaviour in accordance with principles of justice, even within families. Unlike for Honneth, in other words, the moral source of motivation may also inhere in the recognition of the rights and autonomy of the others, and the integration of the family can likewise take place through this form of recognition. This does not oblige Rawls to deny that people typically act out of love in families and that typically the family members are – and should be – guided by the needs of the others in their moral considerations. To this extent, Rawls need not necessarily be read as an alternative to Honneth, but as a more plausible, substantially qualified version of Honneth's model. What for Honneth is a 'normative imperative' has turned into what is 'typical' for Rawls.

Why this is still not satisfactory as a normative model for the modern private family in liberal democracies is brought to light by the previously advanced criticism of Rawls. If we take seriously the consequences of family structures and the determining influence they exert upon the life of the family members, it cannot simply be a matter in principle of recognizing autonomy and justice within families, as Rawls describes. The regulations internal to the institution of the family cannot be entrusted to liberal plurality to the extent envisaged by Rawls. What must be clarified is why and in what way justice must also apply within families, and this means fundamental changes to the *(self-)understanding* and the *(self-) description* of the family. Taking my criticisms of Honneth and Rawls as a starting-point, I should now like to explicate this point by returning to the three different categories we used earlier in the chapter to describe the field of conflict within families: the problem of juridification, the conflict of liberty, and the conflict between love and justice.[86]

Let us start by looking once more at the issue of juridification.[87] It is certainly true that the family would have already lost one of its fundamental functions if its integration were dependent exclusively upon the medium of the law. This is a crucial aspect of Honneth's model that is surely correct. It is thus not the issue here. The point rather is *firstly* to see that the law – symbolically and in other ways – is *always already* intervening in the family and that it is a mistake, therefore, to hold that the family constitutes a social vacuum. What this means is that marriage law, divorce law and family law *in themselves* involve legally regulative interventions in the private sphere of the family, interventions that in part of course have a purely symbolic effect but that nonetheless at least have one. For this reason, the initiative taken by the German Ministers for Gender Equality to change paragraphs 1356ff. of the country's Civil Code,[88] which have to do with the division of family income and the arrangement of joint housekeeping, is of particular significance. Such arrangements regulate perfectly normal family relations, and it is not only once the emotional bond has been destroyed that this occurs. Nor should the symbolical import of the law be underestimated: the cultural self-understanding of a society, including its normative aspects, is known to find expression in its legal system and jurisprudence too. Clearly, changes in the life-projects and moral attitudes of women and men do not come about exclusively on the basis of changes in jurisprudence. But they can and should be encouraged or stimulated by them.[89]

The *second* point is that rights are indeed needed when love is over, when – as Waldron puts it[90] – they have to serve as 'fallback positions' for persons who are otherwise unable to claim the protection they need, as happens in the case of divorce law, maintenance rulings, custody arrangements, etc.[91] Both sorts of legal regulation show that it is misleading to speak of a clear-cut or unbroken separation between public and private, between state and family. Allocations of roles and time, economic structures, etc., also have an immediate and direct effect upon the structure of families, and the gender order – as a form of political order – clearly covers even the most hidden corners of the private domain and the family in particular.[92] As a social institution, the family cannot simply be kept out of social structures, but forms a continuum with them.[93] The issue of juridification is not a matter of publicly regulating the distribution of housework, therefore, but of making use of the medium of the law, which already exists and exerts its influence anyway, in such a way as to ensure that substantive justice between the sexes can in fact be established as far as possible. Where necessary, this may also involve stronger legal interventions, though these may have to be of limited duration.[94]

This brings us to the second of the categories of family conflicts cited above, the conflict between liberty and equality. For Rawls at least, one of the arguments against public, legal or social intrusions upon the privacy of the family was the freedom and the liberal plurality with which family relations can and should be regulated. From one point of view, this is certainly right too: part of the reason we value the privacy of family relations is that here we enjoy the freedom of creation and self-realization that we lack in other social contexts, and we want to regulate the intimate relationships within which we live in our own specific way. But what sorts of conflicts, and what sorts of restrictions are here at issue?[95]

The demands of justice that should play a part in intimate, private relationships and structure these relationships may clash with the interests of individual family members in a variety of different ways. These (moral) conflicts may firstly be between claims to self-realization and family responsibilities, and secondly between different perceptions and interpretations when it comes to the moral assessment of a situation, as when an additional burden assumed by one partner is not perceived or identified as such by the other. None of these *individual* conflicts is in itself resolved by the demand *in principle* for justice in families. In each individual conflict, the attempt must be made to negotiate sensitively between the differing needs and appeals to justice (for example with regard to the allocation of time) in such a way that the latter can be taken into account without the former having to be completely disregarded. This insistence on standards of justice even within families would mean that certain modes of conduct would no longer be morally permissible or socially countenanced. Also, certain arguments would be excluded from the discussion, while others would be recognized as important: arguments based on sexual stereotypes, gender-specific virtues and supposedly 'natural' allocations of roles and work would no longer be considered valid, while appeals to autonomy and the availability of equal scope for freedom would be acceptable.[96] If, therefore, one imposes normative principles based on the equal worth of liberty, in terms, say, of the equal division of housework or family jobs or the equal treatment of boys and girls in family relationships, this may restrict individual liberties in the trivial sense in which morally grounded principles of equality may always restrict individual liberties.[97] Such regulations go beyond what could and should be demanded of the inner life, say, of the Catholic Church. Yet – for the reasons given – one is right to do so.

This still leaves, however, the last of the three expressions of family conflict, the clash between love and justice. What is appealed to in such conflicts, the love or the respect of the other person? And where necessary, should one invoke one's own needs or one's own autonomy? It is certainly true that the source of moral behaviour in affective relationships should be love or care and not respect alone.[98] Out of love, people in such relationships allow themselves to make commitments that they would not recognize in other relationships, commitments involving special forms of consideration, for example. They want not only to *treat the other justly* but also to *do justice to him* – and this seems to be a decisive difference between private and public relationships. People accordingly acknowledge the special moral characteristics of such relationships, considering it justified to care for needs rather than simply respect duties. Yet this does not in itself mean that there has to be a choice or a conflict between love and justice. Indeed, it might be claimed that in relationships of love the reason one wants to comply with the moral requirements of justice is that one loves the other person *and* wants to be just anyway. One might recognize that certain attitudes or modes of behaviour in practice produce or support unjust structures, and this recognition might be based entirely on rationality, respect and a sense of justice and for this reason also move one to make changes.[99] Yet this would not mean that one did not love the other person too. It would simply mean recognizing that emotions such as love need not always necessarily make for attitudes or modes of behaviour that are just, especially since it can be assumed that they themselves do not completely elude social, cultural construction. It is when family relations fail to do justice to such principles that one would say that they are loveless: the love has thus gone when justice is *absent*, not *present*.[100] To this extent, it is difficult to imagine anyway how, from a first-person perspective, a conflict can be generated between feelings of love and a sense of justice with respect to one and the same person in the family.[101]

This threefold perspective changes the normative image of the family in relation to the descriptions set forth by Honneth and Rawls not only in terms of the strength of the demands of justice that are asserted and should be asserted *within* the family – *by* the family and by *society* at large – but also in terms of the self-description of the family itself. Part of both the family's (normative) self-understanding and of society's understanding of the family, therefore, is that in it there is justice between the sexes; that equal liberties and opportunities really are taken seriously; and that *even so* the institution of the family constitutes a very specific social institution, with specific tasks and a specific structure, different from any other institution. Part of the normative self-understanding of this institution is thus also the awareness that the balance between the way the individual person shapes the conditions of her own life and the demands of justice that are valid in general terms is one that is difficult to achieve and difficult to maintain.

I should like now to back up the normative view of the family that I have sketched here with one final point. On various occasions above I have already referred to the fact that the family is also a place where children are brought up, developing their (sexual) identity in part through the images and structures of equality and inequality, power and powerlessness, closeness and distance, self-confidence and insecurity that they experience at home as exemplified by and with their parents. As well as this, I am also taking up the reflections in chapter 3 on the relevance of non-manipulative conditions when it comes to learning and practising autonomy. If the family thus indisputably contributes to the formation of (sexual) identities, such modes of socialization may also contribute to the symbolic reproduction of structural inequalities. The repercussions that the gender-specific division of labour and allocation of roles and the different emphases given to caring for the welfare of others, especially children, have – or may have – on the development of sexual identity and autonomy is something that has frequently (though not with one voice) been investigated and described in feminist psychoanalytic theory.[102] Without being able to go into detail at this point, from this perspective too it can once again be pointed out that family socialization should provide egalitarian, non-manipulative conditions that make it possible for girls (as well as boys) to develop an authentic relationship to their own preferences and generally experience and describe the formation of their own preferences as autonomous. It should provide conditions, in other words, that make it possible for them to acquire an understanding of themselves as people who are autonomous and who value autonomy.

A 'democratization of the private sphere', as Anthony Giddens calls it,[103] would by no means annul the constitutive difference between public and private, between behaviour and attitudes based on happiness and those based on justice. Nor would it invalidate the function of the family that consists in providing us with protection from the demands of public self-presentation and the professional roles we have to play in public for the simple reason that it is public. Nor, moreover, would it superannuate the function of the family that consists in the loving socialization of autonomous, self-reliant, moral individuals with identities that turn out as well as possible. All this remains dependent upon the protection of privacy, and all this continues to show us the value of privacy. This is not lessened by the proposals of justice between the sexes, but increased, because it is extended for all.

Our private home or room, our family, can and should be a refuge, a refuge that we value and look to not only for its own sake, but also and above all because it gives us the opportunity to be on our own, undisturbed and unseen, which seems to be vital for successfully testing, learning and seeking out (aspects of) our autonomy. Being on one's own in order to engage autonomously and authentically in the search for what one wants and who one wants to be is clearly a central aspect of why we seek and value the privacy of seclusion. And to the extent that the private home thus safeguards the seclusion for a person to confront her own life, the dimensions of informational and decisional privacy depend upon this form of privacy too. Yet the private home has its other side too, the side of intimate relationships. This is the context in which intersubjective confrontation and reflection upon goals and projects, ways of life and major decisions are sought, but also in which autonomy is taught as well as learnt or developed. And it is here, therefore, that it comes to the specific conflicts between the protection of privacy and what is supposed to be protected by it. In regard to both aspects of local privacy, it has become clear what is at stake when the protection of privacy is threatened here. It has become clear that strong, *legal* protection of the dwelling must safeguard the right to privacy and that a *moral* right to the possibility of retreating into privacy is legitimately asserted even in intimate, family relations. And it has also become clear that both factors, in terms of their limits and contents, are always conventional in nature and for this reason can always be challenged too.

7 Interfaces: Public and Private

1 Interfaces and ambivalences

The last few chapters have shown how the three dimensions of privacy – overlapping and complementing one another – can protect and develop a person's autonomy and how people are consequently dependent upon the protection of privacy. The liberal proposal of equal freedom has also spotlighted what such protection of privacy for all people alike would mean for the internal structure of liberal societies. And this is precisely what has been at issue in these analyses. The aim has been to make a contribution to the inner configuration of liberal democracy and thus to the self-understanding of liberal theories, a contribution based upon an inquiry into the value of privacy. Seen from the perspective of privacy, this configuration and these theories are shown up in a specific light because the boundary running between private and public dimensions structures liberal society and thus the social relations of the subject in a specific way.

In what follows, I shall not conclude by summarizing for what reasons and in what respects the various dimensions of privacy are valued and how the autonomy of the subject can only be developed through the protection of privacy. I do not, in other words, want to sum up what the value of privacy consists in. Instead of this sort of concluding chapter, I should like to reflect on the ambivalences of privacy where it interfaces with the public realm, for one cannot write about privacy and its value without looking at these interfaces and the ambivalences associated with shifts in the borderline between public and private. When I speak of ambivalences, I mean just this, that is that the points of interface between private and public may bring to expression the dual nature of privacy as something that can be conceived as both liberating and alienating, emancipative and repressive, beneficial and deleterious. These ambivalences warn us that caution is due in any assessment of the problems. The following will thus focus upon two themes: privacy in the public realm, and the relation between the private and the public person. To begin with, section 2 will examine the issue of privacy in the public realm from the standpoint of privacy and with the emphasis on two aspects: firstly, the way privacy is 'staged' *as privacy* in the public sphere, and secondly, the staging of privacy *as its 'publicization'* (*Ver-Öffentlichung*) in the public sphere. The privatization of the public realm can be approached from both these angles. In this way, the ambivalences involved can be elucidated more clearly.

In section 3, the perspective will then be from the public sphere, dealing with questions such as whether the public realm needs to be protected from too much privacy, whether there are some themes that are thus genuinely private and others that are genuinely public, and who it is that actually draws the boundaries between public and private domains. A shift in perspective thus occurs between sections 2 and 3. In section 2, the spotlight is on the perspective of the private person who is staging herself in public, while in section 3 it is on the perspective from the public realm. The conventional nature as well as the functionality of the borderline between public and private have emerged repeatedly over the last few chapters. It is the conventionality of this borderline, its changing course, its constructed nature, and its function that are examined in these two sections. In the final section, I want to look once more at the interfaces between the public and the private from a completely different angle, namely the problem of the identity of the public and the private person. I shall, however, only be sketching or outlining an answer to such questions as how strong such an identity must be considered to be, what practical identity can mean in this context, what the value of privacy can here consist in, and whether the distinction between the private and the public person can in general be understood as a *sui generis* distinction. This sketch will again be paradigmatic, bringing into play a short story by Henry James. Each of the three following sections has much more the character of an outline than an exhaustive discussion. The problems are specified and catalogued rather than resolved. The idea, however, is that they should once again convey three perspectives on the value of privacy.

2 Exposure: the staging of privacy in the public realm

Evaluating the presentation, staging or treatment of privacy in public is a difficult task. This is not just because the field is an extremely heterogeneous one involving completely different social phenomena, but also because the evaluative categories with which the phenomena are analysed and evaluated in turn vary widely and frequently originate from a rather vague cultural critique that views the privatization of the public realm above all as its decline. This critique laments how the most intimate of matters are elevated to the level of a media spectacle and how in this way not only any sense of privacy goes missing, but also the public realm is turned into an 'Arendtian nightmare'[1] that no longer has anything to do with civic commitment to public welfare, or indeed with any notion of 'public'. Mobile phones, reality TV and discussions centring on the affairs of President Clinton, as well as the broad influence of the media on daily life, are then cited as examples of the general blurring of boundaries and the increasing impossibility of distinguishing between the public and private dimensions of life. In this way, runs the critique, social cohesion disappears, and the very foundations of civilization are at risk.[2]

Such present-day diagnoses of the times follow on within a long historiography charting the decline of the public realm through the incursion of the intimate. For a variety of reasons and with a variety of objectives, a tradition of thinking from Arendt to Sennett has registered and lamented in one way or another the degeneration of a better public realm that used to exist.[3] These broad historical studies are interested in the various ways in which the public sphere has been depoliticized by general social developments that are said to have blurred the boundaries between realms that used to be (functionally or naturally) separated and in this way produced a categorical transformation of the basic conditions in which themes of public and of private life are identified and discussed as such. Diagnoses of the current blurring of boundaries can thus follow in these historical lines. In their diagnoses of decline they are likewise interested above all in the loss that such a blurring of boundaries represents for the public realm.[4]

My concern in what follows cannot be with a detailed discussion of the concept of the public sphere, or with its structures and functions, etc. The focus is instead on just one facet, that is the role of privacy in the public sphere. Of course, the two dimensions cannot be separated in precise terms. Yet the public realm is here as it were viewed not directly, but only via the perspective of privacy.[5] To do this, I now want to provide a brief outline of the broad field of public stagings of privacy, in their very different aspects, starting out from a consideration of two particular phenomena: the mobile phone, exemplifying the excessive individualization and atomization of public space, and TV chat shows, exemplifying the incursion of intimacy into public space. In spite of their triviality, these examples will help us discuss diverse aspects of the way privacy is staged in social space. The incursion of intimacy into the public realm of politics – exemplified by the stagings of privacy of and by politicians – will here only play a marginal part. I shall try to show and explain – cautiously and not very excitingly – that what is at issue here are not categorical changes in the concepts and conceptions of private and public, nor an increasing blurring of boundaries between the realms, but rather a *shift* in the boundary, a change in the course the boundary follows, a course that has never been fixed anyway, but is always disputed and is constantly being 'rebuilt'. I shall show that this circumstance might indeed harbour perils, but that these need not in themselves really be regarded as threatening.

Let us start by looking at mobile phones. Few people would dispute that these are an increasingly frequent and in certain contexts also increasingly infuriating phenomenon. Wendy Brown provides a vivid description:

> [I]n Italy, where the cell phone has become so ubiquitous as to be comic, although this comedy may also be a harbinger of ordinary life for all of us [. . .], in Italy cell phones are used everywhere by everyone – shopkeepers, students, children, cleaning women, executives, truck and taxi drivers. Scenes one witnesses every day: Young men navigating heavily trafficked corners on motor scooters, at the same time they are talking on their phones (and smoking). Groups of well dressed young people at a café table, at first glance engaged in lively conversation with each other, but in fact talking on their respective phones to people not at the table. [. . .] Mothers strolling babies and window shopping while simultaneously engaged on the phone. Cell phones ring in parks, movies, busses, elegant restaurants and boutiques, in bathrooms [. . .], anywhere a human might be.[6]

Brown interprets this scenario as an 'Arendtian nightmare': people no longer talk in public *with* one another, let alone about affairs that are of concern to all, about political matters, but instead their talk is solipsistic. Although they do not talk to themselves, it is for themselves. This is part of the reason Brown speaks of the mobile phone as a 'harbinger': just as the culture of mobile phones is already decisively shaping our public life, soon our whole life will be just as incapable of communication and experience.[7] If an attempt is made to situate the phenomenon in a different context, however, mobile phones can be understood – in their origins at least – not only as status symbols but above all as a way of staging privacy in the public domain. After all, telephone conversations were once considered to be particularly private matters. In this sense, they can thus also be understood as an attempt at individualization, as another emblem of such individualization. The fact that they are now available to all irrespective of status and for this very reason no longer have much to do with setting oneself apart from others through individual self-staging is not inconsistent with that original symbolic component, which of course is nonetheless preserved.

How this is interpreted in terms of the meaning of the borderline between private and public clearly depends crucially upon one's normative conceptual framework and upon the history within which one places oneself in making the interpretation. On the one hand, it can thus be seen that in terms of an ideal of successful communication the individuation of 'mobile-phone existence'[8] – as comes to light especially in scenes where there is no conversation among friends, who talk not with one another but with others – must surely be described as a further step in the history of alienation within the public realm. On the other hand, one would be reasonably justified in claiming that even before the invention of mobile phones the public realm was not particularly 'Arendtian' in character. Mobile phones would in these terms be conceived as the sign of a further modernizing step in the individualization, isolation and anonymization of (urban) culture, and in this sense one would here be adopting and endorsing a Simmelian as opposed to an Arendtian point of view.[9] This will become clearer when we look more closely at the concept of privacy that is here involved. For the issue here is not that intimate details are being made public or that private 'knowledge' is being publicized. At issue is a private action, so to speak, that takes place in public. Portrayed in the terminology of the previous chapters, in other words, we are here dealing with an aspect not of informational privacy but of decisional privacy.[10] As a private action within the public realm, the telephone conversation is a private matter that calls for distance – indifference, restraint, reserve – from other people in public. One stages oneself with the mobile phone for others and yet does not want any interference in one's phone call. A person who stages herself in this way is of course playing with the privacy of the phone call: others are not allowed to listen, yet are positively invited to do so. It is a game that comes on top of the genuinely practical functions of the mobile phone, and one that can also be played by means of conversations with another person present in public.

Adopting a Simmelian point of view, it becomes clear that this 'mobile phone culture' also forms part of a different tradition, for the staging of what is private as something private has its own history. It is not only the way a person dresses in public that exemplifies this sort of staging. It can also be asked what the big difference is between sitting in a café and writing letters (or novels, possibly even using a laptop) or reading the paper and making a phone call in public.[11] All these activities are in fact private matters that are transported into the public realm, (partly) because of the distinct self-presentation this permits. This, at least, is one point of view, one that focuses not so much upon the decline of a moribund public realm as upon the changes in the conception and presentation of privacy, upon the shifts, modifications and displacements of the virtual borderline between private and public, and thus also upon the shifts, expansions and appropriations of spaces for autonomous individualization, even though both autonomy and individuality are admittedly limited in the case of mobile phones. I would thus advocate interpreting 'mobile phone culture' as an ambivalent phenomenon, but nonetheless not as a culture that leads to – increasingly individualized – citizens losing any sense of privacy or of the difference between public and private. Rather, it is a culture in which the functions of the public and the private continue to change (as they always have done), the borderline separating them is kept mobile, and the normative codings of the two realms are modified. In this case, however, it is not a blurring of boundaries that takes place, nor is the borderline between the private and the public domains dissolved.

Let us now adopt the other standpoint and turn to the staging of privacy in the form of the 'publicization' of private matters, as exemplified by the chat shows on afternoon television. Our concern here is not with the public staging of privacy *as privacy*, but with the programmatic *exposure of privacy*, the 'publicization' of intimate details that are traditionally still viewed as private. The divergence from the first perspective can also be expressed in different terms, for it is a distinct concept or meaning of privacy that is involved here. If the case of mobile phones is a question of decisional privacy and – despite all the playful, scenic ambiguities we described – always involves a person's entitlement to respect for the privacy of her telephone conversation, in the case of the exposures that take place in chat shows we are dealing with the programmatic revelation of private knowledge. It is a question, that is, of informational privacy, because people communicate things about themselves, reveal things about themselves, that in fact belong within the hidden realm of issues that are broached, if at all, only in the context of close relationships. It is not privacy as privacy, but privacy as a public issue, that now becomes interesting in public.

Once again, it is not clear how this should be interpreted, whether as a decline or as progress.[12] Once again, I should like to approach the question from a first-person perspective, assuming the possible loss of a sense of privacy in an individual who is no longer able to distinguish between private and public (the possible loss of functions of the public realm will thus again only be mentioned in passing).[13] What is happening in these afternoon chat shows, therefore, when participants talk about their weight problems, the difficulties they have accepting their son's homosexuality, their unfulfilled sex life, or their problematic relationship with the in-laws? As we know, a further step beyond these chat shows is taken by so-called reality TV, in which people no longer just talk, but actually live their 'real life' in front of the cameras – marrying, having arguments, making it up afterwards. From reality TV of this sort it is then a natural progression to programmes such as *Big Brother*, which involves a group of people voluntarily shutting themselves away for months in a closed household and allowing themselves to be filmed non-stop.[14]

Here once more I only wish to discuss a small sector of the issue, and I shall do so by looking at two stances. The first of these claims that these developments constitute a disintegration of the distinction between public and private, in that people indiscriminately discuss everything in public. The second claims that what this sort of 'mediazation' of everyday life in fact produces is an invalidation of the distinction between appearance and reality, that is the distinction between genuine daily life and the medium of the film. This thesis is interesting in our context because the loss of this distinction would necessarily entail the loss of the ability to differentiate between private and public, since to the medium *qua* medium everything is public, and a controlled differentiation between what is for me or private and what is also accessible for others (that is for everyone) is made impossible. I want to start by looking briefly into the second of these positions, before turning to the first.

Chat shows, 'reality' shows and 'reality' series are simply a more explicit manifestation of something that is the case anyway, that is the increasing inability of people to distinguish between appearance and reality, a phenomenon that the medium of television not only contributes to but imposes.[15] This stance, as we know, traditionally appears in either an optimistic or a pessimistic version,[16] but it is the optimistic variant that has become rather more influential today. Here categories such as alienation are apparently no longer useful when it comes to explicating the relationship between humans and television. All there is anyway now is what is 'produced by media', and so *a fortiori* the difference between real world and film, between reality and appearance, is no longer relevant.[17] What interests me about this is that the loss of a sense of the separation between public and private here comes to expression in characteristic fashion, for a person who no longer distinguishes between a scene for the film and a scene without the film will no longer be able to distinguish between what is private and what is public either. After all, the film – the medium – is public by definition. The claim made by this stance, propounded first by Jean Baudrillard and subsequently by Wolfgang Welsch, is that we always live as though we were presenting ourselves for television and on television, as though we were being observed by the camera for others. As Welsch puts it,

> people today [. . .] are socialized to such a great degree by televisionary processes that they behave throughout their everyday lives as though television were present. It no longer makes any difference whether television is actually present or not – it has [. . .] 'always been present'. People's behaviour is already coded through and through by television.[18]

Accordingly, Welsch can again coincide with Baudrillard in asserting that 'in our society the only thing that counts as real tends now to be what is produced or reproduced by the media.'[19] A very similar formulation is produced by Norbert Bolz, who writes: 'These days, ubiquitous screens turn two-dimensionality into a criterion of reality, i.e. anything that wants to be certified as real must be crystallized onto monitors.'[20] These writers do not themselves relate this loss of differentiation to the loss of the separation between the private and public spheres, yet the correspondence is patent, for the difference between private and public within the medium *itself* can clearly only ever be an apparent one – the medium knows privacy only as something publicized.[21]

How, therefore, should we assess this stance in empirical and normative terms? Empirically, I consider it to be scarcely sustainable, for in spite of everything most of 'the people' we are here talking about are evidently still fully capable of distinguishing between their daily life and the television, between the private and the public. This is demonstrated, for example, by the otherwise not exactly exhilarating interviews with the participants in the Dutch version of the 'reality' series *Big Brother*, who despite weeks and months playing the game are clearly able to differentiate between daily life in the game and their own daily life and have clearly not lost interest in their own private sphere.[22] The fact that the media exert a major influence on daily life and its changes and modified conventions is as undeniable as it is trivial.[23] Yet this observation cannot support the much less trivial claims that on account of such an influence this distinction can no longer be drawn, that people are no longer able to imagine their life without the perspective of other people upon them, and that they are in general losing any sense of the difference made by the possible presence of this perspective.[24]

However, this does not yet wrap up the normative question of why an increased blurring of the difference between appearance and reality, and with it a loss in the possibility of *controlled* self-presentation that is relevant in our context, should not be desirable. At this point, I am again taking up the earlier reflections on informational privacy and the protection of it. As before, the problem is that a self-determined life – by which I mean a life in which a person has and strives for control over her self-presentations, in which she can differentiate between different relationships and corresponding modes of behaviour, and in which she distinguishes between themes and actions that are only of interest to herself (or to 'specific others') and those that are of interest to all – will cease to be possible if people are no longer in a position, in terms of either the external conditions or their subjective abilities, to distinguish between life that is observed and life that is unobserved because in the 'mediazation' of their daily life everything for them has turned into the 'as if' of film. In this sense, series such as *Big Brother* must indeed be interpreted as a threat. The renunciation of *every* dimension of privacy involves also renouncing intrinsic dimensions of autonomy, and this sort of media development can thus clearly be diagnosed as a mistake.[25] It might of course be objected here that in the course of such developments our very concepts of autonomy, a person's self-relationship, alienation, and successful relationships would change, as in general would the collective assumptions underlying our self-descriptions, concepts and assumptions that are overlaid with the familiar ambivalences anyway. But in these theories such far-reaching normative claims are neither sufficiently explicated nor sufficiently grounded.

Let us now turn to the second of the stances mentioned above. This claims that the self-revelations of afternoon chat shows are the expression of a general blurring of boundaries between public and private realms and the increasing inability to distinguish between private matters or secrets and what is public. At issue here, it is claimed, is the force of cohesion among subjects, which feeds off the 'attraction of their indeterminacy'.[26] It seems to me to be doubtful, however, whether one can draw such broad conclusions concerning people's subjective abilities, ways of life and autonomy on the basis of phenomena such as these chat shows, the (self-) exposures of politicians or in general the incursion of intimacy into the media.[27] On the one hand, the fact that people speak on chat shows about (some of their) intimate problems while others are happy to watch and listen to them doing so need by no means entail that these people have completely lost any sense of the distinction between private and public.[28] I regard it as more likely that they are perfectly capable of such differentiations and not only continue to have an interest in their own 'backstage' after the event, but would not consider themselves entitled, for example, to spy on what goes on in their neighbours' bedroom or talk about their intimate life even among close friends in the way they either do or watch being done on television. The context here seems to be crucial. The *transformation* of one's own private life into an object of public interest on television does not simply leave this private life as it was, but distances it, above all for the people whose intimacy is involved, but also for listeners or spectators. And without such modes of transformation and distancing the private realm remains precisely what it is – private. For this reason, it seems to be jumping to conclusions to infer from the public discussion of intimate matters that boundaries are being blurred between the public and private realms. The individual's sense of privacy and intimacy seems to be more resistant and culturally much more deeply rooted than would be suggested by this sort of chat show or the accompanying cultural critique: not *everywhere* is everything talked about, and not everywhere does everyone *want to* talk about everything. On the other hand, it is evident that while we are not dealing with a general abolition of the difference, we are facing decisive changes in the course of the boundary between private and public, and a shift in the underlying conditions under which themes are differentiated. It has become possible to talk about all these intimate matters in public, and once in the public sphere this must clearly leave its mark there, as well as on each individual's conceptualizations of privacy.[29]

To make it easier to assess the *different* forms in which privacy is staged in public, I should now like briefly to place these forms in a historical perspective. This will enable us to see that the different genesis in each case suggests a different assessment and that the shifts in the boundary can be conceived from completely different angles. One might draw three such historical lines.[30] Firstly, there is the privatization of the public domain through further emblems of individualization in the 'mobile phone culture'. I suggested above that this does not really represent a *blurring of boundaries* between public and private spheres, but should be seen rather from the perspective of the individualization that accompanies processes of modernization. That the broadening of the scope for an autonomous life in the modern era has also brought costs and ambivalences was something already recognized by Simmel, who spoke of 'loneliness as the reverse side of freedom'.[31]

The exposures that take place in chat shows and other incursions of intimacy into the public realm are indicative, by contrast, of a completely different history, for these phenomena can be classified within the (longer) history of confessional literature on the one hand and the (shorter) history of the culture of therapeutic conversation on the other.[32] Both the confession and therapeutic conversation are interested in the growth of individuality and authenticity and achieve this growth by appealing to what is available to everyone in the same but at the same time highly different ways – one's private life. The confessional genre and conversation culture then come to converge infelicitously with the possibilities of the new media and technologies: in days of old, no self-exposure could have presented itself in so public a manner as through television or the internet. Certainly, it can no more be denied that such processes of individualization may also be processes of increasing authenticity than that the culture of therapeutic conversation has also had emancipatory effects or at least intentions. The ambivalences arise when in the act of self-exposure it is not only that authenticity is won (or supposedly won), but that autonomy – in the sense of the ability to differentiate between close and distant relationships and themes – is lost. The broadening and narrowing of a person's scope for autonomous-authentic self-presentation here seem to go hand in hand. The anti-authoritarian and thoroughly emancipatory gesture and impetus of such a break with taboo is one side of the coin, but the other is the (collective) incursion of intimacy into the public realm and the (individual) loss of differentiation regarding the distinct categories of relationships and themes. This ambivalence is undeniable, but it remains just that – an ambivalence, and accordingly cannot be equated with a general blurring of boundaries between the domains.[33]

Finally, the third line I should briefly like to specify goes back to the slogan, 'The personal/private is political.' As we know, the women's movement[34] used this slogan to try to protest against repressive forms of privacy in the family and relationships in general and against forms of privacy that were typecast and coded in terms of woman and nature and had nothing to do with the normative idea of scope for private action. One of the crucial differences with respect to the second line, however, was that this treatment of family conditions was concerned above all with 'types' rather than 'tokens'. Violence against women and children as a *structure* of social conditions and the gender-specific division of labour as a *structure* of domination were to be discussed in public in an attempt not only to bring to light the political dimension of such structures but first of all to construe them as such in normative terms. This also applied to the removal of sexual taboos. It was evident that this had just as much to do with *individual* relations, families and persons, yet these were not necessarily of interest as individual cases, but at most as paradigms. Politicizing private structures by making them public does not aim for individual authenticity but – as a postulate of justice – for the equal worth of freedom. For this reason, cultural critiques that seek to make the women's movement historically responsible, as it were, for the excessive incursion of intimacy into the realm of politics and the media seem naive in historical terms and not particularly interesting in diagnostic terms.[35] This is not contradicted by the fact that even the movement to politicize repressive private structures was unable to steer clear of ambivalences. Yet these reside elsewhere completely, arising when such politicization results in inappropriate juridification and in general when a hermeneutics of suspicion towards private ways of life and relations can discredit these as such.

Seen from the perspective of privacy as set forth in the course of the last few chapters, the blurring of boundaries between the public and private realms in each of these three aspects should be described as *problematic* in such cases where it contributes to the *breakdown*, the *devaluation* or the *destabilization* of *individual autonomy* in the subject's social relations. And this applies both when people communicate too much about themselves and when they fail to respect the privacy of others. From this perspective of individual autonomy, to which the value of privacy is functionally related, it is also possible to diagnose harmful developments such as phenomena of alienation. But not every shift in the conventional borderline between private and public realms has to be described in the same way as dysfunctional. The three forms of such a shift interact and influence one another mutually. Such interaction is bound to make a more precise diagnosis of the privatization of the public realm a complicated matter. Each one of these three forms of shift has its own costs, yet each of these historical lines also suggests positive effects produced by the shifts in the frontier separating public and private domains, dimensions or themes. And the public realm itself, though it has been made to suffer too,[36] has also so far proved to be comparatively resistant. At the same time, the individual's sense of the value of privacy – and thus also, it might be claimed, his sense of individual autonomy and to this extent a rewarding life – has also shown itself to be too robust, like his sense of the function of the public realm, for it to be possible to equate such processes of de-privatization with a general blurring of boundaries or with a loss of the ability to draw the distinction between the two realms.

3 Concealment: the protection of the public realm from private matters

In dealing up to now with the question of privacy in the public sphere, I have adopted above all a first-person perspective, the perspective of a person staging or making a spectacle of her privacy in public. I should now like to discuss the opposite point of view: what does it mean for the third person in the *public* realm, now that what used to be private can be brought out into the open with no holds barred? What should and what must be kept *private* from the standpoint of the public sphere? This is precisely the problem examined in an essay by Thomas Nagel, who starts out from an interpretation of the Clinton–Lewinsky affair and the public scandal it caused.[37] I want to begin by briefly sketching Nagel's position, before then placing this in a broader context in order to establish, at least tentatively, what it means to want to 'protect' the public realm from too much privacy and who it is that draws these lines between public and private dimensions or realms.

Nagel's objective is to defend a stance of 'cultural liberalism',[38] an attitude that neither takes (excessive) note of private, intimate or personal matters in others, nor makes public an inappropriate amount of one's own personal affairs, in other words that is in general able to distinguish competently between what belongs in public and what does not. Such attitudes, abilities and conventions are vitally necessary not only for liberal culture, but for the continued existence of human civilization in general: civilized social life is only possible if, in principle at least, we keep 'our lustful, aggressive, greedy, anxious, or self-obsessed feelings' to ourselves.[39] Nagel distinguishes three functions of the separation between public and private. Firstly, this separation is what makes possible social relations and communication in general, and without it relationships would founder in the chaos of each individual's private thoughts, intentions and the resulting conflicts and insults.[40] Secondly, the separation has the function of protecting each individual's private life from interference on the part of others, thus making human freedom possible in the first place – not only in spatial terms, but also in terms of social distance.[41] Thirdly, the separation opens up an intermediary realm of intimacy, because it is only on the basis of this separation that subjects are able to disclose themselves to specified others in a specific way.[42] These separations are regulated by conventions that inform us of what is to count as private and what as public and above all at what point we are required to show restraint out of consideration for others. The manner and attitude that keeps to these conventions and establishes the greatest possible degree of liberal personal freedom in social space is termed 'civility'.[43] Nagel understands this sort of liberal culture based on a separation of personal and public attitudes and issues as an 'anticommunitarian vision of civility', since it respects in particular a highly individual way of living one's life and seeks to maintain public social space as neutral as possible.[44] The liberal culture Nagel is aiming for would be a 'mature' culture in so far as these conventions were recognized and such civility prevailed: 'In a civilisation with a certain degree of maturity people know what needs to be brought out into the open where it can be considered jointly or collectively, and what should be left to the idiosyncratic individual responses of each of us.'[45]

It is just such a lack of maturity that induces Nagel to write his article, for over the last dozen years in the United States the developments as regards the separation between the private and public realms or dimensions of life have come to pose a threat to a liberal culture of this type. It is not merely the scandalmongering concerning the President that fills him with indignation, but also the new orthodoxy of multicultural and feminist 'political correctness', which – he feels – seeks to control the public realm and can no longer distinguish between what is left to the discretion of each individual and what requires public supervision. Thanks to this new orthodoxy's craving for control, the old days of a 'genuinely neutral way of talking' are over:[46] 'My main point is a conservative one: that we should try to avoid fights over the public space which force into it more than it can contain without the destruction of civility.'[47]

This is the vision of a cultural liberalism that Nagel develops as a complement to his conceptions of political and juridical liberalism, and it is impressive not only in its phenomenological analyses but also in its social-philosophical diagnoses showing the need for a liberal culture in which civility and indifference in the social realm guarantee and organize each individual subject's scope for freedom and autonomy. Nagel's view of the development of civilization as one that has built up an increasing quantity of increasingly useful taboos concerning what is to be granted access to public, shared space and what is to be denied such access is certainly of great explanatory value when it comes to the question of what the dividing line between private and public realms is actually supposed to be protecting. For a start, one might say that Nagel's theory of 'civil liberalism' supports just the sort of approach that attributes to privacy the function of protecting individual autonomy, as has been set forth in the previous chapters. The creation and facilitation of the individual's scope for freedom in the public realm is dependent, among other things, upon persons respecting the privacy of others, not making undue comments, and protecting this privacy by being able to differentiate competently between what belongs on the public agenda and what does not. In fact, this public agenda may be affected by both social contexts such as conversations and larger, political contexts and discussions.[48] The point that the separation between public and private spheres is conventional and functional in nature and that its function is to protect the autonomy of subjects – in their public life as well – is one that Nagel explicitly makes.

Nonetheless, I should like to propose a number of critical qualifications with respect to Nagel, for there seem to be problems and uncertainties in his account when it comes to the question of how one ascertains what treatment of privacy is necessary and useful in the public realm and what is not, that is *how* that dividing line is actually constituted. In what follows, I should like briefly to discuss the neutrality of language and then the neutrality of the 'issues', before thirdly looking into the question of how the boundary between private and public is drawn.[49]

When Nagel speaks of a 'genuinely neutral way of talking', part of the reason that this is surprising is firstly that he himself also claims that 'genuine pluralism is difficult to achieve'.[50] Nagel considers neutral language to be necessary in the social and political public realm because this for him is the only way of guaranteeing a sufficient measure of civility, in the sense both that the individual's scope for action (the way people want to talk as individuals) is not restricted and that things are not talked about in the public realm that are in fact none of the public realm's business. However, it seems problematic to want to speak of the 'neutrality' of language, for a start because in any social space one of the things that is always debatable, or at least can be debatable, is what the appropriate language is in each particular context and what can be talked about together and how. It is undoubtedly true that there are conventions that are in many respects also functional in nature and that do indeed function. Yet some of the examples cited by Nagel, as with the case of politically correct language, relate to circumstances and situations in which the conventions have lost their meaning. One non-neutral way of talking is called into question, and a different, more appropriate way of talking is sought: this, at least, is one way of understanding the efforts being made to combat racist and sexist forms of expression. One may consider the criticism of these conventions to be wrong, one may want to stick to the old descriptions, one may find the new conventions just as restrictive in a different way, etc., yet the idea is still that linguistic conventions – precisely because they are *linguistic* conventions – are not neutral, but are debatable and will remain so. It can be claimed that the style in which people argue about old and new conventions and descriptions may be better or worse, or that cravings for control on the one side and cravings for dominance on the other are of no benefit to the issue itself, but the underlying point remains the same. Neutrality in the social realm is not the same as pluralism. 'Ways of talking' cannot be neutral, because they are always the language of actors within social and cultural contexts and not a mathematical or logical language invented in functional terms and to this extent objective. Through actors that are socially and culturally 'situated', it is always a certain perspective too that is voiced in public. For this reason, the issue of non-neutral language also refers us to the problem of the (unequal) representation of actors in the public realm.[51]

Language is not neutral, but nor are the themes. Of course, even Nagel concedes that it can be difficult distinguishing between themes that belong in public and those where this is the last thing one wants.[52] At this point, however, one can offer two explanatory distinctions that may throw light upon the problem: firstly the difference between diverse aspects of privacy, and secondly the difference, once again, between 'types' and 'tokens'. For good reasons, indeed, in liberalism we consider the *informational* privacy of each individual's thoughts to merit absolute protection, since the function of protecting such privacy is so unequivocally positive, that is the protection of the freedom of thought of the individual. On this point one can surely concur with Nagel's emphasis. The same goes for the emphasis he places on 'mature liberals' also protecting this sort of informational privacy in such a way as not to unduly burden other people with their own private thoughts and opinions. Yet *these* aspects of the protection of privacy are very different from those associated, for example, with privacy in the traditional sense of the private sphere of the household and that concern unjust social structures, which for their part are genuinely bound up with the coding of private and public.[53] The public airing of themes that used to be understood as private contributes decisively to the creation of more just, more egalitarian structures in the public and private realms alike. But it is not just the classic family issues that are relevant in this context, but also other cases of discrimination that have been driven into the seclusion of the private home. Closet homosexuality is but one example here. Of course, Nagel would not dispute these points. Yet the reason he does not discuss them seems to be that he does not pay sufficient attention to the various meanings of privacy and therefore understates the ambivalences in the treatment of private issues in the public realm. The plausible idea that the so-called progress of civilization is tied up with the acquisition of certain taboos and obligations regarding privacy in order to spare other people from one's own private – and not only bodily – matters, and that this also means that people learn in general to behave more or less decently in public,[54] leaves open the question of which taboos of privacy are in fact functional and which are dysfunctional in the sense of having (exclusively) repressive effects.

There is another distinction that helps explain the complex dividing line between private and public, that is the distinction between 'types' and 'tokens'. The fact that there should be public discussion about homosexuals not having to hide their homosexuality, about the possible associations of sexuality with repressive taboos, violence within the family as a structural problem, and child-raising as a task that is not 'by nature' woman's, does not mean that the individual persons involved in each case, with their private problems, should be made a public issue. Whether Mr X or Ms Y is homosexual is indeed their own business. But whether they are forced by society to conceal this is not. The claim that the borderline between private and public might here be challenged does not make it permissible to drag each individual 'token' into the public eye. But it does mean that for each 'type' it is allowed and possibly necessary to ask the question of whether it is legitimate to understand it as a private matter. This brings us to the complicated and oft analysed and interpreted process of public 'agenda-setting' – who puts what on the public agenda? – as well as the processes of emancipation that are associated with changes in the agenda.[55]

However, Nagel sometimes seems to talk as though he were opposed even in principle to public discussion of certain private 'types', as is the case with his comments on homosexuality.[56] What he appears to be underestimating here is the issue of how practical identities, self-understandings and self-descriptions are constituted through the conceptions and regulations concerning what is to count as public and what as private. One of the reasons for this is that when it comes to the – private – question of what projects I wish to pursue in my life and which plans and options are available to me, I rely upon the – public – provision of a 'supply of meaning', without which I would not be able to describe myself as the person I do. Here one need only adduce, for example, the long public refusal to recognize homosexuality as a sexual orientation of equal value, a refusal that naturally proved a decisive influence upon the private lives as well as the public lives of the persons concerned.[57] For this reason, in part, the question of *which public options* are in fact privately available *to whom* and *in what way*, and which are made unavailable, is no trivial one, and it concerns not only the public discussion of themes that used to be private, such as sexuality and sexual orientation, but also once again the problem of the representation of actors and perspectives within the public domain.[58]

This interplay or dialectic of public and private is made even clearer when we turn in greater detail to the discursive constraints and regulations themselves, for what each individual person is entitled to as her private realm may always be a matter of social power structures as well.

A well-known political illustration of this was the hearing of Clarence Thomas prior to his appointment as associate justice of the Supreme Court. I have already referred above to the way in which the de-privatization of Anita Hill's life and the privatization of Clarence Thomas's behaviour were shaped by sexist and racist clichés,[59] and Fraser has provided an exemplary account of the case. In Nagel, the argument concerning the social authority to define what is allowed to be private and what is not – what forms of freedom and autonomy are protected and what are not – goes no further than the comment that Clarence Thomas's 'bad personal conduct' was irrelevant to the problem of whether or not he could be entrusted with political responsibility.[60] But this, of course, was precisely the point. Thomas was a public figure, and one was justified in disputing whether sexual harassment on the part of a figure aspiring to hold one of the most important public offices in the United States could simply be understood as 'bad personal conduct'. What was at stake here, therefore, and rightly so, was a social discussion about where to draw the borderline between public and private.[61]

Is it in general possible, therefore, to protect the public realm? Must some things be hushed up in order to protect it and to protect other people? Why do we value the protection of the private sphere, and why should we stick with this when it comes to public issues as well? The reason is that everyone – and in this we can surely agree with Nagel – wishes to have a life that is self-determined, unobserved, exempt from commentary, a life of their own, and only in this way is it at the same time possible to keep the distances that spare us too immediate a confrontation with the intimacies of other people. As Nagel shows in exemplary fashion, the private sphere protects in two directions: it is protection *of* a person's privacy, and it is protection *from* a person's privacy. Yet this does not alter the fact that in liberal societies the course of the borderline between private and public themes and realms may be constantly open to dispute, and that what should legitimately be private and what should be public may unfortunately only come to light with public discussion.[62] The criteria for assessing what is a suitable borderline for liberal societies relate to the protection of privacy for the sake of protecting equal freedom and equal autonomy. If conventions are called into question, then an enquiry into the value of privacy is also an enquiry into its function in terms of protecting and permitting autonomy.[63] Even so, this cannot mean that every issue is settled *a priori* or can be resolved in advance. It means only that when it comes to major changes in the course of the boundary between private and public realms it is in accordance with these criteria that judgements should be made. The 'mature' liberal culture to which Nagel refers would be one where there was reflection on the conventional and functional nature of this boundary and the fine balance was maintained between respect for the privacy of individuals and the political awareness that conventions for protecting privacy might also be protecting power structures that in fact have nothing to do with the normative concept of privacy.

4 The private and the public person: dissonant identities

A person is autonomous if she is able to identify authentically with the desires that govern her actions and with her objectives and projects, and if she is also able to pursue these objectives. She is autonomous if she in principle reflects on how she wishes to live and what sort of person she wishes to be, and is then able to live accordingly. The protection of privacy is necessary in various aspects and dimensions in order to guarantee the conditions under which she can develop, learn and then practise such autonomy in the first place. This is what I have been contending in the chapters thus far. This notion of autonomy and privacy, however, seems to involve a comparatively strong concept of the unity of the private and the public subject. This subject is autonomous if – in private and public alike – he lives as he has resolved to autonomously and under conditions of authenticity, if he pursues the plans he has developed on his own and with others, and if he authentically can be, and is, the person he wants to be.

Yet how strong and how complete must this unity be between the public and the private person? May there not also be crucial differences between the person privately and for herself on the one hand and the person for others, her public life, plans and actions on the other hand? My concern in this chapter, as I explained at the outset, is with the ambivalences of privacy. For this reason, I now wish to conclude by discussing this ambivalence in the context of the specific problem of the proposed unity of the public and the private person.[64] Once again, this can only be a sketch of the problems.

Before turning to these questions in somewhat greater detail, I should first like to take a step backwards to ask what concept of identity is at stake here.[65] As we know, the question can be approached from a philosophical perspective on the one hand in terms of the theoretical identity of persons. At issue here is the metaphysical-ontological problem of the spatiotemporal continuity of persons. On the other hand, there is the problem of practical identity. The concern here is the moral-ethical question of what sort of person one wants to see oneself as and the question of one's practical self-understanding.[66] While questions of theoretical identity cannot always be conceived independently from questions of practical identity,[67] nor vice versa, we can shelve this complication for the time being because in examining the issue of practical identity that interests us we can proceed as though the problem of theoretical identity were already resolved. Yet even this practical identity can be described in two ways, namely diachronically and synchronically. The heuristic nature of this distinction is of course even more patent than in the case of the distinction between quantitative and qualitative identity. Even so, it can be said that the self-identity of the subject can be considered, by himself as well as by others, both in synchronic and in diachronic terms. There is a meaningful difference between the question, 'what sort of person do I see myself as with this specific biography, with these specific plans, etc.?' and the question, 'what sort of person do I see myself as in the multiplicity of my (present) roles, plans, desires and commitments?'

The question of the identity of the public and the private person seems to be a question concerning the synchronic practical identity of persons. I should like to claim that at least in one particular sense of 'private' one can meaningfully speak of a *sui generis* distinction here. For a start, the difference between the private and the public person is *not* the same as the difference between the self and its roles,[68] an idea that suggests that there is an (authentic) self to which the (inauthentic, public) roles are as it were appended. Yet this is not what is meant by the distinction between the private and the public person. Nor, to this extent, is it the same as the distinction between authentic being-for-oneself and inauthentic being-for-others.[69] Nor is this view of the person the same as the view of the modern (or postmodern) fragmentations of the self,[70] which expresses that it is no longer possible to speak of the *unity* of the subject, however dissonant this might be, because the idea of unity (and of the subject) is questionable as such and *a fortiori* no longer explanatory for practical questions of ethics.[71] Though in fact closely linked to it, Rorty's distinction between the private and the public self is not meant either, for Rorty attributes sharply differing and clearly defined functions both to the private and the public self – that is private self-creation versus the public avoidance of cruelty – without binding them together in the sort of unity that would justify one in speaking of an identity, albeit a dissonant one.[72]

Having begun by distinguishing between the problem of the identity of the private and the public person on the one hand and diverse conceptions of (authentic or inauthentic) fragmentations of the subject on the other, we must now make a further distinction between two approaches to the question of this identity. This distinction relates to what exactly is meant by the concept of privacy. If privacy is conceived *firstly* in terms of the privacy of domestic life, the family, and even friendships or relationships of loyalty to 'specified others' in general, then a conflict of public and private identity would be one where the person's behaviour, opinions and convictions were completely different in this sort of private context from in public contexts.

This general difference between private and public life can again be specified in two distinct ways. The first of these confronts us with a relatively uncomplicated problem. The second confronts us with a complicated problem, which, like the first, nonetheless does not indicate a *sui generis* difference between the private and the public person.

The relatively uncomplicated problem is addressed, for example, by Rawls, when he writes about possible differences between the personal life of citizens and their political identity as citizens of a state: 'It can happen that in their personal affairs, or in the internal life of associations, citizens may regard their final ends and attachments very differently from the way the political conception supposes.'[73] What Rawls is here referring to are possible differences between on the one hand what people in their private convictions and aspirations consider to be right and strive for, and on the other hand what may be demanded of them as state citizens with a 'public identity' (as Rawls calls it) and what they may perfectly well support with this part of their identity.[74] Rawls does not go into possible conflicts between private and public values, opinions and attitudes, but this is presumably simply because differences and even conflicts here are actually provided for and therefore comparatively harmless. Indeed, the very idea of liberal democracies is that one pursues different goals, has different loyalties, and holds different values to be important, depending on whether one is viewing oneself as the citizen of a state or the mother of a family, as engaged in neighbourly help or chairing the works council. The idea is thus that one plays different roles depending on the context one is involved in and on the opinions and convictions one has in that context. Here too, conflicts can of course arise from a first-person perspective: if, for example, I on the one hand consider myself to be a convinced liberal democrat and citizen of the state (and am thus also convinced of the legitimacy of the results of democratic procedures), but on the other hand am a strict Catholic and participate actively in organizations against legal regulations permitting abortion. This difference *could* be described as one between public (civil) and private identity. Yet by no means need it lead to serious cognitive or psychological dissonances. Though from the first-person perspective it is perhaps not a harmless case, it is unproblematic within the context of liberal democracies. It would be a very different matter if someone who publicly espoused equal rights for women and men played the patriarch at home. Yet this would be a problem of the person's general moral-ethical integrity, and it would be inappropriate to describe it in terms of a distinction – let alone a *sui generis* distinction – between public and private identity. Such an appeal to the difference between public and private would here be contingent.

This can be seen even more clearly by looking at the second, comparatively complicated set of problems. This has to do with people who have and display *categorically* different convictions, modes of conduct and attitudes depending on whether they see themselves as private or as public – categorically different from a moral perspective. Here, as we know, we might describe the cases of the Nazis who publicly participated in the crimes of the National Socialists, but in private were apparently devoted fathers (or mothers), or the publicly murderous 'doctors' of the concentration camps, who in private were caring doctors and human beings who kept to their oath.[75] In this issue, however, I do not find the categories of private or public at all helpful. What needs explaining about these cases is not the difference in behaviour between private and public contexts. The fact that these different contexts can also be described as private or public does not seem intrinsic to the real problem, even though it might be claimed that certain ideologies of the private life (privacy as the radically other in relation to a hostile reality) may facilitate such splits and did in fact do so. What needs explanation is rather the psychological and moral split between criminal conduct on the one hand and morally acceptable conduct on the other. These are questions of psychological pathology and moral integrity, but it does not appear to be of any explanatory help trying to explain and interpret these splits by means of the concepts of private and public.[76]

So far we have looked at cases where 'private' refers to the privacy of family life, personal contexts, etc. We may *secondly*, however, consider privacy not in the sense of this private, personal life, but specifically in the sense that the 'private self' is what is only accessible to each individual alone, or what manifests itself when the person is entirely on her own. In contrast, 'public' is here understood to signify any other context, that is any context in which (at least) one other person is present. It then becomes possible to pose the question of the unity of the private and the public person in yet a different way.

In this case, the unity of the private and the public self, or the lack of such unity, has to do with the fact that a person may see herself differently when she is *completely on her own* in private from when she is in public. She can, so to speak, autonomously determine or create herself in such a manner that she acts and thinks (completely) differently in private or in isolation from how she does in public contexts, for and with other people. This sort of broken, dissonant unity need not *necessarily* be inauthentic, providing at least that private and public life are not set apart in such a way that only one of them is conceived as the genuine, deliberate, intentional and desirable one. When Nagel says, apparently straightforwardly, that 'the division of the self protects the limited public space from unmanageable encroachment and the unruly inner life from excessive inhibition',[77] the question that suggests itself is how far this 'division' can be taken and whether it is not inconsistent with the idea of an autonomous, authentic subject and a rewarding, autonomous life. After all, it might be objected (on ethical grounds) that a separation of this sort constitutes an inauthentic double life, or (on moral grounds) that it is hypocritical or sanctimonious or is deceitful towards others.[78]

I should now like to explicate the possibility of such a difference or dissonant unity with the help of the interpretation of a story by Henry James, 'The Private Life'.[79] This not only clarifies the possible significance of such a difference, but also shows why it may not only not be problematic but might possibly even be recommendable. The question is whether this sort of self-division is hypocritical, deceptive, even pathological, or simply a way of living one's life.

'The Private Life' is a short, unusual story about the possible dissociation of the private and the public self, the private and the public person.[80] A small group of six people from London's artistic and intellectual scene meet up in a Swiss health resort for a holiday of leisure.[81] At the centre of attention are the admired and acclaimed poet Clare Vawdrey and, as host, the distinguished Lord Mellifont, a painter. Accompanying them are the latter's wife, Lady Mellifont, as well as Blanche Adney, an actress and star of the London stage, with her husband, a highly respected composer.

The story is narrated from the first-person perspective of a young and ambitious (unnamed) poet during the final days of the holiday. These final days are spent not only going for strolls and idly chatting, but also pressing and finally persuading Vawdrey to read out the last chapter of his work-in-progress. The short story concludes with the whole company departing early due to a storm. The final view is from London, where the six of them find themselves back in their customary social circles again.

The story acquires tension early on through the intimation that there is something the matter with Clare Vawdrey, who – though a gifted poet – is also a surprisingly conventional, indeed a downright boring conversationalist, and finally through the disclosure of his secret: Vawdrey is in fact composed of two 'persons' or 'selves', one of whom writes and the other who appears in public, with others and for others. Yet this is not all. Together with the inquisitive Blanche Adney, the narrator finds out that Lord Mellifont, such a stylish host, in fact only exists in public. Left alone, he simply vanishes or ceases to exist. In spite of these odd circumstances, however, the tone of the tale is not one of agitation, but of ironical amusement. Although it all sounds rather eerie, it does not really come over as a 'ghost story'.

The story's leitmotif or basic theme is established by the first sentence: 'We talked of London face to face with a great bristling primeval glacier.' This is indeed one of those stories in which everything that is to happen or be narrated subsequently is prefigured in the first sentence. Between London and the glacier, culture and nature, sociality and inwardness, between public and private life, the group – the 'we' referred to – sits together and *talks*.[82] They discover to their surprise how 'nice' everyone is away from London ('I had no idea you were really so nice,' says Vawdrey's public self), and this is precisely the issue – 'that revelation of our being after all human'. This is, the narrator adds, 'exactly my story':[83] being human 'after all', at this midpoint between nature and culture, between the inner, private life and the outward, public life of the persons involved. 'Privacy' is here clearly meant in the specific sense in which the 'private self' is what is only accessible to the individual alone.

The focus here is on the poet Vawdrey. Right at the outset, we read this first more detailed account of Vawdrey's public style, in which the poet's irritating tone comes across:

> He never talked about himself. [. . .] [H]e apparently never even reflected. He had his hours and his habits [. . .] but all these things together never made up an attitude. [. . .] *He* was exempt from variations, and not a shade either less or more nice in one place than in another. He differed from other people but never from himself [. . .]. He might have been always in the same company, so far as he recognised any influence from age or condition or sex: he addressed himself to women exactly as he addressed himself to men, and gossiped with all men alike, talking no better to clever folk than to dull. I used to wail to myself over his way of liking one subject – so far as I could tell – precisely as much as another.[84]

This tolerance and the accompanying indifference in Vawdrey's relation to any topic of conversation, the friendly but boring absence of genuine involvement, is a discovery that the narrator finds rather sinister, yet it clearly also has its comic sides. Together with Blanche Adney, he tries to get to the bottom of his perplexity, and it is this search that culminates in the revelation that Vawdrey's writing self is a different one from the self with whom the public world is confronted.

The obvious counterpart to Vawdrey is the figure of Mellifont, who is nothing but his public self, who is 'all public' and has 'no corresponding private life'.[85] He is all 'tone' and 'style', and brilliantly so:

> The handsomest man of his period [. . .] directed the conversation by gestures as irresistible as they were vague; one felt as if without him it wouldn't have had anything to call a tone. This was essentially what he contributed [. . .] above all to English public life. He pervaded it, he coloured it, he embellished it, and without him, it would have lacked, comparably speaking, a vocabulary.[86]

As it emerges, however, there is nothing more to him than this. Unobserved, he ceases to be there at all, as Blanche Adney discovers during a stroll: 'his lordship', she tells the narrator, 'isn't even whole. [. . .] [T]here isn't so much as one, all told, of Lord Mellifont.' The narrator understands at once: 'he struck me as so essentially, so conspicuously and uniformly the public character that I read in a flash the answer to Blanche's riddle.'[87] The narrator, after all, himself also a writer, is a paradigmatically 'integrated' person, a person whose inner life and relationship to himself, his feelings and memories, etc., are not in conflict with his public, social conduct, and who is just as capable of expressing his sensibility and perceptivity in isolation, in privacy or on his own as in his behaviour towards others. This would explain the narrative function of the description of the small excursion he makes on his own into the mountains.[88]

The theme of the story, established on its first page, is the question of what 'being human' means in the face of possible deviations, pathologies, conflicts or ruptures between the private and the public self and also *within* the private or public self. Apart from the narrator (and the composer Adney), all the characters manifest in their personalities or identities a rupture *between* the public and private person or a rupture *within* the public or private person. Yet by no means does this entail the collapse of their personalities. They do not go under on account of these ruptures, and in the cases of Mellifont and Vawdrey the rifts are clearly not even cause for suffering. James is not implying, therefore, that a rewarding life is only possible for personalities who lead their lives without such ruptures, 'aches' or 'maladies'. On the contrary, though the narrator himself – wonderfully integrated person that he is – seems 'good', he also comes over as just a little bit insignificant and somewhat boring.

What James seems to be showing instead is that the chasm between the private and the public self does not point to the need for a person to be perfectly integrated. On the contrary, the decision about what is to count as private and what as public may also be an expression of a successful identity. James describes ruptures between the private and the public self as variations on the daily theme of 'being human'. Concealing oneself as a private person, showing (total) restraint towards others in public, is at any rate not diagnosed as a pathology. Indeed, in the case of Vawdrey – and also, in a different way, with Mellifont – it is the very condition for (artistic) imagination, and as such it subsequently contributes to the enrichment of public life. Even Vawdrey's writings, that is the writings of the private Vawdrey, are read in public, and it is the private Vawdrey of all people who writes *for* the public. It is only by (completely) withholding his private self from public sociality that this self is made available to him in a way that permits him to exert his *true* influence on the public, which is through his books. The fissure in the self here proves to be an enrichment of life, indeed opening up (artistic) possibilities to which the completely integrated person would not have access.

James's scepticism as to whether one's private life must always correspond to one's public life is not to be equated here with Rorty's distinction between private self-creation and the moral public self. James counters any such reading in Rortyan terms through the figure of Mellifont, to whom private self-creation can certainly not be attributed. Nor is James's scepticism directed at the possibility of unity in principle, for each of the 'selves' remains identifiable as *one* person, who, for whatever reasons, simply wants to stage himself as non-integrated.[89] Even a reading of James's figures as embodiments of a (private or authentic) self with various (public) roles is falsified by the variety of modes in which the difference between private and public manifests itself. The ambivalences of such a weak, dissonant conception of the identity of the public and private person come to light, however, in the faint suspicions other people harbour that they are being deceived by these figures. Such is the case not only with Lady Mellifont, who feels cheated by her 'absent' husband, but also with the people who talk or listen to the boring, public Vawdrey. Withholding or refusing to disclose one's (richer) private self may thus assume moral dimensions. Is Mellifont deceiving his wife through his private non-existence? Is he in some way to blame for her 'painless malady'? Is Vawdrey deceiving his listeners by hiding his rich private self from them or at any rate only displaying it in his writings?[90] These ambivalences also come to light when we are given to believe that the private Vawdrey feels neither interest nor approval for his public life. At these points, we sense that the persons in question lead a different and in their eyes better life 'for themselves' than the one – with its goals, projects and practices – that they pursue in public 'for others'. Indeed, their very autonomy seems to be jeopardized to the extent that they do not live authentically – in diverse contexts – as the person they want to be. Finally, ambivalences also come to light where the boundary between everyday dissonances and pathological differences becomes one that is difficult to draw.

Nonetheless, if the rift is conceived in weaker terms and not, to all intents and purposes, as a doubling, there is no need for the dissonance between the private and public self to entail a lack of autonomy. It may be the expression of a life that is fashioned and lived autonomously. James, of course, does not *argue* for such a model. He simply opens up possibilities for interpreting the relationship of the private and public person in this way, but it is an interpretation that would in turn, of course, have to be substantiated with reasons and arguments. I have not done this here, but have merely provided a sketch of the ambivalences. These could not only be further analysed in greater detail, but also taken as a starting point to focus from a different angle on the question of what it is about the autonomous subject that makes this – dissonant – identity possible, what role the imagination must be given, and how the *various* dimensions of privacy fit in to such an identity. Yet all this can and should be no more than an outline.

James's scepticism as to whether one's private life must correspond to one's public life follows on from reflections on the value of privacy as found in the solitude of one's private life history, in being-for-oneself in one's private thoughts as opposed to one's relationships to others, in the seclusion of one's room, in one's own company. For each of the three dimensions of privacy – decisional, informational and local – we have seen that the protection of privacy always has to do both with the protection *of* relations and *within* relations, protection *with* others and protection *from* others. Each of the three dimensions therefore also includes the protection of the solitary subject from all others. Even if an autonomous, good or rewarding life is for the most part a life in and with relations towards others, and even if one's own life-plans and goals – one's own life – always involve other people, the dissonant remainder is still there. Identities do not have to be completely integrated. A rewarding life may be just the sort of life for which the value of privacy comes to light even in such ruptures.

Notes

Chapter 1 Introduction

1 See Bobbio (1989) 1ff. and Weintraub (1997) 1ff.
2 See, for example, Habermas (1992c); see also Arendt (1989) 22ff.
3 Sennett (2002).
4 See Elias (1993); see also Revel et al. (1993). On privacy as compared between cultures (among other things), on the other hand, see Duerr (1994b) 165ff.
5 See the various volumes on the history of private life edited by Ariès and Duby (1987–91), in particular Perrot (1990), on the changes in the structure of the family in the nineteenth century and the transformation of the coding of intimacy in the same period.
6 See Engler (1994), Probst (1998), Mueller-Doohm and Jung (1998).
7 See here, for example, Reichwein et al. (1993), Meyer (1992), also Giddens (1992), Beck and Beck-Gernsheim (2001).
8 See Ariès (1993). It is controversial just how far one can actually speak of a 'fundamental significance' here. For a critical view see, for example, Nelson (1990), also Helly and Reverby (1992). See further below in ch. 6.
9 See here Pateman (1989b) as a starting-point, as well as Landes (1998) and Kerchner and Wilde (1997). I shall return to these theories and debates exhaustively below (ch. 2).
10 See also Davidoff (1998) and Helly and Reverby (1992). However, feminist literature is not the first to experience the private home as oppressive confinement. On conflicts and the privative features of privacy in the nineteenth century, see for example Perrot (1990). For an instructive account of the changes in the interior in painting, see also Gramaccini (1998).
11 See Warren and Brandeis (1984).
12 Shils (1956), Westin (1967), Whitaker (1999). See in detail below in ch. 5, sec. 2.
13 See again Warren and Brandeis (1984); also Turkington and Allen (1999).
14 See here Alexy (1986) 327ff., 334ff.
15 See Schoeman (1992), Benn and Gaus (1983b) and Bier (1980). These will be treated in greater detail below. My work understands itself as a contribution to social and political philosophy. The epistemological and semantic problems of a private language or the privacy of sensations will here accordingly play only a very marginal role.
16 The history of liberal privacy assumes a different appearance depending on when it is taken to begin: with Hobbes and the experiences of the wars of religion, with Locke

and property and liberty, or with Mill and the private freedom from social control. I shall return to these concepts and their inconsistencies in the following chapters.

17 See in greater detail below, ch. 2, sec. 3 and ch. 4, sec. 1.

18 This is also made clear by the various volumes of *A History of Private Life*: Ariès and Duby (1987–91). See Ariès (1993), and, critical of this approach, Nelson (1990). On the history of the concept in general, see for example Elshtain (1981), Westin (1967) 8ff., Weintraub (1997). On individual stages of the philosophical history of the concept, see Saxonhouse (1983), Gobetti (1992), Walton (1983). 'Privacy' or 'private' does not appear as a lemma either in the *Historisches Wörterbuch der Philosophie* (Historical Dictionary of Philosophy) or in *Geschichtliche Grundbegriffe* (Lexicon of Foundational Historical Concepts) (although here the various compounds of 'private-' are broken down in detail in the index).

19 Meaning and definition should be distinguished because the description of the heterogeneous usage – and thus of the meaning – of the concept does not in itself imply an unambiguous definition (while a definition on the other hand naturally does determine an unambiguous meaning). A unified usage (and meaning) can of course be disputed (which is what Thomson does (1974), see ch. 3, sec. 4 below), but this is not what I wish to do. As it happens, according to the *Duden* German dictionary (22nd edn, 2000), the word *Privatheit* (privacy) does not exist in German. I am using the word in spite of this because it is established in everyday German. On the etymology of the German word *privat* see the interesting account in Grimm's German Dictionary.

20 On the following see Inness (1992) 3ff., Allen (1988) 5ff., Benn and Gaus (1983a) 4ff., Bok (1983) 5ff., Gerstein (1978). See also the threefold differentiation of the meaning of 'private' in R. Dworkin (1994) 51ff. See also W. L. Weinstein (1971).

21 For a good account of this see Bok (1983) 10ff. See also Allen (1988) 24f.

22 For this reason, the protection of secrecy is stronger in legal terms than the protection of privacy or of the realm of intimacy (as in the privacy of the post). On this see Branahl (1998). See Wasserstrom (1984), who interprets privacy above all as the realm of what is secret, hidden or concealed and thus seeks to bring to light the connotations of deception and deceit.

23 See here especially Benn and Gaus (1983a) 7ff.

24 It can also be attributed to organizations and institutions, although I am here concerned with the privacy of persons (to this extent itself of course just one sector of the meaning). However, it will become clear that derivative uses of 'private', such as those that refer to institutions, can also be explained using the definition proposed below. On the varied use of 'private' see also Okin (1991) 68ff.

25 See Allen (1988) 5ff., Inness (1992) 95ff.

26 Only on a fourth level do we then find the state itself as a final form of public realm in opposition to all the prior stages. Yet these differences do not all lie on the same scale. On this point see again Okin (1991) 70ff.

27 On this see the very precise account in Benn and Gaus (1983a) 7ff. The question is posed in each case from distinct perspectives: who is affected, who is responsible, who has access to something, who is visible?

28 This type thus incorporates aspects of the second model.

29 Here we find aspects from model one and model two. Diaries belong here too, for they contain 'private knowledge' and to this extent become a private object. For an analysis of these different aspects of 'information', see in greater detail below in ch. 5, sec. 1.

30 This in turn includes aspects of the first model.

31 Further, philosophy is almost alone in its interest in an exact definition of the concept. In other discourses, some notion of privacy (such as the household, or the sphere of intimacy) is usually taken for granted without being defined any more precisely.

32 See here for example Kymlicka (1990a) 248ff.

33 Albeit in conjunction with the idea of privacy as 'intimacy'. See Arendt (1989) 58ff. See in greater detail below in ch. 4, sec. 4.

34 Above all in ch. 2, see secs 1 and 2.

35 See Warren and Brandeis (1984) 76 (original dates from 1890). They relate this very general right to the protection of the 'inviolate personality'; see *passim.* What prompted the article to be written was Warren's anger at the intrusions of the press at his daughter's wedding: 'The press is overstepping in every direction the obvious bounds of propriety and of decency' ((1984) 76). See Prosser (1960) for a brilliant survey of the right to privacy in the United States up until 1960. Prosser concludes his article with the comment: 'All this is a most marvelous tree to grow from the wedding of the daughter of Mr. Samuel D. Warren' ((1960) 423).

36 See Parent (1983).

37 Gavison (1980) 428. Gavison also takes up the three moments to which I shall return later: 'information', 'attention' and 'physical access to X' (ibid.), yet without associating these with the concept of control. See Allen (1988) 11, who here mentions various other *access-definitions*: 'Condition of being protected from unwanted access by others; lack of access to information related to intimacies [. . .] an existential condition of limited access to an individual's life experiences and engagements.'

38 Allen (1988) 15. See 16: 'A person can be inaccessible in at least three senses: physically, dispositionally, and informationally.'

39 For this reason, Schoeman is not particularly convincing either when he writes: 'A man shipwrecked on a deserted island or lost in a dense forest has unfortunately lost control over who has information about him, but we would not want to say that he has no privacy' ((1984c) 3), here arguing against definitions that regard 'control' as a constitutive factor in the definition. Perhaps indeed we would not want to say that he has no privacy, but nor would we claim the opposite – we would be most likely to say that the predicate 'private' has no meaningful use in this context. The moment of conscious control does seem to be constitutive for the meaning of privacy: we can catch ourselves being 'alone', but not being 'private', for this makes no sense semantically.

40 See the confusing account in Westin (1967) 40f., who describes the solitary confinement of prisoners as an example of 'too much' privacy. To speak of privacy here is wrong even in terms of his own definition, for which see the following note.

41 Westin (1967) 7. Yet see also 32: 'privacy is the voluntary and temporal withdrawal of a person from the general society.' Westin is not fully consistent here. See also Gross (1971) 172f.

42 Fried (1968) 482. Two sentences further on we read: 'The person who enjoys privacy is able to grant or deny access to others.' This is clearly not the same definition. Both together, however, specify precisely the dimensions that together go to make up the realm of privacy. I shall return to this shortly. See also Fried (1968) 489f. on the 'privilege' of privacy as contingent (because it can be defined in various ways) and symbolic (because it is an expression of society's will to recognize the idea of privacy on principle and in general).

43 I. Young (1990) 119, 120.

44 Inness (1992) 56. See 69: 'The intimacy of these aspects of privacy constitutes the conceptual focus of privacy.' Accordingly, the next step for Inness must be to define

intimacy, which she does as follows: 'When an agent characterizes an act or activity as intimate, she is claiming that it draws its meaning and value from her love, liking, or care. Intimate decisions concern such matters and, thus, involve a choice on the agent's part about how to (or not to) embody her love, liking, or care' ((1992) 74f.). Privacy is thus conceptually tied to 'love', 'liking' and 'care'. Yet this fails to take central aspects of the concept into account.

45 Bok (1983) 10f. Bok's work is a relatively popular book about secrecy, not privacy. She does not propose a general theory of privacy in it, but outlines, as far as I can see, its most plausible definition.

46 Similar approaches, though less precise in their definitions, are also to be found in Benn and Schoeman. See Benn (1988) 264ff., Schoeman (1992) 11ff. I shall return to both later. See also J. L. Cohen (1992), who uses a very broad concept of privacy with its diverse dimensions, without defining it explicitly.

47 I avoid using Bok's term 'condition' so as to be able to incorporate dwellings and actions as well.

48 Completely different sorts of information may be at issue here. The misconception that we give up all privacy when we go out onto the streets should be dispelled from the outset. On the streets people are protected by other forms – other dimensions – of privacy than at home. See the implausible account in Parent (1983) 344.

49 This conceptual scheme and these dimensions are of course elucidated in greater detail in the following chapters. Yet it is not too soon to point out that drawing boundaries in this way requires subjective abilities. One is not respecting one's own informational privacy, for example, if one reveals too much about oneself in the wrong contexts. Conversely, excessive secretiveness about one's own private life in social contexts can also be interpreted as incompetence in dealing with one's own (informational) privacy. I shall come back to all this later.

50 See again Elias (1993).

51 See Benn (1984), Schoeman (1992) 151ff. See in detail below, ch. 3, sec. 4.

52 That this is only one side of the liberal conceptual scheme, however, will become clear below. See ch. 2, sec. 2.

53 Habermas for one speaks of such a 'family' and of a 'family quarrel' (2002b) 275; see also 50. Waldron likewise speaks of an 'extended family' (1993c) 35. The attempt can also be made to highlight the differences between the positions. In this spirit, see Mendus (1989) 71ff. I must of course keep my sketch of the following four principles very concise.

54 Kymlicka speaks of this (1990a) 50ff., at least as an idea (he calls the position 'liberal equality'). See Brunkhorst (1994) 116ff.

55 See Charles Taylor: the goals of a liberal-democratic society have generally included 'freedom, self-government, and a rule of right founded on equality. A viable liberal society has to take account of all of them [. . .]'; Taylor (1995a) 287. See R. Dworkin (1990) 3 for the distinction between various forms of liberalism. See also Höffe (1994) and Kersting (1997) 397ff.

56 See Habermas (1997), Rawls (1972) 60 ff., R Dworkin (1990) 9ff., R. Dworkin (1978), Waldron (1993c). See in general also Koller (1996).

57 See Mill (1910) 75, Kant (1991) 73ff; Constant (1987); R. Dworkin (1990) 9f. and 19f. On the expansion of liberal civil liberties to all persons and expansion in the sense of a substantiation of social rights, see Forst (2002) 52ff.

58 On the communitarian critique, see below, ch. 4, sec. 2.

59 See ch. 3, secs 2 and 3.

60 And of course it is not only every *liberal* theory that accepts as much. The question is how strongly this has to be interpreted.
61 See again Waldron (1993c) 37ff.
62 R. Dworkin (1983) 2.
63 See R. Dworkin (1981a) and (1981b).
64 See Rawls (1972) 204f. and 76ff.
65 See Habermas (1997), R. Dworkin (1981b). On Rawls, see Hinsch (1997b). See also Okin (1995).
66 Waldron (1993c) 428n; see also Sen (1992).
67 I shall return in detail to the problematic concept of equal liberties in ch. 2, sec. 4.
68 See R. Dworkin (1983) 1: 'Liberals believe [. . .] that government must be neutral in matters of personal morality, that it must leave people free to live as they think best so long as they do not harm others.' R. Dworkin here even seems to be claiming that neutrality must be the 'first principle' of liberalism. On the problems of neutrality in general, see Forst (2002). See also Larmore (1987) 40ff.
69 See Mill (1910) 131ff. See in greater detail below, ch. 4.
70 Rawls distinguishes between various forms of neutrality of procedures, aims and results, see (1999d), (1993). On neutrality see Habermas (1997). See Hinsch (1997a). On the problems inherent in the idea that autonomy and individual freedom always entail the pursuit of very specific 'values', see the communitarian critique by Sandel (1996).
71 Rawls (1999b) 458ff.
72 On the feminist critique of liberal neutrality, see MacKinnon (1989) 155ff., 215ff. See Sandel (1996).
73 See Habermas (1992d), Wellmer (1993), I. Young (1990) 96ff.
74 See Habermas (1997).
75 Also open to dispute is whether it is possible to have a constitutional state without democracy and whether – historically – there has ever existed a connection ('reconciliation') between the two notions. See Habermas (1997) and (2002b), Rawls (1999d).
76 On the theory of democracy see Habermas (1997), Phillips (1991), Mendus (1992a), Bohman and Rehg (1997).
77 See I. Young (1990) 96ff. See also Phillips (1987b) and (1991) 60ff., 120ff. See Lang (1994). In general see also Nussbaum (1999a).
78 In situating myself within such a liberal framework, I am being more optimistic than Carole Pateman, who writes: 'The history of liberal feminism is the history of attempts to generalize liberal liberties and rights to the whole adult population; but liberal feminism does not, and cannot, come to grips with the deeper problems of how women are to take an equal place in the patriarchal civil order' ((1989c) 51; emphasis omitted). I shall justify this optimism in greater detail below (ch. 2).
79 See Nozick (1974).
80 See Sandel (1996), Arendt (1989), Butler (1992). I shall return to each of these positions below.
81 See Westin (1967) 8ff., 23ff. See Moore's historical orientation (1984). See also Ortner (1998).
82 Hall (1990), Duerr (1994b), Shils (1956) 36ff. What is striking is that in the US there have been major studies on (informational) privacy since the 1950s, while comparable studies are not to be found in Germany. This contrasts strangely with the fact that in Germany and Europe – but not in the US – the social interest in the protection of informational privacy is so marked that it has had clear legislative repercussions (as

in the European Union directive, for which see below, ch. 5, sec. 2). On the other hand, in the US there is no study on the public realm comparable (or comparably influential) to Habermas's, even though, for example, the goods of freedom of the press and the right to free speech enjoy much higher legal status in the US compared with the protection of individual personhood.

83 See above on Warren and Brandeis (1984).

84 *Roe v. Wade,* 410 U.S. 113 (1973).

85 On this whole problematic area, see in greater detail below, ch. 4, sec. 1.

86 See the enlightening account in Hall (1990) 123ff.

87 See Allen (2004), and below, ch. 5, sec. 2.

88 BGHZ 26, 349f. (trans. by R. G.). The difference with respect to the US is clearly due above all to the completely different status attached to the freedom of the press and the right to free speech. See the instructive case descriptions in Alderman and Kennedy (1995) 154ff.

89 BGHZ 26, 355.

90 In this case it was admittedly only a federal court, the New York Court of Appeal (*Finger v. Omni*).

91 Alderman and Kennedy (1995) 219. See the exact grounds given in 77 N.Y. 2d 138.

92 On the following see Honneth (1996a).

93 Even procedures that are in this sense constructive are possibly dependent upon the reconstruction of (moral) intuitions in the existing norms. With this distinction between constructive and reconstructive procedures or procedural moments I wish to refer to the different status attached to purely normative grounds, on the one hand, and grounds derived from reflection on social practices, on the other.

94 For a different view see Brown (1995) 154ff.

Chapter 2 Equal Freedom, Equal Privacy

1 Sayers (1984) 169.

2 The history of the pair of concepts 'private' and 'public' has been reappraised very well by feminist criticism. On the following, see for example Benhabib and Nicholson (1988), Okin (1979), (1989b) and (1991), Helly and Reverby (1992), Klinger (1995b). See also Klinger (1996), and more generally also DeCew (1997), Pauer-Studer (1996b), Nagl-Docekal (1996a). See also Ariès and Duby (1987–91), especially the fourth volume (Perrot (1990)), with its articles on the development of private life in the nineteenth century. See also Gramaccini (1998) on the historical transformation of images of privacy in art. That the assignment of women to the world of 'feelings' is not entirely a thing of the past is something that can be corroborated by glancing at any magazine. *Der Spiegel* (11 Oct. 1999, 'Buchmesse Extra') has the title: 'The women are coming! Lots of new stories from the world of feelings.'

3 See Benhabib and Nicholson (1988) 515.

4 On the correlation of nature and culture, women and men, private and public as a cross-cultural phenomenon, see the now classic article by Ortner (1998). See also Tseëlon (1983).

5 See Benhabib and Nicholson (1988) 515: 'The sphere of traditional female life – reproduction, housework and bringing up children – [is] not considered to be an essential component of political life. [. . .] (But) even if it lies outside the political

sphere, the sphere of traditional female life [must] be controlled by politics and subordinate to it' (trans. by R. G.).

6 The practical implementation of this idea, however, has always produced ambiguities in the concept of privacy and uncertainties in the separation of the realms. Along with the private civil liberties, for example, the economy has been and still is regarded as one of the classic realms of privacy, even though the appeal to the concept of privacy in the two contexts – religious freedom and the economy – obviously has a different significance. This is quite apart from the fact that with the development of the welfare state the sphere of private enterprise has been and still is subjected to considerable political intervention. On these various aspects of the term, see Okin (1991). See also Kymlicka (1990a) 250ff.

7 See Mill (1910) 75f., 144f. I shall return to Mill in greater detail shortly.

8 The dilemma can also be expressed in terms of 'head' (or 'reason') and 'heart': 'Hast Du Verstand und ein Herz, so zeige nur eines von beiden. / Beides verdammen sie Dir, zeigst Du beides zugleich', as Hölderlin famously puts it ('If you have reason and a heart, only show one of them. If you show them both at once, the two will be your undoing'). Hölderlin, however, has other conflicts in mind than the ones at issue here.

9 See Ortner again (1998) as the *locus classicus*. Tseëlon speaks of a 'cross-cultural dichotomy between nature and culture. Women are perceived as closer to and are identified with nature, while men are identified with culture. The natural sphere is then designated as the private domain, the home, while the cultural sphere as the public domain, the outside world' ((1983) 111). She also writes: 'Thus two sets of oppositional terms are posited: *nature-private-women* vs. *culture-public-men* which are based on three principles: action (nature/culture), space (private/public), actors (women/men)' (ibid.). Tseëlon criticizes these simple dichotomies as inadequate for an understanding of the symbolic-social construction of 'women'. For an illustration of the question of what is 'naturally' regarded as private, see Held's comment on the cultural construction of the breast-feeding of infants as a (supposedly) purely biological process ((1998) 103). See Meyrowitz ((1985) 312f.) on the change in the coding of privacy in the context of the birth of a child.

10 The facts of the gender-specific division of labour, which is a manifestation of this separation of private and public, are well known. Society's implicit assignment of women and men to the domains of private care on the one hand and public influence on the other is still a commonplace (see for example Bellah et al. (1996) 85ff.). The gender-based segregation of the labour market too reflects the dichotomy between family work and gainful employment, since women, if they work professionally at all, frequently take up the so-called 'social' professions, which are particularly congenial to the supposedly 'feminine' work skills. See Gerlach (1992), Münch (1990).

11 See Aristotle, *Politics* 1253bff., 1259bff. On antiquity, in particular Aristotle, see Swanson (1992). See also Saxonhouse (1983). Concerning history in general see Helly and Reverby (1992) and esp. Okin (1979). See also Coole (1993).

12 See Arendt (1989) 22ff.; also Benhabib (1992).

13 For a critical account, see for example DeCew (1997) 81ff., also Okin (1989b) 89ff. For one example among many of the indiscriminate and sweeping rejection of the distinction between 'private' and 'public' and the concomitant critique of liberalism, see for example Olsen (1991) 378f.: 'Early feminists criticized policies and practices that limited women to the "private sphere": later feminists criticize the entire ideology based on a sharp division or dichotomy between the public and the private. [. . .] women might be better off if society were to recognize the falseness of the

public/private dichotomy and stop using the notion of "privacy" [. . .].' For an equally indiscriminate account, see also Brown (1995) 158.

14 This exclusion has on occasion been more symbolic than real, as we know, despite the gender-specific segregation of the labour market. See also for example Phillips (1991). On the following, see also Rössler (1996).

15 On the historical background see also Davidoff (1998). See also the illuminating but hardly cheering study by Davidoff et al. (1999).

16 See in greater detail for example Minow (1990) and Minow and Shanley (1997).

17 The reference here is to domestic violence. See for example Okin (1989b) 128ff., Kymlicka (1990a) 259f.

18 In this context see for example MacKinnon (1989) 184ff., 215ff. and (1991), also Olsen (1991). See Kymlicka (1990a) 248ff., Nagl-Docekal (1996a), Pauer-Studer (1996b), Benhabib and Nicholson (1988) 515ff. See also Kerchner and Wilde (1997).

19 Klaus (1994) 72. In this connection see also Holland-Cunz (1994) 228, and for a more differentiated account 238ff.

20 For a more general account of this point see Jaggar (1983) 27ff., 173ff.

21 In this connection see also Frazer and Lacey (1993) 74f.

22 See Allen (1988), J. L. Cohen (1992) and (1993). The concept I use of a 'redescription' of privacy comes from J. L. Cohen ('Redescribing Privacy' (1992)).

23 See *Roe v. Wade*, 410 U.S. 113 (1973), esp. 152ff.

24 On this point, see especially Allen (1988) 82ff. I shall return in detail below to the problems associated with grounding a right to abortion in such a right to privacy, see ch. 4, sec. 1.

25 See MacKinnon (1987) 93ff.; also Olsen (1991).

26 MacKinnon is primarily targeting the US jurisprudence on abortion. See again below, ch. 4, sec. 1.

27 See here Cornell's critique of MacKinnon in Cornell (1991).

28 See Glendon (1987).

29 See Elshtain (1981) 228ff. 298ff.; for criticism of her account see Dietz (1985).

30 See the more exhaustive analysis of both forms of critique below in chs 5 and 6.

31 The fact that this ambivalence is common to all the classic liberal theories has been repeatedly discussed in the literature. As a few of many, see again Okin (1979) and (1991), Benhabib and Nicholson (1988), as well as the articles in the first part of Landes (1998). On Habermas, see for example Fraser (1989b), who criticizes Habermas's theory of society (prior to *Between Facts and Norms*) with respect to its 'gender-subtext'. See also, in general, Meehan (1995b).

32 See Pateman (1989b). See Coole (1993) on Hobbes and Locke 53ff., Okin (1979) on Hobbes and Locke 197ff. On rescuing the idea of the social contract in spite of and together with the feminist critique, see the very good account in Hampton (1993).

33 See Pateman (1988) esp. 77ff. and (1989b) and (1989c); also Brennan and Pateman (1998). As an illustration of the fact that Pateman has now become the standard reference text for the reception of the feminist critique of Locke, see Habermas (1992c). See also Coole (1993) 53ff., who looks at Hobbes as well. Indeed, Hobbes himself speaks explicitly of the difference between 'the Common good' and 'the Private' ((1968) 226), as well as employing the traditional, natural concept of privacy.

34 For the following see especially Coole (1994) 193ff. on Locke; Coole (1993) 64ff. here also on the genesis of the *Two Treatises*; Pateman (1989c) and (1988) 77ff.; Elshtain (1981) 108ff., esp. 120ff. For criticism of Pateman's radical critique of Locke and the social contract in general, see for example Hampton (1993) 242f. and Boucher and Kelly (1994a) 27f.

35 Locke (1993) 35f. (*First Treatise* § 48). See Pateman (1989c) 39f. See Coole (1993) 66f., who also gives a meticulous account of the distinct concepts of political, conjugal, paternal and natural power in Locke.

36 Locke (1993) 153 (*Second Treatise* § 78).

37 Locke (1993) 155 (*Second Treatise* § 82).

38 Locke (1993) 157f. (*Second Treatise* § 86–7).

39 This means, moreover, that strictly speaking women remain in the state of nature, because 'those who have no such common appeal [i.e. the legislation of the civil society], I mean on earth, are still in the state of nature' (Locke (1993) 158). But this fails to make sense, if only because Locke disregards the existence of women in the state of nature anyway – at least in terms of the rights to complete freedom that apply in it. The whole construction seems inconsistent.

40 Feminist opinion diverges over how far and for what reasons – strategic motives, negligence, patriarchism – Locke fails to think through the radical implications of his liberal theory. See Pateman (1989c), by contrast with Coole (1994) and with Okin (1979) 199ff.

41 See Locke (1993) 153 (*Second Treatise* § 77).

42 This, moreover, is the reason Pateman conceives her critique of the social contract in such fundamental terms, and not only in relation to Hobbes or Locke. See for example her detailed critique of Freud in (1988) 103ff.

43 Pateman (1989c) 46. This also makes it clear that only one model of interpersonal relations is of genuine social relevance to Locke, that is entering into a contract. Models of relationship such as the one based on care, which also incorporate asymmetrical relations, are not conceived in public or political terms but are 'privatized' by the very concepts they comprise. See for example Coole (1994) 191f.

44 The civil liberties of the man are centred paradigmatically upon a very broadly based concept of *property* in Locke; see Locke (1993) 178ff. (§§ 123ff.).

45 I shall return below to Mill (and to Rorty, who follows a similar line): see ch. 4, sec. 1. On the following see Rössler (1992).

46 More precisely, this explanation is a utilitarian one. This is not entirely without importance, for it shows (contrary to Pateman) that the problematic distinction between private and public is not as such bound to the idea of the social contract. On Mill see Elshtain (1981) 132ff., Coole (1993) 102ff., Okin (1979) 197ff. On the work *On Liberty* see also Skorupski (1989) 337ff.

47 Mill (1910) 75.

48 Mill (1910) 76.

49 See Mill (1910) 140 *passim*. The distinction between private liberty and public control is thus the foremost constituent of liberal theory in Mill. What has come to be called the 'harm principle' (see (1910) 72–3) is the key criterion for differentiating one from another. On private liberty in Mill, see in more detail below, ch. 4, sec. 1.

50 Mill (1984) 298. See also Coole (1993) 110ff. and see Kymlicka (1990a) 248f. See also Elshtain (1981) 135ff., who explains Mill's inconsistencies in terms of his fear of the democratization of intimate relations that is radically justified by his own theory.

51 Pateman is accordingly able to write that the 'dichotomy between the private and the public [. . .] is, ultimately, what the feminist movement is about' (Pateman (1989b) 118).

52 See below, ch. 6, sec. 3, for a constructive, and not solely critical, discussion of the egalitarian structuring of the family and with this a reinterpretation of the private sphere of the household.

53 On the following see Rössler (1992). Especially in the United States there has for several years now been extensive feminist discussion of Rawls's theses. On the following see for example Okin (1989b) 89ff., Green (1986), Kearns (1983), Baehr (1996) e.g. 54 for the difference between a differentiated concept of equality and a simple androcentric concept of equality. Baehr here also criticizes Okin's conception of equality and gender. For criticism of Okin (and Rawls) see also Snitow (1991). On Rawls see also Kittay (1997). See also Pauer-Studer (1996a) 132ff. and *passim*.

54 See Rawls (1972) 7: 'For us the primary subject of justice is the basic structure of society, or more exactly, the way in which the major social institutions distribute fundamental rights and duties [. . .].' The 'monogamous family' is an example of a 'major social institution'. See Rawls (1993), where he mentions the family in the foreword, though not afterwards: 'I do assume that in some form the family is just' (xxix). And slightly later: 'I believe also, though I do not try to show in these lectures, that the alleged difficulties in discussing problems of gender and the family can be overcome' (ibid.).

55 Rawls (1972) 126.

56 Rawls (1972) 300.

57 Rawls (1972) 128.

58 Rawls (1972) 462f., 467f.

59 Rawls (1972) 83f., 300f.

60 The passage where Rawls elucidates the concept of 'fraternity' with reference to the relations within a family, which are characterized, he writes, by the fact that each member has the interests of the others in mind, and where the difference principle thus naturally holds sway, is reminiscent of Sandel's idealization of the family (Rawls (1972) 105); see Sandel (1982) 31ff. For criticism of Rawls see also Kittay (1997), esp. 226ff.

61 Rawls (1972) 462f., 467f.

62 Rawls (1972) 467.

63 On the worth of liberty see Rawls (1972) 204f.

64 For detailed accounts of these authors, see the feminist interpretations of the history of political thought by Okin (1979), Coole (1993), Elshtain (1981) and Benhabib and Nicholson (1988).

65 Rhode (1990) 3. See Scott (1988) 172: 'When difference and equality are paired dichotomously, they structure an impossible choice. If one opts for equality, one is forced to accept the notion that difference is antithetical to it. If one opts for difference, one admits that equality is unattainable.' As one example of many, see also Mendus (1992a) 211ff., and recently also Klinger (1995a).

66 Phillips (1987b) 2. On the following see Rössler (1996).

67 When I here speak of different 'rounds' in a debate, this is, as above, not meant in a strictly chronological sense but a logical one.

68 This applies to the whole range of distinct branches of feminist thought. The controversy over difference and equality was of prominent concern, for example, to feminist ethics: witness the discussion around Carol Gilligan and the conflict over whether – as the theorists of difference held – the 'female' element of 'care' was to be viewed as an alternative to the 'male' universalistic ethic or whether it was to contribute towards or combine with universalistic ethics, as Seyla Benhabib and Alison Jaggar claimed. The divergent stances on difference and equality have here taken the form of an opposition between a particularistic emphasis on care and an integrative universalistic position. On the recent debate over Gilligan see the articles in Nagl-Docekal

and Pauer-Studer (1993). See also Benhabib (1989). For an exhaustive account of the different possible stances in the debate over a 'female ethics', see Pauer-Studer (1996b). Another field of conflict was the debate over a feminist critique of reason. In this case, the positions of 'difference' went so far as to reproach Western logic as such for its 'phallogocentrism' and its focus upon 'male' concepts of identity and unity that excluded women by their very nature (such was the stance taken, for example, by Luce Irigaray). The position of 'equality', by contrast, limited itself to criticizing the *application* of the paradigm of reason together with the accompanying exclusion of women from the realm of reason and their assignment to the realm of feelings (see for example Irigaray (1994)). For criticism see Nagl-Docekal (1996b), who goes beyond this opposition. On the problem see also Ostner and Lichtblau (1992).

69 See for example Jaggar (1983) 173ff., Okin (1989a).

70 See Elshtain (1981) 298ff.

71 See for example the introduction to Bock and James (1992). See also the Milan Women's Bookstore Collective (1990). See Klinger (1995a). The parallel is not entirely justified, given such authors as Nel Noddings, Sara Ruddick and Jean Bethke Elshtain.

72 The corresponding anthologies are no longer titled 'Difference and Equality' (see Gerhard and Jansen, *Differenz und Gleichheit* (1990)), but '*Beyond* Equality and Difference' (see Bock and James (1992)).

73 In this connection, see for example: 'Equality remains of course central to feminist discussion, but its recurrence in the writing signals as much disagreement over its meaning as certainty over its goals. *A commitment to sexual equality does not of itself tell us what shape that equality should take*' (Phillips (1987b) 1, emphasis added). In a similar spirit see also Mendus (1992a).

74 See MacKinnon (1987) 32ff., 93ff., and (1989) e.g. 184ff., 215ff. See Forst (2002) on the feminist critique of the paradigm of equality. See also for example Nussbaum's feminist critique of the feminist critique of liberalism: (1999a) 67ff.

75 MacKinnon (1991) 1297. See also: 'First there must be similarly situated men with whom to compare [. . .]. As a result, when sex inequality is most extreme – most victims of sexual assault with impunity and all those denied legal or funded abortions are women – it drops off the sex inequality map. These are the social practices of dominance which create the gender difference as we know it. When the "similarly situated" assumption is revealed as the white male standard in neutral disguise, the *fist of dominance in the glove of equality* [. . .] dominance essentialised as difference becomes first on the equality agenda rather than last' (ibid., emphasis added).

76 MacKinnon (1991) 1281. See also, in more dramatic terms: 'The distinctive theory forged by this collective movement [the women's movement] is a form of action carried out through words. It is deeply of the world: raw with women's blood, ragged with women's pain, shrill with women's screams. It does not elaborate yet more arcane abstractions of ideas building on ideas. It participates in reality: the reality of a fist in the face, not the concept of a fist in the face. It does not exist to mediate women's reality for male consumption' (MacKinnon (1991) 1285).

77 See Cornell (1991), reviewing MacKinnon (1989).

78 Mendus (1992a) 215.

79 De Lauretis (1993). See Eisenstein (1988) 222f., Benhabib et al. (1994), and in general for example Landweer and Rumpf (1993), Nicholson (1990).

80 See in detail the historical studies by Laqueur (1990), Duden (1993). For the systematic perspective on the social construction of sex, see Hirschauer (1995) and, for a particularly illuminating account, Gildemeister and Wetterer (1992).

[81] See above all Butler (1990), also Butler (1993). On Butler see the discussion in the *Neue Rundschau* (1993) and Benhabib et al. (1994). For a more precise account of the issue, however, see Gildemeister and Wetterer (1992).

[82] See Klinger (1995a), also on what follows.

[83] See for example Butler in Benhabib et al. (1994).

[84] This is not a *petitio* and not a circle: democracy and the constitutional state are also claimed by feminists. Yet this can only go with (at least some idea of) equality of (at least some idea of) rights.

[85] See once again Mendus (1992a) 215.

[86] See once again Okin (1989b) 110ff. and (1991); Kymlicka (1990a) 247ff.

[87] On the family see in full below, ch. 6, sec. 3.

[88] See Fraser (1996c). On the problem see also Allen (1988) 123ff., J. L. Cohen (2004). I shall return below (ch. 7, sec. 3) to this set of problems.

[89] The question, though, is whether one must necessarily hold, like Okin, that in a just society a person's gender will have no more or less importance than the colour of a person's eyes: 'A just future would be one without gender. In its social structures and practices, one's sex would have no more relevance than one's eye color or the length of one's toes' (Okin (1989b) 171). But what are these social practices and structures in which the question of gender becomes totally irrelevant? Should this apply to all social practices and structures or only to some? Nussbaum cautiously opposes Okin, arguing how difficult it would be to free such practices from our deep-seated feelings of maleness and femaleness and suggesting that differences between the sexes might be kept provided they do not result in a hierarchy (Nussbaum (1992b)). One question, therefore, is what is so unappealing about Okin's model of a society in which sexual difference no longer plays any part at all. Another is whether (and if so, how) one can differentiate between contexts in which sexual difference is desirable, in which we regard it as attractive, and those in which it should be dispensed with out of a sense of justice. For the different positions on the issue, see Okin (1989b), Minow (1990), Nussbaum (1992b). For a theory that lays great stress on difference, see Elshtain (1987). See also Fraser (1996a), whose proposed model of society can be conceived as a middle course between approaches such as Elshtain's and Okin's. This question of the relevance of differences in public space also belongs of course to the theory of the public sphere. On this point, see for example Honig (1992), Benhabib (1992).

Chapter 3 Freedom, Privacy and Autonomy

[1] MacCallum (1991) 102. MacCallum is actually only describing a programme, without himself taking this any further here. To take but one theorist who has followed this general definition as a first step of analysis, see Rawls (1972) 202: 'Therefore I shall simply assume that liberty can always be explained by a reference to three items: the agents who are free, the restrictions or limitations which they are free from, and what it is that they are free to do or not to do.' See in general the clear survey in Gray (1990) 12ff. See also Koller (1998) 480f. For criticism of MacCallum, see for example Berofsky (1995) 43ff. I shall look later into Berlin's distinction between negative and positive freedom.

[2] See Skinner (1984) 194f. Incidentally, I consider Skinner's view that MacCallum's triad is more or less the final word on the normative substantialization of what is contained within the concept of freedom to be rather unrealistic. In his explanation

of social and political freedom, Skinner distinguishes between three traditions in the concept of freedom, the negative tradition, the positive one and the republican one. But it is difficult to see why he includes MacCallum's proposed analysis within one of these traditions (the negative one), instead of realizing that the advantage of the triad consists precisely in its initial neutrality with respect to these distinct conceptions. See also Skinner (1991). See also Miller (1991a), who likewise distinguishes between three conceptions or traditions in the concept of freedom, which are again, however, not suitable as an argument against MacCallum. From a liberal perspective such as Rawls's or Habermas's, Skinner's threefold classification of traditions seems to be slightly problematic, since such theorists attempt precisely to combine elements of positive and negative freedom, yet can still not be called republican (nor liberal in the Hobbesian sense with its purely negative conception of liberty).

3 In the following account I shall of course only look at the concept of freedom in so far as it is important to my own argument and to the context in question. Authors frequently identify the concept of freedom with the concept of autonomy, or attempt to define the latter with the help of the former. This is the case with Mendus, for example, who writes: 'These three constituent parts of the concept of autonomy – freedom, rationality and self-determination – must all be explained [. . .]' ((1989) 89). In a similar connection, Raz too suggests dividing the concept of autonomy (though not the concept of freedom) into three component parts and explaining it in terms of these components: appropriate mental abilities, independence and an adequate range of options. These components can clearly be paralleled with the above determinants *x*, *y* and *z*, and conceived as explications of these variables (Raz (1988) 369ff.). In what follows, however, I intend to draw a distinction between on the one hand a certain fundamental form of practical rationality as a necessary but not sufficient condition for us to say of a person that she 'acts freely', and on the other hand a more substantial concept of autonomy. I shall return to Raz, and to this distinction in general, at a later stage.

4 See Tugendhat (1992a) 343; Pothast (1978) 137ff.; the essays in Watson (1982). On the following, see also Gray (1990) 17ff., MacCallum (1991).

5 On the problem of freedom of the will in general, see the articles in Watson (1982) and Pothast (1978). See esp. Strawson (1974), Frankfurt (1989), Taylor (1976), Wolf (1989). I shall not here enter in any further detail into the problem of freedom and determinism, but assume a form of 'compatibilism', which is unproblematic in this context. The general concept of freedom, as I describe it in the following account (as opposed to the concept of autonomy), should not be understood in the sense of Frankfurt's 'wanton' but rather in the sense of Taylor's 'simple weigher of alternatives' (see Frankfurt (1989) and Taylor (1976)).

6 See again Tugendhat (1992a) 334ff.

7 See Benn (1976) 112ff. See also Benn (1984) 229f.

8 For the present I shall speak of the distinction between relevant and less relevant options and the formation of hierarchies of options only in trivial terms. One might say, for example, that it is more relevant to be able to choose between options that really are different. See in more detail below (c).

9 This does not mean that persons without such abilities are not also entitled to civil rights and liberties. The legal issue is clearly to be distinguished from the question of mental abilities. Tugendhat, incidentally, pinpoints 'choice, capacity and opportunity' as the three essential factors in the determination of freedom of action, with the component of choice implying that one is actually able to choose; see Tugendhat (1992c) 356. By 'capacity', Tugendhat here means the ability to carry out the action

in actual fact, in the sense that one is not prevented from carrying it out by anyone or anything. When I refer to 'abilities', however, I mean the more fundamental level of being actually capable of free action (in the sense of Tugendhat's 'choice').

10 Here, of course, only a rather general and vague boundary can be described. Indeed, what I am describing as a failure to fulfil a precondition for freedom is regarded by Raz as a restriction on autonomy, for I am describing a version of what he refers to as *coercion* and *manipulation*, that is restrictions on autonomy in the sense of addictions, drugs, inner compulsions, etc., that can be eliminated by self-instruction and the like (see Raz (1988) 377ff.). Raz here talks of 'independence' and analyses obstacles as 'inner obstacles' to either freedom or autonomy. I believe it is more plausible to cite this form of independence as one of the preconditions for us to describe a subject as free in the first place, rather than as one of the possible obstacles to this freedom. (For a similar position to Raz see also Tugendhat (1992a).) Furthermore, freedom and independence in this sense are also jeopardized when the general 'psychosocial' conditions for an autonomous choice or free action are not present. That is, persons must be able to make decisions under conditions that genuinely correspond to their opinions, assumptions and expectations, etc. (which is meant to rule out the permanent deception of a person).

11 I am borrowing the term 'threshold' concept from Feinberg, who uses it in precisely the opposite way to the way I do, that is in relation to the concept of autonomy. In the case of autonomy, however, I prefer the description 'gradual' concept (following Raz, who calls it a 'matter of degree' (1988) 373). I shall return to this point later on. See Feinberg (1989) 29.

12 See Hobbes (1968) 261ff.; see also Skinner (1984) 194ff. However, in my opinion it is a misconception to see the whole discussion from MacCallum to Rawls exclusively in terms of negative conceptions of liberty. By contrast, it seems more convincing to claim that these authors – by taking into consideration the element of 'freedom to' – went beyond purely negative conceptions. See Tugendhat (1992a) 356f. See also the well-known passage in Freud where he places himself in the Hobbesian tradition and claims that the liberty of the individual is 'no gift of civilization' ((1962) 95).

13 For an analysis of restrictions on freedom see also the categorization in Koller (1998) 481ff.

14 It is, of course, difficult to draw boundaries here: do natural disasters restrict our freedom or our abilities to do something? For an overview see Gray (1990) 22ff., 27ff. A problematic borderline case is that of disabilities. Do they represent a restriction of freedom or a lack of abilities? See Benn and Weinstein (1971) 197f.

15 In other words, certain conditions must hold for the concept of individual freedom not to remain an empty one. This is also the spirit of the arguments in the essays in Nussbaum and Sen (1993); see Nussbaum (1992a) and Sen (1992).

16 See also Tugendhat (1992a) 356f.

17 Berlin (1969) xxxix.

18 See Raz (1988) 373, who here speaks of the need for an 'adequate range of choices'; also 387ff.

19 An absurd alternative, for example, is to cut off an ear. See Benn and Weinstein (1971) 195. An insignificant one is being allowed to choose from between fifteen houses that are all the same. See again Raz (1988).

20 Benn and Weinstein (1971) thus maintain that the extent of freedom depends upon the number of alternatives.

21 Here there is an additional problem, discussed, for example, by G. Dworkin (1988a) 62ff. He provides convincing examples to show that an increase in the number of

options is not always better, because it may raise the costs of the choice in terms of one's responsibility. Dworkin queries, for example, the increase in choice through technology such as amniocentesis or CVS (chorionic villus sampling), cf. (1988a) 67f. He comes to the conclusion that we would not say under all circumstances that more choice is better than less and that criteria are firstly the relevance of the increase in choice (i.e. object-related) and secondly the costs in terms of the responsibility and well-being of the subject making the choice (i.e. related to the subject–object relation).

22 See ch. 2 above. Of course, the existence of a right does not in itself guarantee that it can be realized in actual fact. This is simply a hint of the relevance of social rights for compensating for differences in the realization of negative civil liberties.

23 See Benn (1976) 112ff.; see also Hill (1989) 96ff on Kant; see Taylor (1976). On the history of the concept see the studies by Schneewind (1998).

24 In his book on the concept of autonomy, G. Dworkin ((1988b) 6f.) makes the point that this concept has been explained in extremely different ways in the literature and in the process identified with virtually every similar concept – freedom, individuality, self-legislation, integrity, independence, responsibility and others. He writes accordingly: 'About the only features held constant from one author to another are that autonomy is a feature of persons and that it is a desirable quality to have' ((1988b) 6). And even these two characteristics, as O'Neill has commented, are open to question; see O'Neill (1992) 203. The advantage of the concept's diffuseness, however, is that it makes it more feasible to work out a comparatively open-minded approach to clarifying it.

25 In this spirit, R. Young writes that we should pay closer attention to 'what it is to exercise one's freedom in such a way as to order one's life according to a plan or conception which fully expresses one's own choices since intuitively this is the heart of our notion of autonomy. To this extent autonomy clearly involves more than just being free (even where freedom is construed so as to include both freedom of action and of decision). One must be free to be autonomous, but one can be free and still lack autonomy because it is, for instance, possible freely but mindlessly to mimic the tastes, opinions, ideals, goals, principles, values and preferences of others. So freedom is necessary for autonomy but not sufficient' ((1989) 78).

26 See also below. See Raz (1988) 369ff., Seel (1995) 125ff., Tugendhat (1979).

27 Mill (1910) 75. See also Constant (1987). The well-known passage in Kant runs: 'Man's *freedom* as a human being, as a principle for the constitution of a commonwealth, can be expressed in the following formula. No-one can compel me to be happy in accordance with his conception of the welfare of others, for each may seek his happiness in whatever way he sees fit, so long as he does not infringe upon the freedom of others to pursue a similar end which can be reconciled with the freedom of everyone else within a workable general law – i.e. he must accord to others the same right as he enjoys himself' (Kant (1991) 74). I shall return to the dispute concerning a modern, individualistic concept of freedom in ch. 4, sec. 4.

28 Tugendhat (1979), esp. from 137ff. (all translations from Tugendhat (1979) are by R. G.). Tugendhat here develops his idea of self-determination as a critical response to Heidegger (and Mead). See also Taylor (1976).

29 Tugendhat (1979) 295. See by contrast Tugendhat (1992a), where the concept of autonomy is treated from a different perspective. The concept of autonomy here means something akin to general independence of others (see for example (1992a) 366ff.).

30 Tugendhat (1979) places this connection between one's own good and the good life in an Aristotelian context. Referring to the *Nicomachean Ethics* 1.6, he writes: 'The reflecting person faces the question of how he wants to be – according to his conception of life – and this means that he not only faces the question of what is good for keeping alive, but also the question of the good life.' For a similar view see Taylor, esp. (1976). For discriminating criticism, see Löw-Beer (1994) 121ff.

31 Tugendhat (1979) 146.

32 For example by Habermas, see (1992b). See also, for example, Cooke (1999a). In more recent works on the concept of autonomy, on the other hand, there is of course an (in my view plausible) uncoupling of morality and autonomy. See for example Berofsky (1995) 178f., Christman (1991) and (1989b) 14f. From the perspective of moral responsibility, see also Wallace (1998) 52ff. See, by contrast, Honneth (1994b), who here equates the difference between autonomy and authenticity with the difference between the moral and the ethical orientation of the person. I shall shortly return to this point in greater detail. See also the discriminating definition of the concept of autonomy in Forst (2002). A concept used as broadly as I am doing of course allows for the fact that in certain situations people may autonomously decide to be immoral. Yet this does not strike me as surprising. (Whether a person can autonomously opt *on principle always* to be immoral is another matter.)

33 See Taylor (1976) 281: '(B)eyond the *de facto* characterization of the subject by his goals, desires, and purposes, a person is a subject who can pose the *de jure* question: is this the kind of being I ought to be, or really want to be?' For Taylor, however, the question of what sort of person one wants to be always has a moral component. See Tugendhat's criticism in (1992b). On Taylor see also Rosa (1998) 98ff. I shall return to the question of the connection between morality, ethics and autonomy shortly.

34 Tugendhat (1979) 193.

35 If I were to take for granted conditions that could be altered, this would be tantamount to a flight from the possibility of a self-determined life and ultimately therefore to 'flight from myself'. See Tugendhat (1979) 196: 'The practical question, if posed in fundamental terms, confronts me with myself. [. . .] Evading this freedom is thus a flight from myself. [. . .] The choice to which the practical question is orientated has the character of "choosing oneself" in the double sense that the act of asking and choosing must be performed by me myself (it cannot be taken on by anyone else) and that what I thereby choose is me: in this act I determine what (and how) I shall be.' Menke ((1996) 194f.) here sees Tugendhat's idea of self-determination as crucially underdetermined: in saying, as Tugendhat does, that I myself choose my own life, the description of 'my life' remains 'completely general'; what is lacking, says Menke, is the 'further determination of the individualistic ideal of self-realization', for only with this individualistic ideal is the general idea of the 'freedom of individuality' applied or referred to each individual's actual life. But Tugendhat's idea here is only underdetermined if self-determination is interpreted as moral autonomy, in which case it can indeed only choose the moral, 'common' life (Menke (1996) 195) (trans. by R. G.). Tugendhat's concept of self-determination here, however, does not have a moral component. (Nor does it need to have. See, for his part, Tugendhat (1992b) on the difference between morality and ethics, or rather 'identity', as he calls it here, with regard to the question of how one would like to live.) In this case, however, there is no gap which still needs to be filled by the ideal of individualization. It is always 'my' life that is in question, in relation to which I behave reflectively, making choices. That this is more than just a terminological problem will become even clearer below,

when autonomy is contrasted with authenticity. For the dispute with Menke, see also van den Brink (1997) 135ff.

36 I shall return shortly to the problem of how we are 'situated' within a cultural and social context. See Berofsky (1995) 117ff., and also on the question of whether and how far autonomy consists in reflecting on and evaluating contingently acquired goals and desires etc.: '[The person] will happen to have many goals and ambitions that derive from the contingencies of her life and that were in no sense freely chosen. She may now evaluate those goals and that is what her autonomy basically consists of' (Berofsky (1995) 122; also 129ff).

37 Tugendhat (1979) 197.

38 Tugendhat (1979) 194. For this reason, Habermas's interpretation of Tugendhat as 'decisionistic' is wide of the mark; see Habermas (1992b) 170.

39 This means no autonomy without freedom, and no rewarding life without autonomy (see above). What sorts of considerations here play a part and how important (say) moral duties are by comparison with other points of view, however, is not in itself predetermined by the concept of autonomy.

40 This goes against Kant and against, for example, Christman (see (1989b) 13).

41 However, it will not be until the following chapter (on decisional privacy) that I come to deal in greater detail with those objections to the sort of concept of autonomy I am setting out that oppose the possibility of a substantial concept of autonomy in general (on the basis of the twentieth-century critique of the concept of the subject).

42 See Frankfurt (1989) and (1988a). For criticism of Frankfurt's model for being hierarchical, see for example Bransen (1996). For criticism of Frankfurt's concept of the 'strongest desire' and its function, see G. Taylor (1985) 112ff., also on the concept of identification. The idea that this sort of capacity for reflection is a quintessentially human feature is found in the most diverse of authors, see also C. Taylor (1976). In Korsgaard (1996b) it is defined as the very source of normativity in general, see esp. 90ff.

43 G. Dworkin (1989) 61. Dworkin himself has since revised his theory. See (1988b), esp. ch. 1 (3ff.).

44 See Watson (1989), Christman (1989b) 8ff., S. Wolf (1989). See G. Dworkin's own criticism of his concept of authenticity and identification in (1988b) 15ff. See Berofsky (1995) 99ff., 219ff. See also Geuss (1995) 6, though he is here speaking of freedom rather than autonomy: 'Only someone who does what he really wants to do is in the full sense "free", i.e. someone who acts from a genuine, actual or real desire. The authenticity of the desire motivating the action is thus an essential component of freedom' (trans. by R. G.).

45 On rationality see Lindley (1986) 13ff., Christman (1991) 14ff., Berofsky (1995) 107ff. See in general also Gosepath (1992) 212ff.

46 See Di Stefano (1994).

47 See Lindley (1986) 21f. On the concept of (part)-authorship as a characteristic feature of autonomy, see also Raz (1988) 369ff.

48 On self-deception see in particular Löw-Beer (1990), esp. 62ff.; see also Gosepath (1992) 171ff. On one's orientation towards the truth in general see also Gosepath (1992) 365ff.

49 On the problem of infinite regression, see in particular Frankfurt (1988a) 164ff., where he takes a critical look at the version put forward in (1989) and interprets in more precise (and plausible) terms what it means 'to decide' and 'to make up one's mind'. These processes aim at 'creating an orderly arrangement' ((1988a) 173), in such a way that the process can be stopped and the person as a whole can identify

'whole-heartedly' with the decision or 'arrangement'. On infinite regression, see for example Thalberg (1989), G. Dworkin (1989). See also Mele (1995) 59ff. in the context of the problem of weakness of will. For an instructive account of the problem of reflection in general see Mackenzie (2000).

50 This assumption can of course also be made with regard to the whole process of asking the 'practical question'.

51 For this reason, Feinberg's condition seems too strong, not only because of the demands he makes on rationality ('rational scrutiny') but also because the reflection called for is not just hypothetical in nature ('can and does'): 'One way of being inauthentic, so understood, is to be a habitual and uncritical conformist [. . .] a person is authentic to the extent that [. . .] he can and does subject his opinions and tastes to rational scrutiny' (Feinberg (1989) 32). Christman's version, by contrast, is in my opinion too weak: 'the authenticity condition is met when the agent accepts the desire, value or preference as part of her larger set of desires, beliefs and principles, *whether or not this is done for good reasons*' (Christman (1989b) 7, emphasis added).

52 This will be treated in greater detail below, in ch. 5, sec. 3.

53 On the following, see Taylor (1992b) and (1992c), Menke (1996) 192ff., Rosa (1998) 195ff., Ferrara (1993) and (1994). See also Trilling (1972) 1ff. On the (different) concept in Heidegger, see Guignon (1993) 223ff.

54 See in full, for example, Taylor (1992c).

55 See Polonius's advice: 'to thine own self be true' (discussed in Trilling (1972) 3f.), and of course Herder, on whom Taylor too bases his argument, see Taylor (1992c): 'Jeder Mensch hat ein eignes Mass, gleichsam eine eigne Stimmung aller seiner sinnlichen Gefühle zu einander' ('Each human being has his own measure, as it were an accord peculiar to him of all his feelings to each other'), also quoted in Taylor (1989) 375; see in full 374ff. I shall return later to the problems posed by the underlying theories of the self.

56 Taylor (1992c), secs 1–3 and the two following sections on the problem of the differing conceptions of politics and liberalism that result from this. Taylor is here drawing an opposition between two *normative conceptions* of (liberal) freedom. See also Taylor (1988) 121ff.

57 See again Honneth (1994b). See also Anderson (1994), and Van den Brink (1997) 133ff.

58 In Ferrara (1993) 85ff. and (1994) 242ff. By contrast see also Menke (1996) 193.

59 Ferrara (1994) 243; see also (1993) 88ff.

60 See also Ferrara (1994) 252–3: '[F]or each given identity or work of art there is one optimal way, within the field of the conceivable alternatives, of attaining realization.'

61 This is of course a systematic critique of a conceptual opposition that can only be understood historically. Yet the approaches discussed do not leave the matter at a (convincing) conceptual history, but seek to reformulate this systematically. Furthermore, seen from a politically liberal perspective, quite different problems once more arise, since this conception of positive freedom must be interpreted as a 'comprehensive doctrine' in the Rawlsian sense and this then contradicts the neutrality of the liberal state. Taylor of course conceives his model of the politics of difference precisely as an alternative to models of liberalism such as those of R. Dworkin and Rawls. See, for example, Taylor (1992a).

62 Ferrara could in principle make this claim too in the improbable event that moral autonomy and ethical authenticity came to coincide, so to speak. In the end, it does not seem to help much distinguishing different concepts of autonomy either (as Cooke does (1999b) with the concept of ethical autonomy, and, even more subtly,

Forst (2002)), if only because it can be problematic trying to differentiate between ethical and moral problems anyway. I shall return to this problem below, in ch. 4, sec. 1.

63 On the problem of hierarchies, see for example Berofsky (1995) 51. For criticism of Frankfurt's hierarchical position, see again Bransen (1996) 2ff. In general see also Benson (1991) 395f. The idea of hierarchies does not mean that influences may not work in both directions. It means only that in the end conflicts cannot be left unresolved.

64 Charlotte's renunciation of her love for the Captain in Goethe's *Elective Affinities* would have to be described in these terms, to give just one example.

65 This is known to be in the nature of practical reasons. See the classic essay by Williams (1976a) 166ff. See also Frankfurt (1988a) 172ff.

66 This otherwise implies neither a particularly optimistic nor a particularly rigid concept of autonomy. Yet even assuming that the decision-making 'I' is not entirely the master in his own house and one recognizes that one is never fully transparent in one's desires and needs, one can still try to be as autonomous and reflective as possible. On the problematic nature of the separation of ethics and morality especially in the sphere of private relations, see also below, ch. 4, sec. 1.

67 See for example Nehamas (1985) 170ff. on the idea of self-invention and the notion that 'becoming who one is' should be understood as a constant process of self-correction, self-invention, as the unceasing work of newly producing the self as a unity. I return to the problem of the unity of the person in greater detail below, see ch. 7, sec. 4.

68 Again G. Dworkin (1989) 61. See Christman (1989b) 7f; see also (1988).

69 See Meyers (1987), Friedman (1997), Benhabib (1992).

70 Benson (1991) and (1994).

71 See Griffin (1986) 9f., Hill (1991a). On this problem see in full below, considered from various perspectives, also ch. 5, sec. 3.

72 For this very strong sense of the term, see not only Benson but also Christman (1991). See also Meyers (1987) and Mackenzie and Stoljar (2000a) 17f. on the problem. Nonetheless, I consider it questionable simply to fuse the sociological level of analysis of gender-specific socialization with the individual level. It would clearly be a problem to claim that every man was more autonomous than every woman. On the 'choice' of women in liberal-democratic societies see also Okin (1998).

73 See Christman (1998).

74 One may see oneself as autonomous on the whole even though one may recognize oneself as not particularly autonomous in various *aspects* of life, as when a person proves unable to give up smoking even though she wants to, to give a relatively straightforward example. For such reasons too, it makes sense to treat autonomy as a gradual concept, when applied to oneself and to others alike.

75 See Gray (1990) 101ff., who discusses the putative paradox at length. See also Meyers (1987) and Stoljar (2000). More generally see also below, ch. 4, sec. 3.

76 See also once more the treatment of the family below, ch. 6, sec. 3.

77 Having these projects that are based on 'strong evaluations' means that a person also has the positively evaluated understanding of herself as autonomous, i.e. that autonomy in this sense constitutes a value for her that is associated with other values (evaluations) such as self-esteem, identity, respect for herself and others. Autonomy in this sense cannot be abstracted from the conditions under which it was learnt. One must thus argue against Berofsky ((1995) 161ff.) that the notion of a 'value-free autonomy' is a debatable one, for autonomy is always bound up within a network

of values. Equally, however, one must argue against Taylor that such an 'evaluation' and one's situation within a 'culture' (in a very broad sense) do not in themselves entail predetermined cultural contents. See Taylor (1992a), (1989) 53ff. In the spirit of Taylor see also Rosa (1998) 72ff., 181ff. On the concept and idea of 'strong evaluations', see Taylor (1976) and (1989) 4f., 332ff., etc.

78 Berlin (1969) 131.

79 Of course, certain abilities or capacities are necessary in the subject for him to be able to pursue projects in an autonomous manner. This is a point made by Feinberg, whose analysis of these abilities catalogues twelve 'virtues' (as he calls them) that only together do justice to the whole spectrum of the meaning of autonomy as an ability to make the most of one's own freedom in an independent way. This can be illustrated by the virtue of 'self-reliance': 'being able to rely on oneself if and when others fail. It is indeed a virtue, and not merely a self-regarding one, to have inner resources – strength, courage, ingenuity, toughness, resilience' (Feinberg (1989) 41). To possess self-reliance in this sense constitutes a not merely intellectual 'virtue' (perhaps it would be better to speak of (learnable) abilities), which supports or facilitates the pursuit of goals and projects.

80 This is a point also made by feminist criticism; see for example Nussbaum (1999a).

81 See H. S. Richardson (1997), on the problem of incommensurability in particular, 111ff. See also the observations on the problem of authenticity above.

82 See Sandel (1982) 62f., 179. See also Waldron (1993d) 388ff. See Rawls (1993) 30ff. See also below on the communitarian and feminist critiques of the concept of autonomy, ch. 4, secs 2 and 3. For 'renegade literature' see Koestler (1994) and Semprun (1991). Nonetheless, if (like Rosa (1998) 184ff.) one conceives the 'cultural matrix' within which identities are formed and goals etc. described in such broad terms that every renunciation of an old identity – to the extent that even this renunciation must as such refer to the new identity – is always understood as necessarily within that matrix, then the difference between the communitarian and the liberal understanding of identity-forming and identity-changing processes can scarcely be described.

83 See also below once again, ch. 4, sec. 4.

84 Raz (1988) 394; see also ibid.: 'The conditions of autonomy do not add an independent element to the social forms of a society. They are a central aspect in the character of the bulk of its social forms.' I am, incidentally, here of course disregarding the questions (which actually belong first) of why we would rather be free than unfree and why we regard freedom as a precondition for a rewarding life. On this, see for example Rachels and Ruddick (1989).

85 See Seel (1995) 114ff., 125ff.

86 On the problem of unfortunate contingencies, see also Rössler (1999). For two distinct perspectives on the link between contingency and happiness see Nagel (1982b) 29f. and Adorno (1974).

87 In certain aspects of our life, we may of course decide that we want to act in a way that is not necessarily self-determined, as when a person decides she does not want to be informed of how serious an illness may be. Even so, one can agree in principle with Griffin (1986) 9: 'I certainly want control over my own fate [. . .] I prefer, in important areas of my life, bitter truth to comfortable delusion [. . .] And I should prefer it not because it would be morally better, or aesthetically better, or more noble, but because it would make a better life for me to live.' Critical of this idea but ultimately unconvincing (above all owing to a concept of autonomy that is much too strong as well as to implausible examples), see Arneson (1994), esp. 50ff.

88 There are of course also other classifications to be found in the literature. See for example Inness (1992) 95, who distinguishes between approaches that claim that privacy is valuable for its consequences and those that value it quite independently of its consequences solely on the basis of 'respect for rational choosers'. Yet this categorization disregards a number of approaches and is also internally incoherent. For the general distinction between intrinsic and functional conceptions, see Korsgaard (1996c). On the following in general, see Allen (1988) 35ff.

89 On the following see Thomson (1974), Scanlon (1975), Reiman (1976), Schoeman (1984c), Allen (1988) 41ff., Inness (1992) 28ff.

90 Schoeman (1984c) 26ff.; in this context see also 5ff. on the distinction between a 'distinctiveness thesis' and a 'coherence thesis'.

91 For other sceptical positions, see Prosser (1960). See Schoeman (1984c) 28ff.

92 Thomson (1974). Direct criticism is to be found in Scanlon (1975) and Reiman (1976). Inness criticizes Thomson's position in (1992) 28ff. The objection might here be made that Thomson does not strictly speaking reduce the *value of* privacy, but only a *right to* privacy. Yet she herself is not unambiguous with regard to this distinction.

93 For this reason she employs the 'simplifying hypothesis, that the right to privacy is itself a cluster of rights, and that it is not a distinct cluster of rights but itself intersects with the cluster of rights which the right over the person consists in and also with the cluster of rights which owning property consists in' (Thomson (1974) 306).

94 Scanlon (1975) 320, emphasis in original.

95 In this connection see also Reiman (1976) 30f.

96 Scanlon (1975) 317f., emphasis in original. See also Reiman (1976) 29f. on Scanlon.

97 See in more detail below, ch. 5, sec. 1. There I shall also discuss the extent to which a person's autonomy can be damaged even when she does not know that her privacy has been infringed.

98 See once again Korsgaard (1996c).

99 See also Fried's criticism (1970) 140: 'It is just because this instrumental analysis makes privacy so vulnerable that we feel impelled to assign to privacy some intrinsic significance. But to translate privacy to the level of an intrinsic value might seem more a way of cutting off analysis than of carrying it forward.'

100 'Functional arguments depend on showing that privacy is linked to the promotion of something else that is accepted as desirable,' as Gavison puts it ((1980) 444). Whereas intrinsic answers tend to contain functional elements, functional answers on the other hand run the risk of becoming reductive if the difference between the function of privacy and privacy itself can no longer be explained. This will become clearer below.

101 On the following see Allen (1988) 34ff., who provides a similar analysis of the various proposals present in the literature. In general see Schoeman (1984c) 2ff., Inness (1992) 20ff., 95ff., Okin (1991) 87f., Wasserstrom (1984), DeCew (1997) 46ff., Benn and Gaus (1983a) 7ff., Fried (1968) 482ff. and (1970) 137ff.

102 In other words, there are approaches that are oriented towards relations (such as Rachels, Fried) and those that are oriented towards the individual (such as Reiman, Benn and, exemplarily, Kupfer (1987) 82: 'The most basic claim to be made out is that privacy is essential to the development and maintenance of an autonomous self'). Along with these, there are of course interesting combinations of the two, such as Schoeman's.

103 Inness (1992). I shall also be discussing the relational approaches in detail once more below in ch. 5, sec. 3.

104 Inness (1992) 95.

105 On the privacy of mental conditions and its social function, see for example Wasserstrom (1984) and, more recently, Nagel (1998a).

106 Inness (1992) 112.

107 See Schoeman (1984c) 14f.: '[M]ost significant [...] is the claim that there is a specific privacy interest, connected in a profound way with the recognition of human moral character, and that for historical reasons this interest is more compelling at the present time than it was in the past.' See Benn (1984) and (1976). See also Warren and Brandeis (1984), for whom the value of the 'inviolate personality' is fundamental.

108 See J. L. Cohen (1992), (1993), (1997).

109 See for example J. L. Cohen (1994) 325; the most detailed account, however, is in (1992) 115ff., where she calls the dimensions 'relational privacy', 'decisional autonomy', 'entity privacy' and 'bodily privacy'. Yet she does not go into the connection between these dimensions.

110 J. L. Cohen (1994) 325.

111 See Benn (1988) 264ff., 292ff. See Reiman's criticism of Benn for defining 'respect for persons' in terms of 'persons as choosers', that is for being concerned solely with the idea that persons should be respected in so far as they are capable of rational choice (Reiman (1976) 36f.). Instead of this, says Reiman, it should be seen that privacy is fundamentally bound up with 'personhood': 'Privacy is a social ritual by means of which an individual's moral title to his existence is conferred' ((1976) 39). See also: 'Privacy is necessary to the creation of selves [...]. Privacy is a condition of the original and continuing creation of "selves" or "persons"' ((1976) 39f.).

112 See also, for example, the illuminating account in Benn (1988) 278f.; see also Benn (1984) and Benn and Gaus (1983a).

113 J. L. Cohen (1992) 116, emphasis added. See in greater detail below in ch. 4, Parenthesis, p. 93.

114 See ch. 2 above and in more detail below, ch. 7, secs 2 and 3.

115 See Rawls (1972) 203.

116 All these aspects will be dealt with in greater detail in the following chapters.

117 A third objection, one might think, is that we also respect the privacy of people who do not possess autonomy, whether temporarily so, in the case of people sleeping, or no longer so, in the case of patients in a state of coma or the dead. Yet I believe that we here speak of respect for privacy precisely because we assume an 'as if': we treat such people 'as if' they possessed autonomy, extrapolating attitudes we have towards autonomous people on to cases where this autonomy cannot or can no longer be exercised. The privacy of children can likewise, though in a different way, illustrate this. Although children do not (yet) possess (full) autonomy, the acquisition of autonomy here goes hand in hand with the development of a need for privacy and thus also with the demand for this to be respected.

118 On such phenomena see in more detail below in ch. 7, sec. 2.

119 See Margalit (1996) 201f.

120 See in more detail below in ch. 7, secs 2 and 3.

121 See Margalit (1996) 204ff. See also below, ch. 6, sec. 1. One can of course autonomously decide that one wants to give up one's own autonomy (entirely). Yet as a conceptual problem this is of no more interest to the question of the connection between privacy and autonomy than to a general theory of autonomy itself.

Chapter 4 Decisional Privacy

1 See Allen (1988) and (1998), Turkington and Allen (1999) 585ff., J. L. Cohen (1992) *passim*, all of them in connection with the rulings and terminology of the Supreme Court. See also in more detail the Parenthesis, p. 93 below.

2 See for example Schoeman (1992) 24ff., 151ff., albeit always from the limited and limiting perspective of informational privacy. See also J. L. Johnson (1989b) 20ff., especially on Mill. Here we also find a series of examples and discussions of them. At this point reference can also be made to two further conceptual traditions of 'decisional privacy' that have been lost entirely in the current context of the concept, religion and property, which go back to Hobbes and Locke.

3 Gavison (1980) 448; see also DeCew (1997) 77f.

4 J. L. Johnson (1989a) 158f. cites a similar example to show that a person's privacy is violated merely if another person thinks badly of her. I regard this as going too far, for (as we shall see in more detail in the following chapter) a person's thoughts belong to the most private areas of her life. As long as she does not put them into words, they can thus not violate the privacy of *other people*. Johnson's theory defining privacy as 'immunity from the judgment of others' (ibid.) is therefore not a convincing one.

5 Schoeman (1992), for example 89ff., speaks of 'overreaching' social control. Schoeman too, in other words, is concerned with this sort of private dimension in one's life, but binds this too narrowly to the protection of the various social groups in which the person is involved, arguing against a functional definition of such privacy through the concept of autonomy. On social freedom see also Westin (1967) 32ff.

6 See on the following Mill (1910), Schoeman (1992) 21ff., Skorupski (1989) 337ff. Mill was the first thinker to confront the principles of the complex interrelation of private and public, albeit using a limited concept of privacy (on Mill see above in ch. 2, sec. 3). When Benhabib writes that it is to Hannah Arendt's political philosophy that we owe the insight 'that the public and the private are interdependent' (Benhabib (1996) 213), this refers to a different concept of privacy (the local one), and if it is legitimate, only in this sense is it so (for Mill had already dealt with this interdependence with respect to the concept of decisional privacy). Even granting Benhabib this reduced concept of privacy, however, I do not regard her claim as entirely legitimate. On the contrary, one might say that Arendt – like many other theorists of the public sphere – in fact does not devote enough attention to the interdependence of the two realms or dimensions. On Arendt see below in ch. 4, sec. 4. Indeed it is the feminist theorists (probably since Pateman) who have been the first to reflect on the interdependence of the private and the public in a manner befitting the complexity of the relationship.

7 Mill (1910) 75, 76, 140, 144.

8 Rorty (1989), xv. Rorty is above all concerned to show that every theory that seeks to reconcile the realms of public-political life and private-ethical living has necessarily failed. The aim of public organization is, as he calls it, the liberal avoidance of cruelty, while the private domain is supposed to guarantee the possibility of experimental choice for the good life of each individual. On Rorty's distinction between the private and public sphere, see in more detail Rössler (1992) 107ff. Rorty's theory is interesting here in so far as it has to do with the connection between freedom and privacy. On the identity of the private and the public person in Rorty, see also below in ch. 7, sec. 4.

9 Their outlines are similar not only in the structure of the differentiation between private and public realms (see Rorty (1989) 63: 'J. S. Mill's suggestion that governments

devote themselves to optimizing the balance between leaving people's private lives alone and preventing suffering seems to me pretty much the last word') but also in their conception of private freedom as experimental self-realization. See Rorty (1989) 73ff. and Mill (1910) 114ff.

10 Mill (1910) 75, emphasis added. Given the frequent criticism of Mill's principle, Isaiah Berlin for example points out: 'In so far as I live in society, everything that I do inevitably affects, and is affected by, what others do. Even Mill's strenuous effort to mark the distinction between the spheres of private and social life breaks down under examination. Virtually all Mill's critics have pointed out that everything that I do may have results which will harm other human beings' ((1969) 155). Admittedly, Mill does restrict individual liberty to the point of even regarding it as permissible for 'other people' to use 'advice, instruction, persuasion, and avoidance' as ways of commenting upon a person's private plans (Mill (1910) 149).

11 For the classic account, see Berlin (1969), esp. 121ff. By contrast with Berlin's original idea, which was that negative freedom and positive freedom ground two different political models, the distinction is today commonly understood in such a way that negative freedom means the (politically) guaranteed freedom of the negative civil liberties, while positive freedom is conceived of as this interpretative conception of 'real' or 'true' freedom that may vary from case to case. Rorty's experimental freedom and the rational life-plan of Rawls's *A Theory of Justice* can be viewed as such different positive conceptions. These two forms of the distinction must in turn be separated from Rawls's idea of the difference between liberty and its 'worth' ((1972) 204ff.). This distinction corresponds rather to the distinction between negative civil liberties and social rights (see Habermas (1997)), because both are concerned with the substantial conditions under which civil liberties can be realized by all individuals equally. On this problem see Waldron (1993c) 39ff.

12 See Rorty (1989) 45ff., 120ff. and Rawls (1972) 407ff. as two extremes, both of which nonetheless have to resort to the concept of autonomy.

13 For the communitarian critique see ch. 4, sec. 2.

14 See above, ch. 3, sec. 3. I am here taking up the remarks I made in that section.

15 See above, ch. 3, sec. 3, and below, ch. 4, sec. 3 and ch. 5, sec. 3.

16 On the following see for example the (unsystematic) account in Nagel (1998b). On the role of privacy in these different social contexts see also the detailed account in the following chapter on informational privacy.

17 See in more detail, ch. 5.

18 See the detailed portrayals of (civic) 'inattention' in Goffman (1969) 222ff. See Sennett's concept of 'civility' (2002) 264ff. For another account of the problem see also Schoeman (1992) 151ff.

19 See Simmel (1995) 126: 'mutual reserve and indifference, the spiritual conditions in which broad circles live, are never felt more strongly in their success for the individual's independence than in the densest throng of the city, the bodily proximity and confinement making the spiritual distance all the more palpable' (translations of Simmel by R. G.). See also Lofland (1993). See Lohmann (1991) 30 on Simmel's ambivalence as to whether phenomena of indifference bring about a loss or a gain in freedom. My concern is with the positive side of indifference as a phenomenon that augments freedom. On indifference as an alienating phenomenon in the modern age, see Lohmann (1991) and (1993). On the implications for criticism of culture and modernity, see also below in ch. 7, sec. 2.

20 Simmel (1995) 123; by 'this sort of life' he means life in the city.

21 On the ambivalence of these phenomena, see Simmel's description of freedom as loneliness and indifference as a lack of interest at the wrong time and place, as in

one's dealings with the needy neighbour to whom Simmel refers in (1995) 123. See also Simmel (1995) 126: 'It is clearly just the other side of this freedom when at times there is nowhere one feels so lonely and solitary as in the very throng of the city, for here as elsewhere it is by no means necessary for a person's freedom to be reflected in his emotional life in the form of well-being.' I shall return to the implications of Simmel's remarks in terms of cultural criticism in the final chapter.

22 Nagel (1998a) 5. See also 22: 'Those of us who are not political communitarians want to leave each other some space.' In this essay, Nagel presents a whole host of examples of situations in which people have to show consideration for the privacy of others in public. He also shows the fluid nature of the boundary between questions of decisional privacy (relating to modes of action, behaviour and ways of life) and questions concerning mere manners (bad or otherwise); see 18f.

23 See in more detail below in ch. 7, sec. 3.

24 On this point see Allen (1988) 123ff., in general on privacy in the public domain. See also Benn (1984) 231ff., where he describes a 'man staring at my face' as a violation of privacy.

25 See also Goffman (1971) 44ff., on the 'territories of the self', as well as J. L. Cohen (1992) 59ff.

26 See also above, ch. 2, sec. 5, and below, ch. 7, sec. 3.

27 Here I again refer the reader to ch. 7, sec. 3, where I offer a more detailed interpretation of this sort of conflict.

28 On tolerance see Wolf (1997), Williams (1996), as well as Heyd (1996a).

29 On Mill see Edwards (1988), who draws a distinction (89f.) between indifference and tolerance in so far as Mill's concern is with dispute in public space, which is not a matter of indifference. Yet this only refers to chapter 2 in Mill. In chapters 3 and 4, tolerance as indifference is meant in contrast to social control.

30 In this connection see Walzer (1997) 8f.

31 See Walzer (1997) 8, on 'dissident' or 'eccentric' individuals.

32 See for example Williams (1996) and Wolf (1997).

33 Heyd (1996a) 10f., for example, distinguishes clearly between indifference, tolerance and political commitment, yet without giving indifference its place in social contexts as an attitude towards the scope for an individual's freedom. Indifference can also be demanded with respect to persons as members of groups, as in the case when a man molests a woman.

34 This does not embrace all aspects of decisional privacy (e.g. it does not necessarily incorporate every form of civil inattention), yet it does cover central ones. On the following see also J. L. Cohen (1993) 316ff.

35 Moreover, a parallel is sometimes misleadingly drawn between this distinction and the distinction between private and public, or the two distinctions are even equated; see for example Forst (2002) 94 and Wingert (1993) 150. On the following theme, see in general Forst (2002) 48ff., 90ff., 99ff., 251ff., Habermas (1992b) and (1993), Cooke (1999a) and (1999b), Anderson (1994) and Wingert (1993) 28ff., 131ff. All these approaches presuppose that it is possible to draw a clear boundary between ethical and moral problems and perspectives, or at least fail to question borderline cases and grey areas.

36 See Wingert (1993) in full, 140ff., as well as the detailed account in Forst (2002), both of them similar in their accounts to Benhabib (1989) 463ff., who starts by criticizing the parallel drawn between the private/public distinction and the ethical/moral distinction, but only in so far as problems from the ethical, private realm have to be recognized as public, moral issues and as it were cross over from the one realm to the other. At bottom she continues to hold to the fundamental parallelism.

37 Almost everything about these distinctions is open to dispute, yet for our purposes here these comments are sufficient. What is taken for granted is that it is possible and justifiable to draw a distinction between universalistic morality and individual (or collective) ethical conceptions of the good life. It is not my intention here to call this distinction fundamentally into question, for it makes good sense not only in moral philosophy but also in the context of political philosophy. Yet it would of course be possible to do so. On the discussion of the theme, see for example Wingert (1993) 41ff. For opposition to the view that morality should always be conceived as relativized by ethics, see also Habermas's criticism of Bernstein in Habermas (1998). See also Williams (1983a), Tugendhat (1992b), Pauer-Studer (1996a) 239ff. For a critical and illuminating account, see also Kim (1998), who integrates the moral and the ethical perspective in a critical analysis of Williams.

38 See below on the family in ch. 6, sec. 3. There is surely no theorist writing on the difference between ethics and morality who would wish to dispute that the two perspectives are intertwined in this way. Even so, for the most part it is assumed as unproblematic that a clear-cut separation of the two perspectives is generally possible.

39 Habermas (1992b) 186; see also Habermas (1993).

40 Habermas (1992b) 192, emphases added. See also Taylor's description of identity in terms of one's orientation within 'moral space', esp. (1989) 25ff., 91ff. Cooke speaks of the 'evaluative framework' within which one's plans, etc., must always be able to be situated; see (1999a) 28.

41 See above all Taylor (1989) part 1, esp. 53ff.; see also Taylor (1992a). In particular Forst (2002) also refers to the integration of ethical autonomy within its cultural context.

42 See Habermas (1993). However, Habermas (1992b) 169f. also describes individuality as 'such a self-understanding, articulated in the totality of a life project, [which] stands in need of confirmation by others, whether they be concrete or possible participants in interaction'. For criticism of Habermas, see Cooke (1999a) 30f., Forst (2002), Wingert (1993) 144ff. See also J. L. Cohen (1993) and (1997) 155ff.

43 Cooke (1999a) 34; see also 32: 'A space of one's own may not be sealed against the reflective criticism of other persons and, here, *no person's criticism can be excluded in principle*. The intersubjective dimension of the strong evaluation that is part of autonomous self-authorship implies the need for a private space that is essentially *permeable*' (emphasis added). Although Cooke on the other hand asserts that a 'solitary space' ((1999a) 31) is also necessary for a person, this is qualified directly by the constant possibility of objections from others. See also her drastic requirement that, because they always constitute interpretations of experiences as well, even one's own childhood memories (she cites the example of Martin Walser's) should if necessary be put before a *forum externum* for revision, see (1999a) 36f.

44 Furthermore, it is problematic in phenomenal terms to describe the life-projects and life-plans of particular individuals who have specifically wanted and needed to assert themselves in opposition to *any* judgement on the part of others. The fact that artistic or revolutionary life-projects and life-stories may transcend cultural contexts and cultural recognition, on occasion at high personal cost, and that they may also be devoted to private deliberation on 'how one would like to live', is one that is difficult to reconcile with the reduction of ethical self-realization to possible (public) recognition from (ethical) others.

45 See, for example, the theory of personal identity proposed by Parfit (1987) 245ff., 281ff., for whom the unity of the whole individual life as a linear life-story is not

essential to a person's self-understanding. On Parfit, see Wolf (1986), Dancy (1997). From such a perspective, Habermas's notion of 'vouching' for one's own life-history also seems too strong; see Habermas (1992b) 168. With respect to the synchronic (not the diachronic) demand for ethical recognition and to the private space that eludes this, Nagel's account seems to be more acceptable both in phenomenal and normative terms: 'Everyone is entitled to commit murder in the imagination once in a while, not to mention lesser infractions' (Nagel (1998a) 7). This is something one would be reluctant to justify even to an internalized *forum externum*. Habermas (and Cooke) would be unlikely to want to contest this point either. What is unclear is the status they would be able to grant such reflections in their theories (even though these reflections may perfectly well form part of the ethical self-understanding of a person, who would accordingly understand herself as the sort of person who . . .). Hampshire (1978a) is also concerned with this problem of the discursivity of the ethical dimension; see esp. 36ff, 52f.

46 R. Dworkin (1994) 102.

47 On the following see Tribe (1992) 10ff. and *passim*, J. L. Cohen (1992), Allen (1988) 97ff., DeCew (1997) 95ff., Ely (1973). See especially Turkington and Allen (1999) 630ff. On the history of the case, see in particular Tribe (1992) 27ff.

48 *Roe v. Wade*, 410 U.S. 113 (1973) 153.

49 'Although the Constitution does not explicitly mention any right of privacy, the United States Supreme Court recognizes that a right of personal privacy, or a guarantee of certain areas or zones of privacy, does exist under the Constitution, and that the roots of that right may be found in the First Amendment, in the Fourth and Fifth Amendments, in the Penumbras of the Bill of Rights, in the Ninth Amendment, and in the concept of liberty guaranteed by the first section of the Fourteenth Amendment' (410 U.S. 113 (1973) 153). The Ninth and Fourth Amendments are of relevance in particular when it comes to informational privacy. See Turkington and Allen (1999) 630ff. On the argument put forth by the Supreme Court in *Roe v. Wade*, see Ely (1973) 920f. and R. Dworkin (1994) 105.

50 381 U.S. 479 (1965) and 405 U.S. 438 (1972).

51 405 U.S. 438 (1972) 358 (emphasis added). See also Turkington and Allen (1999) 622ff.

52 On this point, see R. Dworkin (1994) 107.

53 See Allen (1998) 460f.

54 *Bowers v. Hardwick*, 478 U.S. 186 (1986) 144ff. See Turkington and Allen (1999) 733ff., Allen (2004), Sandel (1996) 103ff., DeCew (1997) 110ff.

55 See Ely (1973) 937ff., Dworkin (1994) 118ff.; see also J. L. Cohen (1992) 82ff. and DeCew (1997) 95ff.

56 On both points see again the discussion in Dworkin (1994) 102ff., 118ff., 148ff. See Turkington and Allen (1999) 610ff., 629ff. See Inness (1992) 65ff., who deals in detail with the question of the derivation of decisional privacy from constitutional law.

57 Such as MacKinnon (1987). I shall return to her stance in more detail shortly.

58 See J. L. Cohen (1992) 59 etc.

59 See Sandel (1996) 100ff., Sandel (1989), Glendon (1987), Etzioni (1999) 192ff. On the criticism of Sandel and Glendon, see in full J. L. Cohen (1992) 65ff. See also Forst (2002) 103ff.

60 See MacKinnon (1991) 1311: 'The problem is that while the private has been a refuge for some, it has been a hellhole for others, often at the same time. In gendered light, the law's privacy is a sphere of sanctified isolation, impunity, and unaccountability.

It surrounds the individual in its habitat. It belongs to the individual with power. Women have been accorded neither individuality nor power. [. . .] The private is a distinctive sphere of women's inequality to men.'

61 I am here taking up the reflections laid out in chapter 2, see above, ch. 2, sec. 4.

62 For criticism of MacKinnon and her concept of privacy, see ch. 2, sec. 5.

63 Gavison (1980) 357ff. Gavison flatly dismisses any dimension of decisional privacy, however, and reduces the notion of privacy to its informational and local aspects. Accordingly, I regard her criticism as only partially convincing, that is with respect to the *Roe v. Wade* ruling, but not with respect to her overall theory of privacy. See Allen (1988) 32ff., 97ff.

64 See Ely (1973) 931; see 932: 'I suppose there is nothing to prevent one from using the word "privacy" to mean the freedom to live one's life without government interference.' See (1973) 935ff. for Ely's view that the Supreme Court failed to grasp the complex conflict between foetus and woman correctly because it laid too much emphasis on the notion of individual freedom as privacy. Indeed, Ely argues in general against the Court's attempt to 'invent' a constitutional law in order to impose a particular political viewpoint. For criticism of Ely see R. Dworkin (1994) 114f.

65 Allen (1998) 460 *passim*. See also Turkington and Allen (1999) 585: 'In the United States, the phrase "right to privacy" commonly denotes a right of unfettered, independent decision-making about private life.' See in general Turkington and Allen (1999) 610ff. on the conceptual problems involved.

66 J. L. Cohen (1992) 48, 116, 102 *passim*; see also DeCew (1997) 64 *passim*.

67 See also Tribe (1992) 52ff. for a comparison in international terms. In particular, compare the European jurisdiction, which views homosexual practices but not abortion as protected by privacy, the exact opposite of the US. On this point, see Blok (1999).

68 In Germany, indeed, the obligatory counselling for women considering abortion (see StGB [German Criminal Code] § 218c) can patently be understood as a violation of a woman's (decisional) privacy, for it forces her to talk about her problems with a third party, with someone she might not necessarily wish to involve in her decision.

69 This is incidentally also the line of argument taken by Ely (1973), whose argument against the use of the concept of privacy to ground the right to terminate a pregnancy is thus only an indirect one. By way of explanation, one might at this point refer to an approach such as the one taken by R. Dworkin, who provides a justification for the right to abortion despite recognizing the 'sanctity of life' and in this sense criticizes and reconstructs the justification given by the Supreme Court in *Roe v. Wade*; see R. Dworkin (1994) 102ff., esp. 107f. Yet in this context I shall limit myself to pointing his proposal out, without discussing it. I am not concerned here with the question of which is the best justification for such a right to abortion, but only with the criticism of the one justification based on the right to privacy.

70 This point is made, for example, by Sandel. See in more detail the following section.

71 From this perspective, the Supreme Court's decision concerning *Bowers v. Hardwick* is genuinely inconsistent. See Shanley (1998) 237ff. and Allen (2004).

72 Or at least, they only seem to be of limited relevance. One might for example appeal to decisional privacy in order not to be exposed to comments when buying contraceptives. But this of course is a very different context from the one that Sandel (or the Supreme Court) has in mind.

73 Sandel (1996) 96.

74 See J. L. Cohen (1992) 65ff., Turkington and Allen (1999) 620ff.

75 On this point see above in ch. 1, sec. 4.

76 See Etzioni (1999), Sandel (1996) and (1989). On the following topic, see also Forst (2002) 100ff., J. L. Cohen (1992) 65ff., Shanley (1998) and Allen (2004), writing above all from a juridical perspective. On Sandel in general, see also the anthology edited by Allen and Regan (1998).

77 See Sandel (1996) 103: 'The image of the person as a freely choosing, unencumbered self has only recently come to inform our institutional practice. Whatever its appeal, it does not underlie the American political tradition as a whole.' On the contrast between old and new, 'substantive' and 'voluntarist' forms of privacy, see above all 94ff. and 104ff., the interpretation of the *Griswold* ruling.

78 Sandel (1996) 93.

79 Sandel (1996) 96, emphasis added. In this connection see also Etzioni (1999) 207ff.

80 Sandel (1996) 97: 'Whereas privacy in *Griswold* prevented intrusion into "the sacred precincts of marital bedrooms", privacy in *Eisenstadt* prevented intrusion into *decisions* of certain kinds' (emphasis in original).

81 Sandel (1996) 91ff.; see also Sandel (1982) 47ff. See Turkington and Allen (1999) 607f.

82 On the following theme, see also Pauer-Studer (1996a) 133ff., Waldron (1993b) and (1993d). Here I am of course only focusing on the problem of the concept of privacy, not on other aspects of Sandel's theory.

83 Neutrality, says Sandel, often reflects only the 'voluntarist conception of human agency' ((1996) 92). Allen has pointed out that Sandel is here basing his argument on the traditional image of the family in Warren and Brandeis; see Allen (2004).

84 As a consequence, this point can no longer really be raised as an objection to liberal theory. See for example J. L. Cohen (1992) 97: 'Privacy rights are meant to ensure certain domains of decisional autonomy to every individual, not an atomist or voluntarist conception of the individual. They protect one's decisional autonomy vis-à-vis certain crucially personal concerns, they do not dictate the kinds of reasons one gives for decisions or the reflective processes informing the decision.' See for example Gutmann (1992), to name but one other liberal theorist. See Waldron (1993b) 190ff. (for criticism of Sandel). The idea that the individual is culturally constituted is now part of accepted liberal common sense owing to the influence of communitarian and feminist critiques of the naive concept of the subject and autonomy. Just how far one can or should take the relational nature of autonomy is an issue to which I shall return in the following section on feminist criticism.

85 See Habermas (1992d) for his concept of the 'permeation' of the state by ethics. On neutrality see also Habermas (1997), including his analysis of the communitarian critique. See Waldron (1993d) on Sandel, esp. 388–90.

86 See for example Waldron (1993b).

87 Indeed, Etzioni (1999) can no longer really be read other than as a political programme. See above all the polemical chapter on the problem of enforcing an AIDS test upon newborn babies (17ff.) and on the question of 'Megan's laws' (43ff.), which seek to protect communities against sex offenders charged with child abuse who, once they have served time, are permitted to move about 'freely' again (if 'free' is the right word). For sharp criticism of Etzioni, see also Allen (2004).

88 Etzioni (1999) 199 and 196.

89 Etzioni (1999) 188ff., 207ff.

90 Etzioni (1999) 203ff.

91 Etzioni (1999) 213.

92 This is shown in particular by the rather crudely argued chapter on the individual proposals for laws; see Etzioni (1999), esp. chs 1–3.

93 See Nagel, who criticizes communitarian approaches with the aid of the distinction between public and private spheres, instead seeking to propose 'liberal civility', for, he argues, 'control of the common social space [. . .] involves one of the most effective forms of invasion of privacy – the demand that everyone stand up and be counted' ((1998b) 23).

94 See the very good account in Waldron (1993b) 198f.

95 See above, ch. 3, sec. 3.

96 Jaggar (1983) 131. The quotation comes from her description of the stance of 'socialist feminism'. See Hoagland's comment that individual autonomy is 'a thoroughly noxious concept', cited in Friedman (1997) 44. Nedelsky is similarly radical in her insistence: 'Feminism requires a new conception of autonomy. The prevailing conception stands at the core of liberal theory and carries with it the individualism characteristic of liberalism. Such a conception cannot meet the aspirations of feminist theory and is inconsistent with its methodology [. . .]' ((1989) 219). Even so, Nedelsky continues to hold both to the concept and the value of autonomy. See below on this point. Jessica Benjamin likewise radically challenges the claim to neutrality of the rational, autonomous individual; see Benjamin (1988) 188.

97 On the following see Cooke (1999b), Friedman (1991) and (1997), Keller (1997), Di Stefano (1994) and Mackenzie and Stoljar (2000a).

98 To cite Nedelsky again, feminist criticism insists in general that 'people are not selfmade. We come into being in a social context that is literally constitutive of us' ((1989) 220).

99 See again Jaggar (1983); see West (1997) 259ff.

100 See in full Nussbaum (1999a), esp. 59ff.; 71ff. on the role of feelings and corporeality. On this point see also Bordo (1993) 165ff., 277ff. and Jaggar (2000). See Weir (1996) 43vff., Meehan (1995a), Held (1998) 43ff, Keller once more (1997) and Friedman (1997). See also Benhabib (1989) and (1992). Moreover, see also above on the concept of autonomy in ch. 3, sec. 3.

101 On this point, see above all Friedman (1997), Keller (1997), Kittay (1997), as well as Meyers (1987) and Mackenzie and Stoljar (2000b).

102 See Held (1993) 57ff. and Nedelsky (1989); see also Mackenzie and Stoljar (2000a) 8ff., Friedman (1997) 43ff.

103 See Brown (1995) 135ff., Butler (1992) and (1993). See Gatens (1996) 38ff. In this conceptual context, see also Cornell's illuminating critique of the concept of autonomy and law in her discussion of the issue of abortion, (1995) 31ff., 69ff. In general see also above, ch. 2, sec. 4.

104 Brown (1995) 158. Given the diversity, subtlety and sophistication of the feminist literature on the matter, however, it is remarkable that Brown reproaches 'liberal feminism' with outlining either a one-sided, traditional, male concept of autonomy or a concept of 'difference' that is a product of the same categories: 'Neither approach challenges the gendered division between public and private that locates civic autonomy in opposition to the family, sexuality and reproduction' (ibid.).

105 Butler (1992) 12.

106 See Mackenzie and Stoljar (2000a); see also Stoljar (2000).

107 See Di Stefano (1994) 393, Benhabib (1989). For criticism of Chodorow and the rehabilitation of the idea of 'separation' see Weir (1996), esp. 58ff. On relationality, see also Hill (1987) and O'Neill (1992) 219f.

108 See above, ch. 3, sec. 3.

109 In this connection see Friedman (1997) 55: '[A] little reflection on everyday life reveals that autonomy sometimes results in the severing of relational ties – that it does sometimes disconnect us from others, including those that are closely related to us.'

110 These dimensions of privacy, moreover, protect not only people *in* relations, but also the relations *between* people; see below, ch. 5, sec. 3 and ch. 6, sec. 3.

111 See again Friedman (1997) 51ff.

112 See above, sec. 1 and ch. 3, sec. 3.

113 For this reason it is doubtful whether theories such as Brown's should be included within the 'liberal family', even in terms of their self-understanding. See above for Brown's critique of the concept of autonomy.

114 See ch. 3, sec. 5.

115 Arendt (1989).

116 Arendt (1989) 22ff. *passim*. On the following see Villa (1996) 17ff., 188ff.; Boling (1996) 60ff.; Honig (1992); Benhabib (1994) and (1996) (esp. 198ff. on privacy). On Arendt's concept of freedom and the distinction between public freedom and private necessity, see Pitkin (1981) 331ff. On freedom see the illuminating account in Brunkhorst (1999).

117 Arendt (1989) 45; see also (1989) 58: 'To live an entirely private life means above all to be deprived of things essential to a truly human life: to be deprived of the reality that comes from being seen and heard by others, to be deprived of an "objective" relationship [. . .], to be deprived of the possibility of achieving something more permanent than life itself.'

118 In other contexts, however, Arendt speaks of the equality that has its true place in the public realm of politics, see (1981) 162f.; see also (1959) 50. On this problem, see Honig (1992), Brunkhorst (1999), Elshtain (1997).

119 Arendt (1989) 41, 48f.

120 Arendt (1989) 69.

121 In this connection see also Arendt (1991) 63ff.

122 On the feminist reception of Arendt, see the anthology edited by Honig (1995) and her own introduction to it.

123 Arendt (1989) 73.

124 See above, ch. 2.

125 Arendt (1989) 38, 70f. See Arendt (1991), Brunkhorst (1999), Boling (1996) 62ff. For criticism see also Rawls (1993) 206f.

126 Arendt (1989) 70ff.

127 Arendt (1989) 73.

128 Arendt (1989) 73ff.

129 On this point see the nice account in Honig (1992) 222ff. See also Benhabib (1992).

130 Again see above, ch. 2.

131 One could read Arendt (1989) 72 ('how rich and manifold the realm of the hidden can be under the conditions of intimacy') to be referring to just such a retreat by the word 'hidden'. But she does not make the conceptual link with freedom, but only with the life, necessity or richness of intimacy. In such passages, she is at least ambivalent as far as the value of privacy is concerned.

132 Shils (1956) 21f.

133 This is just a summary of what I set out in greater detail above, in ch. 2, sec. 5.

134 For a rather more detailed account of the public realm, however, see below, ch. 7, sec. 3.

Chapter 5 Informational Privacy

1 For definitions of the term, see the Introduction above and the final section of ch. 3. On the following, see in general Westin (1967), Fried (1968) and (1970) 137ff., Benn (1976), Schoeman (1984c) and (1984b) and Bier (1980).

2 Each of the three dimensions that I have distinguished obviously has its own theoretical tradition that considers the dimension in question to be the true one. See also above ch. 3, sec. 5 and below, ch. 6, sec. 1.

3 Fried (1968) 482. Indeed, Fried also makes an explicit connection between the idea of privacy in the sense of control over information about the person and the concept of freedom: 'Most obviously, privacy in its dimension of control over information is an aspect of personal liberty' ((1968) 483). I shall return to this point below. For criticism see Parent (1983) 343ff. Goffman describes the private sphere in general as an 'information preserve', and as 'the set of facts about himself to which an individual expects to control access while in the presence of others' ((1971) 38–9). In what follows I am taking up such approaches as those adopted by Fried, Benn and Westin because – even though they each employ a restricted concept of only informational privacy – they do make the connection between this and the concept of freedom or autonomy.

4 Westin (1967) 7. See Parent (1983) 343, who writes that Westin's definition is 'cited so often that it could well be called a dogma of contemporary jurisprudence'. Parent then takes issue with this definition, but he seems to be misinterpreting it when he writes that it is unsuitable because one's privacy is not violated every time one goes out on the street and can be seen by others. He appears to be overlooking that what is at stake is not simply the *divulgation* of information, but *control* over the divulgation of information. We saw in the last chapter how one is also entitled to dimensions of privacy on the street, and it will shortly become clear to what extent informational privacy too in the sense of control over information 'on the street' is applicable and relevant. On such 'information-based-definitions' of privacy in general, see Inness (1992) 69f., Allen (1988) 8ff., Schoeman (1984c) 2f.

5 I shall return to this question in detail in the next chapter on local privacy.

6 This is a point recognized by Westin too; see (1967) 52ff. Like subsequent theorists of informational privacy, however, he only looks closely at protection with respect to unspecified third parties.

7 See Gandy (1996) 132.

8 Barth (1988) 319. See Rachels (1975) 323ff.

9 It shows above all why we value the privacy of a room, and would accordingly also belong in the next chapter (see ch. 6, sec. 2). Yet it is not surprising that there should be overlaps between the various dimensions of privacy.

10 Here too a distinction can thus be drawn between whether the deception occurred with or without the knowledge of the person in question. In both cases, albeit differently in each one, possible restrictions in the person's autonomy can be described. The question of why authenticity is important was examined above in the chapter on autonomy, see ch. 3, sec. 3. On the problems involved in the issue, see in more detail sec. 3 below.

11 On this point see the relations theorists Fried (1968) and Rachels (1975), whom I discuss more fully below. See also Goffman (1969) 141ff.

12 This might all seem rather hasty. See the more detailed argument above in ch. 3 and below in sec. 3. This chapter thus spotlights the authenticity of each individual's life as one of the aspects of his autonomy, and not – as in the previous chapter on

decisional privacy – the free space within social relations that secures privacy for particular actions.

13 Benn gives the following description of the case of observation: 'But if he stops merely because he's being watched, the interference is of quite a different kind. He could continue if he chose; being observed affects his action only by changing his own perception of it. The observer makes the action impossible only in the sense that the agent now sees it in a different light, through the eyes, as it were, of the observer' ((1988) 272).

14 For the arguments put forward by the German Federal Constitutional Court, see the ruling on the 1983 National Census Law: 'A person who cannot tell with sufficient certainty what information concerning him is in certain areas known to his social environment, or who is unable to assess in some measure the knowledge of his communication partners, may be substantially restricted in his freedom to make plans or take decisions in a self-determined way' (BVerfGE 65, 1 (43)) (trans. by R. G.). On the jurisprudence of the German Federal Constitutional Court with respect to the connection between the private sphere and civil liberties, see Alexy (1986) 326ff.; see esp. 330ff. for the relevant verdicts returned by the Federal Constitutional Court. On the court's rulings in the case of the *Lauschangriff* (Bugging Operation), see also below, ch. 6.

15 See Benn (1988) 270ff.; see also (1984) and (1976).

16 Individuals may accordingly withdraw into private realms so as not to have to take other opinions, perspectives or positions into consideration without wanting to. On this point, see more fully ch. 6 on local privacy.

17 See Benn (1984) 242: '[R]espect for someone as a person, as a chooser, implies respect for him as one engaged on a kind of self-creative enterprise, which could be disrupted, distorted, or frustrated even by so limited an intrusion as watching. A man's view of what he does may be radically altered by having to see it, as it were, through another man's eyes.' See also 228ff. On Benn see Schoeman (1984c) 1f.

18 In this connection see the enlightening account in Kupfer (1987) 84ff. Kupfer here discusses the question of whether observing a person, unbeknown to that person, can really be described as a violation of informational privacy in the sense of a violation of autonomy. He shows how the belief and the trust that one is *in principle* not being observed (etc.) is intrinsic to autonomy. Even if one only finds out retrospectively that one has been observed or deceived, therefore, the possibility of autonomy in general is threatened because of the need for stability in that social fabric of knowledge and individual control without which self-determined, authentic behaviour is not possible. This association of knowledge, control and autonomy is a point overlooked by G. Dworkin ((1988b) 103ff.), when he claims that if my telephone is bugged it is clearly only my privacy and not my autonomy that has been violated. Looking at this from Kupfer's perspective, it is evident that Dworkin here is wide of the mark (quite apart from the fact that he is inconsistent in conceptual terms too, on the one hand coupling the concept of autonomy with the condition that one must have true opinions about the world, but on the other hand overlooking the false opinions one has if one has false opinions about people listening in on one's phone calls).

19 This is shown by Hall (1990), Westin (1967) 11ff.

20 What persons are willing to recount or divulge about themselves in various contexts differs greatly according to the individual concerned, as well, of course, as the culture. The fact that there are these individual differences clearly has nothing in itself to do with the degree of autonomy in the person. There is obviously a degree of leeway as to whether people are more or less open or reserved, or show a greater or lesser

need to communicate with people. What is intrinsic to autonomy here is the ability and the opportunity in principle to differentiate between close and distant, public and intimate relations. But *how* these lines are drawn depends upon the individuality of the person. The way in which an inability to differentiate between intimate and generally accessible contexts may well also lead to a loss of autonomy is something we shall see in the final chapter (see below, ch. 7, sec. 2).

21 See for example Meyrowitz (1985) 185ff. On recent developments see Agre and Rotenberg (1998), and also on the problem of privacy in the internet. See also Camp (1999) and for a full account of the legal issues, see J. E. Cohen (2000) and Lessig (2000).

22 On this point, see the account, albeit rather a technical one, in Beardsley (1971).

23 Ploeg ((1998) 7) points out the threat, even within the philosophical literature, of allowing the legal discourse to prescribe the themes and set the limits to discussions of informational privacy. The predominance of a legal orientation, which restricts the perspective considerably, is something from which I am attempting to break free by asking the more fundamental question of what sort of infringements and what sort of 'data' are involved. The monographs and anthologies on informational privacy tend to be interested exclusively in the problems of technical surveillance. See Westin (1967), Lyon (1988), Lyon and Zureik (1996a), Gandy (1993), DeCew (1997) and Whitaker (1999).

24 See Allen (2004), Ploeg (1998). See Mayer-Schönberger (1998) on the development of European legislation and Bennett (1998) for an international ('global') perspective. I shall return to this shortly.

25 To a certain extent, this is of course an arbitrary division. When employers eavesdrop on, film or control their employees, this is clearly a case of specified third parties. Yet they will be treated below in section 2, because the context is professional and in principle thus open with respect to unspecified third parties. To a certain degree, a distinction between private and public is here already being taken for granted. My concern, however, is merely to make a meaningful, heuristic subdivision within the continuum of informational privacy ranging from the protection of personal data on the internet (i.e. protection with respect to all possible people) to the protection of relationships and within relationships.

26 The various aspects of informational privacy can be distinguished, that is, in terms of *who* infringes this privacy and *how* they do it. That this tends to be overlooked is shown by Gross ((1971) 170f.), who speaks simply of the loss of privacy that ensues when the bounds of personal affairs are transgressed. Further differentiations are clearly possible.

27 *The Economist* of 1 May 1999 thus bears the title 'The End of Privacy', while *Der Spiegel* two months later (5 July 1999) has the equivalent in German, 'Das Ende des Privaten'. See also *Die Zeit* from 22 July 1999. The monographs on the subject are legion. Recent ones include Whitaker (1999), Lehnert (1999), Etzioni (1999), the two latter being especially up to the minute. To name just two particular pessimists, Levine ((1980) 13ff.) is especially harsh in his criticism of the new technologies, which he regards as the gravest of threats to the protection of privacy, a threat that can no longer be averted. Equally pessimistic is Gottlieb (1996) 156: '[T]he trade-offs where privacy has been sacrificed are now so common that, for all practical purposes, privacy no longer exists.'

28 The notion of the panopticon, introduced by Bentham and developed by Foucault, has been taken up, for example, by Gandy (1993), Reiman (1997b) and Whitaker (1999).

29 On the 'visible human' see for example Gavison (1980) 429ff., Wasserstrom (1984) 329ff. There are countless examples of 'surveillance' and the misuse of data and information even in the earliest studies by Westin (1967) and Shils (1956), as well as in more recent ones, especially Gandy (1993), Whitaker (1999), Agre (1998), and in general Agre and Rotenberg (1998), Lyon (1994), Ploeg (1998), DeCew (1997), Camp (1999), Vedder (2000), and J. E. Cohen (2000). Specifically on surveillance and the infringement of privacy on the internet see Lessig (2000) 142ff.

30 Indeed, *complete* surveillance is not the real danger and in this sense not possible either. See on this point, for example, Gandy (1996). I do not wish to claim either that one could not react to many of these surveillance possibilities with a shrug of the shoulders. Many of the infringements of informational privacy may well not make any difference to a person. However, a shrug of the shoulders may also signal the beginning of a slippery slope, by the bottom of which one is no longer so indifferent in one's reactions.

31 See above all the more recent investigations cited in note 29.

32 By the new information technologies, what is usually meant is the sort of information and communication technology that relies upon microelectronic processes; see Lyon and Zureik (1996a) 2ff.

33 Bentham (1969) 194ff.; see also the introduction by Mack (1969b) viiff. and Mack (1969a) 189ff.

34 On the following see Foucault (1977) 195ff. See also the interesting account in Wunderlich (1999). See Gandy (1993) and (1996), Whitaker (1999), who is very informative on the phenomena of surveillance. See also Reiman (1997b) 170ff. The earliest studies manage without the nightmare imagery; see Westin (1967).

35 Foucault (1977) 200, paraphrasing Bentham (1969) 194. The 'major effect of the Panopticon', writes Foucault, is 'to induce in the inmate a state of conscious and permanent visibility that assures the automatic functioning of power' ((1977) 201).

36 Foucault (1977) 205. See the interesting account in Gandy ((1993) 3ff.) for a (schematic) classification of different theoretical models in terms of their interpretations and assessments of what represents a threat to informational privacy (on Weber, Marx, Foucault and Giddens).

37 Foucault (1977) 204, 201.

38 Bentham (1969) 194.

39 Other people may then even know *more* about me than I know about myself. See Wasserstrom, who wrote as early as 1984 that by putting together all the data collected about him it would be possible to 'produce a picture of how I had been living and what I had been doing [. . .] that is fantastically more detailed, accurate and complete than the one I could supply from my own memory' ((1984) 326). Given that the internet 'forgets nothing', Wasserstrom's comment assumes a new significance.

40 Article 2(a) of Directive 95/46/EC of the European Parliament and of the Council of 24 Oct. 1995 on the protection of individuals with regard to the processing of personal data and on the free movement of such data. The objective of this directive is to guarantee citizens of the European Union a series of important rights, such as the right of access to these data, the right to be informed of the origin of the data, the right to object to transmission of the data (in certain cases), the right to correct false data, etc. There is no comparable directive or law in the United States. On this see Allen (2004), Mayer-Schönberger (1998), J. E. Cohen (2000).

41 Ploeg (1998) 5ff.

42 Gandy (1993) 139, Whitaker (1999). Lyon and Zureik (1996b) 5f. further classify certain places.

43 See Ploeg (1998).

44 Warren and Brandeis (1984). These two justices came to exert great influence on account of the solid and comprehensive (and first) foundation that they provided for a right to privacy guaranteed by constitutional law and based on the principle of an 'inviolate personality' ((1984) 82). See Schoeman (1984c) 16f., (1984b) 204, for an explanatory account of Warren and Brandeis. The various types of infringement they distinguish are classified by Prosser (1960) 389ff. See Schoeman (1984c) 14ff.

45 Schoeman (1984c) 16.

46 Warren and Brandeis (1984) 82.

47 This is a point made by Wasserstrom, see (1984) 321ff.; see also Nagel (1998b).

48 See also ch. 6, sec. 2 on the 'room of one's own' that is important on this account.

49 See Gandy (1993) 139, Camp (1999), J. E. Cohen (2000), Lessig (2000) 142ff.

50 See in more detail ch. 6.

51 See Gandy (1993) 3ff.

52 See Allen (1988) 18ff.; Schoeman (1984c).

53 See the detailed and informative account of the latest methods of surveillance in Whitaker (1999); see also Gandy (1993), Belloti (1998). See also the earlier studies, which have nonetheless lost none of their pertinence, for example Westin (1967) 65ff., 169ff.

54 Yet it was not overlooked by Warren and Brandeis (1984), nor by Benn either (1988) 264ff.

55 See Benn (1988) 271: '[A] fundamental principle in morals [is] a general liberty to do whatever one chooses unless someone else has good grounds to interfere to prevent it, grounds that would appeal to any rational person. The onus of justification, in brief, lies with the advocate of restraint, not on the person restrained.' In the debate in Germany on the *Großer Lauschangriff* (the 'Great Bugging Operation') and other laws of this sort, this onus was inverted – rightly so in the case of the *Großer Lauschangriff,* it has to be said, because the issue here was not a basic justification for the right to privacy, as it was in the case of Warren and Brandeis and the ensuing philosophical discussion, but a restriction upon this state-guaranteed right, imposed in the interests of (what was alleged to be) the public welfare. In other words, the discussion involved a clash between a restriction of individual rights to freedom (in the form of rights to privacy) on the one hand and the interests of public welfare on the other. See also the minutes of the public hearing of the Legal Affairs Committee (101st Session of the Legal Affairs Committee of the German Bundestag (13th legislative term), on 21 Nov. 1997). See also below, ch. 6, sec. 2.

56 This is of course a classically liberal assumption, as has already been made clear by the discussion of the communitarian position (see above, ch. 4, sec. 2).

57 See Lyon, cited in Ploeg (1998) 2: 'From this point of view, the surveillance systems of advanced bureaucratic nation-states are not so much the repressive machines that pessimists imply, but the outcome of aspirations and strivings for citizenship. If government departments are to treat people equally, [. . .] from which other rights follow, then people must be individually identified. The individuation that treats people in their own right [. . .] means freedom from specific constraints but also greater opportunities for surveillance and control on the part of a centralized state.'

58 See Gandy (1996) 123ff. Vedder (2000) also points out dangers of this sort in the even more sensitive context of medical and genetic data. On this issue, see also Lacey (2004).

59 See for example Flaherty (1998).

60 Etzioni (1999), 17ff. and *passim*, describes such conflicts in elaborate terms. However, he does not really describe them as conflicts, since public welfare carries the day over the individual subject anyway in these cases. A much more illuminating account of the costs and benefits is provided by Gandy (1993).

61 See Mayer-Schönberger (1998). See the minutes of the public hearing of the Legal Affairs Committee (101st Session of the Legal Affairs Committee of the German Bundestag (13th legislative term), on 21 Nov. 1997). See Allen (2004).

62 See Allen (2004): '[I]f a U.S. consumer purchases a garden-tool from one company using a credit-card, she can expect her name to go onto a mailing list that will be sold to other companies, with the result that she soon receives catalogues and solicitations from dozens of other companies selling similar or related products.'

63 See Gandy (1996) 132ff.; and Camp (1999), J. E. Cohen (2000), Lessig (2000).

64 This is a very brief summary. See the much more detailed account in Whitaker (1999). On the legal problems see J. E. Cohen (2000). In general see Agre and Rotenberg (1998). On the problem of the privacy of 'public persons' in public , which can here be regarded as a special problem though it in fact constituted the point of departure for the work of Warren and Brandeis, see Warren and Brandeis (1984) as well as Prosser (1960) 383f. See also Allen (1988) 123ff.

65 See Whitaker (1999) 139ff.; he also refers to a 'multicultural panopticon'.

66 See Simmel (1993c) 111ff.; J. L. Cohen (1992) 103ff.

67 This is of course not a sufficient consideration, but this weak reason will do for the present. In this context it is unnecessary to go into the debate about liberal democracy as a whole. On the problem, see Rawls (1999b) and (1999c), as well as Habermas (2002a) and (1997).

68 See Fried (1968) and Rachels (1975).

69 Rachels defines privacy not as informational, but directly as relational; see Rachels (1975) 329f. Fried connects informational privacy with relational privacy on account of the 'exchange' of information; see Fried (1968) 482ff., esp. 484f.

70 See Fried (1968), Rachels (1975). For criticism see Reiman (1976) and Gerstein (1978). This approach to privacy is given various names in the literature, e.g. 'relational privacy' in J. L. Cohen (1992) 63ff., 'commodity theory' in Inness; see Inness (1992) 81ff., who likewise criticizes Fried's theory of intimacy for failing to take the context into account.

71 Fried's argument runs as follows ((1968) 484f.): for a relationship of friendship or love, there must be a voluntary and spontaneous renunciation of a 'necessary something' between the persons involved. This characterizes what is special about the relation in question. In friendship or love, it takes the form of the information that each person tells the other about herself. In intimate relationships, that is, one gives up protection of essential information about oneself by communicating such information to the other. I shall come shortly to the problems of such a 'theory of exchange'. For strong criticism see Reiman (1976) 31f.

72 On the legal context, see Scanlon (1975) and Thomson (1974), as well as Fried and Rachels.

73 Reiman (1976) 31f. Reiman claims that intimate relations and the privacy of such relations are necessary for certain forms of self-invention and self-discovery, arguing in this spirit against Fried and Rachels. See also Allen (1988) 45ff. See also Inness (1992) 74ff., 92ff., who in general upholds a strangely narrow theory of privacy as a protection of love and intimacy.

74 See Schoeman (1984b) 201ff., who makes a logical connection between the constitution of intimate relations and the distinction between public and private to the extent

that for him intimacy entails a renunciation of objectivity, which is only possible if there are no standpoints of detached observation involved in the communication. Schoeman argues that to guarantee this, however, one must have control over the realm of one's 'selective self-disclosure', i.e. control over 'which audiences have access to the various faces we present' ((1984b) 201).

75 On the protection of local privacy see also below, ch. 6, sec. 3.

76 My aim here is by no means to set out a 'generally sufficient' theory of intimate relations. My concern is with the role and function of (informational) privacy, not with the question of exactly how to define 'intimacy' or 'love', etc.

77 Here one could also follow Mead in more fundamental terms; see Mead (1962) 164ff. See also Tugendhat (1979) 245ff., 264ff., Honneth (1996b), Habermas (1992b), Benhabib (1989). Honneth (1996b) describes this process within a theory of recognition.

78 See above, ch. 3, sec. 3 and ch. 4, sec. 3.

79 In this connection, see Tugendhat (1979) 291: 'In reflecting and choosing, each person is thrown back upon himself, and this is the case even if he is reflecting together with others. In this resides the characteristic individuation of independent existence, but this individuation does not mean uniqueness, nor does this being-thrown-back-upon-oneself mean being thrown back upon an I or a self. Rather, it means [. . .] a way of being or a way of behaving' (trans. by R. G.). See also ch. 4, sec. 1 and below, ch. 6, sec. 2.

80 See Schoeman (1992) 136ff. on privacy and gossip; see more generally Bok (1983) 89ff. See also above, ch. 4, sec. 1, on the failure to respect decisional privacy.

81 See Althans (2000) 80ff.

82 Goffman (1971) 338. 'Coalition' too is a technical term. It denotes 'a collaborative arrangement minimally between two parties who use it to control the environment of a third, the arrangement itself not being openly established and recognized in these terms'.

83 The communication between the colluders can take two forms here: 'in one, the participants are not in the presence of the excolluded and therefore need conceal only that they are in touch; in the other, the communication occurs in the immediate presence of the excolluded, typically by means of furtive signs' (Goffman (1971) 333–9).

84 Even in social contexts of friendship we do not tell people everything about what connects us with other people or everything we know about the relations between other people. That is, we may know more about Mrs A than we let on either in what we say or what we do. In this connection, Nagel (1998a) speaks of holding back knowledge, so to speak, for the protection of the public (both general and more specific), which does not have to be confronted with all private knowledge.

85 Goffman (1971) 339.

86 Goffman (1971) 340.

87 See above, ch. 4, sec. 1. Overlaps between the dimensions of privacy are bound to occur here because we are dealing with the various aspects of privacy in public, both the general public and a more specific public.

88 One can follow Goffman in making this claim without necessarily sharing his theory of the 'presentational self' as a whole. For criticism see A. Rawls (1987).

89 Goffman (1971) 340.

90 Goffman (1971) 342.

91 Goffman (1971) 343, 339.

92 See Goffman (1971) 344.

93 For this reason too, G. Dworkin's criticism of the connection of privacy and autonomy ((1988b) 103ff.) fails to convince. For a contrasting account of the problem see Griffin (1986) 9f., who can here be read in direct opposition to Dworkin.

94 U. Johnson (1981). The German title is *Skizze eines Verunglückten* (citations in the text translated from the German original by R. G.). I am of course treating this work as a literary one, even though the autobiographical elements in the story are patent. Von Matt ((1989) 418) nonetheless provides a succinct commentary on all attempts to read the 'Sketch' in purely autobiographical terms: 'Incidentally, Uwe Johnson didn't even kill his wife.' Yet in his *Frankfurter Vorlesungen* (Frankfurt Lectures) ((1986) 451f.), Johnson himself refers to the facts that prompted him to write the 'Sketch': 'In June 1975 it is [. . .] finally revealed to the author that he has been helped in writing *Anniversaries* by a student who had just completed a semester in Prague, whom he merely believed to be his wife, merely thought was his assistant. [. . .] In fact, since autumn 1961 she has been in close contact with a confidant of the StB, the Czechoslovakian state security service. [. . .] Damage to the coronary blood vessels was accompanied by damage to the subject, [. . .] the medium of an author's work' (trans. by R. G.).

95 U. Johnson (1981) 50.

96 U. Johnson (1981) 75.

97 U. Johnson (1981), successive quotations on 57, 9, 11, 10, 76, 29, 7, 69, 68.

98 See von Matt (1989) 416f., in particular on the role of language in Johnson and the connection between the loss of language and the loss of identity. The link with the specific function of communication in the theory of relational privacy, as set out above, is obvious.

99 U. Johnson (1981) 68.

100 U. Johnson (1981) 74.

101 U. Johnson (1981) 45, 56, 52.

102 The ideology of the symbiotic matrimony at times seems a little idiosyncratic in Johnson; see in particular (1981) 20ff.

103 See Simmel (1993a) 317: 'Secrecy offers, so to speak, the possibility of a second world besides the manifest one, and the latter is considerably influenced by the former' (trans. by R. G.). See also Posner (1984) 336: 'At some point nondisclosure becomes fraud.' He continues: 'One consideration relevant to deciding whether the line has been crossed is whether the information sought to be concealed by one of the transacting parties is a product of significant investment.' The language used here may be somewhat disconcerting, but Posner is merely reformulating the problem using economic terms.

104 See above, ch. 3, sec. 3. My concern here is only with this one aspect of deceit in the context of informational privacy, not with the whole phenomenology of intimacy, integrity, imposture and deception.

105 See also Wasserstrom (1984) 323: 'People have the right to have the world be what it appears to be precisely in those cases in which they regard privacy as essential to the diminution of their own vulnerability.' On authenticity see Feinberg (1989) 32, as well as Di Stefano (1994) 388. That the (informational) privacy of Hinterhand is also infringed to the extent that he can assume that private knowledge about him is – probably – used in other contexts than those foreseen or desired by him, i.e. in the relationship between his wife and another man, is just one aspect among many.

106 At this point I refer the reader back to the discussions in ch. 3, see ch. 3, sec. 3.

107 Simmel (1993c) 108 (trans. by R. G.).

108 See below, ch. 7, sec. 4.

Chapter 6 Local Privacy

1 See Duby's foreword to Veyne (1987) viii: 'at all times and in all places a clear, commonsensical distinction has been made between the public – that which is open to the community and subject to the authority of its magistrates – and the private. In other words, a clearly defined realm is set aside for that part of existence for which every language has a word equivalent to "private", a zone of immunity to which we may fall back or retreat, a place where we may set aside arms and armor needed in the public place, relax, take our ease, and lie about unshielded by the ostentatious carapace worn for protection in the outside world.' Once more, one dimension of privacy is singled out as the 'true' one. See above, ch. 5, sec. 1. In opposition to such a de-historicization of the private household, see for example Nelson (1990).

2 It can be assumed, indeed, that transcultural and transhistorical social mechanisms exist, principles that secure and determine the access to and the behaviour (for strangers and residents alike) within (generally) private 'reserves'. On this point see Duerr (1994b) 165ff. See also, for example, Hall (1990) 123ff., 139ff., and Westin (1967) 10ff., who here also looks at studies by Geertz. See Moore (1984) 41ff., 267ff. See also the short but instructive article by Bettelheim (1968). Specifically on changes with respect to the relation of the sexes, see Helly and Reverby (1992), also Davidoff (1998). That these possibilities for being alone need not always necessarily be regarded as self-contained spaces is a point made in particular by Duerr (1994b). In general, of course, it can be said that functional equivalents may exist for private spaces.

3 For clarification of the concepts involved, see for example Christman (1994) 15ff., Waldron (1988) 26ff., Ryan (1983b). See also Arendt (1989) 62ff., 71f. on the grounds for protecting private spaces. Here too it becomes clear that the grounds for such protection are independent of the protection of private property. The following account is not concerned, therefore, with that traditional line in the meaning of 'privacy' that goes back to seventeenth-century ideas on private property and even today is still as relevant as ever on account of such notions as private enterprise and private industry. This aspect of the Lockean tradition is to be left out of account. The question of whether the exercise of freedom always presupposes certain rights of ownership and disposal is one that has to do with the general material and ideological presuppositions of modern societies. On Hegel see Waldron (1988) 343ff., Ritter (1997).

4 On this genesis and the problems associated with it, see above, ch. 2, secs 1 and 2. See also the articles in volumes 4 and 5 of *A History of Private Life* (Perrot (1990) and Prost and Vincent (1991)). For a different approach, see for example Seligman (1998), who traces ideas of private (family) life back not primarily to the nineteenth century, but to the eighteenth century and the emergence of an individualistic morality that ascribes all 'values' to the private sphere.

5 See Ryan (1983b) 241, who here claims that one's office is frequently a more private place than one's home, because at home (but not in the office) one is permanently disturbed by one's children: '[M]any men at least feel that their privacy is a great deal more secure in an office whose door will not be opened by every Tom, Dick and Harry than it is in their own homes, where young Samantha may come bursting through the bedroom or bathroom door at any moment.' Okin points out the not particularly subtle gender subtext in Ryan; see Okin (1991) 89.

6 I am here intentionally not giving this thesis a *very* strong formulation. It does not seem empirically convincing to maintain that there is a *necessary causal* connection

between the possibility of retreating into privacy and the autonomy of an individual. What does seem (both empirically and normatively) plausible is the claim that there is a typical, regular connection between the two factors, i.e. between the privacy of spaces or possibilities for withdrawal (i.e. functional equivalents) in general and autonomy. That this means that the spaces must be used in a specific way is a point to which I return shortly.

7 See Woolf (1977). See below in more detail.

8 See Anja Petz's splendid interpretation of the painting *This is Our Corner* by Lawrence Alma-Tadema (Petz (1998)), which refers to the ambivalence manifest in the portrayal of the children's bedroom, with its opposition between the (individual) meaning bestowed by the children and the (social) restriction imposed by the parents. For the significance of privacy in the development of human personality even in childhood, see for example Fischer (1980).

9 Levinas (1969) 152ff. On the connection between bodies, space, objects and privacy, see for example I. Young (2004). See Gramaccini (1998) on changes in the interior in painting and on the way private life is reflected in the relevant pictures of an epoch, and more specifically on how the 'interior' is mirrored in the private living room as 'exterior'; in particular (1998) 92f.

10 See Heidegger (1978) 138. I have already referred in more detail above (ch. 2) to the reverse side of private space, the oppressive, restrictive aspects of the household, which feminists were not the first to describe. See again volume 4 of *A History of Private Life* (Perrot (1990)) 339ff., 'Scenes and Places', where the origin of the expression 'mur de la vie privée' at the beginning of the nineteenth century is explained. Kumar (2004) also argues against the idealization of the 'room of one's own'.

11 BVerfGE 51, 107. See BVerfGE 80, 373, also BVerfGE 90, 255ff., which deals with the protection of the privacy of objects (in this case letters). See also BVerfGE 32, 71ff., BVerfGE 42, 218ff. Subsequent to the changes dating from 26 Mar. 1998, Article 13 of the German Constitution is from this perspective significantly restricted in its content. See also the minutes of the public hearing of the Legal Affairs Committee (101st Session of the Legal Affairs Committee of the German Bundestag (13th legislative term), on 21 Nov. 1997). (Trans. by R. G.)

12 See for example Fried (1970) 143f. See also Kupfer (1987), and below in more detail. See also: 'The guarantee that one will not be secretly scrutinized within one's own four walls also embraces [. . .] one's right to be able to withdraw [. . .] with one's thoughts and most private expressions to a minimal realm absolutely free from disturbance, in order to belong to oneself alone' (statement by Lisken, see the minutes of the public hearing of the Legal Affairs Committee (cited in previous note) 61). Lisken is thus right to speak of the protection given by Article 13 as a 'non-limitable basic right to respect for my integrity' (ibid., 63).

13 The idea behind this intentionally generous enumeration of similar but not identical concepts is to avoid being pinned down to any one particular theory of the self. On restrictions in this context, however, see above on the 'self' and on autonomy (ch. 3, sec. 3). On the problem see for example Thomä (1998).

14 Orwell (1954). As we know, opinions diverge when it comes to the literary qualities of the novel. See for example Rorty (1989) 169ff. See also Habermas (1992a) 454, where he describes a sign of totalitarian states to be the prevention of *public* discourse by secret services, etc. This is of course *part* of the truth, but it only represents one perspective. On the forms of privacy in 'total institutions', see Goffman (1961).

15 The extent to which the possibility of living life *unobserved* is *in general* essential to the possibility of an autonomous, authentic life is not something I intend to go into again at this point. See the whole discussion in the chapter on informational privacy. My concern here is with a quite specific aspect of the issue, namely how far this interdependence of autonomy and privacy is contingent upon the privacy of a *space.*

16 Orwell (1954) 8.

17 Orwell (1954) 9.

18 Orwell (1954) 10f. In this context, see the especially interesting article by Kharkhordin (1997), which describes and analyses the changes in the concept of privacy following the Russian Revolution.

19 In this connection see Reiman ((1976) 40), who describes privacy as a 'condition of the original and continuing creation of "selves" or "persons"'.

20 Orwell (1954) 200.

21 Here we can again refer the reader to Benn (see ch. 5, sec. 1), who writes: 'A man's view of what he does may be radically altered by having to see it, as it were, through another man's eyes' ((1984) 242); see also 267f. on the issue of private objects such as diaries, private correspondence, etc. See also the instructive approach by Kupfer ('Privacy enables self-knowledge, self-criticism, and self-evaluation') in (1987) 83.

22 Fried (1970) 143.

23 The close connection between self-invention and self-presentation is pointed out by Gross: 'Respect for privacy is required to safeguard our changes of mood and mind, and to promote growth of the person through self-discovery and criticism. We want to run the risk of making fools of ourselves and be free to call ourselves fools, yet not be fools in the settled opinion of the world, convicted out of our own mouths' ((1971) 176).

24 See the quotation from Duby above (note 1), even if the battle metaphor does seem somewhat exaggerated.

25 Here I am again taking up the discussions in the last chapter (see ch. 5, sec. 1). On this aspect, see the fine accounts by Thomas Nagel and Harry Frankfurt. Nagel writes ((1998b) 18): 'The awareness of how one appears from outside is a constant of human life, sometimes burdensome, sometimes an indispensable resource. But there are aspects of life which require that we be free of it, in order that we may live and react entirely from the inside. They include sexual life in its most unconstrained form and the more extreme aspects of emotional life – fundamental anxieties about oneself, fear of death, personal rage, remorse, and grief. All these have muted public forms, and sometimes, as with collective grief, they serve an important function for the inner life, but the full private reality needs protection – not primarily from the knowledge, but from the direct perception of others.' See also Nagel (1998a) 14ff. And Frankfurt writes ((1988a) 163): 'It is a salient characteristic of human beings, one which affects our lives in deep and innumerable ways, that we care about what we are. This is closely connected both as cause and as effect to our enormous preoccupation with what other people think of us. We are ceaselessly alert to the danger that there may be discrepancies between what we wish to be (or what we wish to seem to be) and how we actually appear to others and to ourselves.'

26 Westin thus speaks of the 'emotional release' necessary in complex societies; see (1967) 34. See also Okin (1991) 87f.

27 Goffman (1969), esp. 109ff. Although Goffman is frequently called as a witness in the literature on privacy, this is almost entirely – and legitimately so – in connection with his work on asylums (Goffman (1961)). In general he provides a rich source

of empirical support for normative reflections on privacy. See the critical analysis of Goffman's distinction between 'front regions' and 'back regions' in Meyrowitz ((1985) 93ff., 135ff., 167ff. etc.), who nonetheless sometimes seems to be claiming, unconvincingly, that changes in what is 'back' and what is 'front' invalidate the distinction as a whole.

28 Goffman (1969) 114f.

29 Cornell (1995) gives an instructive account of the need for an 'imaginary domain' to safeguard the bodily integrity of women (see e.g. 31ff.). The idea of 'a room of one's own' and of a protected space can *also* be interpreted (though Cornell herself does not do so) as providing the preconditions for this feeling of bodily integrity, for this would be just such a realm in which one does not have to present oneself in any way. Woolf, by contrast, had the possibilities for intellectual creativity in mind (see (1977) e.g. 76ff.). At this point, one can again refer to Sennett, who considers the possibilities for retreating into privacy as intrinsic to the playful identity of the subject; see (2002) 266ff.

30 See for example Bordo (1993) 165ff. on the element of cultural construction. See also Gatens (1996) 60ff. and Honig (1992). For a historical account see Chartier (1993) and Prost and Vincent (1991). See also Landweer (1999) 98ff. On the change in notions of intimacy in general see Giddens (1992).

31 See Elias (1993) 414ff., Duerr (1994a) 256ff. For an illuminating account of the differences between Elias and Duerr, see Schlossberger (2000).

32 On the dual nature of privacy (as protection from others but also as protection for others) see also below, ch. 7, sec. 3. On prescribed privacy see also, for example, DeCew (1997) 68f., Etzioni (1999) 196ff. On the progress of civilization see Nagel (1998a).

33 Sartre (1958) 252ff. I am not in general interested in the place of this theory of intersubjectivity within Sartre's book. On this see for example Morris (1999). What Sartre intends to be read in fundamental terms as ontology, I read literally and 'ontically'.

34 Sartre (1958) 257, 263.

35 Sartre (1958) 264f.

36 As mentioned above, I here make no claim to be reconstructing Sartre's intentions. Indeed, there are passages that show, by contrast, that forms of privacy that I take to be intrinsic to autonomy and freedom run directly counter to Sartre's intentions. See for example: 'if the Other-as-object is defined in connection with the world as the object which *sees* what I see, then my fundamental connection with the Other-as-subject must be able to be referred back to my permanent possibility of *being seen* by the Other' (Sartre (1958) 256, emphasis in original).

37 Emphasis in the original. See also: 'if we happen to appear "in public" to act in a play or to give a lecture, we never lose sight of the fact that we are looked at, and we execute the ensemble of acts which we have come to perform *in the presence of* the look; better yet we attempt to constitute a being and an ensemble of objects *for* this look' (Sartre (1958) 281, emphases in original). On the *evaluative* aspect of the look, which always represents a judgement as well, see Sartre (1958) 267ff. Reversing the direction in which the look is considered, the same of course applies: 'I am fixing the people whom I see into objects; [. . .]. In looking at them I measure my power' ((1958) 266).

38 Honneth (1995b) 158ff.

39 Here one could tie in Sartre's reflections on the look with the issue of shame, as Sartre himself does; see (1958) 261ff.

40 This has already become clear on various occasions; see above, ch. 1, sec. 5 and ch. 5, sec. 1.

41 I am again not giving the thesis a very strong formulation, see above note 6. See also Kupfer (1987), one of the few to reflect on the empirical claim of his normative theses.

42 See above, ch. 3, sec. 3.

43 The privacy of the confessional, incidentally, can be located exactly midway between these two forms of privacy (persons as individuals and persons in relations), for it is not the protection of a private relation that is here being sought, nor the protection of the person in herself, but rather the person in her relation to God. It can be seen here that for this exceptional form of privacy the Christian Church (Catholic and Protestant alike) makes a normatively plausible appeal, based on the freedom of worship, to a particular interpretation of Article 13 of the German Constitution and thus the protection of the private home: 'Any person who confides himself and his deeds to God in confession in the presence of an official witness of the Church – the priest – must be able to be absolutely certain that there is nobody else listening. The religious act of confession does not permit of further participants' (statement by Löwe, see the minutes of the public hearing of the Legal Affairs Committee (cited in note 11 above) 3f.).

44 At this point, we could also return to an objection *in principle* to this conception of local privacy and freedom or autonomy, an objection that completely denies this connection between the elements concerned. According to this view, the realm of privacy – and especially the private home – is anything other than a place of freedom or autonomy, but rather a place of necessity, of reproductive work. It is not a place where one can freely 'realize oneself', that is, but a place where one only does what is needed for the reproduction of biological life. This, again, is Hannah Arendt's objection. We have already seen in the chapter on decisional privacy, however, why Arendt's Aristotelian theory of privacy as a realm (exclusively) of necessity and reproduction is not particularly convincing if one assumes a modern, liberal, individualistic concept of freedom and autonomy. It can now be seen from a different perspective why Arendt's strict separation of realms and activities is inappropriate both in phenomenal and normative terms. Both conceptually and phenomenally, Arendt is unable to take into account the solitary privacy of reflection, to assign it a place that is theoretically or normatively relevant. This seems, however, to indicate a deficient theory of *modern* privacy. On Arendt see above, ch. 4, sec. 4.

45 See above all Meyrowitz (1985) *passim*. See also Kumar (1997); Koch (2000). I shall return to these questions concerning the way privacy has changed under the influence of the media in the final chapter.

46 See for example Knops (1999) 16ff. At first sight, the hermit too is renouncing his privacy, exposing himself to the possibility of no longer distinguishing between the public and the private dimensions of his life. If for the webcammer everything is public, for the hermit everything is private.

47 On the (decreasing) difference between private and public modes of behaviour in the context of the new media, see again Meyrowitz (1985) 93ff.

48 Viewed from a distinct perspective, of course, the problems are very different, for webcammers may be renouncing their privacy completely, while television spectators may attach great value to their privacy, albeit using it in a specific way. I treat the renunciation of privacy in greater detail in the chapter on informational privacy and above all in the final chapter. It is thus not my concern at this point.

49 This objection may claim two things: either that one may lead an autonomous life even without using privacy in this way to achieve individual autonomy, or that autonomy is not needed for a rewarding life anyway (not to the extent I suggested).

50 The television can also be viewed from a different perspective, however, which sees it as facilitating processes of self-invention and self-dialogue in search of autonomy. This is how Koch (2000) describes the private experience of the solitary use of the medium of television. See also below, ch. 7, sec. 2.

51 See the article in the Dutch daily newspaper *Het Parool* from 12 June 1999, 'Inkijk: Wat bezielt de webcammer?', where a number of interviews with webcammers are cited. This of course categorically distinguishes webcammers from the participants in the TV series *Big Brother*.

52 We could at this stage also attempt to articulate a further objection, roughly following Rorty and Foucault. According to such an objection, the form of self-invention that I have described does not go nearly far enough, for it continues to cling to the notion of a unitary, autonomous self, one that can be reached, for example, by writing a diary: the idea of self-creation implied by the modern conception of freedom must be conceived in much more radical and experimental terms than Winston righteously writing his diary. Yet firstly (from an epistemological standpoint), there is no need here to presuppose a strong, unitary self, not even in the case of Winston. One can consistently posit perfectly plausible theories of the unity of the self in its becoming, a unity conceived exclusively as a 'regulative idea' for a plural self, etc. (On this problem see for example Nehamas (1985), part 2, esp. 170ff.). And secondly (from the standpoint of political science), one can and should understand such ideas of self-creation and experiment as possibilities that are compatible with, and indeed are opened up by, a theory of freedom as autonomy of the sort I have been describing here. If they were to be seen as a strong, radical alternative and conceived as the (only) possibility for a rewarding life, they would clearly have to be viewed as a 'comprehensive doctrine' (see for example Rawls (1999d) 450f.), with all the associated difficulties this entails for a liberal theory. See sec. 1 above.

53 See ch. 2, sec. 3.

54 Horkheimer (1972) 114. The family, he continues, to this extent 'cultivates the dream of a better condition for mankind'. Yet the contrast drawn by Horkheimer also contains a significant ideological component. See again Klinger (1995b). In this context see also Benhabib and Nicholson (1988) 551f., Nagl-Docekal (1993).

55 This is the normative perspective on the family. As is well known, the traditional, conventional perspective is in many respects antithetical to this normative view. I have looked at this point in detail above (ch. 2).

56 Kumar ((1997) 222) thus cites the relevant statistics for Great Britain indicating that the traditional classic nuclear family now accounts for only 15 per cent of all families. On the decline in marriages in Germany and the change in family structures, see for example the well-documented article in *Der Spiegel* 43 (1996) 78ff. See McLanahan (1997) and Schwinger (1995) on the diversification of family structures. The disappearance since the 1960s of the bourgeois nuclear family as the norm for small-scale social organization is described thoroughly in the empirically and statistically well-documented study by Meyer (1992) 67ff. See also Coontz (1997) 109ff.

57 I. Young (1997) 196. See also Brown (1995) 135ff., though her critique of liberalism is unconvincing. On the history of the family, the types of family members, the relevant social contexts and the permeability of boundaries, see the instructive book by Davidoff et al. (1999). On the history of the family see also Sennett (2002) 177ff.

See Luhmann (1998) 129ff., and in general on the historical development of the social difference between personal and impersonal relationships, 152ff.

58 On the 'juridification of the private sphere' and the 'colonization of the life-world' see for example Habermas (1987) 367–73; on the term 'juridification' (*Verrechtlichung*) see (1987) 357.

59 See Fraser (1989b), Anderson (1998), Kleingeld (1998). A particularly enlightening account is also provided by Berghahn (1996), including her masterly dismissal of a variety of critics of juridification. See Klinger (1995b) 18ff. on Habermas's concept of privacy and family and in general on the tradition of the Frankfurt School.

60 See for example the clear account in Sennett (1998), ch. 1.

61 See Kumar (1997), for example, for an account of the profound effect such changes can have on family life.

62 See Gildemeister and Wetterer (1992) 222ff.

63 These forms of discrimination of course go beyond the paradigm of distributive justice to the extent that they also have to do with structures of recognition, dominance and victimization that are difficult to operationalize. See I. Young (1990) 15ff. On the final point in particular see Benjamin (1988) esp. 196ff., and Weir (1996) 65ff. See also Kymlicka (1990b).

64 Honneth (forthcoming a). On Honneth see also Pauer-Studer (2004).

65 Honneth (forthcoming a).

66 It is questionable whether Honneth is here being fair towards Kant, to whom he attributes a model of matrimony that is 'without any emotional bonding' (forthcoming a). Yet this does not mean we should regard the Kantian model as any more convincing. See Herman (1995), esp. 982f.

67 Honneth (forthcoming a).

68 Honneth (forthcoming a); see also (1994a) 99.

69 Honneth (forthcoming a).

70 See the particularly clear account in Honneth (1994a) 98f. The two are here connected.

71 See Struehning (1996) and the very good account in Kleingeld (1998). See also Anderson (1998) 363: 'Unless one assumes that particular structures for living together are ordained by God or biology, it is an open question whether the increase in single-parent households or common-law marriages represents a problem. What clearly would represent a problem, however, are developments that threaten to rob family life of its meaning and purpose'; such developments lead to disintegration if they produce a 'lack of contact between family members' (363ff.).

72 One might also consider problematic Honneth's reference to (uncriticized) 'needs' that at all events have to be met within the family. This seems to be going too far. In the family as in all (social) contexts, people may have needs that can be criticized or that call for criticism.

73 On the three forms of recognition see in particular Honneth (1996b) 92ff.

74 In this connection see also Pauer-Studer (2004).

75 And of course whenever – in objective terms – an intimate relationship is (extremely) inequitable and exploitative in character. Postulates of justice are also involved when one shifts attention from the relationship between partners to the parent–children relationship, for parents are often unable on purely logical grounds to do justice to the conflicting *needs* of children and must therefore attempt to act justly, for reasons of and according to a yardstick of justice.

76 See Hampton (1993) 240: 'One cannot distribute the pain that a parent feels when her teenage child gets into trouble, the happiness felt by someone because of the

accomplishments of her friend, the suffering of a woman because of the illness of a parent. But one can distribute the burdens of caring for an infant or running a household, the costs of correspondence, the work involved in a project jointly undertaken by two friends. These nonaffective costs and benefits that the relationship itself creates or makes possible must be distributed fairly if the relationship is to be just.'

77 See ch. 2, sec. 3.

78 In (1999b) Rawls devotes a substantial section to the family, 595ff.

79 See Rawls (1972) 60ff., 75ff.

80 Rawls (1999b) 597, emphasis added.

81 See Rawls (1999c) 596f. and 598f.

82 Rawls (1999c) 596f.

83 Rawls (1972) 212, emphasis added.

84 Rawls of course also sets forth this argument himself in describing the development of one's sense of justice; see (1972) 462ff.

85 See Rawls (1999c) 599f. on the issue of the gender-specific division of labour, which is (only) fair if it was chosen by oneself. Yet he leaves open the exact conditions under which one might here *appropriately and legitimately* say that something has been chosen by oneself.

86 On the following see, for example, Okin (1989b) 134ff., 170ff. See also Hampton (1993), esp. 236ff., Berghahn (1996).

87 See the classic passage in Habermas (1987) 372–3: 'The point is to protect areas of life that are functionally dependent on social integration through values, norms, and consensus formation, to preserve them from falling prey to the systemic imperatives of economic and administrative subsystems growing with dynamics of their own, and to defend them from becoming converted over, through the steering medium of the law, to a principle of sociation that is, for them, dysfunctional.' See also Habermas (1997).

88 See the bill proposed in the German state of Baden-Württemberg, Bundesrat Document 268/99, dated 4 May 1999.

89 In this connection see also Berghahn (1996). For a critical view see Olsen (1994).

90 Waldron gives convincing grounds for this. The structures of social behaviour, he says, should not be identified too closely with the affective ties of existing communities, for in a human world it can always come about that people want to break free from these existing affective ties and take 'new initiatives' in the attempt to make a bearable life possible for themselves. See Waldron (1993d) 379ff. ('we find that, far from destroying or replacing affective ties, fallback rights may be their precondition, at least in an imperfect world' (387)). See also in general his dispute with the communitarians in (1993d) 381ff.

91 In this respect especially, the analyses and proposals made, for example, by Okin seem reasonable. These concern measures that affect the economic situation of housewives by legally safeguarding their participation in the family income and above all provide legal and financial cover for women and children in the case of divorce. Yet Okin is also concerned with the organization of child supervision and ultimately the complete restructuring of working life; see (1989b), esp. 149ff., 170ff.; also (1989c).

92 See for example Minow (1997), esp. 266ff., on the connection between maintenance rights and duties within the family, as well as on the role of the state (which is not neutral, because it – rightly – supports families).

93 I refer the reader once more to the individualization of lifestyles, in that the nuclear family no longer exists as such anyway; see Schwinger (1995). On the politics of the

family, see Gerlach (1992), who also provides relevant statistics on the disappearance of traditional family structures, especially in big cities ((1992) 265ff.). See also the anthology by Lüscher et al. (1990), and also Beck-Gernsheim (1994) 8ff. Giddens speaks of the 'everyday social experiments, with which wider social changes more or less oblige us to engage' ((1992) 8).

94 By way of example, one might here mention the regulation (already in force in some European countries) that grants three years' paid leave for new parents – but only provided that this is claimed jointly by both parents. See in general Gerlach (1992).

95 In fact, we must here of course make a distinction between three groups of relationships: firstly, the relationship between one partner and the other, together with the obligations (and conflicts) entailed by a relationship based on partnership; secondly, the parent–child relationship, with the obligations that parents have towards their children, and children towards their parents; and thirdly, the relationship of siblings, with the obligations of brothers and sisters towards one another. For the sake of simplicity, I concentrate on the first case. The two other cases are possibly even more complicated. On the second case, see for example the anthology edited by O'Neill and Ruddick (1979), especially Held (1979). See also the more recent anthology edited by Narayan and Bartkowiak (1999).

96 There is a further factor that results from the distinction between ethics of care and ethics of justice, with its stereotypical gender-specific connotations of a moral orientation based on care in women and one based on principles in men. Paradoxically, in the fabric of relations and actions making up the family, this can put women at a further disadvantage in structural terms because their moral orientation makes them less able to bring their own interests and their own – perfectly legitimate – standpoint to bear than men, who find it easier to do so on account of their moral perspective centred upon principles. This is shown by Herrmann (1999).

97 Such a position might result in difficulties in the liberal contexts of multiculturalism, for the claim is that boys and girls are entitled to equal treatment within their family, even though this might run counter to certain religious positions. Yet this is merely the consequence of a concept of individual autonomy that is essential to liberal democracy, in conjunction with the specific character of the institution of the family.

98 For a more detailed analysis of this connection, we should also require a more detailed analysis of 'love'. See for example the volume edited by Lamb (1997) and the enlightening article by Velleman (1999), which interprets and analyses love as itself constituting a moral emotion.

99 See Velleman (1999), esp. 19ff.

100 See again Honneth (forthcoming a). In the background here there seems to be a symbiotic idea of love that has been criticized in general on several occasions. See Friedman (1997), Tugendhat (1993) 263ff., Giddens (1992). One might instead claim that love always includes the recognition of the autonomy of the other, and for this reason is *also* a source of moral behaviour. One example of such a theory is provided by Tugendhat, following on from Fromm; see Tugendhat (1993) 272ff.

101 Such a view of the family attempts to avoid a sentimentalization of the family of the sort present in a rather extravagant form, for example, in Sandel; see (1982) 31ff. On this point see also, for example, Pauer-Studer (1996b) 140f.

102 On the normative problem see again Benjamin (1988), whose criticism of the traditional family one may find convincing without thereby agreeing with her critique of the concept of autonomy. See also Weir (1996) 65ff., Meehan (1995a) and Friedman (1997). See Mackenzie and Stoljar (2000a). See also the contributions to the

discussion of feminist psychoanalysis in Benjamin (1995). See also Dausien (1999) on the change in the meaning of the concept of 'gender-specific socialization'. On the feminist critique of the concept of autonomy, see ch. 4, sec. 3.

103 Giddens (1992) 184; see also 184ff. As long as there are blatant injustices in this private sphere, men will remain – to use a formulation of Fraser's – the 'free riders' (Fraser (1996a)) of liberal democracy. Even so, I want to emphasize once more that establishing the conditions under which a family is a just one can of course not tell us anything about the conditions under which family life can really succeed. Justice in families is not a panacea for all their problems.

Chapter 7 Interfaces

1 Brown (2004).

2 See Mueller-Doohm and Jung (1998) 145, Engler (1994), Probst (1998), all of whom follow in the tradition of Sennett (2002), albeit with varying degrees of authority. See also the other articles in Imhof and Schulz (1998). See also the essayistic account by Lehnert (1999). It is interesting to note that this discourse on the loss of privacy as a symptom of the times is completely independent of the discourse on the loss of informational privacy. The former laments that 'people' are no longer interested in privacy and have lost their sense of privacy. The latter, by contrast, ascertains that 'people' lament the threat to their interests in privacy posed by the development of information technology.

3 See Sennett (2002), Arendt (1989). Of course, Habermas too writes a history of the decline of the public realm. But in his case the explanation is a different one and has nothing to do with such privatization and the incursion of intimacy. See Habermas (1992c), also on Sennett. On the fact that histories of the public realm are almost without exception histories of rises and falls, see Benhabib, who speaks of a 'certain nostalgia' in these studies ((1997) 26).

4 Sennett has both in mind, but is less interested in a differentiated concept of privacy than in the public realm; see (2002) esp. 259ff. On Arendt, see also above, ch. 4, sec. 4.

5 I shall also be making a few comments on the concept and function of the public realm in what follows. Apart from this, however, I shall be treating it as a 'residual category', as indeed I have been throughout so far.

6 Brown (2004). For a very detailed and very enlightening account of the various functions – to be assessed in various ways – of the mobile phone and the different forms of 'communication interference' that it causes, see Burkart (2000).

7 For Brown this is above all a sign of the complete emptying of the concept of experience. See Brown (2004).

8 Mueller-Doohm and Jung (1998) 146.

9 See Lohmann (1992) and (1993) on Simmel and the ambivalences of urban culture.

10 Although one should in fact describe the privacy of a telephone call as informational privacy in that it has to do with the protection of certain knowledge about the person, the staging of the phone call in the public realm puts the spotlight on that other dimension of privacy, especially as these mobile phone conversations should not be overestimated anyway. They are as a rule either completely trivial or, as business conversations, completely incomprehensible, and of course on the other hand have a genuine practical function.

11 See in more detail Buckart (2000), who also describes all the other major aspects of 'mobile-phone culture' (accessibility, supervision, mechanization of culture, etc.) that do not necessarily have anything to do with the difference between private and public.

12 Even Westin ((1967) 52ff.) points out that threats to privacy reside not only in the supervision made possible by the new information technologies, but also in people's willingness to dispense with their privacy.

13 I shall return to this point in greater detail shortly, in the discussion of Nagel.

14 On the Dutch *Big Brother* series, see Hille (2000), which must be termed more of a celebration of the programme than a critical analysis, but which does provide ample material on 'events in the house', the associated commercial interests and, implicitly, the possible conflicts.

15 On the following see Keppler (1994) 11ff. and (1998), Bolz (1998), Welsch (1991b), Baudrillard (1990).

16 The pessimistic version is to be found, for example, in Adorno and Horkheimer (1979). Midway between such optimistic and pessimistic versions of the cultural critique of the media, a sober stance can be found in Koch (2000), who describes positive effects of television and film precisely with regard to the distinction between public and private, yet without becoming euphoric. See also Cavell (1979).

17 See Baudrillard (1990) 257ff.

18 Welsch (1991b) 58 (trans. by R. G.). He continues: 'Reality – not only external reality, but even the inner reality of one's self-understanding and social programming – is today largely constituted through perception of the mass media.' Of course, one should here distinguish in much greater detail between the (indisputable) influence that the media have on our daily lives and the (disputable) abolition of the difference said to accompany this. For a closer analysis of the thesis from the perspective of media theory, see Keppler (1994) 16ff.

19 Welsch (1991b) 58. Welsch and Baudrillard seem to welcome this.

20 Bolz (1998) 131 (trans. by R. G.). Bolz describes these processes in a more reproachful tone.

21 On informational privacy see also above, ch. 5, secs 1 and 2.

22 See again the descriptions in Hille (2000), e.g. 79f.

23 See for example Thompson (1995) 125ff. and 207ff., and also, once more, Meyrowitz (1985).

24 Welsch speaks of the 'reality [that has] itself become software' ((1991a) 58f.). See the very enlightening account in Wasserstrom (1984) 323ff. on the issue of what would go missing if we were permanently to adopt the perspective that we were being filmed.

25 This lack of autonomy in the sense of independent control over one's own life is illustrated in Peter Weir's film *The Truman Show*. See also above on 'webcammers' in ch. 6, sec. 2 and on informational privacy in ch. 5, sec. 1. Conversely, see the reflections by Reemtsma (1999) on the loss of autonomy in *forced* privacy.

26 Mueller-Doohm and Jung (1998) 145 (trans. by R. G.). Their interpretation is that there is 'a mixing of the private and the public. This falling away of the boundary between the private and the public can be [. . .] seen by the obscene way, in terms of media communication, in which television puts the spotlight on the most private of inner lives.' The 'bizarre urge to give private and intimate matters the status of a public event', they write, is an indication that 'social cohesion' is disappearing because as a result of the widespread removal of taboos people can no longer grasp the difference between secrets, taboos and exposures that is intrinsic to social relations. See also

the account in Sennett (2002) 6f., though this is broader in the range of phenomena it covers: 'The world of intimate feeling loses any boundaries; it is no longer restrained by a public world in which people make alternative and countervailing investment of themselves. The erosion of a strong public life therefore deforms the intimate relations [. . .].'

27 See in general Sennett (2002) 269ff., Imhof and Schulz (1998), Liebert (1999), and the classical account in Meyrowitz (1985), here esp. 160ff.

28 I do not mean to play down the predominantly grotesque tastelessness and embarrassment of these shows. Nor would I deny the possibility of analysing these media phenomena using (among other things) concepts such as 'privacy', 'alienation' or a 'rewarding life'. Here I am merely arguing against the exaggerated thesis that these phenomena justify talk of a general erosion of the difference between private and public spheres.

29 That this is so is as obvious as it is interesting. On the drastic changes in conventions since the nineteenth century and the way in which such forms of exhibitionism may also be associated with the falling of masks of excessive piety, see for example Perrot (1990). See also Foucault (1979).

30 This is of course only a very brief sketch. These three lines correspond to the three dimensions of privacy that were described in the last chapter.

31 Simmel (1995) 126 (trans. by R. G.). See also Lohmann (1992) and (1993).

32 See Sennett (2002). However, in *The Fall of Public Man* Sennett does not have a marked interest in these lines, and for this reason deals neither with Richardson's *Pamela* nor with Rousseau's *Confessions*, for example.

33 For a completely different, very pessimistic account, see Ross (1998).

34 See Nuber (1993), esp. 134ff.

35 As in the case, for example, of Engler (1994).

36 As happened in the Clinton–Lewinsky affair, during the course of which virtually nothing else was discussed in public.

37 On the following see Nagel (1998a) and (1998b).

38 Nagel (1998a) 23.

39 Nagel (1998b) 15.

40 This is argued particularly succinctly in Nagel (1998b). See also Nagel (1998a) 4: '[T]here is much more going on inside us all the time than we are willing to express, and civilisation would be impossible if we could all read each other's mind.'

41 'The more complicated people's lives become, the more they need the protection of separate private domains' (Nagel (1998a) 9).

42 On intimacy see Nagel (1998a) 20ff.

43 Nagel also speaks of 'reticence' or 'nonacknowledgment'. On these forms of restraint, also as described by other authors, see above in ch. 4, sec. 1.

44 Nagel (1998a) 29, 23.

45 Nagel (1998a) 14.

46 Nagel (1998a) 24.

47 Nagel (1998a) 22f.

48 Incidentally, Nagel too provides another example of the fact that theories of the public realm always appear in the guise of theories of decline; see above, note 3.

49 On the following see Fraser (1992) and (1996c), Benhabib (1994) and (1997), Liebert (1999), and the now classic account by I. M. Young (1990), esp. 96ff.

50 Nagel (1998a) 25.

51 This problem is not treated by Nagel either. However, Nagel is the author of a relevant essay on the quota system; see (1982c). On the problem, see Phillips (1993) 90ff., Sauer (1994) and (1997).

52 See Nagel (1998a) 23, where he writes that sometimes a 'cultural war' is necessary. Yet it remains unclear *when* this should be the case.
53 See in greater detail above, ch. 2.
54 See Nagel (1998a) 18f. on the avoidance of bad manners in public.
55 See Fraser (1992) and (1996c); see Habermas (1992c); and in general Peters (1994).
56 See Nagel (1998a) 28f.
57 See above, ch. 2, sec. 5.
58 See again, for example, I. M. Young (1990) 96ff., 196ff.
59 See above, ch. 2, sec. 5.
60 Nagel (1998a) 26.
61 With Clinton–Lewinsky, this was not the problem, as it was not a case of sexual harassment. For this reason, Lewinsky has not turned the affair into a scandal either.
62 Even Nagel does not deny, for example, the positive effects of removing sexual taboos. The problem, however, is that once themes have come into the public eye, they cannot simply be modified and returned to the private sphere. See Nagel (1998a) 5ff.
63 This, at least, is what I have tried to show over the last few chapters.
64 On this problem see Benn (1988) 271ff., Wasserstrom (1984). For a special version of the issue see also Rorty (1989). See Schoeman (1984c) 409ff.
65 On the following see Noonan (1989), Quante (1995), A. O. Rorty (1976b). See also the classic article by Perry (1976), as well as Wolf (1986). See Williams (1976b) 1ff., 46ff., Flax (1990) 187ff., Parfit (1987) 245ff.
66 See Tugendhat (1979), 234f., 272f., 284f.; Rawls (1993) 31f.
67 See Quante (1995) 43ff.; Parfit (1987) 199ff.
68 See Ryan (1983a); see also above, ch. 3, sec. 3, on theories of the self.
69 As with Schoeman (1984c) 409ff.
70 See Flax (1990) 222ff.; Foucault (1987).
71 See Butler (1992). On Rorty see also Guignon and Hiley (1990) 350f. See also Nancy (1990) 5 *passim.*
72 Rorty (1989) 65, 73 and *passim*. See Guignon and Hiley (1990) *passim* on the concept of the self as a 'network'. See also Hollis (1990) 249f. on the 'network' and the dissolution of identity.
73 Rawls (1993) 31.
74 'They affirm the values of political justice and want to see them embodied in political institutions and social policies. They also work for the other values in non-public life and for the ends of the associations to which they belong' (Rawls (1993) 31).
75 See Lifton (1986), esp. 417ff., 430ff.
76 In this connection see also Vetlesen (1993) and Löw-Beer (1993).
77 Nagel (1998b).
78 Wasserstrom thus cautiously argues that the differences between one's disorderly thoughts and the respectable expression they are given might also represent a lack of 'forthrightness, honesty, and candour'; see (1984) 331.
79 James (1986); on the following see Rössler (1998).
80 On the genesis of the story, see James's own preface to the New York edition in James (1986) 50ff. See also the foreword by the editor Kermode in James (1986), esp. 18ff. On the story 'The Jolly Corner' as one of the 'ghost stories', mentioned by James himself in connection with 'The Private Life', see the introduction by Zabel in James (1958) 24ff., as well, of course, as 'The Jolly Corner' itself, in James (1958) 314ff. On the relevant period in James (1888–97), see Sicker (1980) 73ff. On this theme in James see also Samuels (1971).
81 On the significance of the setting, the Swiss Alps, see Hasler (1966) 108ff.

82 In what follows, I shall only be interpreting certain aspects of the story. I shall not, for example, be looking into the role of language and its constitutive function in the fractured identities of the two protagonists Vawdrey and Mellifont. Vawdrey, after all, is a poet and writes (himself) only as a private self, while Mellifont, the painter, takes care of the public 'vocabulary'; see James (1986) 199.

83 James (1986) 192.

84 James (1986) 193f.

85 James (1986) 215.

86 James (1986) 199.

87 James (1986) 214, 215. Blanche Adney and Lady Mellifont are in a certain sense also counterparts to Vawdrey, albeit in a different way. Blanche is so because she has a rupture *within* her *public* self, and Lady Mellifont because her private life, and thus her *private* self, is fissured. Lady Mellifont's identity is affected detrimentally by the mysterious self-relationship of her husband: 'She had a secret, and if you didn't find it out as you knew her better you at least felt sure she was gentle and unaffected and limited, as well as rather submissively sad. She was like a woman with a painless malady' ((1986) 195). The character of Blanche Adney, by contrast, has its rupture in her public life, in her suffering at being typecast within the world of comic acting, in her longing *as an actress* to play a serious role and her longing thus to be taken seriously as a *public* person: 'This was the canker in the rose, the ache beneath the smile' ((1986) 200). The public view of her – from the perspective of others as well as her own – is complete and utterly dominant. Owing to this dominance, the rupture weighs all the heavier: 'The perspective of the stage made her over, and in society she was like the model off the pedestal' ((1986) 201).

88 'My story isn't closely concerned with the charming hours I passed there – hours of the kind that make intense memories' (James (1986) 209). This harmony between private and public has its counterpoints in the inability of Vawdrey (the 'public' Vawdrey) to think, feel or talk about anything different whether in the open countryside or indoors, that is above all social gossip ((1986) 228), as well as in the discovery that Mellifont vanishes as soon as he is on his own, which also takes place in the most beautiful natural surroundings.

89 If James's text were a philosophical text, it would here of course be necessary to enquire in greater detail into its semantic and epistemological implications. But it is a literary text and can thus be interpreted and taken seriously in a different manner.

90 However, James does not appear to be concerned with moral problems in this tale. Incidentally, these questions illustrate once more, from a different and special angle, how difficult it is to make a clear-cut separation between ethics and morality. Is it a moral problem if one does not wish to let others, even 'intimate others', participate in one's rich inner life? Nagel speaks of the 'full private reality' of feelings and fears that require the *protection* of privacy (Nagel (1998a) 18). It is clearly impossible to draw a definite borderline between this legitimate protection and 'deceit and hypocrisy' (Schoeman (1984c) 3).

References

Adorno, T. W. (1974) *Minima Moralia: Reflections from Damaged Life*, trans. E. Jephcott, London.

Adorno, T. W. and Horkheimer, M. (1979) *Dialectic of Enlightenment*, trans. J. Cumming, London.

Agre, P. E. (1998) 'Introduction', in Agre and Rotenberg (1998).

Agre, P. E. and Rotenberg, M. (eds) (1998) *Technology and Privacy: The New Landscape*, Cambridge, Mass.

Alderman, E. and Kennedy, C. (1995) *The Right to Privacy*, New York.

Alexy, R. (1986) *Theorie der Grundrechte*, Frankfurt-am-Main.

Allen, A. L. (1988) *Uneasy Access: Privacy for Women in a Free Society*, Totowa.

Allen, A. L. (1998) 'Privacy', in A. Jaggar and I. M. Young (eds), *A Companion to Feminist Philosophy*, Oxford.

Allen, A. L. (2004) 'Privacy in American Law', in Rössler (2004).

Allen, A. L. and Regan, M. (eds) (1998) *Debating Democracy's Discontent: Essays on American Politics, Law, and Public Philosophy*, Oxford.

Althans, B. (2000) *Der Klatsch, die Frauen und das Sprechen bei der Arbeit*, Frankfurt-am-Main.

Anderson, J. (1994) 'Starke Wertungen, Wünsche zweiter Ordnung und intersubjektive Kritik: Überlegungen zum Begriff ethischer Autonomie', *Deutsche Zeitschrift für Philosophie* 1.

Anderson, J. (1998) 'Is Equality Tearing Families Apart?', in M. May, S. Collins-Chobanian and K. Wong (eds), *Applied Ethics: A Multicultural Approach*, Upper Saddle River, N.J.

Arendt, H. (1959) 'Reflections on Little Rock', *Dissent* 6(1).

Arendt, H. (1981) 'Es gibt nur ein einziges Menschenrecht', in O. Höffe, G. Kadelbach and G. Plumpe (eds), *Praktische Philosophie/Ethik, Reader zum Funk-Kolleg*, vol. 2, Munich.

Arendt, H. (1989) *The Human Condition*, Chicago and London.

Arendt, H. (1991) 'Freedom and Politics', in Miller (1991b).

Ariès, P. (1962) *Centuries of Childhood: A Social History of Family Life*, trans. R. Baldick, New York.

Ariès, P. (1993) 'Introduction', in Chartier (1993).

Ariès, P. and Duby, G. (gen. eds) (1987–91) *A History of Private Life*, 5 vols, Cambridge, Mass.

Arneson, R. J. (1994) 'Autonomy and Preference Formation', in J. L. Coleman and A. Buchanan (eds), *In Harm's Way: Essays in Honor of Joel Feinberg*, Cambridge, Mass.

Baehr, A. (1996) 'Toward a New Feminist Liberalism: Okin, Rawls and Habermas', *Hypatia* 2(1).

Barck, K. H. et al. (eds) (1990) *Aisthesis. Wahrnehmung heute oder Perspektiven einer anderen Ästhetik*, Stuttgart.

Barry, B. (1989) *Democracy, Power and Justice: Essays in Political Theory*, Oxford.

Barth, J. (1988) 'The End of the Road' (1958), in J. Barth, *The Floating Opera and The End of the Road*, New York.

Baudrillard, J. (1990) 'Videowelt und fraktales Subjekt', in Barck et al. (1990).

Beardsley, E. L. (1971) 'Privacy: Autonomy and Selective Disclosure', in Pennock and Chapman (1971).

Beck, U. and Beck-Gernsheim, E. (eds) (2001) *Individualization: Institutionalized Individualism and its Social and Political Consequences*, London.

Beck-Gernsheim, E. (1994) 'Auf dem Weg in die postfamiliale Gesellschaft', *Aus Politik und Zeitgeschichte*, 29–39.

Bellah, R. N. et al. (1996) *Habits of the Heart: Individualism and Commitment in American Life*, Berkeley and Los Angeles.

Belloti, V. (1998) 'Design for Privacy in Multimedia Computing and Communications Environment', in Agre and Rotenberg (1998).

Benhabib, S. (1989) 'Der verallgemeinerte und der konkrete Andere. Ansätze zu einer feministischen Moraltheorie', in List and Studer (1989).

Benhabib, S. (1992) *Situating the Self: Gender, Community and Postmodernism in Contemporary Ethics*, New York.

Benhabib, S. (1994) 'Feministische Theorie und Hannah Arendts Begriff des öffentlichen Raums', in Brückner and Meyer (1994).

Benhabib, S. (1996) *The Reluctant Modernism of Hannah Arendt*, Thousand Oaks and London.

Benhabib, S. (1997) 'Die gefährdete Öffentlichkeit', *Transit* 13.

Benhabib, S. and Cornell, D. (eds) (1987) *Feminism as Critique*, Minneapolis.

Benhabib, S. and Nicholson, L. (1988) 'Politische Philosophie und die Frauenfrage', in H. Münkler and I. Fetscher (eds), *Pipers Handbuch der politischen Ideen*, Munich.

Benhabib, S., Butler, J., Cornell, D. and Fraser, N. (eds) (1994) *Feminist Contentions: A Philosophical Exchange*, New York.

Benjamin, J. (1988) *The Bonds of Love: Psychoanalysis, Feminism and the Problem of Domination*, New York.

Benjamin, J. (ed.) (1995) *Unbestimmte Grenzen. Beiträge zur Psychoanalyse der Geschlechter*, Frankfurt-am-Main.

Benn, S. (1976) 'Freedom, Autonomy and the Concept of a Person', *Proceedings of the Aristotelian Society* 76.

Benn, S. (1984) 'Privacy, Freedom and Respect for Persons', in Schoeman (1984a); also in Pennock and Chapman (1971).

Benn, S. (1988) *A Theory of Freedom*, Cambridge.

Benn, S. and Gaus, G. (1983a) 'The Public and the Private: Concepts and Action', in Benn and Gaus (1983b).

Benn, S. and Gaus, G. (eds) (1983b) *Public and Private in Social Life*, New York.

Benn, S. and Weinstein, W. L. (1971) 'Being Free to Act and Being a Free Man', *Mind* 80.

Bennett, C. (1998) 'Convergence Revisited: Toward a Global Policy for the Protection of Personal Data?', in Agre and Rotenberg (1998).

Benson, P. (1991) 'Autonomy and Oppressive Socialization', *Social Theory and Practice* 17(3).

Benson, P. (1994) 'Free Agency and Self-Worth', *Journal of Philosophy* 91(12).

Bentham, J. (1969) 'Panopticon Papers', in Mack (1969a).

Berghahn, S. (1996) 'Die Verrechtlichung des Privaten – allgemeines Verhängnis oder Chance für bessere Geschlechterverhältnisse?', *Leviathan* 1.

Berlin, I. (1969) 'Two Concepts of Liberty', in I. Berlin, *Four Essays on Liberty*, Oxford.

Berofsky, B. (1995) *Liberation from Self: A Theory of Personal Autonomy*, Cambridge.

Bettelheim, B. (1968) 'The Right to Privacy is a Myth', *Saturday Evening Post*, 27 July, pp. 8–9.

BGHZ, *Amtliche Sammlung der Entscheidungen des Bundesgerichtshofs in Zivilsachen* (Official Collection of the Rulings of the German Federal Supreme Court in Civil Proceedings), cited by volume and page.

Bier, W. C. (ed.) (1980) *Privacy: A Vanishing Value?* New York.

Biester, E. et al. (eds) (1994) *Demokratie oder Androkratie?* Frankfurt-am-Main.

Blok, P. (1999) 'Het recht op privacy in het EVRM', MS.

Bobbio, N. (1989) 'The Great Dichotomy: Public/Private', in N. Bobbio, *Democracy and Dictatorship: The Nature and Limits of State Power*, Cambridge.

Bock, G. and James, S. (eds) (1992) *Beyond Equality and Difference: Citizenship, Feminist Politics, Female Subjectivity*, London.

Bohman, J. and Rehg, W. (eds) (1997) *Deliberative Democracy: Essays on Reason and Politics*, Cambridge, Mass.

Bok, S. (1983) *Secrets: On the Ethics of Concealment and Revelation*, New York.

Boling, P. (1996) *Privacy and the Politics of Intimate Life*, Ithaca, N.Y.

Bolz, N. (1998) *Chaos und Simulation*, Munich.

Bordo, S. (1993) *Unbearable Weight: Feminism, Western Culture and the Body*, Berkeley.

Boucher, D. and Kelly, P. (1994a) 'Introduction', in Boucher and Kelly (1994b).

Boucher, D. and Kelly, P. (eds) (1994b) *The Social Contract from Hobbes to Rawls*, London and New York.

Branahl, U. (1998) 'Der Schutz des Privaten im öffentlichen Diskurs', in Imhof and Schulz (1998).

Bransen, J. (1996) 'Identification and the Idea of an Alternative of Oneself', *European Journal of Philosophy* 4.

Brennan, T. and Pateman, C. (1998) ' "Mere Auxiliaries to the Commonwealth": Women and the Origins of Liberalism', in Phillips (1998).

Brink, B. v. d. (1997) *The Tragedy of Liberalism (De tragiek van het liberalisme. Met een samenvatting in het Nederlands*), Utrecht.

Brown, W. (1995) *States of Injury: Power and Freedom in Late Modernity*, Princeton.

Brown, W. (2004) 'The Subject of Privacy: A Comment on Moira Gatens', in Rössler (2004).

Brückner, M. and Meyer, B. (eds) (1994) *Die sichtbare Frau. Die Aneignung der gesellschaftlichen Räume*, Freiburg.

Brunkhorst, H. (1994) *Demokratie und Differenz*, Frankfurt-am-Main.

Brunkhorst, H. (1999) 'Equality and Elitism in Hannah Arendt', MS.

Burkart, G. (2000) 'Mobile Kommunikation. Zur Kulturbedeutung des "Handy" ', *Soziale Welt* 51.

Butler, J. (1990) *Gender Trouble: Feminism and the Subversion of Identity*, New York and London.

Butler, J. (1992) 'Contingent Foundations: Feminism and the Question of "Postmodernism" ', in Butler and Scott (1992).

Butler, J. (1993) *Bodies that Matter: On the Discursive Limits of 'Sex'*, New York and London.

Butler, J. and Scott, J. (eds) (1992) *Feminists Theorize the Political*, New York and London.

BVerfGE, *Amtliche Sammlung der Entscheidungen des Bundesverfassungsgerichts* (Official Collection of the Rulings of the German Federal Constitutional Court), cited by volume and page.

Camp, J. L. (1999) 'Web Security and Privacy: An American Perspective', *The Information Society* 15.

Cavell, S. (1979) *The World Viewed: Reflections on the Ontology of Film*, Cambridge, Mass.

Chartier, R. (ed.) (1993) *Passions of the Renaissance*, trans. A. Goldhammer, Cambridge, Mass.; vol. 3 of Ariès and Duby (1987–91).

Christman, J. (1988) 'Constructing the Inner Citadel: Recent Work on the Concept of Autonomy', *Ethics* 99.

Christman, J. (ed.) (1989a) *The Inner Citadel: Essays on Individual Autonomy*, Oxford and New York.

Christman, J. (1989b) 'Introduction', in Christman (1989a).

Christman, J. (1991) 'Autonomy and Personal History', *Canadian Journal of Philosophy* 21(1).

Christman, J. (1994) *The Myth of Property: Toward an Egalitarian Theory of Ownership*, Oxford.

Christman, J. (1998) 'Autonomy and Self-Reflection', MS.

Cohen, J. E. (2000) 'Examined Lives: Informational Privacy and the Subject as Object', *Stanford Law Review* 52 (May).

Cohen, J. L. (1992) 'Redescribing Privacy: Identity, Difference and the Abortion Controversy', *Columbia Law Journal* 3.

Cohen, J. L. (1993) 'Zur Neubeschreibung der Privatsphäre', in C. Menke and M. Seel (eds), *Zur Verteidigung der Vernunft gegen ihre Liebhaber und Verächter*, Frankfurt-am-Main.

Cohen, J. L. (1994) 'Das Öffentliche und das Private neu denken', in Brückner and Meyer (1994).

Cohen, J. L. (1997) 'Rethinking Privacy: Autonomy, Identity and the Abortion Controversy', in Weintraub and Kumar (1997).

Cohen, J. L. (2004) 'Personal Autonomy and the Law: Sexual Harassment, Privacy and the Dilemmas of Regulating "Intimacy"', in Rössler (2004).

Constant, B. (1987) 'The Liberty of the Ancients compared with that of the Moderns', in B. Constant, *Political Writings*, trans. B. Fontana, Cambridge.

Cooke, M. (1999a) 'A Space of One's Own: Autonomy, Privacy, Liberty', *Philosophy and Social Criticism* 25(1).

Cooke, M. (1999b) 'Questioning Autonomy: The Feminist Challenge and the Challenge for Feminism', in R. Kearney and M. Dooley (eds), *Questioning Ethics: Contemporary Debates in Philosophy*, London and New York.

Coole, D. (1993) *Women in Political Theory: From Ancient Misogyny to Contemporary Feminism*, Boulder, Colo.

Coole, D. (1994) 'Women, Gender and Contract: Feminist Interpretations', in Boucher and Kelly (1994b).

Coontz, S. (1997) *The Way We Really Are*, New York.

Cornell, D. (1991) 'Sexual Difference, the Feminine and Equivalency: A Critique of MacKinnon's *Toward a Feminist Theory of the State*', *Yale Law Journal* 100.

Cornell, D. (1995) *The Imaginary Domain: Abortion, Pornography and Sexual Harassment*, London.

Dancy, J. (ed.) (1997) *Reading Parfit*, Oxford.

Dausien, B. (1999) '"Geschlechtsspezifische Sozialisation" – Konstruktiv(istisch)e Ideen zur Karriere und Kritik eines Konzepts', in B. Dausien et al. (eds), *Erkenntnisprojekt Geschlecht. Feministische Perspektiven verwandeln Wissenschaft*, Opladen.

Davidoff, L. (1998) 'Regarding Some "Old Husbands' Tales": Public and Private in Feminist History', in Landes (1998).

Davidoff, L., Doolittle, M., Fink, J. and Holden, K. (1999) *The Family Story: Blood, Contract and Intimacy 1830–1960*, London and New York.

DeCew, J. Wagner (1997) *In Pursuit of Privacy: Law, Ethics and the Rise of Technology*, Ithaca, N.Y.

Di Stefano, C. (1994) 'Trouble with Autonomy: Some Feminist Considerations', in Okin and Mansbridge (1994).

Dietz, M. (1985) 'Citizenship with a Feminist Face', *Political Theory* 13.

Duby, G. (ed.) (1993) *Revelations of the Medieval World*, trans. A. Goldhammer, Cambridge, Mass.; vol. 2 of Ariès and Duby (1987–91).

Duden, B. (1993) *Disembodying Women: Perspectives on Pregnancy and the Unborn*, trans. L. Hoinacki, Cambridge, Mass.

Duerr, H. P. (1994a) *Intimität*, vol. 2 of *Der Mythos vom Zivilisationsprozeß*, Frankfurt-am-Main.

Duerr, H. P. (1994b) *Nacktheit und Scham*, vol. 1 of *Der Mythos vom Zivilisationsprozeß*, Frankfurt-am-Main.

Duerr, H. P. (1999) *Der erotische Leib*, vol. 4 of *Der Mythos vom Zivilisationsprozeß*, Frankfurt-am-Main.

Dworkin, G. (1978) 'Privacy and the Law', in Young (1978).

Dworkin, G. (1988a) 'Is More Choice Better than Less?' (1982), in Dworkin (1988b).

Dworkin, G. (1988b) *The Theory and Practice of Autonomy*, Cambridge, Mass.

Dworkin, G. (1989) 'The Concept of Autonomy', in Christman (1989a).

Dworkin, R. (1977) *Taking Rights Seriously*, London and Cambridge, Mass.

Dworkin, R. (1978) 'Liberalism', in Hampshire (1978b).

Dworkin, R. (1981a) 'What is Equality? Part One: Equality of Welfare', *Philosophy and Public Affairs* 10.

Dworkin, R. (1981b) 'What is Equality? Part Two: Equality of Resources', *Philosophy and Public Affairs* 10.

Dworkin, R. (1983) 'Neutrality, Equality and Liberalism', in D. MacLean and C. Mills (eds), *Liberalism Reconsidered*, Totowa.

Dworkin, R. (1990) 'Foundations of Liberal Equality', in R. Dworkin and G. B. Peterson (eds), *Tanner Lectures on Human Values II*, Salt Lake City.

Dworkin, R. (1994) *Life's Dominion: An Argument about Abortion, Euthanasia and Individual Freedom*, New York.

Edwards, D. (1988) 'Toleration and Mill's Liberty of Thought and Discussion', in Mendus (1988).

Eisenstein, Z. (1988) *The Female Body and the Law*, Cambridge, Mass.

Elias, N. (1993) *The Civilizing Process: The History of Manners, and State Formation and Civilization*, trans. E. Jephcott, Oxford.

Elshtain, J. B. (1981) *Public Man and Private Woman: Women in Social and Political Thought*, Princeton.

Elshtain, J. B. (1987) 'Against Androgyny', in Phillips (1987a).

Elshtain, J. B. (1997) 'Political Children: Reflections on Hannah Arendt's Distinction between Public and Private Life', in M. L. Shanley and U. Narayan (eds), *Reconstructing Political Theory: Feminist Perspectives*, University Park, Pa.

Ely, J. H. (1973) 'The Wages of Crying Wolf: A Comment on Roe v. Wade', *Yale Law Journal* 82.

Engler, W. (1994) 'Was ist privat, politisch, öffentlich?', *Leviathan* 14.

Estlund, D. M. and Nussbaum, M. (eds) (1997) *Sex, Preference and the Family: Essays on Law and Nature*, Oxford.

Etzioni, A. (1999) *The Limits of Privacy*, New York.

Farge, A. and Foucault, M. (eds) (1982) *Le désordre des familles. Lettres de cachet des Archives de la Bastille*, Paris.

Feinberg, J. (1989) 'Autonomy', in Christman (1989a).

Fergus, M. C. (1980) 'Promotion of Openness in a Democracy', in Bier (1980).

Ferrara, A. (1993) *Modernity and Authenticity: A Study of the Social and Ethical Thought of Jean-Jacques Rousseau*, New York.

Ferrara, A. (1994) 'Authenticity and the Project of Modernity', *European Journal of Philosophy* 2(3).

Ferrara, A. (1998) *Reflective Authenticity: Rethinking the Project of Modernity*, London.

Fischer, C. T. (1980) 'Privacy and Human Development', in Bier (1980).

Flaherty, D. H. (1998) 'Controlling Surveillance: Can Privacy Protection be Made Effective?', in Agre and Rotenberg (1998).

Flax, J. (1990) *Thinking Fragments: Psychoanalysis, Feminism, Postmodernism in the Contemporary West*, Berkeley, Los Angeles and Oxford.

Forst, R. (2002) *Contexts of Justice: Political Philosophy beyond Liberalism and Communitarianism*, trans. J. Farrell, Berkeley.

Foucault, M. (1977) *Discipline and Punish: The Birth of the Prison*, trans. A. Sheridan, Harmondsworth.

Foucault, M. (1979) *The History of Sexuality, Volume I: An Introduction*, trans. R. Hurley, Harmondsworth.

Foucault, M. (1987) *The Thought from Outside*, trans. B. Massumi, New York.

Frankenberg, G. (ed.) (1994) *Auf der Suche nach der gerechten Gesellschaft*, Frankfurt-am-Main.

Frankfurt, H. G. (1988a) 'Identification and Wholeheartedness', in Frankfurt (1988b).

Frankfurt, H. G. (1988b) *The Importance of What We Care About*, Cambridge.

Frankfurt, H. G. (1989) 'Freedom of the Will and the Concept of a Person' (1971), in Christman (1989a).

Frankfurt, H. G. (1999a) 'On the Necessity of Ideals', in Frankfurt (1999b).
Frankfurt, H. G. (1999b) *Necessity, Volition and Love*, Cambridge.
Fraser, N. (1989a) *Unruly Practices: Power, Discourse and Gender in Contemporary Social Theory*, Minnesota.
Fraser, N. (1989b) 'What is Critical about Critical Theory', in Fraser (1989a).
Fraser, N. (1992) 'Rethinking the Public Sphere', in C. Calhoun (ed.), *Habermas and the Public Sphere*, Cambridge, Mass.
Fraser, N. (1996a) 'After the Family-Wage: A Post-Industrial Thought Experiment', in Fraser (1996b).
Fraser, N. (1996b) *Justice Interruptus: Critical Reflections on the 'Postsocialist' Condition*, London.
Fraser, N. (1996c) 'Sex, Lies, and the Public Sphere: Reflections on the Confirmation of Clarence Thomas', in Fraser (1996b).
Frazer, E. and Lacey, N. (1993) *The Politics of Community*, New York and London.
Freud, S. (1962) 'Civilization and its Discontents', in S. Freud, *The Standard Edition of the Complete Psychological Works*, vol. 21, trans. J. Strachey, London.
Fried, C. (1968) 'Privacy', *Yale Law Journal* 77.
Fried, C. (1970) *An Anatomy of Values*, Cambridge, Mass.
Friedman, M. (1993) *What Are Friends For? Feminist Perspectives on Personal Relationships and Moral Theory*, Ithaca and London.
Friedman, M. (1997) 'Autonomy and Social Relationships: Rethinking the Feminist Critique', in Meyers (1997).
Friedman, M. (1999) 'Romantic Love and Personal Autonomy', in P. A. French and H. Wettstein (eds), *Midwest Studies in Philosophy XXII: Philosophy of Emotions*, Notre Dame, Ind.
Gamarnikow, E. et al. (eds) (1983) *The Public and the Private*, Aldershot.
Gandy, O. H. (1993) *The Panoptic Sort: A Political Economy of Personal Information*, Boulder and San Francisco.
Gandy, O. H. (1996) 'Coming to Terms with the Panoptic Sort', in Lyon and Zureik (1996a).
Gatens, M. (1996) *Imaginary Bodies: Ethics, Power and Corporeality*, London and New York.
Gavison, R. (1980) 'Privacy and the Limits of the Law', *Yale Law Review* 77.
Gerhard, U. and Jansen, M. et al. (eds) (1990) *Differenz und Gleichheit. Menschenrechte haben (k)ein Geschlecht*, Frankfurt-am-Main.
Gerlach, I. (1992) 'Aktuelle Fragen der Familienpolitik', in P. Kerenhörster and D. Thränhardt (eds), *Herausforderung an den Wohlfahrtsstaat,* Studien zur Politikwissenschaft 74, Münster and Hamburg.
Gerstein, R. (1978) 'Intimacy and Privacy', *Ethics* 89.
Geschäftsstelle der deutschen Nationalkommission für das Internationale Jahr der Familie (Administrative Office of the German National Commission for the International Year of the Family) (ed.), *Familienreport*, Trier.
Geuss, R. (1995) 'Auffassungen der Freiheit', *Zeitschrift für philosophische Forschung* 49.
Giddens, A. (1992) *The Transformation of Intimacy: Sexuality, Love and Eroticism in Modern Societies*, Cambridge.
Gildemeister, R. and Wetterer, A. (1992) 'Wie Geschlechter gemacht werden. Die soziale Konstruktion der Zweigeschlechtlichkeit und ihre Reifizierung in der Frauenforschung', in G. A. Knapp and A. Wetterer (eds), *Traditionen, Brüche. Entwicklungen feministischer Theorie*, Freiburg.

Glendon, M. A. (1987) *Abortion and Divorce in Western Law*, Cambridge, Mass.
Gobetti, D. (1992) *Private and Public: Individuals, Households and Body Politic in Locke and Hutcheson*, London and New York.
Goffman, E. (1961) *Asylums: Essays on the Social Situation of Mental Patients and Other Inmates*, New York.
Goffman, E. (1967) *Interaction Ritual: Essays on Face-to-Face Behaviour*, New York.
Goffman, E. (1969) *The Presentation of Self in Everyday Life*, Harmondsworth.
Goffman, E. (1971) *Relations in Public: Microstudies of the Public Order*, Harmondsworth.
Gosepath, S. (1992) *Aufgeklärtes Eigeninteresse. Eine Theorie theoretischer und praktischer Rationalität*, Frankfurt-am-Main.
Gottlieb, C. C. (1996) 'Privacy: A Concept whose Time has Come and Gone', in Lyon and Zureik (1996a).
Gould, C. C. (1984) 'Private Rights and Public Virtues: Women, the Family and Democracy', in C. C. Gould (ed.), *Beyond Domination: New Perspectives on Women and Philosophy*, Totowa.
Gramaccini, N. (1998) 'Die Freuden des privaten Lebens. Das Interieur im historischen Wandel', in Schulze (1998).
Gray, T. (1990) *Freedom*, London.
Green, K. (1986) 'Rawls, Women and the Priority of Liberty', *Australasian Journal of Philosophy* 64, suppl.
Greenawalt, K. (1995) *Private Consciences and Public Reasons*, Oxford.
Griffin, J. (1986) *Well-Being: Its Meaning, Measurement and Moral Importance*, Oxford.
Gross, H. (1971) 'Privacy and Autonomy', in Pennock and Chapman (1971).
Guignon, C. (1993) 'Authenticity, Moral Values and Psychotherapy', in C. Guignon (ed.), *The Cambridge Companion to Heidegger*, Cambridge.
Guignon, C. and Hiley, D. R. (1990) 'Biting the Bullet: Rorty on Private and Public Morality', in A. R. Malachowski (ed.), *Reading Rorty*, Oxford.
Gutmann, A. (1992) 'Introduction', in C. Taylor (1992b).
Habermas, J. (1984) *The Theory of Communicative Action, Volume 1: Reason and the Rationalization of Society*, trans. T. McCarthy, Boston.
Habermas, J. (1987) *The Theory of Communicative Action, Volume 2: Lifeworld and System: A Critique of Functionalist Reason*, trans. T. McCarthy, Boston.
Habermas, J. (1992a) 'Further Reflections on the Public Sphere', in C. Calhoun (ed.), *Habermas and the Public Sphere*, Cambridge, Mass.
Habermas, J. (1992b) 'Individuation through Socialization: On George Herbert Mead's Theory of Subjectivity', in J. Habermas, *Postmetaphysical Thinking: Philosophical Essays*, trans. W. Hohengarten, Cambridge, Mass.
Habermas, J. (1992c) *The Structural Transformation of the Public Sphere: An Inquiry into a Category of Bourgeois Society*, trans. T. Burger, Cambridge.
Habermas, J. (1992d) 'Struggles for Recognition in the Democratic Constitutional State', trans. S. W. Nicholsen, in C. Taylor (1992b); also in Habermas (2002a).
Habermas, J. (1993) 'On the Pragmatic, Ethical and Moral Employments of Practical Reason', in J. Habermas, *Justification and Application: Remarks on Discourse Ethics*, trans. C. P. Cronin, Cambridge, Mass.
Habermas, J. (1997) *Between Facts and Norms: Contributions to a Discourse Theory of Law and Democracy*, trans. W. Rehg, Cambridge.

Habermas, J. (1998) 'Reply to Symposium Participants, Benjamin N. Cardozo School of Law', in M. Rosenfeld and A. Arato (eds), *Habermas on Law and Democracy: Critical Exchanges*, Berkeley.

Habermas, J. (2002a) *The Inclusion of the Other: Studies in Political Theory*, ed. C. Cronin and P. De Greiff, Cambridge.

Habermas, J. (2002b) 'Reconciliation through the Public Use of Reason', in Habermas (2002a).

Hall, E. T. (1990) *The Hidden Dimension*, New York.

Hampshire, S. (1978a) 'Public and Private Morality', in Hampshire (1978b).

Hampshire, S. (ed.) (1978b) *Public and Private Morality*, Cambridge.

Hampton, J. (1993) 'Feminist Contractarianism', in L. M. Antony and C. Witt (eds), *A Mind of One's Own*, Oxford.

Hasler, J. (1966) 'Switzerland in the Life and Work of Henry James', Diss. Basel.

Hegel, G. W. F. (1991) *Elements of the Philosophy of Right*, trans. A. Wood and H. Nisbet, Cambridge.

Heidegger, M. (1978) *Being and Time*, trans. J. Macquarrie and E. Robinson, Oxford.

Held, V. (1979) 'The Equal Obligation of Mothers and Fathers', in O. O'Neill and W. Ruddick (eds), *Having Children*, Oxford.

Held, V. (1993) *Feminist Morality: Transforming Culture, Society and Politics*, Chicago and London.

Held, V. (1998) 'Feminist Reconceptualizations in Ethics', in J. A. Kourany (ed.), *Philosophy in a Feminist Voice: Critiques and Reconstructions*, Princeton.

Helly, D. O. and Reverby, S. M. (eds) (1992) *Gendered Domains: Rethinking Public and Private in Women's History. Essays from the Seventh Berkshire Conference on the History of Women*, Ithaca and London.

Henkin, L. (1974) 'Privacy and Autonomy', *Columbia Law Review* 74.

Herman, B. (1995) 'Ob es sich lohnen könnte, über Kants Auffassungen von Sexualität und Ehe nachzudenken?', *Deutsche Zeitschrift für Philosophie* 6.

Hermann, M. (1999) 'Geschlechterethik und Selbstkonzept. Moralphilosophische Folgerungen aus der Kohlberg & Gilligan-Kontroverse', in B. Dausien et al. (eds), *Erkenntnisprojekt Geschlecht. Feministische Perspektiven verwandeln Wissenschaft*, Opladen.

Heyd, D. (1996a) 'Introduction', in Heyd (1996b).

Heyd, D. (ed.) (1996b) *Toleration: An Elusive Virtue*, Princeton.

Hill, T. (1987) 'The Importance of Autonomy', in Kittay and Meyers (1987).

Hill, T. (1989) 'The Kantian Conception of Autonomy', in Christman (1989a).

Hill, T. (1991a) 'Autonomy and Benevolent Lies', in Hill (1991b).

Hill, T. (1991b) *Autonomy and Self-Respect*, Cambridge.

Hill, T. (1991c) 'Weakness of Will and Character', in Hill (1991b).

Hille, K. et al. (2000) *Big Brother. Het Boek*, 's-Gravenhage and Amsterdam.

Hinsch, W. (1997a) 'Die Idee der öffentlichen Rechtfertigung', in Hinsch and Philosophische Gesellschaft Bad Homburg (1997).

Hinsch, W. (1997b) 'Politischer Konsens in einer streitbaren Welt', in Hinsch and Philosophische Gesellschaft Bad Homburg (1997).

Hinsch, W. and Philosophische Gesellschaft Bad Homburg (eds) (1997) *Zur Idee des politischen Liberalismus. John Rawls in der Diskussion*, Frankfurt-am-Main.

Hirschauer, S. (1995) 'Die soziale Fortpflanzung der Zweigeschlechtlichkeit', *Kölner Zeitschrift für Soziologie und Sozialpsychologie* 46.

Hobbes, T. (1968) *Leviathan*, ed. C. B. Macpherson, Harmondsworth.

Höffe, O. (1994) *Political Justice: Foundations for a Critical Philosophy of Law and the State*, trans. J. C. Cohen, Cambridge.

Holland-Cunz, B. (1994) 'Öffentlichkeit und Intimität: demokratie-theoretische Überlegungen', in Biester et al. (1994).

Hollis, M. (1990) 'The Poetics of Personhood', in A. R. Malachowski (ed.), *Reading Rorty*, Oxford.

Honig, B. (1992) 'Toward an Agonistic Feminism: Hannah Arendt and the Politics of Identity', in Butler and Scott (1992).

Honig, B. (ed.) (1995) *Feminist Interpretations of Hannah Arendt*, University Park, Pa.

Honneth, A. (1994a) *Desintegration. Bruchstücke einer soziologischen Zeitdiagnose*, Frankfurt-am-Main.

Honneth, A. (1994b) 'Einführung in den Schwerpunkt Autonomie und Authentizität', *Deutsche Zeitschrift für Philosophie* 1.

Honneth, A. (1995a) *The Fragmented World of the Social: Essays in Social and Political Thought*, ed. C. Wright, Albany.

Honneth, A. (1995b) 'The Struggle for Recognition: On Sartre's Theory of Intersubjectivity', in Honneth (1995a).

Honneth, A. (1996a) 'Pathologies of the Social: The Past and Present of Social Philosophy', trans. J. C. Swindal, in D. Rasmussen (ed.), *Handbook of Critical Theory*, Oxford.

Honneth, A. (1996b) *The Struggle for Recognition: The Moral Grammar of Social Conflicts*, Cambridge, Mass.

Honneth, A. (forthcoming a) 'Between Justice and Affection: The Family as a Field of Moral Disputes', trans. J. M. M. Farrell, in Honneth (forthcoming c).

Honneth, A. (forthcoming b) 'Love and Morality: On the Moral Content of Emotional Ties', trans. J. Ben-Levi, in Honneth (forthcoming c).

Honneth, A. (forthcoming c) *The Morality of Recognition*, Cambridge.

Horkheimer, M. (1972) 'Authority and the Family', in M. Horkheimer, *Critical Theory: Selected Essays*, trans. M. J. O'Connell, New York.

Imhof, K. and Schulz, P. (eds) (1998) *Die Veröffentlichung des Privaten – die Privatisierung des Öffentlichen*, Opladen and Wiesbaden.

Inness, J. (1992) *Privacy, Intimacy and Isolation*, Oxford.

Irigaray, L. (1994) *Thinking the Difference: For a Peaceful Revolution*, trans. K. Montin, London.

Jaggar, A. (1983) *Feminist Politics and Human Nature*, Totowa.

Jaggar, A. (ed.) (1994) *Living with Contradictions: Controversies in Feminist Social Ethics*, Boulder, Colo.

James, H. (1958) *In the Cage and Other Tales*, ed. M. D. Zabel, London.

James, H. (1986) 'The Private Life', in *The Figure in the Carpet and Other Stories*, ed. F. Kermode, London.

James, S. (2000) 'Feminism in Philosophy of Mind: The Question of Personal Identity', in M. Fricker and J. Hornsby (eds), *Feminism in Philosophy*, Cambridge.

Johnson, J. L. (1989a) 'Privacy and the Judgment of Others', *The Journal of Value Inquiry* 23.

Johnson, J. L. (1989b) 'Privacy, Liberty and Integrity', *Public Affairs Quarterly* 3(3).

Johnson, P. (1993) *Frames of Deceit: A Study of the Loss and Recovery of Public and Private Trust*, Cambridge.

Johnson, U. (1981) *Skizze eines Verunglückten*, Frankfurt-am-Main.
Johnson, U. (1986) *Begleitumstände. Frankfurter Vorlesungen*, Frankfurt-am-Main.
Kant, I. (1991) 'On the Common Saying: "This may be true in theory, but it does not apply in practice"', in H. Reiss (ed.), *Kant: Political Writings*, trans. H. B. Nisbet, Cambridge.
Kant, I. (1996) *The Metaphysics of Morals*, trans. M. J. Gregor, Cambridge.
Kant, I. (1997) *Critique of Practical Reason*, trans. M. J. Gregor, Cambridge.
Kant, I. (1998) *Groundwork of the Metaphysics of Morals*, trans. M. J. Gregor, Cambridge.
Kearns, D. (1983) 'A Theory of Justice – and Love: Rawls on the Family', *Politics (Australian Political Studies Journal)* 18(2).
Keller, J. (1997) 'Autonomy, Relationality and Feminist Ethics', *Hypatia* 12(2).
Kenngott, E. (1995) 'Feminismus und Demokratie', *Leviathan* 23.
Keppler, A. (1994) *Wirklicher als die Wirklichkeit. Das neue Realitätsprinzip der Fernsehunterhaltung*, Frankfurt-am-Main.
Keppler, A. (1998) 'Das Private ist politisch. Die Veröffentlichung des Privaten – eine ambivalente Medienstrategie', in Imhof and Schulz (1998).
Kerchner, B. and Wilde, G. (eds) (1997) *Staat und Privatheit. Aktuelle Studien zu einem schwierigen Verhältnis*, Opladen.
Kersting, W. (1997) *Recht, Gerechtigkeit und demokratische Tugend*, Frankfurt-am-Main.
Kharkhordin, O. (1997) 'Reveal and Dissimulate: A Genealogy of Private Life in Soviet Russia', in Weintraub and Kumar (1997).
Kim, S. (1998) 'Kantische Moral und das gute Leben', in H. Steinfath (ed.), *Was ist ein gutes Leben? Philosophische Reflexionen*, Frankfurt-am-Main.
Kittay, E. F. (1997) 'Human Dependency and Rawlsian Equality', in Meyers (1997).
Kittay, E. F. and Meyers, D. T. (eds) (1987) *Women and Moral Theory*, New York.
Klaus, E. (1994) 'Von der heimlichen Öffentlichkeit der Frauen', in *Geschlechterverhältnisse und Politik*, ed. K. Pühl, Frankfurt-am-Main.
Kleingeld, P. (1998) 'Just Love? Marriage and the Question of Justice', *Social Theory and Practice* 24(2).
Klinger, C. (1995a) 'Über neuere Tendenzen in der Theorie der Geschlechterdifferenz', *Deutsche Zeitschrift für Philosophie* 5.
Klinger, C. (1995b) 'Zwischen allen Stühlen. Die politische Theoriediskussion der Gegenwart in einer feministischen Perspektive', MS.
Klinger, C. (1996) 'Private Freiheiten und öffentliche Ordnung: Triumph und Dilemma einer modernen Denkfigur', in W. Weidenfeld (ed.), *Demokratie am Wendepunkt: Die demokratische Frage als Projekt des 21. Jahrhunderts*, Berlin.
Knops, L. B. C. (1999) 'Privacy. Waar ligt de grens?', MS.
Koch, G. (2000) 'A Private Point of View: Privacy in and via the Media', in *Brief: Privacies*, ASCA Yearbook, Amsterdam.
Koestler, A. (1994) *Darkness at Noon*, New York.
Koller, P. (1996) 'Freiheit als Problem der politischen Philosophie', in K. Bayertz (ed.), *Politik und Ethik*, Stuttgart.
Koller, P. (1998) 'Grundlinien einer Theorie gesellschaftlicher Freiheit', in Nida-Rümelin and Vossenkuhl (1998).
Korsgaard, C. M. (1996a) *Creating the Kingdom of Ends*, Cambridge.
Korsgaard, C. M. (1996b) *The Sources of Normativity*, Cambridge.

Korsgaard, C. M. (1996c) 'Two Distinctions in Goodness', in Korsgaard (1996a).

Kumar, K. (1997) 'Home: The Promise and Predicament of Private Life at the End of the Twentieth Century', in Weintraub and Kumar (1997).

Kumar, K. (2004) 'Bringing It All Back Home: A Comment on Iris Young', in Rössler (2004).

Kupfer, J. H. (1987) 'Privacy, Autonomy and Self-Concept', *American Philosophical Quarterly* 24(1).

Kupfer, J. H. (1990) *Autonomy and Social Interaction*, Albany.

Kupferman, T. (ed.) (1990) *Privacy and Publicity: Readings from Communications and the Law*, 2, London.

Kymlicka, W. (1990a) *Contemporary Political Philosophy: An Introduction*, Oxford.

Kymlicka, W. (1990b) 'Rethinking the Family', *Philosophy and Public Affairs* 20.

Lacey, N. (2004) 'Interpreting Doctrines of Privacy: A Comment on Anita Allen', in Rössler (2004).

Lamb, R. (ed.) (1997) *Love Analyzed*, Boulder, Colo.

Landes, J. B. (ed.) (1998) *Feminism: The Public and the Private*, Oxford and New York.

Landweer, H. and Rumpf, M. (1993) 'Zur Kritik der Kategorie "Geschlecht"', *Feministische Studien* 11(2).

Landweer, H. (1999) *Scham und Macht. Phänomenologische Untersuchungen zur Sozialität eines Gefühls*, Tübingen.

Lang, S. (1994) 'Politische Öffentlichkeit und Demokratie. Überlegungen zur Verschränkung von Androzentrismus und öffentlicher Teilhabe', in Biester et al. (1994).

Laqueur, T. (1990) *Making Sex: Body and Gender from the Greeks to Freud*, Cambridge, Mass.

Larmore, C. (1987) *Patterns of Moral Complexity*, Cambridge, Mass.

Lauretis, T. de (1993) 'Der Feminismus und seine Differenzen', *Feministische Studien* 11(2).

Lehnert, G. (1999) *Mit dem Handy in der Peepshow. Die Inszenierung des Privaten im öffentlichen Raum*, Berlin.

Lessig, L. (2000) *Code and Other Laws of Cyberspace*, New York.

Levinas, E. (1969) *Totality and Infinity: An Essay on Exteriority*, trans. A. Lingis, Pittsburgh.

Levine, M. H. (1980) 'Privacy in the Tradition of the Western World', in Bier (1980).

Liebert U. (1999) 'Grenzen liberaler Öffentlichkeit. Zur feministischen Demokratietheorie im Diskurs um die Clinton-Lewinsky-Affäre', in W. Merkel and A. Busch (eds), *Demokratie in Ost und West. Für Klaus von Beyme*, Frankfurt-am-Main.

Lifton, R. J. (1986) *The Nazi Doctors: Medical Killing and the Psychology of Genocide*, New York.

Lindley, R. (1986) *Autonomy*, London.

List, E. and Studer, H. (eds) (1989) *Denkverhältnisse. Feminismus und Kritik*, Frankfurt-am-Main.

Locke, J. (1993) *Two Treatises of Government*, ed. M. Goldie, London.

Lofland, L. (1993) 'Urbanity, Tolerance and Public Space: The Creation of Cosmopolitans', in L. Deben et al. (eds), *Understanding Amsterdam*, Amsterdam.

Lohmann, G. (1991) *Indifferenz und Gesellschaft. Eine kritische Auseinandersetzung mit Marx*, Frankfurt-am-Main.
Lohmann, G. (1992) 'Fragmentierung, Oberflächlichkeit und Ganzheit individueller Existenz. Negativismus bei Georg Simmel', in E. Angehrn et al., *Dialektischer Negativismus*, Frankfurt-am-Main.
Lohmann, G. (1993) 'Die Anpassung des individuellen Lebens an die innere Unendlichkeit der Großstädte. Formen der Individualisierung bei Simmel', *Berliner Journal für Soziologie* 2.
Löw-Beer, M. (1990) *Selbsttäuschung. Philosophische Analyse eines psychischen Phänomens*, Freiburg and Munich.
Löw-Beer, M. (1993) 'Zum Verhältnis emotionaler und politischer Gleichgültigkeit', *Babylon* 12.
Löw-Beer, M. (1994) 'Sind wir einzigartig? Zum Verhältnis von Autonomie und Individualität', *Deutsche Zeitschrift für Philosophie* 1.
Luhmann, N. (1998) *Love as Passion: The Codification of Intimacy*, trans. J. Gaines and D. L. Jones, Stanford.
Lüscher, K., Schultheis, F. and Wehrspann, M. (eds) (1990) *Die 'postmoderne' Familie: Familiale Strategien und Familienpolitik in einer Übergangszeit*, Constance.
Lyon, D. (1988) *The Information Society: Issues and Illusions*, Cambridge.
Lyon, D. (1994) *The Electronic Eye: The Rise of Surveillance Society*, Cambridge.
Lyon, D. and Zureik, E. (eds) (1996a) *Computers, Surveillance and Privacy*, Minneapolis and London.
Lyon, D. and Zureik, E. (1996b) 'Surveillance, Privacy and the New Technology', in Lyon and Zureik (1996a).
MacCallum, G. C. (1991) 'Negative and Positive Freedom', in Miller (1991b).
Mack, P. M. (ed.) (1969a) *A Bentham Reader*, New York.
Mack, P. M. (1969b) 'Introduction', in Mack (1969a).
Mackenzie, C. (2000) 'Imagining Oneself Otherwise', in Mackenzie and Stoljar (2000b).
Mackenzie, C. and Stoljar, N. (2000a) 'Introduction: Autonomy Refigured', in Mackenzie and Stoljar (2000b).
Mackenzie, C. and Stoljar, N. (eds) (2000b) *Relational Autonomy: Feminist Perspectives on Autonomy, Agency, and the Social Self*, Oxford and New York.
MacKinnon, C. (1987) *Feminism Unmodified: Discourses on Life and Law*, Cambridge, Mass.
MacKinnon, C. (1989) *Toward a Feminist Theory of the State*, Cambridge, Mass.
MacKinnon, C. (1991) 'Reflections on Sex Equality under Law', *Yale Law Journal* 100.
Maresch, R. and Werber, N. (eds) (1999) *Kommunikation, Medien, Macht*, Frankfurt-am-Main.
Margalit, A. (1996) *The Decent Society*, trans. N. Goldblum, Cambridge, Mass. and London.
Mayer-Schönberger, V. (1998) 'General Development of Data Protection in Europe', in Agre and Rotenberg (1998).
McLanahan, S. (1997) 'The Consequences of Single Motherhood', in Estlund and Nussbaum (1997).
Mead, G. H. (1962) *Mind, Self and Society: From the Standpoint of a Social Behaviorist*, ed. C. W. Morris, Chicago and London.

Meehan, J. (1995a) 'Autonomy, Recognition, and Respect: Habermas, Benjamin, and Honneth', in Meehan (1995b).

Meehan, J. (ed.) (1995b) *Feminists Read Habermas: Gendering the Subject of Discourse*, London and New York.

Mele, A. R. (1995) *Autonomous Agents: From Self-Control to Autonomy*, New York and Oxford.

Mendus, S. (ed.) (1988) *Justifying Toleration: Conceptual and Historical Perspectives*, Cambridge.

Mendus, S. (1989) *Toleration and the Limits of Liberalism*, London.

Mendus, S. (1992a) 'Losing the Faith: Feminism and Democracy', in J. Dunn (ed.), *Democracy – the Unfinished Journey*, London.

Mendus, S. (1992b) 'Strangers and Brothers: Liberalism, Socialism and the Concept of Autonomy', in Milligan and Miller (1992).

Menke, C. (1996) *Tragödie im Sittlichen. Gerechtigkeit und Freiheit nach Hegel*, Frankfurt-am-Main.

Meyer, T. (1992) *Modernisierung der Privatheit. Differenzierungs- und Individualisierungsprozesse des familialen Zusammenlebens*, Frankfurt-am-Main.

Meyers, D. T. (1987) 'The Socialized Individual and Individual Autonomy: An Intersection between Philosophy and Psychology', in Kittay and Meyers (1987).

Meyers, D. T. (ed.) (1997) *Feminists Rethink the Self*, Oxford.

Meyrowitz, J. (1985) *No Sense of Place: The Impact of Electronic Media on Social Behaviour*, Oxford.

Milan Women's Bookstore Collective (1990) *Sexual Difference: A Theory of Social-Symbolic Practice*, trans. P. Cicogna and T. De Lauretis, Bloomington and Indianapolis.

Mill, J. S. (1910) 'On Liberty', in *Utilitarianism, Liberty and Representative Government* (Everyman's Library), London and New York.

Mill, J. S. (1984) 'The Subjection of Women', in *Collected Works of John Stuart Mill*, vol. 21, ed. J. M. Robson, Toronto.

Miller, D. (1991a) 'Introduction', in Miller (1991b).

Miller, D. (ed.) (1991b) *Liberty*, Oxford.

Milligan, D. and Miller, W. W. (eds) (1992) *Liberalism, Citizenship and Autonomy*, Oxford.

Minow, M. (1990) *Making All the Difference: Inclusion, Exclusion and the American Law*, Ithaca and London.

Minow, M. (1997) 'All in the Family and in All Families: Membership, Loving and Owing', in Estlund and Nussbaum (1997).

Minow, M. and Shanley, M. L. (1997) 'Revisioning the Family: Relational Rights and Responsibilities', in M. L. Shanley and U. Narayan (eds), *Reconstructing Political Theory: Feminist Perspectives*, University Park, Pa.

Moore, B. (1984) *Privacy: Studies in Social and Cultural History*, London and New York.

Morris, P. Sutton (1999) 'Sartre on Objectification: A Feminist Perspective', in J. S. Murphy (ed.), *Feminist Interpretations of Jean-Paul Sartre*, University Park, Pa.

Mouffe, C. (1992) 'Feminism, Citizenship and Radical Democratic Politics', in Butler and Scott (1992).

Mueller-Doohm, S. and Jung, T. (1998) 'Das Tabu, das Geheimnis und das Private – Vom Verlust der Diskretion', in Imhof and Schulz (1998).

Münch, U. (1990) *Familienpolitik in der Bundesrepublik Deutschland*, Freiburg.

Nagel, T. (1982a) 'Moral Luck', in Nagel (1982b).
Nagel, T. (1982b) *Mortal Questions*, Cambridge.
Nagel, T. (1982c) 'The Policy of Preference', in Nagel (1982b).
Nagel, T. (1998a) 'Concealment and Exposure', *Philosophy and Public Affairs* 27(1).
Nagel, T. (1998b) 'The Shredding of Public Privacy: Reflections on Recent Events in Washington', *Times Literary Supplement*, 14 Aug.
Nagl-Docekal, H. (1993) 'Die Kunst der Grenzziehung und die Familie', *Deutsche Zeitschrift für Philosophie* 6.
Nagl-Docekal, H. (1996a) 'Feministische Vernunftkritik', in K. O. Apel and M. Kettner (eds), *Rationalitäten*, Frankfurt-am-Main.
Nagl-Docekal, H. (1996b) 'Gleichbehandlung und Anerkennung von Differenz: Kontroversielle Themen feministischer politischer Philosophie', in Nagl-Docekal and Pauer-Studer (1996).
Nagl-Docekal, H. and Pauer-Studer, H. (eds) (1993) *Jenseits der Geschlechtermoral. Beiträge zur feministischen Ethik*, Frankfurt-am-Main.
Nagl-Docekal, H. and Pauer-Studer, H. (eds) (1996) *Politische Theorie: Gleichheit, Differenz, Lebensqualität*, Frankfurt-am-Main.
Nancy, J. L. (1990) 'Introduction', in E. Cadava et al. (eds), *Who Comes After the Subject?* London and New York.
Narayan, U. and Bartkowiak, J. (eds) (1999) *Having and Raising Children: Unconventional Families, Hard Choices and the Social Good*, University Park, Pa.
Nedelsky, J. (1989) 'Reconceiving Autonomy: Sources, Thoughts and Possibilities', in A. C. Hutchinson and L. J. M. Green (eds), *Law and the Community: The End of Individualism?* Toronto.
Nehamas, A. (1985) *Nietzsche: Life as Literature*, Cambridge, Mass.
Nelson, J. L. (1990) 'The Problematic in the Private', *Social History* 15(3).
Neue Rundschau (1993), special edition *Den Körper neu denken*. Gender Studies (special editor P. Eggers) 104(4).
Neville, R. C. (1980) 'Various Meanings of Privacy: A Philosophical Analysis', in Bier (1980).
Nicholson, L. (ed.) (1990) *Feminism/Postmodernism*, New York.
Nida-Rümelin, J. and Vossenkuhl, W. (eds) (1998) *Ethische und politische Freiheit*, Berlin and New York.
Noonan, H. (1989) *Personal Identity*, London.
Nozick, R. (1974) *Anarchy, State and Utopia*, New York.
Nuber, U. (ed.) (1993) *Wir wollten alles . . . Was haben wir nun? Eine Zwischenbilanz der Frauenbewegung*, Stuttgart.
Nussbaum, M. (1992a) 'Human Functioning and Social Justice: In Defence of Aristotelian Essentialism', *Political Theory* 20.
Nussbaum, M. (1992b) 'Justice for Women!', *New York Review of Books*, 8 Oct.
Nussbaum, M. (1999a) 'The Feminist Critique of Liberalism', in Nussbaum (1999b).
Nussbaum, M. (1999b) *Sex and Social Justice*, Oxford and New York.
Nussbaum, M. and Sen, A. (eds) (1993) *The Quality of Life*, Oxford.
O'Neill, O. (1992) 'Autonomy, Coherence and Independence', in Milligan and Miller (1992).
O'Neill, O. and Ruddick, W. (eds) (1979) *Having Children: Philosophical and Legal Reflections on Parenthood*, New York.
Okin, S. Moller (1979) *Women in Western Political Thought*, London.

Okin, S. Moller (1989a) 'Humanist Liberalism', in N. Rosenblum (ed.), *Liberalism and the Moral Life*, Cambridge, Mass.
Okin, S. Moller (1989b) *Justice, Gender and the Family*, New York.
Okin, S. Moller (1989c) 'Reason and Feeling in Thinking about Justice', *Ethics* 99.
Okin, S. Moller (1991) 'Gender, the Public and the Private', in D. Held (ed.), *Political Theory Today*, Cambridge and Stanford.
Okin, S. Moller (1995) 'Politics and the Complex Inequality of Gender', in D. Miller and M. Walzer (eds), *Pluralism, Justice and Equality*, Oxford.
Okin, S. Moller (1998) 'Feminism and Political Theory', in J. A. Kourany (ed.), *Philosophy in a Feminist Voice: Critiques and Reconstructions*, Princeton.
Okin, S. Moller and Mansbridge, J. (eds) (1994) *Feminism*, 2 vols, Aldershot.
Olsen, F. E. (1991) 'A Finger to the Devil: Abortion, Privacy and Equality', *Dissent* (summer).
Olsen, F. E. (1994) 'The Myth of State Intervention in the Family', in Okin and Mansbridge (1994), vol. 1.
Ortner, S. B. (1998) 'Is Female to Male as Nature is to Culture?' in Landes (1998).
Orwell, G. (1954) *1984*, Harmondsworth.
Ostner, I. and Lichtblau, K. (eds) (1992) *Feministische Vernunftkritik*, Frankfurt-am-Main.
Parent, W. A. (1983) 'Recent Work on the Concept of Privacy', *American Philosophical Quarterly* 20.
Parfit, D. (1987) *Reasons and Persons*, Oxford.
Pateman, C. (1988) *The Sexual Contract*, Stanford.
Pateman, C. (1989a) *The Disorder of Women*, Oxford.
Pateman, C. (1989b) 'Feminist Critiques of the Public/Private Dichotomy', in Pateman (1989a).
Pateman, C. (1989c) 'The Fraternal Social Contract', in Pateman (1989a).
Pauer-Studer, H. (1996a) *Das Andere der Gerechtigkeit. Moraltheorie im Kontext der Geschlechterdifferenz*, Berlin.
Pauer-Studer, H. (1996b) 'Geschlechtergerechtigkeit: Gleichheit und Lebensqualität', in Nagl-Docekal and Pauer-Studer (1996).
Pauer-Studer, H. (2004) 'Justice as a Precondition of Affection and Care: A Comment on Axel Honneth', in Rössler (2004).
Pennock, J. R. and Chapman, J. W. (eds) (1971) *Privacy*, New York.
Perrot, M. (ed.) (1990) *From the Fires of Revolution to the Great War*, trans. A. Goldhammer, Cambridge, Mass.; vol. 4 of Ariès and Duby (1987–91).
Perry, J. (1976) 'The Importance of Being Identical', in A. O. Rorty (ed.), *The Identities of Persons*, Berkeley and London.
Peters, B. (1994) 'Der Sinn von Öffentlichkeit', in F. Neidhardt (ed.), *Öffentlichkeit, öffentliche Meinung, soziale Bewegungen*, special edition 34 of *Kölner Zeitschrift für Soziologie und Sozialpsychologie*, Opladen.
Petz, A. (1998) 'Lawrence Alma Tadema, Das ist unsere Ecke', in Schulze (1998).
Peuckert, R. (1991) *Familienformen im sozialen Wandel*, Opladen.
Phillips, A. (ed.) (1987a) *Feminism and Equality*, Oxford.
Phillips, A. (1987b) 'Introduction', in Phillips (1987a).
Phillips, A. (1991) *Engendering Democracy*, Oxford.
Phillips, A. (1993) *Democracy and Difference*, London.
Phillips, A. (ed.) (1998) *Feminism and Politics*, Oxford.

Pitkin, H. (1981) 'Justice: On Relating Public and Private', *Political Theory* 9(3).
Ploeg, I. v. d. (1998) 'Keys to Privacy: Translations of "The Privacy Problem" in Information Technologies', MS.
Posner, R. A. (1984) 'An Economic Theory of Privacy', in Schoeman (1984a).
Post, R. C. (1995) 'The Social Foundations of Privacy: Community and Self in the Common Law Tort', in R. C. Post, *Constitutional Domains: Democracy, Community, Management*, Cambridge, Mass.
Pothast, U. (ed.) (1978) *Seminar: Freies Handeln und Determinismus*, Frankfurt-am-Main.
Probst, L. (1998) 'Politisierung des Privaten, Privatisierung des Politischen', *Blätter für deutsche und internationale Politik* 43(10).
Prosser, W. (1960) 'Privacy', *California Law Review* 48(3).
Prost, A. and Vincent, G. (eds) (1991) *Riddles of Identity in Modern Life*, trans. A. Goldhammer, Cambridge, Mass., vol. 5 of Ariès and Duby (1987–91).
Quante, M. (1995) 'Die Identität der Person: Facetten eines Problems. Neuere Beiträge zur Diskussion um personale Identität', *Philosophische Rundschau* 42.
Rachels, J. (1975) 'Why Privacy is Important', *Philosophy and Public Affairs* 4.
Rachels, J. and Ruddick, W. (1989) 'Lives and Liberty', in Christman (1989a).
Rawls, A. W. (1987) 'The Interaction Order Sui Generis: Goffman's Contribution to Social Theory', *Sociological Theory* 5.
Rawls, J. (1972) *A Theory of Justice*, Oxford.
Rawls, J. (1993) *Political Liberalism*, Cambridge, Mass.
Rawls, J. (1999a) *Collected Papers*, ed. S. Freeman, Cambridge, Mass.
Rawls, J. (1999b) 'The Idea of an Overlapping Consensus', in Rawls (1999a).
Rawls, J. (1999c) 'The Idea of Public Reason Revisited', in Rawls (1999a).
Rawls, J. (1999d) 'The Priority of Right and Ideas of the Good', in Rawls (1999a).
Raz, J. (1988) *The Morality of Freedom*, Oxford.
Raz, J. (1990) 'Facing Diversity: The Case of Epistemic Abstinence', *Philosophy and Public Affairs* 19(1).
Reemtsma, J. P. (1999) *In the Cellar*, trans. C. B. Janeway, New York.
Reichwein, R., Cramer, C. and Buer, F. (eds) (1993) *Umbrüche in der Privatsphäre: Familie und Haushalt zwischen Politik, Ökonomie und sozialen Netzen*, Bielefeld.
Reiman, J. H. (1976) 'Privacy, Intimacy and Personhood', *Philosophy and Public Affairs* 6; also in Reiman (1997a).
Reiman, J. H. (1997a) *Critical Moral Liberalism. Theory and Practice*, Lanham and London.
Reiman, J. H. (1997b) 'Driving to the Panopticon: A Philosophical Exploration of the Risks to Privacy Posed by the Information Technology of the Future', in Reiman (1997a).
Revel, J. et al. (1993) 'Forms of Privatization', in Chartier (1993).
Rhode, D. (1989) *Justice and Gender*, Cambridge, Mass.
Rhode, D. (ed.) (1990) *Theoretical Perspectives on Sexual Difference*, New Haven.
Richards, A. J. (1989) 'Rights and Autonomy', in Christman (1989a).
Richards, J. R. (1986) 'Separate Spheres', in P. Singer (ed.), *Applied Ethics*, Oxford.
Richardson, H. S. (1997) *Practical Reasoning about Final Ends*, Cambridge, Mass.
Richardson, S. (1975) *Pamela, or Virtue Rewarded: In a Series of Familiar Letters from a Beautiful Young Damsel to her Parents* (1740), London.
Ricoeur, P. (1992) *Oneself as Another*, trans. K. Blamey, Chicago.

Ritter, J. (1997) 'Person und Eigentum. Zu Hegels Grundlinien der Philosophie des Rechts (§§ 34–81)', in L. Siep (ed.), *G. W. F. Hegel, Grundlinien der Philosophie des Rechts*, Berlin.
Rorty, A. O. (ed.) (1976a) *The Identities of Persons*, Berkeley and London.
Rorty, A. O. (1976b) 'A Literary Postscript: Characters, Persons, Selves, Individuals', in Rorty (1976a).
Rorty, R. (1989) *Contingency, Irony and Solidarity*, Cambridge.
Rorty, R. (1991) 'Feminism and Pragmatism', *Michigan Quarterly Review* 30(2).
Rosa, H. (1998) *Identität und kulturelle Praxis. Politische Philosophie nach Charles Taylor*, Frankfurt-am-Main and New York.
Ross, D. (1998) 'Die Regression des Politischen. Die Massenmedien privatisieren die Öffentlichkeit', in Imhof and Schulz (1998).
Rössler, B. (1992) 'Der ungleiche Wert der Freiheit', *Analyse und Kritik*, 14(1).
Rössler, B. (1996) 'Feministische Theorien der Politik', in K. v. Beyme and C. Offe (eds), *Politische Theorien in der Ära der Transformation*, Opladen.
Rössler, B. (1998) 'The Ache beneath the Smile. Literarische Texte und philosophische Imagination', in E. Angehrn and B. Baertschi (eds), *Interpretation und Wahrheit*, Studia Philosophica 57, Bern.
Rössler, B. (1999) 'Unglück und Unrecht. Grenzen von Gerechtigkeit im liberalen Rechtsstaat', in H. Münkler and M. Llanque (eds), *Konzeptionen der Gerechtigkeit: Kulturvergleich – Ideengeschichte – Moderne Debatte*, Baden-Baden.
Rössler, B. (ed.) (2004) *Privacies: Philosophical Evaluations*, Stanford.
Rousseau, J.-J. (2000) *Confessions*, trans. A. Scholar, Oxford.
Ryan, A. (1983a) 'Private Selves and Public Parts', in Benn and Gaus (1983b).
Ryan, A. (1983b) 'Public and Private Property', in Benn and Gaus (1983b).
Samuels, C. T. (1971) *The Ambiguity of Henry James*, Urbana, Ill.
Sandel, M. (1982) *Liberalism and the Limits of Justice*, Cambridge, Mass.
Sandel, M. (1984) 'The Procedural Republic and the Unencumbered Self', *Political Theory* 12.
Sandel, M. (1989) 'Moral Argument and Liberal Toleration: Abortion and Homosexuality', *California Law Review* 77.
Sandel, M. (1996) *Democracy's Discontent: America in Search of a Public Philosophy*, Cambridge, Mass.
Sartre, J.-P. (1958) *Being and Nothingness: An Essay on Phenomenological Ontology*, trans. H. E. Barnes, London.
Sauer, B. (1994) 'Was heißt und zu welchem Zwecke partizipieren wir? Kritische Anmerkungen zur Partizipationsforschung', in Biester et al. (1994).
Sauer, B. (1997) ' "Die Magd der Industriegesellschaft". Anmerkungen zur Geschlechtsblindheit von Staats- und Institutionentheorien', in Kerchner and Wilde (1997).
Saxonhouse, A. (1983) 'Classical Greek Conceptions of Private and Public', in Benn and Gaus (1983b).
Sayers, D. (1984) *Gaudy Night*, London.
Scanlon, T. (1975) 'Thomson on Privacy', *Philosophy and Public Affairs* 4.
Schlossberger, M. (2000) 'Rezeptionsschwierigkeiten. Hans Peter Duerrs Kritik an Norbert Elias' Historischer Anthropologie', *Leviathan* 1.
Schneewind, J. B. (1998) *The Invention of Autonomy: A History of Modern Moral Philosophy*, Cambridge.

Schoeman, F. (ed.) (1984a) *Philosophical Dimensions of Privacy: An Anthology*, New York.

Schoeman, F. (1984b) 'Privacy and Intimate Information', in Schoeman (1984a).

Schoeman, F. (1984c) 'Privacy: Philosophical Dimensions of the Literature', in Schoeman (1984a).

Schoeman, F. (1992) *Privacy and Social Freedom*, Cambridge.

Schulze, S. (ed.) (1998) *Innenleben. Die Kunst des Interieurs. Vermeer bis Kabakov*, Frankfurt-am-Main.

Schwinger, E. (1995) 'Der kulturelle Bedarf an Fürsorglichkeit. Familiale Lebensgemeinschaften und die Verantwortlichkeit politischer Steuerung', *Deutsche Zeitschrift für Philosophie* 6.

Scott, J. (1988) *Gender and the Politics of History*, Cambridge, Mass.

Seel, M. (1995) *Versuch über die Form des Glücks. Studien zur Ethik*, Frankfurt-am-Main.

Seligman, A. (1998) 'Between Public and Private', *Society* 35(3).

Semprun, J. (1991) *Netschajew kehrt zurück*, Berlin.

Sen, A. (1992) *Inequality Reexamined*, New York and Cambridge, Mass.

Sennett, R. (1994) *Flesh and Stone: The Body and the City in Western Civilization*, New York.

Sennett, R. (1998) *The Corrosion of Character: The Personal Consequences of Work in the New Capitalism*, New York and London.

Sennett, R. (2002) *The Fall of Public Man*, Harmondsworth.

Shanley, M. Lyndon (1998) 'Unencumbered Individuals and Embedded Selves: Reasons to Resist Dichotomous Thinking in Family Law', in Allen and Regan (1998).

Shils, E. A. (1956) *The Torment of Secrecy*, Glencoe, Ill.

Sicker, P. (1980) *Love and the Quest for Identity in the Fiction of Henry James*, Princeton.

Silber, J. R. (1971) 'Masks and Fig Leaves', in Pennock and Chapman (1971).

Simmel, G. (1990) *The Philosophy of Money*, trans. D. Frisby and T. Bottomore, London.

Simmel, G. (1993a) 'Das Geheimnis. Eine sozialpsychologische Studie', in Simmel (1993b).

Simmel, G. (1993b) *Georg Simmel. Aufsätze und Abhandlungen 1901–1908*, vol. 2, ed. A. Cavalli and V. Krech, Frankfurt-am-Main.

Simmel, G. (1993c) 'Psychologie der Diskretion', in Simmel (1993b).

Simmel, G. (1995) 'Die Großstädte und das Geistesleben', in *Georg Simmel. Aufsätze und Abhandlungen 1901–1908*, vol. 1, ed. R. Kramme, A. Rammstedt and O. Rammstedt, Frankfurt-am-Main.

Skinner, Q. (1984) 'The Idea of Negative Liberty: Philosophical and Historical Perspectives' in R. Rorty, B. Samunina and Q. Skinner (eds), *Philosophy in History*, Cambridge, Mass.

Skinner, Q. (1991) 'The Paradoxes of Political Liberty', in Miller (1991b).

Skorupski, J. (1989) *John Stuart Mill*, London and New York.

Snitow, A. (1991) 'Talking to the Brothers', *Dissent* (winter).

Steiner, H. (1991) 'Individual Liberty', in Miller (1991b).

Stoljar, N. (2000) 'Autonomy and the Feminist Intuition', in Mackenzie and Stoljar (2000b).

Strawson, P. F. (1974) 'Freedom and Resentment', in P. F. Strawson, *Freedom and Resentment and Other Essays*, London and New York.

Struehning, K. (1996) 'Feminist Challenges to the New Familialism: Lifestyle Experimentation and the Freedom of Intimate Association', *Hypatia* 11(1).
Swanson, J. A. (1992) *The Public and the Private in Aristotle's Political Philosophy*, Ithaca, N.Y.
Taylor, C. (1976) 'Responsibility For Self', in Rorty (1976a).
Taylor, C. (1988) 'Der Irrtum der negativen Freiheit', in C. Taylor (ed.), *Negative Freiheit? Zur Kritik des neuzeitlichen Individualismus*, Frankfurt-am-Main.
Taylor, C. (1989) *Sources of the Self: The Making of the Modern Identity*, Cambridge.
Taylor, C. (1992a) *The Ethics of Authenticity*, Cambridge, Mass.
Taylor, C. (1992b) *Multiculturalism and 'The Politics of Recognition'*, ed. A. Gutmann, Princeton.
Taylor, C. (1992c) 'The Politics of Recognition', in Taylor (1992b); also in Taylor (1995b).
Taylor, C. (1995a) 'Liberal Politics and the Public Sphere', in Taylor (1995b).
Taylor, C. (1995b) *Philosophical Arguments*, Cambridge, Mass.
Taylor, G. (1985) *Pride, Shame and Guilt: Emotions of Self-Assessment*, Oxford.
Thalberg, I. (1989) 'Hierarchical Analyses of Unfree Action', in Christman (1989a).
Thomä, D. (1998) *Erzähle dich selbst. Lebensgeschichte als philosophisches Problem*, Munich.
Thompson, J. B. (1995) *The Media and Modernity: A Social Theory of the Media*, Cambridge and Stanford.
Thomson, J. J. (1974) 'The Right to Privacy', *Philosophy and Public Affairs* 4.
Tribe, L. H. (1992) *Abortion: The Clash of Absolutes*, New York.
Trilling, L. (1972) *Sincerity and Authenticity*, Cambridge, Mass.
Tseëlon, E. (1983) 'Women and the Private Domain: A Symbolic Interactionist Perspective', *Journal for the Theory of Social Behaviour* 21(2).
Tugendhat, E. (1979) *Selbstbewußtsein und Selbstbestimmung. Sprachanalytische Interpretationen*, Frankfurt-am-Main.
Tugendhat, E. (1992a) 'Der Begriff der Willensfreiheit', in Tugendhat (1992d).
Tugendhat, E. (1992b) 'Koreferat zu Charles Taylor: "What is Human Agency?" ', in Tugendhat (1992d).
Tugendhat, E. (1992c) 'Liberalism, Liberty and the Issue of Economic Human Rights', in Tugendhat (1992d).
Tugendhat, E. (1992d) *Philosophische Aufsätze*, Frankfurt-am-Main.
Tugendhat, E. (1993) *Vorlesungen über Ethik*, Frankfurt-am-Main.
Turkington, R. C. and Allen, A. L. (eds) (1999) *Privacy Law: Cases and Materials*, St. Paul, Minn.
Vedder, A. (2000) 'Medical Data, New Information Technologies and the Need for Normative Principles Other than Privacy Rules', in M. Freeman (ed.), *Current Legal Issues: Medicine and Law*, Oxford.
Velleman, J. D. (1999) 'Love as a Moral Emotion', MS.
Vetlesen, A. (1993) 'Die Rolle der Empathie für die Wahrnehmung. Moralphilosophische Überlegungen am Beispiel der Massenvernichtung', *Babylon* 12.
Veyne, P. (ed.) (1987) *From Pagan Rome to Byzantine*, trans. A. Goldhammer, Cambridge, Mass.; vol. 1 of Ariès and Duby (1987–91).
Villa, D. R. (1996) *Arendt and Heidegger: The Fate of the Political*, Princeton.
von Matt, P. (1989) *Liebesverrat. Die Treulosen in der Literatur*, Munich.
Waldron, J. (1988) *The Right to Private Property*, Oxford.

Waldron, J. (1993a) *Liberal Rights: Collected Papers 1981–1991*, Cambridge.

Waldron, J. (1993b) 'Particular Values and Critical Morality', in Waldron (1993a).

Waldron, J. (1993c) 'Theoretical Foundations of Liberalism', in Waldron (1993a).

Waldron, J. (1993d) 'When Justice Replaces Affection: The Need for Rights', in Waldron (1993a).

Wallace, R. J. (1998) *Responsibility and the Moral Sentiments*, Cambridge, Mass. and London.

Walton, A. S. (1983) 'Public and Private Interests: Hegel on Civil Society and the State', in Benn and Gaus (1983b).

Walzer, M. (1997) *On Toleration*, New Haven and London.

Warren, S. D. and Brandeis, L. D. (1984) 'The Right to Privacy' (1890), in Schoeman (1984a).

Wasserstrom, R. (1984) 'Privacy: Some Arguments and Assumptions', in Schoeman (1984a).

Watson, G. (ed.) (1982) *Free Will*, Oxford.

Watson, G. (1989) 'Free Agency', in Christman (1989a).

Weinstein, M. A. (1971) 'The Uses of Privacy in the Good Life', in Pennock and Chapman (1971).

Weinstein, W. L. (1971) 'The Private and the Free: A Conceptual Inquiry', in Pennock and Chapman (1971).

Weintraub, J. (1997) 'The Theory and Politics of the Public/Private Distinction', in Weintraub and Kumar (1997).

Weintraub, J. and Kumar, K. (eds) (1997) *Public and Private in Thought and Practice: Perspectives on a Grand Dichotomy*, Chicago.

Weir, A. (1996) *Sacrificial Logics: Feminist Theory and the Critique of Identity*, New York and London.

Wellmer, A. (1993) 'Bedingungen einer demokratischen Kultur. Zur Debatte zwischen Liberalen und Kommunitaristen', in M. Brumlik and H. Brunkhorst (eds), *Gemeinschaft und Gerechtigkeit*, Frankfurt-am-Main.

Wellmer, A. (2000) 'Models of Freedom in the Modern World', in A. Wellmer, *Endgames: The Irreconcilable Nature of Modernity*, trans. D. Midgley, Cambridge, Mass.

Welsch, W. (1991a) *Ästhetisches Denken*, Stuttgart.

Welsch, W. (1991b) 'Zur Aktualität ästhetischen Denkens', in Welsch (1991a).

Welsch, W. (1996) *Grenzgänge der Ästhetik*, Stuttgart.

West, R. (1997) *Caring for Justice*, New York and London.

Westin, A. F. (1967) *Privacy and Freedom*, New York.

Whitaker, R. (1999) *The End of Privacy: How Total Surveillance is Becoming a Reality*, New York.

Williams, B. (1976a) 'Ethical Consistency', in Williams (1976b).

Williams, B. (1976b) *Problems of the Self. Philosophical Papers 1956–1972*, Cambridge.

Williams, B. (1983a) *Moral Luck. Philosophical Papers 1973–1980*, Cambridge.

Williams, B. (1983b) 'Persons, Character and Morality', in Williams (1983a).

Williams, B. (1996) 'Toleration: An Impossible Virtue?' in Heyd (1996b).

Wingert, L. (1993) *Gemeinsinn und Moral. Grundzüge einer intersubjektivistischen Moralkonzeption*, Frankfurt-am-Main.

Wolf, S. (1989) 'Sanity and the Metaphysics of Responsibility', in Christman (1989a).

Wolf, U. (1986) 'Was es heißt, sein Leben zu leben', *Philosophische Rundschau* 33(3–4).
Wolf, U. (1997) 'Übergreifender Konsens und öffentliche Vernunft', in Hinsch and Philosophische Gesellschaft Bad Homburg (1997).
Wolfe, A. (1997) 'Public and Private in Theory and Practice: Some Implications of an Uncertain Boundary', in Weintraub and Kumar (1997).
Woolf, V. (1977) *A Room of One's Own*, London.
Wunderlich, S. (1999) 'Vom digitalen Panoptikum zur elektrischen Heterotopie. Foucaultsche Topographien der Macht', in Maresch and Werber (1999).
Young, I. M. (1990) *Justice and the Politics of Difference*, Princeton.
Young, I. M. (1997) *Intersecting Voices: Dilemmas of Gender, Political Philosophy and Policy*, Princeton.
Young, I. M. (2004) 'A Room of One's Own: Old Age, Extended Care and Privacy', in Rössler (2004).
Young, J. (ed.) (1978) *Privacy*, New York.
Young, R. (1989) 'Autonomy and the Inner Self', in Christman (1989a).
Zahlmann, C. (ed.) (1992) *Kommunitarismus in der Diskussion*, Berlin.

Index

www.ingramcontent.com/pod-product-compliance
Ingram Content Group UK Ltd.
Pitfield, Milton Keynes, MK11 3LW, UK
UKHW020145250726
13967UKWH00002B/866